DO ALL THE GOOD YOU CAN

DO ALL THE GOOD YOU CAN

How Faith Shaped
Hillary Rodham Clinton's Politics

GARY SCOTT SMITH

**UNIVERSITY OF
ILLINOIS PRESS**
Urbana, Chicago, and Springfield

Library of Congress Cataloging-in-Publication Data
Names: Smith, Gary Scott, 1950– author.
Title: Do all the good you can: how faith shaped Hillary
    Rodham Clinton's politics / Gary Scott Smith.
Description: Urbana: University of Illinois Press, [2023]
    | Includes bibliographical references and index.
Identifiers: LCCN 2023003599 (print) | LCCN
    2023003600 (ebook) | ISBN 9780252045318 (cloth) |
    ISBN 9780252054839 (ebook)
Subjects: LCSH: Clinton, Hillary Rodham—Religion.
    | Clinton, Hillary Rodham—Political and social
    views. | Presidents' spouses—United States—
    Biography. | Legislators—United States—
    Biography. | Women presidential candidates—
    United States—Biography.
Classification: LCC E887.C55 S585 2023 (print) | LCC
    E887.C55 (ebook) | DDC 973.929092 [B]—dc23/
    eng/20230310
LC record available at https://lccn.loc.gov/2023003599
LC ebook record available at https://lccn.loc.gov/
    2023003600

Contents

Preface

Hillary Rodham Clinton is one of the most important women in American history. Although she narrowly and surprisingly lost the 2016 presidential election, through her campaign and other political roles, Clinton cracked the glass ceiling holding women back and helped pave the way for them to serve in varied positions of responsibility in politics, business, and society. Clinton promoted many progressive causes and cogently presented positions on numerous issues that continue to be both contentious and significant today.

Clinton's faith is extremely important to her. She was raised in a staunchly Methodist home and faithfully participated in Sunday school, worship services, and a youth fellowship group. She had a close relationship with her youth pastor, Don Jones, that began when she was in ninth grade and lasted until his death in 2009. She has prayed and read the Bible frequently, perused dozens of issues of religious magazines, and devoured hundreds of religious books. As the first lady of Arkansas, Clinton taught Sunday school and gave numerous lectures throughout the state on Methodism and her personal religious convictions. As the nation's first lady, she participated actively in Foundry United Methodist Church in Washington and a women's prayer group. Clinton attended a Senate prayer group during the eight years she represented New York in that chamber. Her faith helped shape her character, determine her priorities, deal with personal and professional difficulties, and devise political positions. Motivated by her Methodist heritage and the Bible, she has made improving the lives of women and children one of her principal political concerns. From 1993 to 2016, Clinton spoke frequently to congregations and religious assemblies (usually to promote her candidacy for the Senate and the presidency). She also discussed her faith in numerous speeches and with several journalists.

Individuals holding varied political perspectives have testified that Clinton's faith is strong and authentic. Her sole religious biographer to date, political scientist Paul Kengor, argued that Clinton unquestionably "is a sincere, committed Christian and has been since childhood." Journalist Carl Bernstein called Clinton "a deeply religious person" who "carries a Bible with her, underlines it frequently, [and] believes in the Methodist creed of being called to service." Former Republican governor of Arkansas Mike Huckabee insisted that Clinton's faith is genuine. "Her social concern and her political thought rest on a spiritual foundation," Don Jones avowed. Faith is an essential part of Clinton's life, asserted Burns Strider, who served as a faith outreach director for her 2008 presidential campaign.[1]

Although scores of books and thousands of articles have been written about Clinton, the role of faith in her life has been underappreciated, especially by scholars. Most biographers have paid little attention to Clinton's Methodist faith in describing her life and work. The role of religion in her campaigns for the Senate and the presidency has also been insufficiently examined.

Hillary Rodham Clinton's faith has significantly influenced her personality, perspective on life, political policies, and concept of public service. It has helped her cope with the immense challenges she faced as a female political pioneer, an activist and controversial first lady, a champion of women and children's rights, an admired US senator, a globe-trotting secretary of state, and a two-time presidential candidate. Her faith gave her the strength to deal with her husband's sexual unfaithfulness, especially the public spectacle caused by his dalliance with Monica Lewinsky, and her devastating loss in the 2016 presidential election. Religious factors and issues were very important in her 2000 campaign for the US Senate, her attempt to obtain the Democratic presidential nomination in 2008, and her 2016 battle against Donald Trump. During both presidential campaigns, Clinton was lauded as a social gospel Methodist and denounced as tantamount to Lucifer. Had she devoted more time, energy, and resources to appealing to religious constituencies during the 2016 campaign, she very likely would have captured the presidency, yet scholars have provided scant analysis of this probability. The most comprehensive chronicle of Clinton's quest to become chief executive, Jonathan Allen and Amie Parnes's *Shattered: Inside Hillary Clinton's Doomed Campaign* (2017), provides no analysis of Clinton's faith, the religious aspects of key issues in the election—abortion, gay marriage, religious liberty, or the appointment of Supreme Court justices—or her efforts to appeal to religious groups.

Studying Clinton's religious convictions and practices and how her faith impacted her life sheds light on many important aspects of contemporary America, including the relationship between religion and politics, the strategies and tactics of political campaigning, the functions of government, US foreign policy, the role of women in American society, sexism, and racism. It also helps illuminate the priorities and principles of and problems faced by American religious communities, especially white and Black evangelicals, mainline Protestants, and traditional Catholics.

To accentuate Clinton's Methodist heritage and convictions, every chapter title in this book contains a quotation from John Wesley, the founder of Methodism.

Acknowledgments

As my endnotes detail, my book relies heavily on the books, articles, and opin-ion pieces written about Hillary Clinton by dozens of scholars and pundits. Their excellent work has made my task much easier. Especially valuable is *God and Hillary Clinton* (2006), penned by my longtime colleague Paul Kengor.

My debt to various individuals is substantial. Joyce Kebert and Conni Shaw, staff at Buhl Library of Grove City College, procured many articles and inter-library loan books for me. I am very grateful to Christopher Evans, Professor of History of Christianity and Methodist Studies at Boston University, for his thorough review of my manuscript and numerous helpful suggestions for revision. Margaret Bendroth, former Executive Director of the Congregational Library and Archives, also read my entire manuscript and provided much valu-able analysis. Timothy Larsen, Fred McManis Chair of Christian Thought at Wheaton College, helped me in the early stages of my research and writing. Mark David Hall, Professor of Politics at George Fox University, and John Fea, Professor of American History at Messiah University, supplied thoughtful assessment of my concluding chapter. Special thanks go to Alison Syring, my editor at the University of Illinois Press. She shepherded my book through the press's approval process and made dozens of suggestions to enhance the manuscript. I also want to thank other members of the press who worked on my book: Jennifer Argo, Angela Burton, Jennie Fisher, Kevin Cunningham, and Roberta Sparenberg. I am especially grateful to Rachel Paul for her outstanding copyediting. For the fourth time in the last four years, my friend Bruce Barron expertly copyedited a religious biography I wrote, substantially improving its prose. He helped ensure that my facts were correct and prodded me to think critically about numerous arguments I made. As always, my wife Jane provided wise counsel about my book.

Introduction

"Stay in Love with God"

In January 2016, when pushed by an Iowa voter to describe her beliefs, Hillary Rodham Clinton responded, "I am a person of faith. I am a Christian. I am a Methodist."[1] Indeed, she described her religious convictions numerous times in campaign statements and speeches, interviews, and books. Nevertheless, Donald Trump told a group of Christian leaders in June 2016, "We don't know anything about Hillary in terms of religion. Now, she's been in the public eye for years and years, and yet . . . there's nothing out there."[2] Trump's assertion is patently false, but many other Americans seem to know little about Clinton's faith.

What Jon Meacham wrote in 2008 is still true: "Though Hillary Rodham Clinton has been on the periphery or in the middle of national life for decades," she is one of the "least understood figures in American politics."[3] Clinton's religious convictions are especially misconstrued. Although her religious views have been frequently denounced by the leaders of the religious right, they are shared by millions of mainline Protestants, including United Methodists. Clinton's faith is more deeply rooted and fervent than many supporters, opponents, pundits, and biographers have recognized.

America's Most Controversial and Important Female Politician

During the past fifty years, only two women have been more important on the global scene than Hillary Rodham Clinton: Margaret Thatcher and Angela

Merkel. Thatcher was the United Kingdom's prime minister from 1979 to 1990, and Merkel was Germany's president from 2005 to 2016. Both strong-willed women served their nations effectively and advanced the world's welfare. Although Clinton did not become the United States' chief executive, she has been a prominent first lady, a productive US senator, a respected secretary of state, a two-time presidential candidate, and a pathbreaking female political leader.

In the 1980s, Clinton was already ranked as one of the top hundred lawyers in the United States. As the first lady of Arkansas, she led an educational initiative that significantly raised the standards of the state's public schools and the academic achievement of their students. Clinton was arguably the most influential first lady in our nation's history; she was certainly the most controversial one. Before she was elected a US senator from New York in 2000, only twenty-seven women, many of whom had been appointed for short periods, had served in this capacity. In 2008, Clinton became the first woman to nearly win the presidential nomination of a major political party. From 2009 to 2013, she served as the nation's third female secretary of state. Other women had previously run for the presidency, including Victoria Woodhull in 1872, Belva Lockwood in 1884 and 1888, Margaret Chase Smith in 1964, Shirley Chisholm in 1972, Patricia Schroeder in 1988, and Elizabeth Dole in 2000, but Clinton was first to have the name recognition and fund-raising capability to be a viable candidate, and in 2016 she became the first woman to receive the nomination of a major political party. Although she won almost three million more votes than Donald Trump, she lost the 2016 election, surprising most pollsters and pundits.

Clinton has done more than any other US politician to publicize the problems and promote the rights of women and children around the world. Through all these activities, she has blazed a trail for other women to follow. Arguably, Clinton is the most important woman in American political history.

Simultaneously the most esteemed and abhorred woman in America, Clinton evokes strong passions in many. Twenty-two times between 1993 and 2017, Gallup polls proclaimed her the most admired woman in America. Few American figures have garnered more attention or have been as frequently attacked as Clinton. While mudslinging has been common in American history, perhaps no politician has been subject to as much vitriol and abuse as Clinton. She has been accused of murder, lying, financial misconduct, numerous cases of conflict of interest, improperly firing White House Travel Office employees ("Travelgate"), inappropriately accessing hundreds of FBI background reports on former Republican White House employees ("Filegate"), using personal e-mail accounts to conduct official federal government business while serving as secretary of state, and staying in a failed marriage to preserve her political prospects. Not since Richard Nixon has a politician been viewed in so many conflicting ways. Moreover, few people have had every facet of their lives as scrutinized as she has. Her husband's infidelities have been widely publicized, and her marriage and sex life have been discussed frequently. For example, in 2006, a front-page *New York Times* story estimated the number of conjugal encounters the Clintons had each month.[4]

Biographer Christopher Anderson called Clinton the "most controversial, most complex, most loved-hated-admired-reviled woman—perhaps person—in America."[5] "No president of the United States and no first lady," journalists Joe Conason and Gene Lyons maintained, "have ever been subject to the corrosive combination of personal scrutiny, published and broadcast vilification, and official investigation and prosecution" the Clintons endured.[6] Hillary has been described as brilliant, compassionate, conniving, ruthless, and arrogant, as a saint, a victim, and a schemer. Many have viewed her as a heroic character, a combination of Joan of Arc and Eleanor Roosevelt.[7] To millions of others, however, she is a demon who, if elected president, would have destroyed American society and undermined its values. She has been mocked as a witch, a bitch, a feminazi, a slut, a daughter of Satan, a whore, a castrating ball-breaker, and a Marxist. Many men saw her as a combination of evil female archetypes: Jezebel, Snow White's stepmother, Lady Macbeth, Marie Antoinette, and Nurse Ratched. Conservative radio personality Don Imus repeatedly referred to Hillary as Satan, while Glenn Beck labeled her the antichrist. Conservative columnist Ann Coulter ridiculed Clinton as "white trash."[8] From being held responsible for all the failures of her husband's administration to being denounced as "crooked Hillary" by Donald Trump, who called for her incarceration, Clinton has dealt with a torrent of invective and derision. "She has survived personal and professional traumas that would have destroyed nearly anyone else—all in the public eye."[9] After Bill publicly confessed to having had an inappropriate sexual relationship with Monica Lewinsky in 1998, *New York Times* columnist Maureen Dowd called Hillary the "most degraded wife in the history of the world."[10]

Sexism has intensified the challenges Clinton has faced throughout her political career and contributed to making her such a target. Her assertiveness has challenged the perceptions of many Americans, especially religious conservatives, regarding women's roles in society. When women politicians display "political competence and ambition," they are often viewed "as suspect, even dangerous." A woman who goes "beyond the conventional boundaries of her sex," asserted novelist Susanna Moore, is called "ambitious or calculating or insincere or lesbian."[11] Successful women, avowed journalist Sady Doyle, "have always been penalized vigilantly and forcefully, and turned into spectacles."[12]

Moreover, few Americans have been as mocked for their moral convictions or have had the sincerity of their faith questioned as much as Clinton. Hating Hillary has been a national pastime—primarily for Republicans but also for some Democrats—since 1993, when some derisively called her the nation's copresident. One journalist proposed using the verb "Hillarating" to describe the ridicule she has endured. Conservative talk radio host Michael Savage called Clinton "the most Godless woman in the Senate" and asserted that her policies were taken "right out of the Marxist playbook." Religious right leader Jerry Falwell professed hope at a 2006 Values Voter Summit that Democrats would select Clinton as their 2008 presidential candidate because "if Lucifer ran, he wouldn't energize" evangelicals as much as Clinton. Derogatory jokes and hate marketing fueled a "Hate Hillary" campaign in 2008. Millions purchased bumper stickers, T-shirts, voodoo dolls, and "No Way in Hellary" BBQ aprons to display their animus toward Clinton. Dozens of websites denounced Clinton's alleged crookedness, while bloggers castigated her as Hitlery and Hilldabeast and many political conservatives described her as "Slippery Hillary."[13]

The attack on Clinton intensified in 2016. At the Republican National Convention, New Jersey Governor Chris Christie led the delegates through "a mock indictment" of the Democratic presidential nominee for various alleged crimes as the crowd repeatedly responded, "Guilty!" In the ensuing campaign, crowds at Trump rallies often yelled "Trump that bitch" and called for her imprisonment. Her treatment during the campaign, Susan Bordo argued in *The Destruction of Hillary Clinton*, "was almost medieval." T-shirts and coffee mugs displayed Trump holding Clinton's severed head, "like Perseus from ancient Greek mythology, lifting high the head of Medusa." Clinton was understandably dismayed by this "flood of hatred." She asserted that she "had left the State Department [as] one of the most admired public servants in America," but that "now people seemed to think I was evil." Dozens of websites, author Margaret Atwood declared, claimed that "Hillary was actually a Satanist with demonic powers."[14]

The Faith Factor

While numerous factors have shaped Clinton's personality, sense of calling, and political agenda, her faith has played a major role. "You can't understand Hillary Clinton if you don't understand her religion and its place in her life," declared famous journalist Carl Bernstein, one of her leading biographers. Her relationship with God, he added, is at the core of her being; it is "the north star of her moral compass."[15] Clinton has been called a political progressive, a radical feminist, "a disciplined political operative," a cautious moderate, an efficient working mother, and her husband's closest confidant. But many years before she became a Democrat, a lawyer, a politician's wife, or a stateswoman, Clinton became a Methodist. And as many who know her well insist, that is how she is best understood. As Kenneth Woodward argued, "She thinks like a Methodist, talks like a Methodist and wants to reform society just like a well-Sunday-schooled Methodist churchwoman should."[16] Her Methodist faith, Clinton testified, has "been a huge part of who I am and how I have seen the world, and what I believe in, and what I have tried to do in my life."[17]

Clinton professes to have a close personal relationship with God that determines her beliefs and directs her life. Unlike most evangelicals, many other Protestants, and some Catholics, Clinton does not claim to have had a distinct moment of conversion, a born-again experience. Like many other mainline Protestants and numerous Catholics and Orthodox Christians, she explains that her commitment to Christ developed gradually as she was raised by Christian parents and nurtured in the Methodist faith by faithfully attending worship services, Sunday school classes, and youth group meetings. "Hillary's faith," one of her aides contended, supplied "the missionary zeal with which she attacks her issues" and her "extraordinary self-discipline and focus."[18] Like many other social gospel–oriented mainline Protestants, post–Vatican II Catholics, and left-wing evangelicals, Clinton's faith has "focused on the moral dimensions of everyday experience" and the importance of doing good works to accomplish God's purposes on earth.[19]

Throughout her life, Clinton has been driven by a dictum often attributed to John Wesley, the founder of Methodism: "Do all the good you can, by all the means you can, in all the ways you can, in all the places you can, at all the times you can, to all the people you can, as long as ever you can."[20] Don Jones, Clinton's youth minister in Park Ridge, Illinois, asserted that caring for the poor and disadvantaged and working to achieve social justice have been a "continuing thread" in her life.[21] Clinton's pro bono activities as a Yale Law School student, work with the Children's Defense Fund, endeavors to improve public education in Arkansas, efforts as first lady to reform health care, and quest to end the mistreatment of and provide full human rights for children and women have all expressed her religiously motivated mission to fulfill Wesley's maxim and bring God's kingdom on earth.

Clinton's religious convictions are consistent with those of most mainline Protestants—long-established, overwhelmingly white denominations that for much of the twentieth century were the nation's largest, most successful, most visible communions. These denominations include the American Baptist Church (USA), the Disciples of Christ, the Episcopal Church USA, the Evangelical Lutheran Church in America, the Presbyterian Church (USA), the Reformed Church in America, the United Church of Christ, and Clinton's own United Methodist Church. Also called mainstream Protestant and old-line Protestant, these denominations differ from evangelical, fundamentalist, and Pentecostal bodies in their history, theology, liturgy, and social activism. From the 1920s to the 1960s, mainline denominations claimed the largest number of adherents, significant moral authority, and substantial societal respect. They constituted the "standard brand religion," "the normative, the taken-for-granted, the standard for judging other groups." They were viewed as the religious establishment and helped define America's core values; their members dominated the nation's politics and business.[22] Historian Mark Lempke argued that by 1960 most mainline ministers espoused progressive Christianity, which he described as "a program of political and spiritual reform built around four precepts": a prophetic critique of American society, efforts to aid the marginalized, advocacy of peace and social justice, and a commitment to ecumenism. In that year, nearly half of all voters belonged to mainline Protestant denominations. Many theologically liberal mainline leaders spent the 1960s promoting peace, arms control, and affordable housing, antagonizing many of their parishioners who did not share their priorities and who complained that the clergy were ignoring their congregants' spiritual needs.[23]

Membership in mainline churches began to decline in the later 1960s and continued to do so until the 2010s. In *Why Conservative Churches Are Growing*, Dean Kelley attributed this loss in membership to their failure to supply satisfying explanations of the meaning of life, nurture their parishioners' faith, and provide the accountability, discipline, and camaraderie that characterized successful evangelical congregations. Because of their loss of millions of members, the authority and social impact of mainline communions, although still substantial, have diminished. Nevertheless, their "values and sensibilities, . . . especially interfaith openness, social tolerance, respect for civil and human rights, and psychological and mystical spiritualties," have continued to gain ground in American society.[24] Mainline Protestantism has been theologically and ideologically pluralistic, with theological moderates predominating, but its key leaders and denominational stances have usually been theologically liberal, ecumenically engaged, and socially activist.[25]

Methodists, who were the nation's largest denomination during most of the nineteenth century, strove energetically to shape American moral norms and social practices. Many Methodists embraced the social gospel, the adherents of which worked diligently from the 1880s to the 1920s to alleviate social ills, reform American society, and bring the kingdom of God on earth.[26] Today the United Methodist Church is the nation's third-largest denomination behind Roman Catholics and Southern Baptists. Its membership peaked in the 1960s at about 11 million and is currently approximately 7.5 million. In the early 1960s, when Hillary Rodham joined the youth group of the First Methodist Church in Park Ridge, a Chicago suburb, the denomination's social concerns had shifted from the nineteenth-century emphasis on prohibiting alcohol, gambling, and secular activities on the Sabbath and the early-twentieth-century focus on curbing social and industrial ills to combating racism and sexism.[27] Clinton grew up in a Methodist church whose ministers and members were generally optimistic, theologically moderate, and socially progressive. As part of the nation's largest Protestant denomination in the 1960s, many of them participated in the civil rights and antiwar movements and supported feminism, environmental stewardship, an expanded welfare state, and independence for former European colonies. Many Methodists also called for abortion rights. For thousands of Methodist pastors and laypeople, by the 1960s, social amelioration had become more important than evangelism and spiritual formation.[28]

Methodism helped shape the political philosophy and inspire the social activism of not only Clinton but three older Democratic politicians—South Dakota Senator George McGovern and Minnesotans Hubert Humphrey and Walter Mondale, both of whom served as a US senator and then as vice president. All four were motivated by Methodism's quest for reform, reinforced by expectations that God's kingdom would triumph in this world, which helped fuel political progressivism's drive to create a just and egalitarian society through political action.[29] As the Democratic presidential nominee in 1972, McGovern, the son of a Methodist minister and a graduate of a Methodist college, who had himself studied to become a Methodist minister and taught at his Methodist alma mater before entering politics, helped make Methodist priorities those of the Democratic Party.[30] Beginning in that year, Democratic Party platforms were very similar to the positions the United Methodist Church adopted at its 1972 quadrennial General Convention. Both groups demanded the immediate withdrawal of US troops from Vietnam and called for "wholesale transformation of political, economic and social institutions." Throughout the remainder of the twentieth century, Democrats' planks on evolving culture-war issues paralleled the stances taken by Methodists (as well as those of the Roman Catholic and Jewish social-justice traditions).[31] In addition, Clinton's positions on abortion and same-sex marriage generally paralleled those of the United Methodist Church until 2016, when the denomination voted to withdraw from the Religious Coalition for Reproductive Choice and to oppose both homosexual marriage and ordination to the ministry.[32]

Throughout her life, Clinton's faith has helped her cope with challenges and difficulties that might have otherwise devastated her or at least prevented her from continuing to serve in the political arena. Clinton and several aides and friends insisted that her faith played a crucial role in enabling her to endure with her husband's unfaithfulness and the public shame his actions caused.

Critics predictably evaluate Clinton's faith more negatively. One argued that since her time as Arkansas's first lady, Clinton's deep-seated Methodist values had made her "strident," "off-putting," and blatantly disapproving of those who frequented bars, smoked, or told racy jokes.[33] Another complained that Clinton's religious convictions helped explain "her moral certitude" and "righteousness that brooks no modification of her ideas."[34] This contributed to her belief that she knew what was best for people and her difficulty in compromising (including on health care reform as first lady). Biographer William Chafe contended that these traits made it difficult to reconcile the two Hillarys. One was thoughtful and sensitive, caring deeply about people and "the ultimate concerns of the human condition." The other was contemptuous and combative, continually at war with enemies whom she assessed as deserving little respect.[35] Leaders of the religious right scorned Clinton for being neither sufficiently submissive to her husband nor properly maternal.[36] They also deplored her quest to use the federal government to promote a progressive understanding of social and moral justice. Secular pundits attacked her for advocating flaky new-age spiritual blather, while some Democratic Party leaders criticized her for injecting religion into policies and thereby antagonizing some prospective voters.[37]

For a variety of reasons, Clinton's faith, although strongly held and sometimes explicitly expressed, has been underappreciated. The secularity and disinterest of the media, widespread dislike of George W. Bush's outspokenness about his faith, the belief that many politicians used religious rhetoric for ulterior purposes, her reluctance to discuss her personal life, and the animosity of the religious right all contributed to Clinton's faith being either neglected or misconstrued. Right-wing media outlets often claimed that political liberals could not be true Christians, while left-wing journalists criticized debate moderators for even asking candidates about their personal faith. Although Clinton's stated religious views have been quite consistent throughout her life, many people expressed surprise and sometimes suspicion whenever she mentioned her faith. Dozens of political conservatives argued during both the 2008 and 2016 presidential campaigns that Clinton's faith was "duplicitous and disingenuous," a façade employed to win the votes of religious Americans. Cynics complained that she professed belief in Christian teaching and traditional moral values during these campaigns solely for political reasons. Numerous polls, including ones conducted in 2014 and 2016 by the *Washington Post* and ABC News, reported that about 50 percent of Americans did not think that she was very religious or trustworthy.[38] During both presidential campaigns, Clinton struggled to present herself as authentic and personable. Talking more about her faith could have helped her appeal to religiously devout voters, but it also might have made some of them warier about her. That possibility, coupled with Clinton's hesitancy to discuss her private life, often led her to refrain from discussing her faith in speeches or personal conversations.

As a Democrat, Clinton has faced greater challenges in speaking about her faith than her Republican counterparts. About a quarter of liberal voters in 2016 had no religious affiliation, and many of them disliked candidates discussing their faith. Constituting 21 percent of American adults, "nones" were as large a voting bloc in 2016 as any religious group, including evangelicals and Catholics. On the other hand, in that year 64 percent of African Americans, another major Democratic constituency, thought that political candidates said too little about their faith. Moreover, most evangelicals and Catholics disagreed with the Democratic Party's stance on abortion, increasing Clinton's difficulty in winning their votes despite sharing their emphasis on having a deep personal relationship with God.[39]

During her 2016 campaign, Clinton hired a religious outreach director, discussed her faith in numerous speeches and Black churches, addressed several Black religious assemblies, met with some Black church leaders, highlighted religion at the Democratic National Convention, and selected a running mate, Tim Kaine, who was well known as a devout Catholic. However, she turned down requests for interviews with religious publications, including *Christianity Today*, and invitations to meet with evangelical leaders and groups, and she did not hire anyone to coordinate her efforts to reach evangelicals. The outcome of the 2016 election might have been different if Clinton had focused more on wooing religiously committed voters. As a twice-divorced casino mogul who had rarely attended church, knew little about the Bible, and had bragged about behaviors that clashed with biblical morality, Trump was potentially repulsive to most evangelicals.[40] Russell Moore, the head of the Southern Baptist Ethics and Religious Liberty Commission, and several other prominent evangelicals excoriated him in interviews, op-eds, and tweets. Had Clinton met with evangelical leaders and groups, listened to their concerns, talked more about issues that mattered to them, assured them that she would protect their religious freedom, and promised to give them a voice in her administration, she "might have peeled away religious voters looking for a reason not to vote for Trump" and won the election.[41] Three states Clinton lost by very small margins—Pennsylvania, Wisconsin, and Michigan—had numerous mainline Protestant and Catholic voters. Many of these voters either did not recognize the depth or importance of Clinton's faith or thought that it was not genuine because she did not emphasize it. Had Clinton focused more on faith outreach to these groups and been more outspoken about her Christian convictions, she might have won these states, which would have given her enough electoral votes to become president.[42]

Clinton's Methodist faith has played a substantial role in her life, and religious factors have been very important in her work as Arkansas's first lady, the nation's first lady, a US senator, secretary of state, and a presidential candidate. Unpacking the nature and influence of Clinton's faith is crucial to understanding her priorities, motives, and actions in various stages of her life.

1

"I Felt My Heart Strangely Warmed"

Clinton's Spiritual Roots

On October 26, 1947, Chicago natives Hugh and Dorothy Rodham welcomed their first child, Hillary. The Rodhams and their church, First Methodist in Park Ridge, would have a powerful influence on Clinton's personality, faith, and life of public service. Born in 1911, Hugh Rodham grew up in a staunchly Methodist home in Scranton, Pennsylvania, whose members traced their lineage back to the denomination's eighteenth-century founders, John and Charles Wesley.[1] His father, Hugh Sr., was the sixth of eleven children; he worked for five decades at the Scranton Lace Company, ending his career as a supervisor. The 6-foot-2, 230-pound Hugh Jr. majored in physical education at Penn State University and was a third-string tight end for the perennial football power. After graduating in 1935, Hugh worked briefly at the Scranton Lace Company, then moved to Chicago where he sold drapery fabrics throughout the Midwest. During World War II, he supervised new recruits in the navy's Gene Tunney program. Named for the former heavyweight boxing champion who headed it, this program helped make soldiers more physically fit. When the war ended, Hugh started a drapery fabric business called Rodrik Fabrics that operated in the Merchandise Mart in Chicago's Loop.

Born in Chicago on June 4, 1919—the day Congress passed the Nineteenth Amendment to give women the right to vote—Dorothy Rodham had a childhood filled with adversity. Her mother, Della Murray, was fifteen and her father, Edwin John Howell Jr., a fireman, was seventeen at her birth. They boarded for a while with four other families in crowded quarters in a hardscrabble Chicago neighborhood. Dorothy's parents often neglected her and moved several times, forcing her to switch elementary schools. The unhappily married couple quarreled frequently, sometimes violently, and divorced in 1927.

After being awarded custody of eight-year-old Dorothy and her three-year-old sister, Isabelle, Edwin sent them unescorted on a four-day train ride to live with his parents—Edwin Howell Sr. and Emma Howell—in Alhambra, a Los Angeles suburb. Edwin, a former British sailor, worked as a machinist in an auto plant. Emma reluctantly agreed to care for her two granddaughters but provided little love or nurture during the ten years Dorothy lived there. Hillary Clinton reported that Emma was "a severe woman who wore black Victorian dresses and resented and ignored my mother except when enforcing her rigid house rules." During this period, Dorothy rarely saw her father and never saw her mother.[2] By the mid-1930s, the Howells were relying on assistance from relief agencies to cover their expenses. After graduating from high school, Dorothy went to live in Chicago with Della, who had recently remarried and promised to pay for her college education; however, she actually wanted Dorothy to serve as her housekeeper and provided no funds for college, crushing Dorothy's dreams of attending Northwestern University and of experiencing her mother's love. Disillusioned, Dorothy took an office job earning $13 a week and moved into a small apartment.[3]

Hugh and Dorothy met in 1937 and, after a five-year courtship, married in 1942. In 1950, the Rodhams moved to a two-story brick home in Park Ridge, fifteen miles northwest of downtown Chicago, near what is today the O'Hare International Airport. Hugh was a self-made businessman and resolute Republican who embraced a gospel of self-reliance, social conservatism, and anticommunism. Although his drapery business was lucrative and Hugh bought a new Cadillac every year, he did not enjoy the respect of his upper-middle-class neighbors, who were primarily physicians, lawyers, and businessmen, and did not socialize with them. Strongly prejudiced against African Americans and Catholics, Hugh suffered from discontentment and depression, which ran in his family. In 1948, Hugh discovered his brother Russell trying to hang himself in the attic of their parents' home and cut him down. Russell became an alcoholic, descended into a deep depression, and died in a fire in 1962. Overwhelmed by despair after their father's death in 1965, Hugh's other brother Willard died of coronary thrombosis five weeks later. A journalist described Rodham as "a tyrant and a tightwad" and "a very demanding and domineering father and husband."[4] Hugh had a disagreeable disposition and was unfulfilled and tightfisted (among other acts of miserliness, he often turned off the heat during winter nights to save money), and the Rodham family had few friends.[5]

The surly, confrontational curmudgeon was difficult to please and "often treated his children with a condescension that bordered on contempt."[6] They "suffered his relentless, demeaning sarcasm and misanthropic inclination, endured his embarrassing parsimony, and silently accepted his humiliation and verbal abuse of their mother."[7] Hugh rarely praised Hillary or her two brothers—Hugh (born in 1950) and Tony (1954)—while constantly prodding them to do better. When Hillary had trouble with math in fourth grade, Hugh woke her early every morning to grill her on multiplication tables. On the other hand, if she received an A, he sneered, "You must go to a pretty easy school." If Hillary or her brothers asked their father for an allowance for doing their many household chores, he bluntly responded, "I feed you, don't I?"[8] Hillary's childhood friend Betsy Ebeling asserted that Hugh was "always pushing buttons." He "made provocative statements" and challenged anyone who disagreed to "defend your position."[9] Numerous friends and relatives complained that Hugh's treatment of his children "amounted to the kind of psychological abuse and adversity that might have crushed some children."[10] Hugh's tenacity, unremitting competitiveness, and constant demands for perfection strongly affected his children.[11] Hillary described her father as a highly opinionated, "rock-ribbed, up-by-your-bootstraps, conservative Republican." She added that "he was a tough taskmaster, but we knew he cared about us."[12] Hugh taught his only daughter that she could do anything boys did, including playing sports.

Hillary loved and respected her father despite his unpleasant demeanor, harsh discipline, and emotional unavailability, but she had a much closer relationship with her mother, a homemaker who served as a spiritual role model, provided "unconditional love and support," and taught her to be confident and caring. Dorothy was determined to help Hillary avoid the privation and pain that plagued her own childhood. She worked to ensure that Hillary had positive experiences and valuable opportunities. Hillary praised her mother's "unlimited affection and encouragement."[13] Hillary declared that "my mother" inspired her through "her devotion, imagination and great spirit."[14] "Above all, Dorothy taught Hillary never to underestimate her talents, her potential, or the value of her education."[15]

Both Hugh and Dorothy helped shape Hillary's personality, faith, and future path. Her father influenced her to be "combative, determined and scrappy." Her friend and White House press aide Lisa Caputo suggested that Hillary derived much of her discipline, drive, and work ethic from Hugh.[16] On the other hand, Clinton has often been criticized for displaying some of the same traits that characterized her father, including emotional detachment, harshness, and lack of charm.[17] "Both my parents," Clinton explained, "conditioned us to be tough in order to survive whatever life might throw at us."[18] Despite their very different personalities and perspectives, Hugh and Dorothy both taught their children that through self-control, hard work, and the aid of their parents, school, and church, they could accomplish almost any dream.[19] Hillary struggled as a child to reconcile her father's "insistence on self-reliance and independence" with her mother's "concerns about social justice and compassion."[20] As an adult, she continued to grapple with this challenge.

Hugh rarely attended church with his family, but Hillary noted that the "gruff former Navy man" prayed "on his knees . . . by his bed every night" and declared that "seeing him humble himself before God" made "a big impression on me as a young girl."[21] His model contributed to making prayer "a source of solace and guidance for me even as a child."[22] Dorothy, by contrast, was very involved in the ministry of First Methodist Church. She attended faithfully with her children, taught Sunday school for many years, and helped raise money to support home and foreign missions.[23] Her mother's example encouraged Hillary to participate actively at First Methodist and motivated her to help the indigent and vulnerable. "My mother," Hillary explained, "was very concerned about injustice and unfairness" and "kept that on the forefront of our minds."[24] Even in her nineties, Hillary testified, "Mom never lost her commitment to social justice, which did so much to mold and inspire me."[25]

Despite Hugh's lack of church attendance, Clinton insisted that "our spiritual life as a family was spirited and constant." The family "talked with God, walked with God, ate, studied, and argued with God. Each night, we knelt by our beds to pray before we went to sleep. We said grace at dinner, thanking God for all the blessings" he bestowed. "God was always present to us, a much-esteemed, much addressed member of the family."[26] From her earliest days, as she dealt with life's ups and downs and especially in tough times, Clinton found prayer to be "a very important replenisher."[27]

Hillary Rodham's Youth

As a youth, Rodham engaged in many activities, displaying the traits, interests, and achievements that would later propel her into the political arena and limelight. At age ten, she organized a neighborhood "Olympics," charging friends twenty-five cents to compete in events to raise money for destitute children in Chicago. Rodham "was determined to be the most active, most visible, and most accomplished student" in her high school class.[28] Childhood friends report that she was intelligent, witty, warm, tenacious, and loyal.[29] Serious about academics, gregarious, and athletic, Rodham played field hockey, softball, and volleyball, excelled in tennis, swimming, skating, and ballet, and held numerous summer jobs. Respected for "her toughness, competitiveness, and strong convictions," Rodham belonged to the National Honor Society, was elected junior class president, served on the student council and the "cultural values" committee, wrote for her high school's newspaper and yearbook, and participated on the "It's Academic" quiz show team, which competed against other high schools on a local television program.[30] As a senior, she performed in the school's two-hour variety show "Americana," which portrayed American history from the Pilgrims to the twist. Her "force of will, intense preparation, and dutiful study," biographer Carl Bernstein argued, made her an honor-roll student, and "her prodigious memory" and extensive preparation made her a formidable opponent in classroom debates.[31]

In the fall of 1964, Rodham debated classmate Howard Primer in front of the entire student body, with Clinton playing the Republican nominee, Arizona Senator Barry Goldwater, and Primer playing Democratic nominee President Lyndon Johnson. They spent hours preparing, and contrary to the national vote, Rodham's Goldwater trounced Primer's Johnson in a student vote after the debate. Hillary won her high school's first "good citizen" award, sponsored by the Daughters of the American Revolution (DAR). She was "selected for her citizenship qualities of dependability, service, leadership and patriotism," the local newspaper reported.[32]

Rodham did not wear makeup and went on few dates; imagining the class of 1965 ten years in the future, her school newspaper depicted her as a nun named "Sister Frigidaire."[33] "While her girlfriends had crushes, stared at boys, [and] padded their bras, Hillary talked about politics, Sputnik and sports," a journalist asserted.[34] She graduated fifteenth in a class of a thousand, was a National Merit Scholar finalist, and was voted the female student most likely to succeed. Outside the classroom, Rodham won numerous Brownie and Girl Scout badges and DAR community service awards and was an active young Republican and a Goldwater girl, "right down to my cowgirl outfit and straw cowboy hat emblazoned with the slogan 'AuH$_2$O.'"[35] Describing her confident and accomplished daughter, Dorothy Rodham declared, "Hillary has never had a self-esteem problem."[36]

As a child and teenager, Rodham was very involved in the worship, fellowship, and outreach of the three thousand–member First Methodist Church
of Park Ridge, a large Tudor-style structure four blocks from the Rodham
home. She faithfully attended Sunday school and Vacation Bible School; participated regularly in youth group meetings, church athletic competitions,
potluck suppers, and Christmas and Easter pageants; and cleaned the altar in
the sanctuary on Saturdays. At age eleven, she joined the church after reading
her confirmation essay, "What Jesus Means to Me," before the entire congregation.[37] "My active involvement" in the congregation, Clinton later explained,
"opened my eyes and heart to the needs of others and helped instill a sense of
social responsibility rooted in my faith."[38] The message and ministry of Park
Ridge, which embodied the long-standing Methodist emphasis on the social
implications of the gospel, forced her "to confront the reality of inequity and
injustice."[39] Her enthusiastic participation in the church, she argued, was "a
critical part of my growing up." In many ways "it influenced me, and helped
me develop as a person, not only on my own faith journey, but with a sense
of obligation to others." First Methodist's ministers and lay leaders taught
her "about the connection between my personal faith and the obligations I
faced as a Christian, both to other individuals and to society." The church was
Rodham's second home, and its activities and spiritual nurture were incredibly important to her. "We discussed what our faith meant in the world," she
explained, "and I am so grateful for those lessons and those opportunities."[40]

The Impact of Don Jones

Rodham's understanding of Christianity and passion for helping others deep-
ened after the charismatic Don Jones came to Park Ridge to serve as the
church's youth minister in September 1961, as she began ninth grade. Jones
had grown up during the Depression, primarily in South Dakota, and attended
South Dakota State University but dropped out, enlisted in the navy, and
fought in the Korean War. After his military service, Jones finished his BA at
Augustana College, a Lutheran institution in Sioux Falls, South Dakota, and
then enrolled at Drew Divinity School in New Jersey in 1958. Remarkably,
First Methodist of Park Ridge, which had many John Birchers in its pews and
was a bastion of social conservatism during much of the 1960s, hired a social
liberal whose theology was Neo-Orthodox.[41] Jones drove his red 1959 Chevrolet
Impala convertible to visit the church's youth and used books, films, and field
trips to expose them to the world beyond Park Ridge. First Methodist, Jones

complained, was a "homogeneous cocoon" that taught youth to "be nice, don't drink, don't smoke, don't say dirty words, don't pierce your ears and don't be contaminated by the world outside."[42] Park Ridge was an all-white, predominantly Protestant community of upwardly mobile families, and its population doubled from 16,500 to 33,000 during the 1950s. Liquor sales were prohibited, divorce was rare, and the civil rights struggle was only a distant rumble, but regular air raid drills reminded children that atomic bombs could disrupt if not destroy their world. Its residents assumed that honesty, caring for others, and hard work would be rewarded.[43] While Rodham attended high school in the early 1960s, Park Ridge was more *Happy Days* than *Easy Rider*.[44]

Jones encouraged his charges to study the Bible and the Methodist heritage and to accept Christ as their Savior, but he also strove to lift them above "pious escapism" to engage in "an authentic and deep quest for God and life's meaning." At his Sunday and Thursday evening classes, which youth dubbed "The University of Life," he sought to connect Christian theology with pop culture, art, and social issues. He exposed them to existentialism, abstract art, the music of Bob Dylan, and the radical politics of the 1960s counterculture.[45] Clinton and her peers read the poems of e. e. cummings, T. S. Eliot, and W. H. Auden, and the works of Danish philosopher Søren Kierkegaard, Russian novelist Fyodor Dostoyevsky, German pastor Dietrich Bonhoeffer, and American theologians Paul Tillich and Reinhold Niebuhr. Jones discussed with them Kierkegaard's "leap of faith," Bonhoeffer's "religionless Christianity," and Niebuhr's "unsentimental view of history."[46] Rodham learned from Bonhoeffer that Christians should be totally engaged in the world to promote human development and from Niebuhr about balancing "a clear-eyed realism about human nature" with "an unrelenting passion for justice and social reform."[47]

Jones challenged youth group members to express their faith through their actions as these prominent theologians and pastors and Methodist founder John Wesley had done. Jones used prints of Vincent van Gogh's *The Starry Night* and Pablo Picasso's *Guernica* to examine God, nature, violence, and war. He rented Rod Serling's *Requiem for a Heavyweight*, a film about a washed-up boxer who wrestles with the meaning of life, and Francois Truffaut's *The 400 Blows*, the story of a troubled Parisian youth confined at a center for delinquents. The youth group discussed these movies and numerous controversial topics, including crime, drugs, and teen pregnancy. Jones arranged a debate between an atheist and a Christian on the existence of God. He brought his youth to a nearby synagogue to hear its rabbi discuss Judaism and Israel. He took them to meet Black and Hispanic inner-city teenagers, many of whom were gang members. Jones also arranged a meeting with social activist and organizer Saul Alinsky, who denounced the American power structure.

Hillary later insisted that going with her youth group to hear Martin Luther King Jr. preach on "Remaining Awake through a Great Revolution" and meeting him after his sermon was a pivotal experience for her. King exhorted Christians to confront the two great challenges of their age—racism and poverty—and insisted that "the end of life is not to be happy, but to do the will of God come what may."[48] Until she heard King speak, Hillary had been only "dimly aware of the social revolution occurring in our country." She later asserted that King's charge impacted her like God's striking of the apostle Paul on the road to Damascus "and challenged our indifference."[49] Clinton declared that King's words and "the power of his example affected me deeply," reinforcing Jones's admonition "to face the world as it is, not as we might want it to be" and "to commit ourselves to turning it into what it should be." Bill Clinton argued in 2016 that King's sermon changed the course of Hillary's moral and political life. Transforming the world, he had realized when they first met, "is really what motivates her."[50]

Perhaps just as importantly for Clinton's public career, youth group members engaged in social activism. They organized food drives to aid the destitute, visited the elderly in nursing homes, and babysat the children of migrant farmworkers camping in fields west of Chicago. Jones, she recalled, fervently argued that being "a Christian did not just mean you were concerned about your own personal salvation."[51] The discussions Jones led with the youth group were not "just an intellectual enterprise." The youth pastor, Clinton explained, forced them to consider "What does this mean to you as a Christian? What does this mean to you as a person?"[52] Jones exposed them to literature and theology that portrayed human life as "filled with tragedy and alienation." When people realized this, Jones contended, "human flourishing" became possible. According to Rosalie Bentzinger, First Methodist's director of Christian education, Rodham concluded as a youth that Christians were required to provide for people's social and material needs.[53] These experiences helped instill in Rodham a concern for unprivileged children that drove her work as an adult.[54] "My church gave me concrete experiences that forced me to confront the reality of inequity and injustice."[55] It "taught me [that] because I had those blessings [from my church family], I owed something back. And for me that took the shape early on of caring about children," Clinton told *Good Housekeeping* magazine in December 1992.[56]

Hillary's relationship with Jones deeply affected her. Jones became for her a "father figure, adored brother, and knight-errant"; Dorothy Rodham regarded him "as a kindred spirit," "a brother in Christ."[57] Jones and Hillary had lengthy, serious discussions about the books she read. "She was curious" and "insatiable," he observed.[58] Clinton later explained that "Jones's influence" was "mind-blowing." Learning about the world beyond Park Ridge "was exciting and challenging," which Jones "linked to our faith."[59] Jones, she added, opened "our eyes to injustice in the wider world" beyond our "sheltered, middle-class, all white community."[60] He helped her develop "a sense of social mission" and "a personal commitment to faith" that was "very unifying."[61] According to Roger Morris, her conversations with Jones stimulated "the first fitful awakenings of critical intellect and sensibility in a spiritually minded young woman." As the cautious, politically conservative teenager was developing her worldview, Jones provided acceptance, direction, and encouragement.[62]

Don Jones was not the only adult who sought to influence the heart and mind of the bright, precocious teenager. Her ninth-grade social studies teacher, Paul Carlson, a member of First Methodist Church, also strove to educate her about the world beyond tranquil Park Ridge and challenge her complacency. An even more ardent anticommunist than Hugh Rodham, Carlson warned his students about the threat of the Soviet Union, communists in America, and counterculture radicals. Delighted by Rodham's conservative ideology and interest in politics, he introduced her to Barry Goldwater's *The Conscience of a Conservative* (1960). Rodham was inspired by Goldwater's defense of individual rights, which mirrored her father's views. She wrote a seventy-five-page term paper for Carlson's "History of Civilization" class on the conservative political movement. In addition, Rodham participated in Carlson's after-school history club, which focused on patriotism and free enterprise.[63] Carlson also introduced Rodham to refugees from the Soviet Union, helping reinforce her staunch anticommunist perspective.[64]

Rodham felt caught between the political positions of Jones on one hand and her father and Carlson on the other. "Though my eyes were opening, I still mostly parroted the conventional wisdom of Park Ridge's and my father's politics," Clinton later explained. While Jones provided "'liberalizing' experiences," Carlson "reinforced my already strong anti-communist views."[65] In high school, Clinton recognized that preserving people's dignity while helping them improve their lives was challenging and could be considered either a politically liberal or conservative approach, given the various ways in which these ideologies were defined.[66] Influenced by Jones and Carlson, her two mentors, who "were locked in a battle for my mind and soul," Rodham affirmed both political orientations, a stance that would continue throughout her college years.[67] By the time she got to Wellesley College, she wondered "if it's possible to be a mental conservative and a heart liberal."[68]

"More than anyone else," Jones prodded Rodham "to question the traditions and prejudices of her Park Ridge upbringing." He challenged her to view "the Bible as a basis for political action," which eventually helped root "her politics in the tradition of the Christian left." Jones insisted that John Wesley taught that Christians must "engage in political activity to promote human flourishing," which helped convince Rodham that the government played a major role in alleviating social ills.[69] According to Jones, Niebuhr helped her understand "the truth of the human condition" and perceive "that the use of power to achieve social good is legitimate."[70]

Clinton insisted that Jones "opened up a new world to me" and "helped guide me on a spiritual, social and political journey" that would last for more than forty years. After leaving Park Ridge, Jones earned a PhD at Drew University and taught religion there from 1966 to 2002. Clinton and Jones corresponded frequently about theological issues and personal matters. When Jones died in 2009, Clinton stated, "Don taught me the meaning of the words 'faith in action' and the importance of social justice and human rights. I will miss him and will be grateful forever [for] his intelligence, counsel, kindness and support over many years." Childhood friend Ernest Ricketts insisted that Jones's impact on her was "life altering." She absorbed all the religious experiences and philosophical discussions of her youth and greatly benefited from Jones's "really positive influence."[71]

Surprisingly, given the political and cultural conservatism of many of First Methodist's members, they initially had little opposition to Jones's theology and methods.[72] Even taking his protégés to hear Alinsky, who employed tactics such as picketing executives' homes and staging "fart-ins" to gain concessions from corporations, did not produce a major controversy.[73] However, the competing perspectives of Jones and Carlson eventually surfaced at the Park Ridge church when the teacher accused the youth minister of making his charges feel guilty about the difficulties their minority peers experienced, which, Carlson insisted, were not their fault.[74] In response, Jones complained that Carlson was stuffing the church's pews with "alarmist anticommunist literature." Upset with Jones's theology, political perspective, and the University of Life curriculum, Carlson pushed First Methodist to dismiss him.[75] He convinced a majority of church members that the "freethinking" Jones was a dangerous influence on the Park Ridge youth, and the church forced him to leave after just two years on its staff.[76]

Nevertheless, Jones's impact on Clinton continued. Jones would serve as her major counselor for more than two decades as they discussed the capriciousness of human nature and the teachings of Christianity. Jones helped equip Clinton to handle adversity and soothe her "troubled soul" by doing good works. Almost every time she experienced pain, rejection, or humiliation as an adult, Clinton would respond by engaging in social activism.[77] As a youth, Rodham embraced her father's fervor for free enterprise, Carlson's vigilance against communist aggression, her mother's compassion for the poor and oppressed, and Jones's outrage about inequality.[78] At Wellesley College near Boston, these commitments and others she held would be challenged; some would grow weaker while others became stronger. By the time she went to Wellesley in September 1965, Bernstein argued, the essential elements of Clinton's adult character were evident—her keen intellect, intense ambition, idealism, messianism, seriousness of purpose, belief in public service, and "perhaps, above all, the balm, beacon and refuge of religion."[79]

Clinton grew up in a community that, like the United States as a whole, was predominantly white and Protestant. Church membership and attendance were at an all-time high in the 1950s. Individuals strongly committed to or at least loosely affiliated with mainline Protestant denominations controlled the three branches of the federal government, the business community, America's major cultural institutions, and many state and local organizations. The Christian worldview still provided the intellectual framework for most Americans, and Protestant mores prevailed in most areas of society.[80] The social upheaval and intellectual ferment of the second half of the 1960s would challenge and change American life and society while Clinton attended Wellesley.

2

"Let Your Light Shine to All"

From Wellesley to the White House

Leaving her sheltered suburban enclave, Hillary Rodham joined a group of extremely talented young women at Wellesley College, situated in a Boston suburb, in the fall of 1965. Harvard, Yale, and the other Ivy League universities still excluded female students. Wellesley was part of a consortium of women's colleges, including Barnard, Bryn Mawr, Mount Holyoke, Smith, Radcliffe, and Vassar, that mirrored the Ivies. Dubbed the Seven Sisters, these institutions attracted some of the nation's brightest, most accomplished young women. Rodham was also admitted to Radcliffe, Vassar, and Smith, but she chose Wellesley partly because one of her favorite high school teachers was a Wellesley graduate.[1] Many of Rodham's classmates had attended private boarding schools, were in the top 1 percent of their graduating classes, had traveled extensively, were fluent in foreign languages, and were quite sophisticated for their age. Nevertheless, Rodham distinguished herself at Wellesley through her academic performance, extracurricular contributions, and personal traits, and was selected as the college's first student commencement speaker. In her speech, Rodham gained national notoriety by critiquing the commencement address of African American senator Edward Brooke (R-MA).

As for many young people, Rodham's college years were a time of self-examination and questioning inherited beliefs and values. During her four years at Wellesley, her political and religious convictions were strongly challenged, and some of them changed. She gradually abandoned the political conservatism of her father and Paul Carlson, and solidified her commitment to a social gospel Protestantism, the aims of which coincided with those of many idealistic youths during the tumultuous 1960s. "My world exploded when I got to Wellesley," she told a PBS interviewer.[2] Don Jones, formerly her youth pastor at Park Ridge, helped Rodham navigate the intellectual terrain and spiritual trials she faced in college.

Following her graduation from Wellesley in May 1969, Rodham spent four years at Yale Law School, where she further distinguished herself through her scholarship, campus leadership, internships, and pro bono work. After completing her degree at Yale in 1973, Rodham worked for seven months with the Children's Defense Fund and then for eight months on the staff of the House Judiciary Committee, which was leading the impeachment investigation of President Richard Nixon. In 1974, she moved to Fayetteville, Arkansas, to be with Bill Clinton, whom she had begun dating at Yale and married in October 1975. During her years in New Haven, Connecticut, and Washington, DC, and her first six years in Arkansas, she rarely attended church.[3] In 1980, however, after the birth of Chelsea, her only child, and Bill's traumatic loss in his second gubernatorial race, she became deeply involved in the life and ministry of First United Methodist Church in Little Rock, and her faith motivated some of her activities as Arkansas's first lady. Hillary played an important though controversial role in the 1992 presidential election.

Wellesley College

When Rodham arrived on campus, Wellesley in some ways was still mired in the Victorian age. Wellesley was, as it had been for decades, "a staid, prestigious conservative institution."[4] A *Time* magazine article "described Wellesley students as a breed of wholesome creatures, unencumbered by the world's woes, whose education and personalities destined them to the inspiring life of a 'well-adjusted housewife.'" Many Wellesley seniors were determined to get their "ring by spring!" Women were required to wear a skirt to dinner, allowed to have male visitors in their rooms only from 2:00 to 5:00 p.m. on Sundays, and had to be back in their rooms every evening by midnight or occasionally 1:00 a.m.[5]

Wellesley's campus life and its students' expectations would change dramatically, however, during the next four years as Americans experienced social upheaval, political turmoil, protest movements, and intellectual ferment and as Rodham and her classmates pressured Wellesley's administrators to change some of the college's policies. President Lyndon Johnson sought to implement his

Great Society program, while African Americans, Native Americans, and women strove to obtain equality. Colonies around the world fought to gain their independence. Apartheid reigned in South Africa. Throngs of demonstrators protested racial and sexual discrimination and the Vietnam War. In 1968, riots erupted in Paris, the Soviets crushed an uprising in Prague, and Martin Luther King Jr. and Robert Kennedy were assassinated. Students at hundreds of institutions called for changes in the curriculum and campus life, and the counterculture gained adherents and attention. Many questioned the bedrock assumptions and values of American life and society. Meanwhile, Wellesley students attended classes, developed deep friendships, dated male students at nearby colleges and universities, and reevaluated their belief systems. Rodham's political science professor Alan Schechter explained that "the aura of the martyred [John F.] Kennedy was strong" on campuses, and everyone talked passionately about alleviating racism or joining the Peace Corps. "The mood was one of youthful idealism."[6]

Time magazine named the whole cohort of Americans twenty-five and under its 1966 "Man of the Year," asserting, "Never have the young been so assertive or so articulate, so well educated or so worldly [or] enmeshed so early or so earnestly in society." Members of this generation embraced "every philosophy from Anarchy to Zen." Many of them were participating in the civil rights movement and cared deeply about "deprived and spurned citizens" at home and abroad, and some were protesting the war in Vietnam. They criticized the older generation's materialism, greed, and despoiling of the environment and strove to create a kinder, more equitable society. *Time* contended that no organized movement, including the Christian church, had the power to inspire them. Harvard chaplain Paul Santmire lamented that most young Americans had "been fed a Milquetoast gospel" and viewed "religion with a certain anthropological sophistication." However, he added, "they really would like to believe." *Time* insisted that younger Americans possessed "a built-in bunk detector" that enabled them to sniff out "dishonesty and double standards." Members of this generation, *Time* predicted optimistically, "will land on the moon, cure cancer and the common cold, [build] smog-free cities, enrich the underdeveloped world and, no doubt, write finis to poverty and war." They would also supply "a new sense of morality, a transcendent and contemporary ethic that could infinitely enrich" society.[7] Only the first aspect of *Time*'s prophecy was fulfilled, but the magazine's assessment illustrates the high expectations many had for the Baby Boomer generation.

Like most other colleges established in nineteenth-century America, Wellesley has religious roots. Chartered in 1870 by Congregationalist Henry Fowle

Durant, a Boston lawyer and businessman, and his wife, Pauline, it welcomed its first students in 1875. Famed evangelist Dwight L. Moody served as a spiritual mentor to Henry Durant and was a member of the college's board from 1876 until 1899. Durant sought to help women obtain full equality in American society. In an 1877 sermon, he declared, "We revolt against the slavery in which women are held by the customs of society—the broken health, the aimless lives, the subordinate position, the helpless dependence, the dishonesties and shams of so-called education. The High Education of Women is one of the great world battle-cries for freedom. . . . It is the assertion of absolute equality."[8] Durant wanted the college to be led by women, and Wellesley has always had a female president. He designed Wellesley to be a distinctively Christian college. Its early curriculum was centered around the study of the Bible and church history. The Bible, Durant insisted, should always be studied with "profound reverence" and a "heartfelt prayer that our heavenly Father would give us help and strength from above, that we might read aright and learn its lessons in simplicity and in truth."[9] Shortly before dying of Bright's disease in 1881, he charged the faculty to "have faith, work and pray, and be co-laborers with God." He exhorted students similarly to "try to lead souls to God. [Make] Christ first in all things and always."[10] Over the years, Wellesley, like hundreds of other American colleges, deemphasized its Christian roots and the teaching of the Bible and became a largely secular institution, although it still had a chaplain and a required Bible course when Rodham attended.[11]

Situated next to Lake Waban, Wellesley's beautiful five hundred–acre campus includes hills, woodlands, meadows, and an arboretum. Wellesley has long had an outstanding academic reputation. For many years, it has been ranked among the nation's top-five national liberal arts colleges and often has been the highest-ranking women's college in this category. Its many distinguished alumni include Katharine Lee Bates, an 1880 graduate and longtime Wellesley English professor, who penned "America the Beautiful." Other notable alumnae are Soong Mei-ling (also known as Madame Chiang Kai-shek), who was first lady of China and then of Taiwan; the first female US secretary of state Madeleine Albright; astronaut Pamela Melroy; author Nora Ephron; composers Elizabeth Bell and Natalie Sleeth; journalists Callie Crossley, Diane Sawyer, and Cokie Roberts; and three US ambassadors.

During her four years at Wellesley, which she called "among the most exhilarating and informative of my life," Rodham questioned both her religious and political beliefs, changing some and solidifying others.[12] She played a major role in Wellesley's student government as a class officer and as president her senior year, helping change some of the college's educational and student life policies. After serving as the president of Wellesley Young Republicans during her freshman year, Rodham gradually became a Democrat, although she continued to support some Republican candidates. Each academic year, she rethought some issues and grew firmer in her convictions.[13] Rodham "struggled to reconcile competing visions of the good—to bring together her intellectual realism with her spiritual compassion."[14] She grappled with racial injustice, women's rights, abortion, and US foreign policy (especially the Vietnam War), all of which would later be major issues in her political career. Like countless other college students, she doubted some of her religious convictions, even though they were more strongly grounded than those of many of her peers. Although she continued to attend church and participate in a campus religious organization, her life did not revolve around Christian activities as it had in Park Ridge.

As a campus leader, Rodham had good relationships with student groups as varied as sororities and Students for a Democratic Society. Eschewing extremism, she adopted a moderate, pragmatic approach and communicated effectively with faculty and administrators. Many of her classmates insisted that Rodham displayed "the same character, political style and outlook" at Wellesley as she did later as first lady.[15] After examining Wellesley's archives, minutes of student government meetings, and reports about its actions in the student newspaper and interviewing numerous professors, classmates, and contemporaries, Michael Kruse argued that the "political personality that has defined" Rodham throughout her political career was evident at Wellesley: "centrist, cautious, respectful of authority, progressive but never at the expense of maintaining access to the seats of power." She was the principal "intermediary between her increasingly radicalized fellow students and a change-resistant faculty and administration." Some of her classmates complained that she had been coopted by the administration and was far "too mainstream," but others judged her pragmatic style to be effective in the tumultuous atmosphere of the late 1960s.[16]

Early in her freshman year, Rodham met Geoffrey Shields, a junior at Harvard, and they dated for more than two years. She discussed many of the era's most controversial topics with Shields and his classmates. Rodhan became very animated, Shields remembered, when debating "racial issues, the Vietnam War, civil rights, civil liberties." She had little interest in abstract philosophical questions or literature, Shields added, but she loved to argue about whether morality is relative to "a particular time or circumstance or whether there are absolute moral principles." Shields concluded that "she was a [moral] relativist" at this point in life.[17] Rodham, however, told a friend that "I believe there are some absolute truths," but she was unsure whether people could discover them.[18] Many Wellesley women and Harvard men, Carl Bernstein asserted, believed that Rodham "had a self-righteous streak," but it was not a major aspect of her character.[19]

Clinton attended worship services and the meetings of the college's interdenominational chapel society frequently while at Wellesley. As noted, she questioned aspects of her religious socialization and belief system, especially the alleged connection between biblical teaching and political conservatism. However, she rejected the more radical political and ideological positions espoused by the counterculture during the turbulent 1960s. While moving to the left politically, she remained a committed Methodist, influenced by her church experiences as a youth, Methodist social activism, her ongoing relationship with Don Jones, and *motive* magazine, a liberal Methodist journal designed primarily for college students. She took Wellesley's required course in the Bible, for which she later professed gratitude. By the late 1960s, the Methodist Church was no longer admonishing youth to avoid dancing and alcohol consumption, but Clinton drank sparingly. In a letter to Jones, she noted that she was having "as much fun as any good Methodist can."[20] Her college friends testified that she did not smoke marijuana, drink to excess, or embrace the era's hedonism.[21] Rodham called herself "a moral Methodist" and "a progressive, an ethical Christian and a political activist."[22]

Rodham's interest in social issues led her to participate in the chapel society instead of the campus's branch of the evangelical InterVarsity Fellowship. Led by Paul Santmire, the college's chaplain, this organization focused on discussing social problems and the jeremiads of Old Testament prophets against injustice.[23] Clinton's faith also helped prompt her to tutor low-income students in Roxbury, a Boston suburb, in reading. She praised Wellesley's emphasis on service; its motto was "'Not to be ministered unto, but to minister'—a phrase in line with my own Methodist upbringing."[24] "My activist faith was sharpened by the social upheavals of the 1960s and 1970s," she wrote later. "In college and law school, my friends and I spent many long nights debating the morality and efficacy of civil disobedience, dodging the draft, and other forms of resistance."[25]

Jones continued to have a significant impact on Rodham's worldview during her years at Wellesley. Through their correspondence, he served as her "confessor, partner in Socratic debate, and spiritual adviser." When she dealt with depression during her freshman year and considered dropping out, she turned to Jones for comfort and counsel, as she would many more times during the next three decades. In a letter to her that year, Jones discussed Edmund Burke's emphasis on individual responsibility and asked "whether someone can be a Burkean realist about history and human nature and at the same time have liberal sentiments and visions." "It is an interesting question you posed," Clinton responded. "Can one be a mind conservative and a heart liberal?" She would grapple with this issue for the next fifty years.[26]

Meeting Black students as part of her high school youth group experiences led Rodham to want to learn more about African Americans and the challenges they faced. Wellesley had no Black faculty, and only six of the more than four hundred women in Rodham's freshman class were African Americans. Early in her first semester, she took a Black classmate with her to an otherwise all-white church service at Christ Church Methodist in Wellesley. When Rodham called some friends in Park Ridge to tell them what she had done, they reprimanded her for what they deemed a political act. Rodham complained in a letter to Jones that these people "thought she did this not out of goodwill but as a symbolic gesture to [challenge] a lily-white church." Had someone done the same thing a year earlier, Rodham confessed to Jones, she would have concluded, "Look how liberal that girl is trying to be going to church with a Negro."[27] By bringing her Black friend to church, Rodham told Jones, "I was testing me as much as I was testing the church."[28]

Motive Magazine

When Rodham went to Wellesley, her home church gave her a subscription to *motive*, a magazine published monthly during the academic year by the Methodist Student Movement. *Motive* was founded in 1941 by Harold Ehrensperger, a friend of Mohandas Gandhi who helped establish India's first school of journalism and later headed the creative arts and religion program at Boston University. During the second half of the 1960s, the arts-and-culture magazine served as "the virtual national magazine of the entire student Christian movement" of mainline Protestant churches.[29] In 1966, *Time* declared that it stood out from other religious publications "like a miniskirt at a church social."[30] *Motive* contained articles and poems on varied social issues, usually written from a Methodist social-justice perspective consistent with Rodham's personal faith.[31] *Motive* featured some of the world's most prominent politicians, theologians, activists, and public intellectuals, including Democratic senator J.

William Fulbright, chair of the Senate Foreign Relations Committee; Columbia University professor and future secretary of state Zbigniew Brzezinski; Argentine Methodist liberation theologian Jose Miguez Bonino; Jurgen Moltmann, professor of systematic theology at the University of Tubingen; Paul Ramsay, who taught ethics and religion at Princeton University; Harvard Divinity School theologian Harvey Cox, author of the controversial *The Secular City* (1965); civil rights activist Julian Bond; Eldridge Cleaver, minister of information for the Black Panther Party and author of *Soul on Ice* (1968); and socialist Howard Zinn, who taught political science at Boston University and later penned *A People's History of the United States* (1980). *Motive* articles demanded an end to the war in Vietnam, questioned the dominant explanation of the Cold War, classified the United States as an imperialist power, strongly supported the civil rights movement, and exhorted college students to reform society. Other articles discussed the "death of God" movement, the negative impact of technology, violence in Africa, racial justice, African American history, civil disobedience, protests at American universities against racism and war, and the US government's responsibility to help the poor. Many progressive Methodist leaders were upset by *motive*'s increasingly radical religious and political positions in the later 1960s. As Rodham was graduating from Wellesley, the May 1969 *motive* special issue on women's liberation was removed from the presses because of the controversy caused by its use of vulgarity and discussion of lesbianism.[32] In 1972, the United Methodist Church discontinued funding the magazine; *motive*'s final two issues focused on lesbianism, feminism, and male homosexuality.

As Rodham began her freshman year at Wellesley, *motive* contained an article discussing free speech on college campuses and protests against *in loco parentis* (school officials acting in the place of parents), demanding that students have a greater voice in determining what they studied and that education be made more relevant to their future enterprises.[33] Other articles in this issue described the revolt of some college students against middle-class American values, urged readers to reform the ecumenical movement, and protested that American leaders believed that might makes right.[34] Many college students, Julian Bond exulted, were foregoing diplomas, jobs, adult approval, and personal security to participate in the civil rights struggle.[35] Another author rejoiced that at almost every American college, a core group of students was fighting to end racial discrimination, alleviate poverty, promote peace, and improve education.[36] In a review of Clark Kerr's *The Uses of the University* and Harvey Cox's *The Secular City*, Roger Shinn, professor of applied Christianity at Union Theological Seminary, exhorted students to stimulate, learn from, criticize, and help direct the social and political revolutions of their day.[37] An article titled "A Student Manifesto: A Model for Revolutionary Mission" asserted that students confronted "radically new possibilities" for "freedom or bondage, creation or destruction." The "Christ event" had "shattered the first century ethos," made believers children of God, and given them "the awesome responsibility of administering the affairs of the world in the name of God." Christian revolutionaries realized that their lives were inextricably intertwined with those of people living in Selma, Alabama, Cuba, and Vietnam. Colleges, the manifesto declared, must prepare visionaries to move beyond the church "to meet the Lord" in the midst of the world's "social, political, and economic upheaval."[38] Strongly affected by the left-leaning articles she read, Rodham would take up some of these challenges in her years at Wellesley. She would respond to others later through her work as a lawyer, governor's wife, first lady, US senator, secretary of state, and presidential candidate.

As first lady, Clinton noted that she still had all the issues of *motive* she had received as a college student and asserted that the article that had most affected her during these years was one by New Left leader Carl Oglesby. "It was the first thing I had ever read that challenged the Vietnam War," Clinton recalled. Her growing opposition to the war contributed to her switching from being a Goldwater Republican to a McGovern Democrat.[39] After working in a military industry job, Oglesby joined Students for a Democratic Society (SDS) and served as the organization's president in 1965 and 1966. His antiwar speech at a rally in Washington in November 1965, titled "Let Us Shape the Future," is widely regarded as "a landmark of American political rhetoric."[40] Oglesby complained that many Americans self-righteously denounced communist tyranny while ignoring the "right-wing tyrannies that our businessmen traffic with and our nation profits from every day."[41] Under his leadership, SDS, which had 100,000 members by 1968, fueled opposition to the Vietnam War.

In his *motive* article, Oglesby repudiated the conventional arguments for US intervention in Vietnam and elsewhere. The basic reason, he argued, was that the United States sought to make the world safe for American businessmen to operate everywhere "on terms always advantageous, in environments always protected by friendly or puppet oligarchies." Americans might "rather effectively disguise our imperialist motives from ourselves," but "we have an empire that is administered around the world by the business community and guarded by the government."[42]

Oglesby averred that every American with a television set knew about the devastating effects of our nation's saturation bombing of North Vietnam. If the United States refused to stop this carnage, it would be as culpable as the "decent Germans" who ignored Adolf Eichmann's slaughter of the Jews at Auschwitz. He urged the United States to leave Vietnam immediately, pay reparations to both North and South Vietnam equal to as much as one-tenth of what had been spent to destroy these countries, and "promise never again to intervene in a revolutionary struggle." He also implored Americans to make revolutions unnecessary by restoring "the principle of no-aid-to-tyrants that was originally the heart of the Alliance for Progress" and by reducing the power of international corporations.[43]

Why, Oglesby asked, were so many people willing to rebel against their oppressors, face terror and brutality, and risk death? People did "not take up arms for stupid reasons learned from a Marxist handbook," but rather because of the horrible conditions under which they lived. They were motivated by the same reasons that led Fanny Lou Hamer and other American activists to fight for basic civil rights despite the bombing of churches, murders of children, lynchings of men, and brutal responses to their demonstrations and marches.[44]

Rodham spent the summer of 1966 at a cottage on the Lake Michigan shore, babysitting and doing research for Christopher Beal, a former Wellesley professor who was editing a book about the Vietnam War, which was published in 1968 as *The Realities of Vietnam: A Ripon Society Appraisal* (the Ripon Society was a liberal Republican movement founded in 1964). By the end of the summer, Rodham was adamantly opposed to the war, even though the antiwar movement had just begun and she identified as a (Nelson) Rockefeller Republican.[45]

Saul Alinsky

Rodham majored in political science at Wellesley and planned to go to law school. Alona Evans, chair of Wellesley's Political Science Department and a specialist in international criminal law and refugee issues, introduced Rodham to the work of radical activist and Chicago organizer Saul Alinsky, whom Rodham had met as a high school student.[46] Alinsky was one of the American left's most revered leaders. He was celebrated by some and reviled by others for his use of boycotts, picketing, rent strikes, and dramatic gestures to confront city officials, corporate executives, and slum landlords.[47]

Wayne Leys argued in *Christian Century* that Alinsky was "Machiavelli in Modern Dress"; he contended that Alinsky's 1946 book *Reveille for Radicals* implied that "power can be used for good ends, even though it be built up by deception," and called for alliances between Christians and atheistic

communists.[48] A 1965 *Christian Century* editorial insisted that Alinsky's methods "are ineffective, divisive and ethically sub-Christian."[49] Despite such criticisms, in the 1960s Alinsky became respectable, even revered by some. Protestant church leaders in Rochester, New York, invited him to help extinguish
the city's smoldering fires of racial unrest that had erupted in riots during
the summer of 1965. In that year, *The Nation* praised Alinsky as America's
"leading hellraiser," and *Harper's* published a laudatory interview calling him
a "professional radical."[50] Responding to the *Harper's* piece, *Christian Century*
lamented that a small number of influential urban leaders and a surprisingly
large number of Protestant and Roman Catholic clergymen had "mistakenly
swallowed Mr. Alinsky's theories of community organization." The editors
agreed that American urban society must be radically restructured to eliminate
unjust and harmful social arrangements, but they protested that Alinsky's
policies and practices contradicted "Judeo-Christian concepts of human rights
and human values."[51]

Rodham spent many hours during her senior year writing an honors thesis
on the efforts of Alinsky and others to reduce poverty. Her ninety-two-page
thesis reads "like a capstone of her own intellectual and ideological evolution
at Wellesley."[52] Alinsky, Rodham argued, claimed to be a moral relativist, but
he believed in human goodness and insisted that if fear and privation were
eliminated, people would live in peace.[53] Upon her graduation, she was invited by Alinsky to work with him as an organizer in a predominantly African
American neighborhood in Oakland, California; despite her admiration for
him, she declined the offer and instead enrolled in Yale Law School. In her
thesis, Rodham criticized Lyndon Johnson's Great Society programs for not
sufficiently including input from its intended beneficiaries—the poor—while
also contending that Alinsky's bottom-up, community-organizing approach
would not produce significant long-term comprehensive changes.[54] In her
2003 memoir, *Living History*, Clinton insisted that although she and Alinsky
agreed about "the value of empowering people to help themselves," they differed about how to effect social change. He "believed you could change the
system only from the outside," she wrote. "I didn't."[55]

Changing Wellesley and Political Activism

Led by Rodham, the class of 1969 changed Wellesley's academic program and
campus life more than any other in the college's history. As a member of the
student government, Rodham worked, like student leaders on many other

campuses during the late 1960s, to institute a pass-fail option for courses, reduce the number of required courses, and increase visitation hours in the dorms. She also encouraged Wellesley to recruit and admit more students of color, appoint more Black faculty, create more Black studies courses, and devise a summer Upward Bound program for minority children.[56] The college stopped requiring women to wear skirts at dinner and when going into town, and it introduced interdisciplinary majors.[57] Showing signs of her future prominence, Rodham stood out among Wellesley's "many intelligent, accomplished women," classmate Nancy Gist argued, because of her charisma, leadership, ability to focus, and maturity.

Rodham's confrontational nature was also evident at Wellesley. The college president, Ruth Adams, declared that dealing with her was challenging for anyone "disagreeing with her. She could be very insistent." In classroom discussions, classmate Gale Lyon-Rosenberger observed, Rodham's comments were sometimes "a little cutting." Rodham welcomed the approbation brought by her efforts to improve Wellesley's academic and social life. "Recognition was important to her," Geoff Shields averred.[58]

Rodham was deeply disturbed by the assassination of Martin Luther King Jr. on April 4, 1968. After hearing about his death, a classmate reported, she hurled her bookbag across the room. She cried, yelled, asked questions, and declared, "I can't stand it anymore." She called the head of Wellesley's Black student organization to express her condolences. A month later, Rodham participated in a two-day strike during which numerous Wellesley students attended workshops and teach-ins on racism and war instead of going to classes.[59] Wearing a black armband, she also marched with protesters in Boston.

Although Rodham helped organize antiwar rallies and participated in sit-ins and teach-ins, she was not a radical. She was influenced by the books and articles of Will Herberg, a conservative Jewish social philosopher and professor at Drew University, who denounced the spiritual rootlessness of America's 1960s "flower power" culture as a fleeting trend that was doomed to die because it had been cut off from its spiritual roots in Judeo-Christian teaching on "freedom, brotherhood, justice, and personal dignity."[60] Herberg helped convince Rodham that instead of tearing down American society, people should work to make it more just and responsive to the needs of all groups.[61] Rodham reported that she also read books by Neo-Orthodox theologian Karl Barth and Anglican apologist C. S. Lewis.[62]

During the summer of 1968, Rodham had an internship with the House Republican Conference in Washington. Working for Wisconsin congressman

Melvin Laird, who later served as secretary of defense under Richard Nixon, she wrote a position paper analyzing American options in Vietnam. Rodham argued that Lyndon Johnson had not properly assessed the human and financial costs of escalating the war. In March 1968, Rodham traveled to New Hampshire to campaign for Eugene McCarthy, an antiwar candidate challenging Johnson for the Democratic nomination. Still undecided about her political affiliation, in early August, she went to the Republican National Convention in Miami to support Nelson Rockefeller's eleventh-hour campaign to pilfer the party's presidential nomination from Richard Nixon. In late August, Rodham took a train to the Democratic National Convention with her friend Betsy Ebeling and was shocked by the violent protests they witnessed, which Ebeling described as "mayhem."[63]

A Controversial Commencement Speech

Rodham's address as Wellesley's first student commencement speaker on May 31, 1969, catapulted her into the limelight for the first time. *Life* magazine included excerpts of her speech as part of an article on the year's most noteworthy commencement addresses, subtitled "With Eloquent Defiance, Top Students Protest Right through Commencement." Major newspapers, including the *Washington Post, New York Times*, and *Chicago Tribune*, also discussed her speech, and Rodham was interviewed on the nationally televised *Irv Kupcinet Show*. Her speech provides a glimpse into Rodham's perspective on life as she graduated from college and probably contributed to her belief that she had a future in politics.

What made Rodham's speech memorable was her response to the commencement address of Republican senator Edward Brooke. Her political science professor Alan Schechter called Rodham's prepared speech, which she read to him before commencement, "a perfect example of youthful idealism at the time."[64] Upset by Brooke's address, however, Rodham added extemporaneous remarks, criticizing Brooke's complacency toward America's social ills. "The entire tone" of the senator's speech, she explained later, was "very discouraging."[65] Brooke applauded the nation's incremental progress and insisted that "the overwhelming majority of Americans will stand firm on one principle: Coercive protest is wrong," especially "because it is unnecessary."[66] In *Living History*, Clinton argued that Brooke's speech "sounded like a defense of President Nixon's policies, notable more for what it didn't say than what it did."[67] As one of her classmates put it, "Senator Brooke basically told us everything was fine and that people who were protesting were elite ne'er-do-wells. I remember sitting in my seat fuming."[68]

Articulating aspects of social gospel theology, the social concerns of her generation, and her own uncertainty about many issues, Rodham attacked middle-class American values. Her speech, however, was "more of a manifesto of moderation than a revolutionary's battle cry."[69] Rodham's disjointed and rambling remarks expressed the confusion, angst, and disappointment of her generation, especially about the widespread lack of trust, integrity, and respect in American society. During their four years at Wellesley, Rodham explained, she and her classmates had confronted a large gap between their expectations and social realities and had questioned "basic assumptions underlying our education." She was pleased that she and her classmates had reduced the gap between their aspirations and actual conditions and had gained a voice in "the process of academic decision making." Rodham lamented the futility of America's "prevailing, acquisitive, and competitive corporate life," expressed her generation's desire to escape "the burden of inauthentic reality," and urged her classmates to grapple "with some of the inarticulate maybe even inarticulable things that we're feeling." Rodham protested that for "too long our leaders have viewed politics as the art of the possible." She urged Americans to instead "practice politics as the art of making what appears to be impossible possible." Quoting a poem by her classmate Nancy Scheibner, she concluded that the members of her generation were called "not to save the world in a glorious crusade," but rather to use their skills to promote trust, integrity, and respect and effect meaningful changes in society.[70] Rodham's rhetoric seems mild in retrospect, but her boldness in challenging a US senator made it unforgettable to her classmates. Impressed by her courage and thrilled by her critique, they gave her a seven-minute standing ovation.[71]

Not everyone was pleased by Rodham's speech. Some Wellesley administrators were upset that she had disparaged a renowned politician. The *Chicago Tribune* hoped that "youngsters of 21 and less who now find courtesy and patience and reliance on 'nonviolent political change' impossible" would someday become mature and "exemplify these badly needed virtues."[72]

After graduating from Wellesley, Rodham, seeking adventure, spent the summer of 1969 in Alaska. While 400,000 young people listened to music at Woodstock and millions around the world watched Neil Armstrong walk on the moon, Rodham washed dishes at the Mt. McKinley Park Hotel in Denali National Park and gutted salmon at a cannery in Valdez, wearing hip boots and an apron. She was fired for complaining too vehemently about the unhealthy pastiness of some of the salmon. Rodham joked in 2007 that this job was the "best preparation for being in Washington that you can possibly imagine."[73]

Yale Law School

Rodham was accepted at both Yale and Harvard law schools but chose Yale because many of its faculty championed using the law as a major agent of social change, a perspective that resonated with her life goals. The courts, she believed, had done more than presidents, Congress, or state legislatures to desegregate the nation and protect civil liberties.[74] Rodham also decided against Harvard after a law school professor, mirroring the 1973 movie *The Paper Chase*, dismissively told her, "We don't need any more women at Harvard."[75] At Yale Law School, Rodham's worldview continued to be informed by her Methodist social-justice commitments, but she rarely attended church. A minor celebrity because of her commencement address, she stood out in the classroom and fought to improve conditions on campus and beyond. Rodham urged the administration to provide tampon machines in women's restrooms and was one of the school's leading student opponents of the Vietnam War. She worked to help children who were being treated for various mental and physical problems at Yale New Haven Hospital. Rodham also worked pro bono at the New Haven Legal Assistance Association, specializing in child abuse cases.[76]

Rodham excelled academically and served on the board of editors of the *Yale Review of Law and Social Action*. The law school had other outstanding students who went on to contribute significantly to American society, including future secretary of labor Robert Reich, Supreme Court Justice Clarence Thomas, and Bill Clinton. In fact, these four took a civil liberties class together. According to Reich, every time the professor asked a question, Rodham's hand went up first, and whenever she was called on, she answered correctly. Reich often volunteered answers, which were right about half the time. Thomas never said a word, and Clinton spent much more time doing political work than attending class.

Rodham and Clinton began to date during the spring of 1971. Hillary could have graduated a year before Bill, who had spent two years at Oxford University on a Rhodes scholarship after graduating from Georgetown University. However, because of their relationship, Rodham decided to stay in New Haven for a fourth year. She had begun to develop a specialty in children's law and spent the year studying child development at the Yale Child Study Center. As part of her work there, she wrote an article on the rights of children that was published in the *Harvard Educational Review* in 1973 and would later cause controversy.

Rodham's summer experiences during her years in law school helped shape her subsequent life. In May 1970, she spoke at a League of Women Voters convention and met the keynote speaker, Marian Wright Edelman, whom Rodham revered for her work in helping children. Edelman, the daughter of a Baptist minister, shared Rodham's belief that Christians were obligated to serve the needy. A graduate of Yale Law School and eight years older than Rodham, Edelman had worked with the NAACP Legal Defense Fund in New York and Mississippi. In early June, Rodham moved to Washington to work for a new organization Edelman had created, the Washington Research Project, a public interest law firm. Edelman assigned Rodham to work with a Senate subcommittee headed by Walter Mondale of Minnesota that was investigating the working and living conditions of migrant farm laborers and their families. Rodham had firsthand experience with this issue from babysitting the children of migrant workers near her Park Ridge home as a teenager. Her work focused on researching the health and education of migrant children, primarily in the South. Rodham helped document migrants' inadequate housing and deplorable sanitation facilities and the lack of schooling provided to many of their children. Her report supplied some of the most compelling testimony at the hearings Mondale convened, but the subcommittee's work did not lead to any legislation, reinforcing Rodham's negative perception of electoral politics. Her summer experience helped convince her to eschew corporate law and instead focus on studying how laws affected children.[77]

During the summer of 1971, Rodham interned with the Oakland, California, law firm of Treuhaft, Walker, and Bernstein. She was attracted to the firm because of its focus on constitutional rights and civil liberties and its commitment to combating racial discrimination and social injustice, which resonated with her Methodist social gospel ideals.[78] Its specialties included defending various radical causes, and two of its four partners were current or former Communist Party members. The firm's leading partner, Robert Treuhaft, married to English author Jessica Mitford, had belonged to the American Communist Party, and the House Un-American Activities Committee had considered him one the nation's most subversive attorneys. After becoming disenchanted, however, he left the party in 1958. Nevertheless, the firm defended some Black Panthers, left-wing labor leaders, and other radicals, and was frequently accused of having communist connections.

The next summer, 1972, Rodham worked for fellow Methodist and South Dakota Senator George McGovern as he campaigned for the Democratic presidential nomination. Gary Hart, McGovern's campaign manager and a 1964 Yale Law School graduate, assigned her to San Antonio, Texas, where she worked with Bill Clinton; Taylor Branch, an assistant editor at *The Washington Monthly*, later to achieve fame for his three-volume biography of Martin Luther King Jr.; and Sara Ehrman, who lived with Rodham. In campaigning for McGovern, Rodham strove to "combine her Methodist commitment to making the world right through good works and her thoroughly ingrained liberal political ideology." Ehrman, a Jewish congressional aide to McGovern, who grew up in Queens and was twenty-nine years older than Rodham, described her as a "progressive Christian" who wanted to use "litigation to do good, and to correct injustices" and sought "to live by a kind of spiritual high-mindedness." Rodham read her Bible constantly, often marking verses that were especially important to her, and frequently brought it along while electioneering. She strove to garner support for McGovern by going door to door in hardscrabble neighborhoods to persuade Hispanic residents to vote. Rodham, Ehrman insisted, was indomitable, fearless, and passionate, and believed that God was on her side.[79]

The Children's Defense Fund and the House Judiciary Committee

After graduating from Yale, Rodham, inspired in part by her Christian faith, decided to work for Edelman's newly created Children's Defense Fund (CDF) rather than a prestigious law firm. As noted, Rodham had interned with another organization Edelman headed in Washington in summer 1970, and the activist served as a mentor, role model, and soulmate for Rodham, who shared her Christian convictions and desire to help children.[80] Both women strove to make improving the lives of children a national priority.[81] Rodham went undercover to investigate the problems experienced by children with disabilities in New England and children harmed by systemic racism in the Deep South. She interviewed juvenile offenders in South Carolina who were incarcerated in adult state prisons and knocked on doors in Bedford, Massachusetts, trying to determine why a large discrepancy existed between the number of school-age children recorded by the census and the number enrolled in schools.[82] Rodham worked for the CDF for only seven months, but her long-standing interest in children's welfare led her to subsequently join the CDF's board, which she chaired from 1986 to 1992.

In January 1974, Rodham took a job with the House Judiciary Committee special counsel overseeing the impeachment inquiry into President Richard Nixon triggered by the Watergate scandal. Rodham was one of forty-four attorneys on the staff who had recently graduated from the nation's most highly ranked law schools. They worked seven days a week, sometimes as many as twenty hours per day.[83] After Nixon resigned in August, Rodham rejected offers from prominent law firms in Washington and Manhattan and moved to Arkansas.

In July 1973, Rodham took the District of Columbia bar exam along with 816 other law school graduates. A total of 550 (62 percent) passed, but amazingly Rodham did not. For the first time in her life, the bright, diligent, zealous graduate of one of the nation's top law schools failed spectacularly.[84] Rodham had taken the Arkansas bar exam, which she passed, before sitting for the District of Columbia's more difficult one, and she did not publicly reveal that she had flunked this exam until her 2003 memoir, *Living History*, in which she explained that her failure helped persuade her to move to Arkansas. "I had taken both the Arkansas and Washington, DC, bar exams during the summer," she wrote, "but my heart was pulling me toward Arkansas. When I learned that I passed in Arkansas but failed in DC, I thought that maybe my test scores were telling me something." She added, "Despite the satisfaction of my work, I was lonely and missed Bill more than I could stand."[85] Clinton joined many other luminaries who failed the bar exam, including Franklin Roosevelt, Michelle Obama, California governors Jerry Brown and Pete Wilson, and John F. Kennedy Jr. During the 2016 presidential campaign, Donald Trump would ridicule Clinton for this failure.[86]

While working for the special counsel, Rodham rented a room from Sara Ehrman. When she decided to move to Arkansas to live with Clinton, her landlord offered to drive her there. But Ehrman had ulterior motives; during their 1,193-mile, two-day trip, she painstakingly tried to convince Rodham to return to Washington. Clinton was teaching at the University of Arkansas Law School in Fayetteville, and Ehrman insisted that "she was crazy to go to that Mickey Mouse state to marry a country professor." Ehrman warned Rodham that she was giving up a "promising career for an uncertain future." She saw Rodham as a young, eager, vulnerable, fearful woman who would not fulfill her potential if she moved to Arkansas. To every objection Ehrman raised,

Rodham responded, "I love him, and I want to be with him."[87] Ehrman was right that Rodham's decision to move would be life-altering; she was wrong that it would confine Rodham to a cultural outback where she could not fully use her gifts. A mutual friend asserted that "ultimately Hillary made the decision to join Bill Clinton and to help him change the world." The impact of their partnership would be unprecedented.[88]

First Lady of Arkansas

When Rodham arrived in Arkansas in the summer of 1975, the state had only 2.16 million people and Little Rock, its largest city, was home to 258,000 residents. Walmart had been founded in Arkansas in 1962, but the state was widely regarded as an economic, political, social, cultural, and educational backwater. Betsey Wright, Bill Clinton's chief of staff while he was governor, argued that both Hillary and Bill passionately believed they were called "to make a difference in this world."[89] Carl Bernstein contended that Rodham wanted "to do good on a huge scale." Since adolescence, she had sought "to determine what was right" and "to make it happen." Looking heavenward and inspired by John Wesley's emphasis on service, she brought "an almost messianic sense of purpose" to her marriage to Bill and her work as an attorney and as Arkansas first lady. Her "high-mindedness and purity of vision" transcended "the conventionally political."[90]

After living together off and on for several years, Hillary and Bill, who were now both teaching at the University of Arkansas School of Law, wed on October 11, 1975, in their modest home in Fayetteville. Only fifteen people attended the ceremony performed by Vic Nixon, the pastor of the Central United Methodist Church in Fayetteville. Hillary was the university's second female law professor. While teaching there, she helped open a legal aid clinic at the university, secured funding for it, and served as its first director. In its first year, the clinic provided three hundred clients with student lawyers. In 1977, Rodham became the first female associate at the Rose Law Firm, the nation's third-oldest law practice, founded in 1820, sixteen years before Arkansas became a state. She became the firm's first female partner in 1979 and worked there until 1992, although she took leaves to head an education reform task force and campaign for her husband. Most of her work involved family law and domestic dispute cases, but Rodham also represented a crop duster whose airplane injured a farmworker, a forty-one-year-old factory worker accused of raping a twelve-year-old girl, and a canning company sued by a man who found the rear end of a rat in his pork and beans.[91] *The National Law Journal* named her one of America's hundred most influential lawyers in 1988 and 1991.

In 1976, thirty-year-old Bill Clinton was elected Arkansas's attorney general, and two years later, he was elected governor. After losing the 1980 gubernatorial race, Bill was again elected governor in 1982 and then reelected in 1984, 1986, and 1990. In addition to serving as Arkansas's first lady and specializing in corporate litigation and family law at Rose Law, Hillary engaged in numerous other enterprises. Motivated by her faith, her desire to provide greater opportunities for women, and her quest to improve the lives of children, she chaired the board of the Children's Defense Fund as well as the American Bar Association's Commission on Women in the Profession. She also served on the board of the Legal Services Corporation, a government organization that provided legal aid to the poor, as well as on the boards of the Children's Television Workshop, Southern Development Bancorporation, and Walmart. She cofounded Arkansas Advocates for Children and Families in 1977 and played an active role in the organization. Clinton helped bring a parenting skills program to the state, create a home-instruction program for parents of preschoolers, establish a neonatal care unit at the Arkansas Children's Hospital, and acquire two fully equipped helicopters for hospital use.[92] In addition, she created a six-week summer Governor's School for four hundred gifted, rising high school seniors, held at Hendrix College, a Methodist institution in Conway, which invited her in 1980 to serve as its president.[93]

For the Clintons, 1980 was a pivotal year. Their daughter, Chelsea, was born in February, and in November, Bill lost his reelection campaign. Both events caused Bill and Hillary to reassess their goals, faith, and involvement in the church. After Bill's defeat, the financially strapped Clintons struggled with self-doubt and stress. Shattered at his rejection by the voters, Bill sulked and played the country song "I Don't Know Whether to Kill Myself or Go Bowling" on the jukebox. Hillary held their fragile family together, used the money she had made trading cattle futures in 1978 to buy a small house in Little Rock, and filled it with furniture from thrift stores. Her salary as a lawyer enabled them to pay their bills. The almost $100,000 Hillary earned in a ten-month period through her trading would be scrutinized and widely criticized during the early years of Bill's presidency, as would her investment in the Whitewater real-estate development on land in the Ozarks.[94]

Like many other younger adults, the Clintons ceased attending church for several years while pursuing their careers but resumed their involvement in the church after becoming parents. Many viewed Bill's decision to return to the church as politically motivated because Republican savings and loan executive Frank White, who narrowly defeated him in the 1980 gubernatorial race, was an evangelical Christian who had campaigned aggressively among religious voters and declared his triumph "a victory for the Lord."[95] Many Arkansas voters complained that Hillary "had no religion" and had not been attending church; some even denounced her as a godless liberal. Therefore, one of her motives for returning to church may have been to help Bill's political career.[96] On the other hand, Hillary's faith had been important to her since her childhood and had helped sustain her through many trials. David Brock's contention that Hillary "genuinely seemed to be seeking spiritual guidance and a renewed sense of purpose" by returning to church rings true.[97] David Maraniss argued that religion played "an increasingly important role" in the lives of both Clintons throughout the 1980s. Their faith "eased the burden" of their high-profile lives, "sometimes offering solace and escape from the contentious world of politics, at other times providing theological support for their political choices."[98]

Unlike most couples returning to church, Bill and Hillary chose to participate in different congregations based on their religious backgrounds and convictions. Bill joined Immanuel Baptist Church, a four thousand–member Southern Baptist congregation in Little Rock, and began singing in the choir. Hillary joined First United Methodist, a more theologically liberal congregation attended by scores of younger, affluent professionals, especially lawyers, including many of Little Rock's most prominent ones. Hillary quickly became involved in numerous church activities. Clinton, a local Methodist bishop declared, was "a vibrant and vital part of the life" of First United Methodist "as a Sunday school teacher, a worker with youth, [and] a faithful worshiper."[99] In addition, she served on the church's administrative board and did pro bono legal work on the church's behalf. For several years, Clinton also represented the Methodist Conference of Arkansas. Nancy Wood, chair of the Arkansas State Board of Education and a member of the Sunday school class Clinton taught, insisted, "She's great. She never uses a note. It just pours out." Her classes were discussion-oriented; Clinton presented positions and then solicited reactions from class participants. She "handled people who disagreed with her well."[100] Years later, her pastor, Ed Matthews, vividly remembered one of Clinton's lessons explaining that forgiveness is God's gift, not a human attribute.[101] Clinton strongly supported the church's establishment of a day-care center that by the early 2020s provided full-time and after-school childcare for more than three hundred children.[102]

Clinton also gave a stump speech throughout the state explaining why she was a Methodist, discussing her personal faith and the theology and ministry of John Wesley. She noted that Wesley emphasized both individual salvation and social justice as he implored societies to meet the needs of all their residents and exhorted everyone, if possible, to provide for themselves. She frequently quoted her favorite Wesley statement, which would become her campaign slogan in 2016: "Do all the good you can, by all the means you can, in all the ways you can, in all the places you can, at all the times you can, to all the people you can, as long as you ever can."[103] Clinton spoke at churches belonging to other denominations, including a Baptist church in North Little Rock, where she discussed "Women Armed with the Christian Sword—to Build an Army for the Lord." Her speeches demonstrated that her political perspective drew strength from her religious commitments.[104] In a lecture at Drew University in New Jersey in April 1987, Clinton expressed some of her chief religious convictions. She denounced materialism, selfishness, and excessive individualism, and lamented that America was experiencing a spiritual crisis. Clinton called the 1980s a "Decade of Greed" and, echoing the social-justice message of the religious left, attacked the dangers of capitalism. However, she also expressed alarm about issues that religious conservatives highlighted, including increases in pornography, promiscuity, marital infidelity, divorce, and abortion.[105]

When Chelsea was born, Clinton "prayed that I would be a good enough mother for her."[106] Hillary reported that she and Bill "spent a lot of time talking about our religious faith and beliefs." They agreed that "the most important thing is [having a] personal relationship with God" and viewed their respective churches as places where their faith could grow as they fellowshipped with other Christians.[107] According to Bill, they often discussed "what it meant to live a good life and the nature of life after death."[108] "When Bill is home, he prays with Chelsea every night," Hillary reported. "We say grace at meals. When we cannot get to church, we often have a devotional."[109] Hillary and Bill tried to help Chelsea develop her own spiritual life. When she was young, both parents read her children's versions of Cain and Abel, David and Goliath, Esther, the Good Samaritan, and other Bible stories. The Clintons wanted her to be "part of the fellowship and framework for spiritual development that church offers." After spending time at both of her parents' churches, Chelsea decided at age ten to be confirmed as a Methodist.[110]

Marital problems caused by Bill's unfaithfulness led Hillary to rely deeply on her faith during her years as Arkansas's first lady. It is unclear when Bill's extramarital affairs began exactly, but certainly they started by the early 1980s. Ed Matthews explained that Bill's behavior broke Hillary's heart and prompted her to seek comfort by reading the Psalms. To deal with their problems, the Clintons received counseling from Matthews and prayed together. Bill promised to stop his infidelity but did not do so.[111]

One issue with religious aspects that troubled Hillary in the 1980s was the implementation of the death penalty. A legal brief protesting capital punishment that she wrote in the early 1980s helped prevent the death of a man with an intellectual disability. Meanwhile, Bill had endorsed the death penalty as he moved toward the political center. When Don Jones came to see Hillary in Little Rock soon after she wrote her brief, he argued that the Judeo-Christian tradition provided "fairly strong support for punitive justice," so the death penalty could not be ruled out. Moreover, he insisted, if the just-war theory was morally acceptable, so was capital punishment. Hillary agreed with Jones's reasoning and confessed, "It is agonizing, but I think [some people] have forfeited the right to life." She also agreed with Jones that capital punishment was acceptable not "as a deterrent but [only] as something some people deserve."[112]

The most significant initiative Clinton undertook as Arkansas's first lady was a campaign to reform the state's public schools, which according to Clint Burleson, one of her pastors at First United Methodist, was "grounded in Methodist social concerns."[113] In 1983, Bill appointed her to chair the Arkansas Education Standards Committee, a task force charged with reexamining the state's educational standards. Arkansas's public schools were among the lowest-performing ones in the country.

In speeches promoting education reform at PTA meetings, Kiwanis luncheons, and other venues in towns across the state, Hillary sought to persuade Arkansas residents to accept a sales tax to pay for improving their schools.[114] In so doing, she articulated "some of the same centrist, values-oriented themes of the New Democrat philosophy that Bill would later embrace." Recognizing the need to appeal to Arkansas's many culturally conservative citizens, the state's first lady emphasized personal responsibility and discipline, themes derived from her Methodist heritage, her relationship with Don Jones, and the biblically based social activism of Marian Wright Edelman. Hillary insisted that Arkansas schools could not be effectively reformed until families became stronger and more stable and residents embraced "shared values." Much of what she advocated was similar to the motifs promoted by US Senator Dan Quayle (R-IN) and political commentator William Bennett before these themes became nationally prominent.[115]

Hillary chaired seventy-five committee meetings in three months, visited every county in the state, and heard as much as nine hours of testimony a day.[116] The committee adopted many of the standards devised by the 1983 Reagan commission on education and published in *A Nation at Risk: The Imperative for Educational Reform*. Whereas the Reagan plan called for decentralization, Clinton's plan entailed "centralized command and control" and mandated that any school not meeting state standards could be dissolved or annexed. Every school would have to "conform to a set of elaborate, state-imposed 'standards' designed by Hillary and an elite cadre of education experts and policy wonks." Her plan called for giving the state more power than many Democratic members and almost all Republican members of the state legislature usually wanted to do.[117] Nevertheless, the Arkansas legislature passed all the committee's recommendations. All students were required to take tests to evaluate their academic achievement at the end of third, sixth, and eighth grade; all teachers had to pass a competency test; and a sales tax was enacted to increase education funding, provide equal aid to urban and rural school districts, and raise teachers' salaries by three thousand dollars a year. Although teachers appreciated their higher pay, many of them vociferously complained about having to pass basic skills tests.

When Hillary presented the task force's proposed educational reforms to a legislative committee in 1983, state representative Lloyd George quipped, "I think we've elected the wrong Clinton."[118] Hillary's work on education reform was "a public-relations bonanza," especially because she had been previously considered "something of an oddity in her adopted state." Many had viewed her as a midwestern hippie and a feminist who had kept her maiden name, dressed unfashionably, and pursued her own career.[119] John Robert Starr, editor of the *Arkansas Democrat-Gazette*, claimed that countless Arkansas residents went "from resenting Hillary to really caring a great deal about her." Her friend Diane Blair asserted that her devotion to school reform and children's advocacy causes helped make Hillary popular in the state.[120] Some Arkansas citizens urged her to run for office, and Bill called his wife "one of the best arguments for re-electing me."[121] The state's adoption of these education reforms improved Arkansas's reputation and gave Hillary standing as "a serious player" in politics and policy.[122]

Numerous biographers have argued that Hillary played a major role in helping elect Bill as both governor and president and to perform effectively in both roles. "To Bill's charm, outgoingness, political charisma, and intellectual genius," William Chafe asserted, "she brought direction, stability, discipline, and a personal center." During their years in Arkansas, Hillary "disciplined his impulses, honed his political messages," and helped him create an effective political operation.[123] Starr contended that Hillary was Bill's "number one adviser" while he was governor. Often when discussing political issues with the editor, Bill would say, "Well, Hillary thinks. . . ."[124]

During her years as Arkansas's first lady, many praised Clinton's character. Friends described her as kind, smart, funny, warm, loyal, and tenacious. They insisted that she never complained or discussed the pain Bill's infidelities caused her. Female friends reported that she frequently asked what books they were reading and inquired about their husbands' lives. Hillary knew what schools their children were attending and about the health of their elderly parents.[125] Starr, one of Bill's fiercest critics, extolled Hillary. "She has backbone, he doesn't," he declared. "She has integrity, he doesn't. Bill Clinton will tell you what you want to hear and Hillary will look you in the eye and tell you the truth whether you want to hear it or not, but she'll tell it to you in a way that makes you like it."[126] Roger Morris, by contrast, accused Hillary of failing to condemn exploited labor in Arkansas and owning "highly lucrative stocks in a corrupt commodities market and in companies profiting from racism in South Africa."[127]

Despite Bill's infidelities, Hillary insisted that by 1991, "I'd gotten what I'd always dreamed of—a loving family, a fulfilling career, and a life of service to others—plus more that I had never imagined." But the future would bring even greater accomplishments and challenges.[128]

The 1992 Presidential Campaign

Hillary became an issue in the 1992 presidential campaign because of statements she and Bill made, her personality, an article she had written about children's rights, and what she represented to many Americans. On the other hand, her defense of her husband against accusations of a long-standing affair with Gennifer Flowers and her effective campaigning helped him win the election.

Rarely in presidential campaigns has a candidate's wife been attacked, but Hillary often was. Speakers at the 1992 Republican National Convention castigated Bill as "a skirt chaser and draft dodger" and Hillary as a nontraditional, unfeminine woman.[129] Many were troubled by the Clintons' repeated refrain that if Bill was elected, the nation would get a "copresidency." "Buy one, get one free," the Clintons proclaimed. "You vote for him, you get me," Hillary frequently declared. Critics complained that the Clintons were promoting the idea of an "unprecedented partnership in the White House."[130]

Two comments Hillary made during the 1992 campaign caused considerable controversy. On January 26, 1992, on CBS's *60 Minutes*, immediately following the Washington Redskins' victory in the Super Bowl, Hillary responded aggressively to questions about her marriage and Bill's alleged twelve-year affair with Flowers by invoking Tammy Wynette's 1968 country hit "Stand by Your Man." She told an estimated audience of fifty million viewers, "I'm not sitting here [as] some little woman standing by my man like Tammy Wynette." Instead, she added, "I'm sitting here because I love him, and I respect him, and I honor what he's been through and what we've been through together." Many Americans complained that Clinton's remark belittled both traditional marriages and country artists. However, pundits agreed that Hillary's spirited defense of her husband against accusations of sexual infidelity was critical to his electoral success. Hillary sought to show her independence, which alienated many traditionalist voters, while supporting her husband—an approach that, especially because of later revelations about Bill's infidelity, was widely viewed "as a kind of surrender."[131]

Hillary stirred more controversy seven weeks later. Responding to questions about whether a conflict of interest existed between her work as a lawyer and her husband's position as governor, she snapped, "I suppose I could have stayed home and baked cookies and had teas, but what I decided to do was to fulfill my profession, which I entered before my husband was in public life." Many were offended by Hillary's apparent condescension toward women who did not work outside the home. Clinton insisted that her remark had been misunderstood and that she had been referring only to the ceremonial duties of the first lady, not the homemaking role. *New York Times* columnist William Safire accused Hillary of violating a fundamental principle of campaigning: "You do not defend yourself from a conflict-of-interest charge by insulting a large segment of the voting public." Safire added that Clinton came "across as a political bumbler" by appearing to express "contempt for women who work at home."[132] Her comments sparked debate over what role women should play at home, at work, and in politics, as would her presidential campaigns in 2008 and 2016.[133]

Republicans strove to make Hillary's influence on Bill a campaign issue. Even though Nancy Reagan helped run the nation and Barbara Bush had a significant voice in her husband's administration, Republicans mined "fears as old as Adam and Eve about the dangers of an assertive, ambitious woman speaking into the ear of her man."[134] They portrayed her as "a hard-bitten careerist" who stayed with Bill, despite his infidelity, only to capture the White House.[135] Republicans lambasted Hillary as an arrogant, abrasive radical feminist who demeaned stay-at-home mothers.[136] Some journalists called Hillary the "H-bomb" factor of the campaign, and *US News and World Report* castigated her as an "overbearing, yuppie wife from hell."[137]

Republicans also denounced her "unorthodox legal writings," which argued that children deserved legal rights and that some decisions about their lives "should not be made unilaterally by parents."[138] Sociologist Christopher Lasch accused Clinton of seeking to redefine the family and reduce the authority of parents. She allegedly wanted to make children equal to adults before the law and to empower the state to assume many parental responsibilities. Her writings, Lasch argued, implied that the family stymied children's development, whereas the state set them free.[139] Conservative columnist Cal Thomas slammed Clinton as a Lady Macbeth who brought "toil and trouble" to the American family.[140] Republicans often quoted statements from her legal articles out of context to depict Clinton as an enemy of the traditional family.[141] Speaking at a ministers' gathering in Cleveland in late October 1992, Clinton defended her position by citing a pastoral letter from the National Conference of Catholic Bishops. Everyone agreed that "the family is the primary developer of the values and the mindset of a child," she declared. "But as the Catholic bishops said, a child is a result both of his or her family's values and the policies of the nation in which that child resides."[142]

On the night Bill announced his candidacy in October 1991, his family and friends sang his favorite hymn, "Amazing Grace,"[143] and during the campaign both Bill and Hillary insisted that their faith was important to them. Bill declared, "I pray virtually every day, usually at night, and I read the Bible every week." He testified that he believed strongly in the "constancy of sin, the possibility of forgiveness, [and] the reality of redemption."[144] Hillary explained that Methodism's emphasis on people's "scripturally ordered responsibility" to help others had inspired her to work for two decades to improve the lives of children.[145] Don Jones argued that "the key to understanding Hillary is her spiritual center." Both her social concern and political thought rested on "a spiritual foundation."[146] She believed that politics and individuals' vocations could be "instruments for helping people," Jones added.[147] Bill denounced

George H. W. Bush in August 1992 for questioning Democrats' commitment to God and comparing his values with those of film producer Woody Allen. Clinton declared Bush's implication that "Democrats are somehow Godless is deeply offensive to me, to Senator [Al] Gore and to all of us who cherish our religious convictions."[148]

Patt Morrison asked in the *Los Angeles Times* if Americans were ready to have a feminist first lady. How Clinton was viewed, she argued, was "as much a verdict on the role of women in the '90s as a judgment of her style and achievements." Morrison avowed that the discomfort many felt about Clinton reflected their ambivalence about "women, power, work and marriage." An organization called Citizens Against Clinton castigated her as "a radical feminist who has little use for religious values or even the traditional family unit" and "total contempt for traditional American women."[149]

Hillary's first-name recognition, Morrison asserted, was close to that of musical superstar Cher. The corporate lawyer, mother, feminist, educational reformer, and children's activist had "strong ideas and the will to carry them out." Many Americans thought she should be the Democratic presidential nominee. Others, however, saw Clinton as bossy, arrogant, and humorless, prompting her to try to appear kinder, more gentle, less ambitious and manipulative, and as a working mom who was "as down-home likable as she is intellectually admirable."[150] To counter depictions of Clinton as a militant feminist, some popular and women's magazines pictured her teaching Sunday school and taking care of Chelsea at home. These competing portraits of Hillary would continue after she became first lady while her policy role in Bill's presidency caused more controversy.

Michael Kelly astutely observed that the public debate over Hillary during the 1992 campaign focused on how politically liberal and power hungry she was and ignored her concerns about morality, values, and the meaning of life. Kelly described Hillary as a political liberal who supported a "generally 'progressive' social agenda with a strong dose of moralism," driven by her "abundant faith in . . . the redeeming power of love." "American women don't need lectures from Washington about values," she declared during the presidential race. "We don't need to hear about an idealized world that was never as righteous or carefree as some would like to think."[151] Despite such statements, Clinton believed that values and moral issues played a crucial role in improving public life. The extensive criticism she faced during the campaign led most Americans to ignore or misunderstand her core values, which she would express more transparently in her work as first lady, especially in her 1993 "politics of meaning" speech.

After Bush conceded on election night, Hillary reported, "Bill and I went into our bedroom, closed the door and prayed together for God's help as he took on this awesome honor and responsibility."[152] As in earlier phases of her life, Clinton's faith would be a driving force in determining her priorities and coping with the great political and personal challenges she would confront as first lady.

3

"Light Yourself on Fire with Passion"

America's First Lady

Hillary Clinton is arguably the most renowned, influential, and despised first lady in American history. She has competitors for the designation as most famous: Martha Washington, Abigail Adams, Dolley Madison, Eleanor Roosevelt, Jackie Kennedy, and Nancy Reagan. She has rivals for the most politically powerful: Adams, Edith Wilson, Roosevelt, Reagan, and Barbara Bush. But she has no close contenders for the title of most reviled first lady.

During the 1992 campaign, the Clintons repeatedly insisted that if Bill were elected, they would be copresidents. Hillary allegedly declared in 1993, "I'm not going to have some reporters pawing through our papers. We are the president."[1] Bill solicited her advice and considered her opinion in making many political decisions and in crafting numerous policies. She led the initiative to make health care more available and affordable, although it proved to be a political disaster for the Clinton administration. Her influence was reinforced by what some termed Hillaryland—a coterie of extremely dedicated aides, primarily women, who helped give the first lady an independent power center in the White House.[2] Her 1996 book, *It Takes a Village*, zoomed to the top of the best-seller list, and throughout her tenure, she was in great demand as a speaker and regularly attracted throngs of admirers when traveling abroad.[3]

Americans have "a long tradition of ridicule and criticism . . . of first ladies who voiced political opinions," argued Edith Mayo, who designed the "First Ladies, Political Role and Public Image" exhibit at the Smithsonian Museum.[4] Clinton's formidable political influence led her to be criticized for many of the administration's failures. The first two years of her husband's presidency were plagued by problems, many of which have been attributed to Hillary. Carl Bernstein argued that she was primarily responsible for the health care fiasco, "the inept staffing of the White House, the disastrous search for an attorney general, the Travel Office fiasco, the Whitewater land deal, the so-called scandal over her commodities trading, [and] the alienation of key senators and congressmen." By the 1994 midterm elections, their "dual administration" appeared to be ruined and repudiated.[5] The Clintons, however, rebounded. Bill was reelected handily in 1996, and his administration is highly ranked by most historians and political scientists.

Clinton was the nation's sixth Methodist first lady following Eliza Johnson, Julia Grant, Lucy Hayes, Ida McKinley, and Florence Harding. The heritage and doctrines of Methodism are very important to her. As Kenneth Woodward put it, "She thinks like a Methodist, talks like a Methodist and wants to reform society just like a well-Sunday-schooled Methodist churchwoman should." "I am," Clinton professed in 1994, "an old-fashioned Methodist."[6] "Hillary views the world through a Methodist lens," Don Jones asserted. "And we Methodists," he added jokingly, "know what's good for you."[7] Shortly after her husband was elected, Hillary declared, "As a Christian, part of my obligation is to take action to alleviate suffering." Methodism's explicit recognition of this duty, she explained, "is one reason I'm comfortable in this church."[8] Clinton complained in 1994, however, that the Methodist church had become "too involved in the social gospel" and was not paying "enough attention to questions of personal salvation and individual faith. It is, for me, both a question of grace and of personal commitment."[9] Preaching, Clinton contended, "is a distant second to practicing"—that is, to promoting such biblical values as "compassion, courage, faith, fellowship, forgiveness, love, peace, hope, wisdom, prayer, and humility."[10]

In May 1997, as Clinton later explained in one of her books, she and British prime minister Tony Blair discussed "the connection between our religious faith and public service. Both of us rooted our political beliefs in our faith, which molded our commitment to social action. I talked about John Wesley's invocation, which I had taken to heart when I was confirmed in the Methodist faith—Live every day doing as much good as you can, in every way you can—and about what theologians have described as 'the push of duty and the pull of grace.'"[11] Clinton told an interviewer that she often consulted the Methodist *Book of Resolutions*, the denomination's official handbook, when assessing social and political issues.[12] Strikingly, no president, including the devout Presbyterian Woodrow Wilson, has reported reviewing the official manual of his denomination to help him determine his political positions and policies.[13]

To cope with political and personal difficulties and defeats as first lady, Clinton read the Bible and reflected upon Wesley's dictum. Clinton's faith helped her deal with the barrage of criticism, disappointments, and heartaches she faced as first lady, especially the Monica Lewinsky affair. "I'm blessed with the kind of religious faith and upbringing," she professed in 1996, "that has given me a lot that I can fall back on."[14]

Like many other aspects of her life and personality, Clinton's religious convictions have been seen differently by her critics and admirers. Her supporters argued that her religious commitments inspired her many acts of compassion and service. Her detractors claimed that her religious beliefs gave her "a messiah-like self-perception" and "a license to do whatever she pleased in the name of God."[15]

Great Expectations

After Bill Clinton was elected, many Americans debated how Hillary should perform the role of first lady. Some stressed the opportunities the position offered to the nation's most visible professional woman, while others emphasized the inherent constraints it involved. Melanne Verveer, executive director of People for the American Way, a progressive organization, who would later serve as Hillary's chief of staff, expressed the ambivalence many felt. If Clinton played a leadership role in her husband's administration, she warned, many Americans would be resentful, but if Hillary did not do so, "extraordinary numbers of people are going to be keenly disappointed." Susan Estrich, a law professor at the University of Southern California, insisted that "most feminists are delighted to see a strong woman in the White House."[16] Hillary's friends and advisers reported that she was wrestling with how to balance being a "ceremonial spouse and Presidential partner."[17] How would Americans respond if she continued to be outspoken and independent, expressing strong opinions on many matters?

Clinton began her tenure as first lady, a journalist asserted, as "loved and hated, feared and admired." Millions of Americans, especially young women, viewed her as "a role model and exemplar" of modern womanhood, "a latter-day Joan of Arc." Conservative critics, by contrast, saw her "as the embodiment of American decline, a 'feminazi,' a symbol of abortion and gay rights, a '90s version of the biblical Witch of Endor."[18] Americans had frequently embraced first ladies when they displayed vulnerability; many admired Betty Ford, Nancy

Reagan, and Barbara Bush when they disclosed that they struggled with addiction, cancer, and depression.[19] But Clinton was very reluctant to open up about her personal life.

The first lady has no specified constitutional duties, but Hillary knew everyone would judge how she performed the role. Many people viewed her as a "Rorschach test" for the American public.[20] She had the potential to be one of the most powerful voices in the federal government. No first lady entered the White House with higher and more competing expectations.

Although Abigail Adams, Eleanor Roosevelt, Bess Truman, and Rosalynn Carter, among others, had considerable backstage influence, Clinton was expected, given campaign statements, her personality, and her career as a lawyer, to participate more actively in politics than any of her predecessors.[21] Other first ladies exerted influence primarily through "pillow talk," but Clinton would likely function as a presidential advisor and policy advocate.[22] Being first lady was a fairy-tale role, the closest one a democracy has to being queen, but some commentators contended that Hillary aspired to be king. She initially described her role as serving as "a voice for children," which had been a major component of her public career.[23] Driven by her Methodist social conscience, Clinton, aides predicted, would work to improve the lives of families and children, especially impoverished ones. She had long supported the Children's Defense Fund's call for the federal government to protect children from abuse and provide more financial aid for prenatal maternal health, early childhood education, and childhood immunization programs.[24] "Her Methodist faith," a journalist insisted, underlies "her philosophy of advocating help for the needy" while demanding that aid recipients work diligently to help themselves.[25]

Another journalist predicted that given her extensive church involvement, occasional lay preaching, and study of prominent theologians, Clinton might serve as a White House "theologian-in-residence."[26] Friends testified that "she is a deeply religious woman who carries favorite scriptures—including passages from Corinthians, Proverbs and Psalms—in her purse." Family friend Carolyn Staley avowed that Hillary "has a deep, personal spirituality" and "gets power from her faith."[27] "Her spiritual commitment," Don Jones insisted, was "interwoven in the fabric of her private and public" life. Jones was amazed that Clinton had spent hours underlining and thoroughly annotating a book about renewal in the Methodist Church.[28] Ed Matthews, her principal pastor in Little Rock, maintained that Clinton's robust religious convictions motivated her "to make this world a better place."[29] Her close friend Diane Blair called Clinton "a devoted reader of the Bible."[30]

Clinton's Tenure Begins

The stakes for Hillary's role were immense as Bill's presidency began. If health care reform succeeded, Democrats might be able to gain the loyalty of a new generation of working-class and middle-class voters just as the adoption of Social Security had prompted an earlier generation to support the party from Franklin Roosevelt to Lyndon Johnson. However, if this reform failed, Clinton advisers feared it could discredit the first lady and bring down the administration.[31]

Clinton dove headfirst into her role, quickly demonstrating that she would be the most activist first lady since Eleanor Roosevelt. As head of a task force charged with restructuring America's health system, she traveled around the country to hold seminars on health care and meet with dozens of lawmakers to discuss the nation's health care problems. Meanwhile, she tried to give Chelsea as normal a life as possible, and Clinton discussed books she had read and movies she had watched with close friends. Clinton, a *Chicago Tribune* columnist argued, appeared to never sleep and to be "the best time manager in the world"; she made "Wonder Woman look like a wimp." Some friends and colleagues praised "her so effusively that she seems one miracle short of Mother Teresa."[32]

Throughout the Clinton administration, critics protested that Hillary had too much power. Mary Hancock Hinds, a policy analyst for George H. W. Bush, compared her influence with that of Oliver North, who, as a National Security Council staff member during the Reagan administration, had "operated secretly and unchecked within the confines of the White House."[33] In the early months of the Clinton administration, Hillary became the butt of comedians' jokes while rumors circulated that she had hurled a lamp at the president, that she and Bill slept in separate beds, and that she was a lesbian.[34]

Martha Sherrill argued in the *Washington Post* that Clinton had "much more depth, intellect and spirituality" than most politicians. Much of the debate about Hillary, she noted, had centered on the question of "How Left Is She?" based on the assumption that she was more liberal than Bill. Meanwhile, Hillary often talked about "virtue" and having a "higher purpose"; Sherrill maintained that she served as "a White House moral compass."[35] Although her critics strongly disagreed, Clinton considered herself "very conservative."[36] She insisted that her political views were "an amalgam."[37] She rejected the "aggressively individualistic, pro-market, anti-government ideology" of many Reaganites, but she believed "strongly in individual responsibility" and that families should play the leading role in transmitting values and culture. Unlike

Reagan conservatives, she wanted government to limit the power of other institutions, especially large corporations, and to curb "the sometimes destructive power of free markets" to promote community and preserve families. Her stance, Clinton maintained, was based on "a set of deeply held religious beliefs." Her Methodist faith had opened "her eyes to the problems of others." She objected to most liberals' tendency to downplay the importance of religion in public life. Faith, Clinton declared, "is a wonderful gift of grace" that "gives you a sense of being rooted in meaning and love that goes far beyond your own life" and helps determine "what is really important."[38]

The Politics of Meaning

One of the most philosophical, poignant, and painful episodes of Clinton's tenure as first lady was her April 6, 1993, address at the University of Texas in Austin, often dubbed her "politics of meaning" speech, and its aftermath. Although Clinton had spoken from many Methodist pulpits, she had never "preached so grandly" as she did in Austin, and no first lady had ever delivered a more "audacious" public address.[39] As she spoke to 14,000 people at the university's field house, Clinton was under great emotional pressure. Health care reform was going poorly, her financial practices in Arkansas were being investigated, and her father had just been removed from life support and would die the day after her speech. Influenced by Michael Lerner, a rabbi and political activist, and invoking the penitent remarks of a dying Lee Atwater, an adviser to both Ronald Reagan and George H. W. Bush, and a jeremiad of African missionary Albert Schweitzer, Clinton argued that the United States was experiencing a grave national "crisis of meaning and spirituality . . . a sleeping sickness of the soul." America's cities "filled with hopeless girls with babies and angry boys with guns" were only the most obvious sign that our nation was crippled by "alienation and despair and hopelessness."[40]

Mixing ancient wisdom, biblical teaching, communitarian thinking, and the pragmatism of theologian Reinhold Niebuhr,[41] Clinton exhorted Americans to work together to enhance their spiritual fulfillment, insisting that everyone should help redefine what our lives should be. Clinton challenged citizens to stop seeking salvation through big government or the market economy. Americans should instead adopt "a new ethos of individual responsibility and caring" and recognize that "we are all part of something bigger than ourselves."[42] Her call for "remodeling society by redefining what it means to be a human in the 20th century" was "fully consonant with the Methodists' liberal social creed."[43] However, the negative reaction to her speech by many members of the media made her reluctant to bare her soul again about her philosophical and religious beliefs.

Clinton quoted Atwater at length in her speech. The Republican declared, "The eighties were about acquiring—acquiring wealth, power, prestige. . . . But you can acquire all you want and still feel empty. What power wouldn't I trade for a little more time with my family? What price wouldn't I pay for an evening with friends?" It required "a deadly illness," Atwater asserted, "to put me eye-to-eye with that truth, but it is a truth that the country, caught up in its ruthless ambitions and moral decay, can learn on my dime." Whoever led the nation through the 1990s, he concluded, must address "this spiritual vacuum at the heart of American society—this tumor of the soul."[44]

Building on Atwater's dying remarks, Clinton asked, why did a nation as affluent as the United States have such an "undercurrent of discontent," a sense that "economic growth and prosperity, political democracy and freedom are not enough?" Why did "we lack, at some core level, meaning in our individual lives and meaning collectively—that sense that our lives are part of some greater effort, that we are connected to one another, that community means that we have a place where we belong no matter who we are?"[45]

In discussing her speech with journalist Michael Kelly, Clinton admitted that she did not have a "coherent explanation" for the human predicament, but she offered a "tentative definition" of her beliefs. The core of her worldview, she explained, was that everyone had inherent worth because God fashioned people as spiritual creatures. She noted that she had given many talks in Arkansas about "the underlying principles of Methodism" that stressed how timeless scripture resonated with "what we now know about human beings." The Golden Rule and Christ's commandment to "love your neighbor as yourself" both assumed that people would value themselves and thereby act responsibly, which, in turn, would motivate them "to respect and care for other people."[46] Her speech, Verveer insisted, expressed how Clinton's "religious values infused her sense of public service."[47]

On the other hand, Clinton contended that no "core thing" or "unifying theory" explained the perennial problems of human beings and how to solve them.[48] Many Christians would counter that humanity's fundamental problems spring from sin and that personal salvation is the basic solution for them. Clinton, however, was speaking in a public setting as America's first lady and strove to be sensitive to the nation's religious and ideological pluralism. Therefore, she emphasized spirituality and used little explicitly Christian language.

But nowhere privately did she make the common Christian argument that unless people come to know God personally, they will never be truly satisfied no matter how much wealth, power, or fame they achieve.

"Balancing the conservative-mind, liberal-heart equation" that Clinton had grappled with since her freshman year at Wellesley and seeking to help people fill the "spiritual vacuum" that Lee Atwater had experienced on his deathbed, Clinton sought to express "for herself, her husband, and their presidency an overarching, benevolent . . . governmental philosophy that embraced both traditional notions of family and individual responsibility, as well as" the importance of compassionate government programs designed "to help those less able to help themselves." Her speech sounded, Carl Bernstein argued, as if the Clintons had "a presidential partnership with God."[49] Kelly contended that both Clintons combined "a generally 'progressive' social agenda with a strong dose of moralism" fueled by a deep "faith in the capacity of the human intellect and the redeeming power of love." Rather than a politics of the left or right, the Clintons espoused "the politics of do-good ism" based on the principles of the social gospel and the teachings of liberation theology and Protestant liberalism.[50] Since Jimmy Carter, who had been widely viewed by Democratic moguls as hopelessly naïve and had been lampooned for applying his faith to political issues, most Democratic politicians had been reluctant to even mention God or traditional moral virtues, enabling Republicans, especially right-wing ones, to dominate the discussion of religious values. Hillary wanted to Democrats to reengage in the conversation.[51]

Don Jones contended that Clinton's speech displayed the influence of theologian Paul Tillich's writings on alienation and meaninglessness. She realized that "you cannot depend on the basic nature of man to be good and you cannot depend entirely on moral suasion to make it good. You have to use power." As a Christian, Jones asserted, Clinton understood that using "power to achieve social good is legitimate."[52] Reinhold Niebuhr's analysis of human nature, society, and the role of power in effecting social change seems even more important in Clinton's argument than the writings of Tillich.

The press savagely attacked Clinton's analysis of the nation's moral and spiritual problems. The first lady declared that "my critics were divided between conservatives who suspect I did not mean what I said and liberals who feared that I did."[53] In his *New York Times Magazine* article, Kelly called her "Saint Hillary," while another newspaper skewered her speech as "psychobabble."[54] Both liberal and conservative pundits denounced what they referred to as "religious moralisms wrapped in New Age language."[55] Although often asserting that Clinton's remarks were closely aligned with the biblically inspired social gospel tradition in American politics advanced by Harriet Beecher Stowe, Jane Addams, and Dorothy Day, the secular liberal elite expressed great discomfort with her focus on the spiritual dimension.[56] This derision deeply hurt Clinton as she dealt with her father's death. Lissa Muscatine, Clinton's speechwriter, insisted that the first lady felt "blindsided and misunderstood." She was ridiculed for trying to be "thoughtful in a personal way."[57]

Prior to delivering her speech, Clinton had met several times with Michael Lerner, the editor and publisher of *Tikkun*, a Jewish journal that combined liberal cultural commentary, post-Marxist analysis, Talmudic principles, and new-age rhetoric. Some pundits referred to Lerner as Clinton's guru.[58] Lerner called for a new politics that sought "to build a society based" not on profit and power but on "ethical and spiritual sensitivity and a sense of community, mutual caring and responsibility."[59] Lerner complained that the government had done little to supply individuals' spiritual needs or help Americans participate in "an ethically based spiritual community" that linked them "to a higher purpose."[60] While most Christians saw churches and faith-based organizations as the primary vehicle for changing culture and society, Lerner and Clinton maintained that "a spiritually motivated, 'caring' government" could play a major role in this endeavor.[61] As Clinton put it, the government could help create conditions that enabled people "to take responsibility for themselves and therefore participate fully in this search for meaning."[62]

Lerner praised Clinton for modeling what religion entailed rather than "telling people they have to be religious." She showed people that their values should guide every aspect of their lives. Journalist Martha Sherrill argued similarly that the lifelong Methodist embodied her denomination's values, social perspective, sense of purpose, and emphasis on global missionary work. Like John Wesley, Sherrill stressed, Clinton labored to help social outcasts, the underprivileged, and children.[63]

After Clinton's speech, Lerner complained that much of the media had belittled their shared conviction that most Americans hungered "for a society that supports rather than undermines loving relationships, ethical life and communities that provide a framework for transcending the individualism and me-firstism of the competitive marketplace." Many journalists, Lerner protested, were portraying Clinton and him as claiming to be on "a higher moral plane than other Americans." He and Clinton did not believe, however, "that the problem is the low moral level of the American people." They argued instead that the nation's economic, social, and political institutions hindered the desire of most Americans for society to promote "ethical sensitivity" and for life to transcend material self-interest. By calling for "the politics of meaning," Clinton sought to change the dominant American discourse "from the language of selfishness to the language of caring, social responsibility." Thousands of politicians and people in other vocations, Lerner contended, could translate "the discourse of caring" into policy if Clinton promoted this paradigm shift. Her task was made difficult, however, by "a hostile media" who treated human beings as motivated only by material self-interest.[64]

The most insightful and discussed analysis of Clinton's address was Michael Kelly's "Saint Hillary" article. Since discovering at age fourteen that the world "could be very cruel" to the less fortunate, Kelly asserted, Clinton had worked "to make things right." Although some might view her childhood idealism as "naive or trite or grandiose," Clinton continued to espouse this goal with no "apparent sense of irony or inadequacy." She wanted people to apply the Golden Rule, do good "on a grand scale," and "make the world a better place." According to Kelly, Clinton was searching not merely for "programmatic answers but for The Answer," for something that would explain "the Meaning of It All." She sought a solution that would "marry conservatism and liberalism, and capitalism and statism, that would tie together practically everything . . . the faults of man and the word of God, the end of Communism and the beginning of the third millennium, crime in the streets and on Wall Street . . . the cynicism of the press and the corrupting role of television, the breakdown of civility and the loss of community." Clinton wanted to redesign how Americans did politics and government. Her message, Kelly maintained, was "an old and very American" one that went "beyond the normal boundaries of politics into the territory of religion." It focused not only on what government should do but on how people should behave. It stressed "values, not programs. It is the message of the preacher," a role Clinton had "filled many times delivering guest sermons from the pulpits of United Methodist churches." Kelly concluded, however, that much of what Clinton saw as wrong with the American way of life actually stemmed from "the liberal experiments in the reshaping of society" that "the intellectual elite" of her generation had conducted.[65]

Kelly posed two questions. First, if society needed to be remade, why should Clinton get the job? After all, she was part of the cohort that had rejected traditional moral absolutes and conventional societal standards. Second, how could the ethical teachings of the Bible be expressed in government policies? Lerner urged the Clinton administration to require every government agency to examine how any proposed piece of legislation or new program would impact "the ethics and the caring and sharing of the community." However, Kelly argued, any proposal to improve public values clashed with "the fundamentals of social liberalism that are the guiding ethos of Democratic policies." Social conservatives, he granted, could "speak bluntly about what is morally right and what is not. Conservatism is purposely, explicitly judgmental." Social liberalism, by contrast, had increasingly rejected the concept of judgment and instead espoused "the expansion of rights and the tolerance of diversity." Making moral judgment a basis for governmental policy, Kelly insisted, would require restricting what liberals widely regarded as sacrosanct rights and admitting that tolerance had limits.[66] David Brock argued that Kelly's critique conveyed the position of "many liberal journalists and intellectuals who cringed at the idea of invoking a religious justification for progressive policies and dismissed" her search for meaning as evidence that Clinton was becoming unhinged.[67]

A month after her speech at the University of Texas, Clinton expressed empathy for the members of the religious right who often lamented that many Americans had lost a sense of purpose and become "amoral decision-makers" with no overriding values. She asserted that "the search for meaning cut across all kinds of religious and ideological boundaries." No group has "a corner on God."[68] After demonizing her enemies for several months and portraying herself as the savior of righteous liberals, William Chafe contended, in making this comment, Clinton reasserted a perspective "much more consistent with the spiritual leadership she had learned with Don Jones than with the warrior role she had taken on as First Lady."[69]

In February 1994, Clinton confessed to a National Prayer Luncheon that she was hesitant to discuss religious ideas again. She "was astonished to realize" that many people thought "spirituality should be confined to events like this, and not brought out into the public arena." Rejecting this perspective, she rejoiced that many people agreed that spiritual renewal was necessary and were willing to "work in good faith together to fill that sense of emptiness with the Word and with an outreach that is grounded in real Christian values."[70] The negative response to her Austin speech had made Clinton reticent to discuss her religious convictions publicly. Nevertheless, the themes she discussed in that speech would continue to motivate her work for the next twenty-five years.

Troubles

During her first year in the White House, Hillary's father died, her good friend Vince Foster committed suicide, Bill's mother died of cancer, and Hillary and Bill "were attacked daily from all directions." Following Foster's death, Hillary reported, she suffered immense emotional pain and stumbled along by "sheer willpower." To cope, she turned to her religious beliefs, husband, and friends. Hillary reported, "I reread favorite scriptures, quotations, and writings that had touched me in the past."[71]

Clinton also dealt with numerous difficulties in 1994. Numerous groups attacked her for many different reasons. The constant questioning of her integrity made her angry and frustrated. Family friend Betsey Wright explained, "Her whole life [had been dedicated] to the social precepts of the Methodist church and the commitment to serve people she had learned at the feet of Don Jones. Now she felt under 'siege,' [and] her very character [was] under assault by a Washington culture that seemed bereft of anything moral or decent."[72] As the 1994 midterm elections approached, the Clinton administration was praised for reducing the deficit, providing family leave, establishing AmeriCorps, and passing the Brady Bill to reduce the violence caused by handguns and the North American Free Trade Agreement to increase US trade with Canada and Mexico. But these achievements were overshadowed by Foster's suicide, Travelgate, the culture war between the Washington establishment and the Clinton White House, the 1993 tax bill passed without any Republican votes in Congress, and the failed effort to provide universal health care.[73]

Democrats suffered a crushing defeat in the midterm elections as Republicans gained eight seats in the Senate and 54 seats in the House of Representatives, taking control of both houses of Congress for the first time since 1952. Propelled by the Contract with America engineered by Representative Newt Gingrich of Georgia, the "Republican Revolution" also gave the party a net increase of ten governorships and control of many state legislatures. Republicans attacked the Clinton administration's income tax increase, ban on assault weapons, allowing of homosexuals to serve in the military, and especially its push for universal health care, which they denounced as a "government takeover" of one-seventh of the US economy.[74] Chastened by the resounding Democratic defeat and strident personal criticism, Hillary told an interviewer in February 1995 that she was going to take a back seat in her husband's administration.[75]

In dealing with these blows, Clinton again relied on her faith. "During the stresses of 1993 and 1994," she later wrote, "I had read my Bible and other books about religion and spirituality."[76] She primarily perused the works of popular evangelical authors, including Tony Campolo and Gordon MacDonald, and books on spiritual formation by Dutch Catholic priest Henri Nouwen. Surprisingly, she regularly read the evangelical monthly *Christianity Today* rather than the mainline periodical *Christian Century*, which expressed theological and social perspectives much closer to hers.[77] Her family attended Foundry Methodist Church, "and I drew great sustenance from the sermons and personal support offered by the congregation and its senior minister, Rev. Dr. Phil Wogaman. My prayer group continued to pray for me, as did countless other people around the world. It all helped so much." She was especially moved by Nouwen's admonition to practice "the discipline of gratitude." Clinton declared, "I had so much to be grateful for, even in the midst of lost elections, failed health care reform efforts, partisan and prosecutorial attacks, and the death of those I loved. I just had to discipline myself to remember how blessed I was."[78]

Saint or Sinner?

Throughout Bill's first term, Hillary attracted a huge amount of media attention and was depicted in contradictory ways. In 1994, *Newsweek* inquired whether Hillary was a saint who had "radiated spirituality" as she delivered her impassioned message exhorting Americans to awaken from their "sleeping sickness of the soul" or a sinner who had engaged in shady stock trading in Arkansas to miraculously transform $1,000 into $100,000.[79] "Who is the real Hillary Clinton?" journalist David Brock asked similarly in 1996. "Is she the articulate lawyer and political activist" or "The Lady Macbeth of Little Rock?" Was she a latter-day Joan of Arc who strove to provide health care coverage for everyone? Was she "Saint Hillary, exponent of 'the politics of meaning'? The Ivan Boesky of cattle-futures trading?" Or was she "a virtual recluse" who channeled "the spirit of Eleanor Roosevelt"? More than almost anyone else in recent American history, Hillary had evoked radically different reactions— "impassioned paeans from her supporters and vitriolic attacks from her foes."[80]

Brock noted that Clinton had been compared to Leona Helmsley (convicted of federal income tax evasion in 1989), Ma Barker (a ruthless crime matriarch), Adolf Hitler's mistress Eva Braun, and anti-Semitic Nation of Islam leader

Louis Farrakhan.[81] A Clinton aide called her a "dragon lady" and "the house SOB." Kenneth Walsh and Bruce Auster argued that she had trouble combining the disparate roles of "public advocate and power broker" with the traditional first lady function of "national comforter."[82] FBI agent Gary Aldrich lambasted Clinton as "a deranged power-mad emasculator," while Roger Morris portrayed her as "a deeply cynical, ruthless shrew" in *Partners in Power*. In *Blood Sport* (1996), James Stewart called Clinton "a selfish, money-grubbing cheat," and *Washington Post* columnist Sally Quinn declared, "There's just something about her that pisses people off."[83]

Public perception of Clinton reached its nadir in 1996. Conservative columnist William Safire called her "a congenital liar," and almost half of Americans agreed; only 43 percent of Americans viewed her positively—the lowest rating of any first lady in twentieth-century surveys.[84] Although first ladies have rarely been attacked by their husbands' political opponents, Hillary was assailed by both George H. W. Bush and Robert Dole at the 1996 Republican National Convention. As the election approached, Hillary had few advocates. Safire argued that Clinton had lied about the 10,000 percent profit she made in 1979 commodity trading, Vince Foster's death, Travelgate, and other matters and had suborned "lying in her aides and friends," ensnaring them "in a web of deceit."[85] In his generally sympathetic biography, Carl Bernstein averred that during Bill's first term, Hillary was "more rigid, secretive, combative, deceptive and angry" than at any other time in her life.[86] This barrage of criticism stung Clinton and made her reluctant to discuss her private life, including her faith.

Foundry Methodist Church

On the morning of January 20, 1993, a few hours before Bill was inaugurated as president, the Clintons' faith was on display at an ecumenical worship service at the Metropolitan African Methodist Episcopal Church, which blended their Baptist and Methodist faiths. Bill, Hillary, and Vice President Al Gore planned the service, the first preinaugural service held at an African American church. The Metropolitan AME Church had been a major center of Black worship and activism for nearly 150 years. Frederick Douglass's funeral was conducted there in 1895, as was that of Rosa Parks in 2005.[87] A dozen religious leaders, including both Bill's and Hillary's Little Rock pastors—Southern Baptist Rex Horne and Methodist Ed Matthews—as well as Rabbi Eugene Levy, Imam Wallace Mohammed, African American Gardner Taylor of Brooklyn's Concord Baptist Church, and the Greek Orthodox dean of Holy Trinity Cathedral in New York spoke briefly to the two thousand attendees. Billy Graham prayed for Hillary and Tipper Gore because they would "bear so much of the responsibilities and burdens" of their husbands.[88]

After Bill was elected president, numerous District of Columbia pastors wrote letters and made telephone calls inviting the Clintons to worship with their congregations. First Baptist Church, a thousand-member congregation where Jimmy Carter had worshipped, seemed to have the inside track, but Foundry United Methodist, two blocks from First Baptist, was also a major contender. First Baptist's senior minister declared that its worshippers would again happily tolerate the inconveniences connected with having the nation's first family attend its services. J. Philip Wogaman, senior pastor of the 1,400-member Foundry church, asserted that welcoming the Clintons would be a "great privilege."[89] During the first two months of Bill's presidency, they visited several churches. Unlike some of his predecessors, including Ronald Reagan, Bill was determined to attend church regularly to set a good example, provide for his own spiritual nourishment, and reap political benefits.

On the weekend of March 12–14, 1993, a foot of snow fell on Washington and the Clintons were feeling "stir crazy," Hillary recalled. They tramped a mile through the blizzard to visit Foundry, located in the Dupont Circle neighborhood, for the first time. During his first year as president, Bill worshipped at Foundry, First Baptist, and St. John's Episcopal Church. Hillary occasionally went with Bill to First Baptist, but after a conflict between the church's older and newer members led First Baptist's senior pastor to resign in December 1993, the Clintons made Foundry their church home, remaining there for the next seven years.[90] By Wogaman's estimate, the Clintons attended about one hundred services during Bill's presidency (less than 25 percent of the total) and always sat three rows from the front. Following Hillary's example at Park Ridge, Chelsea participated regularly in Foundry's youth group. The Clintons attended meetings for parents of youth group members and helped plan a youth mission trip to Appalachia. When Foundry members were hospitalized, Hillary and Bill often called to check on their health. For Hillary, Foundry became a safe haven, a place for fellowship and spiritual renewal.[91] At Foundry, she declared, "we were, not 'the First Family'—we were just our family." In this religious community, Hillary explained, "we could worship, study, contemplate, be of service, get some good pastoral advice, and step outside all the commotion of life in the White House and Washington. That was very, very precious to us."[92]

Wogaman became Foundry's senior pastor in July 1992 after teaching Christian ethics for twenty-six years, during eleven of which he also served as dean, at Wesley Theological Seminary, a Methodist institution in Washington. Founded in 1814 by Henry Foxall, a wealthy Georgetown foundry owner grateful to God that the British had not destroyed his business during the War of 1812, it had previously been the home church of President Rutherford B. Hayes. When the Clintons began attending, former US senator and 1972 Democratic presidential nominee George McGovern worshipped there, as did Sen. Bob Dole (R-KS) and his wife Elizabeth, the president of the American Red Cross.

Wogaman, a theological liberal, often clashed on social and political issues with Methodist evangelicals and theological conservatives in other denominations. Wogaman frequently denounced racism, led a task force that investigated Nestlé's sale of infant formula to the indigent in the developing world, called for providing sanctuary to Central American refugees, advocated abortion rights, and served as president of the Interfaith Alliance, a group formed in 1994 to counterbalance the political influence of the religious right. In his sermons, Wogaman supported feminism, denounced the mistreatment of gays, and endorsed health care reform. Reflecting Wogaman's commitments, a church newsletter criticized numerous aspects of the GOP's 1994 Contract with America.[93]

Foundry was enmeshed throughout the 1990s in conflict over homosexuality, abortion, and theology. Wogaman served on a Methodist Church committee that studied how the Bible viewed homosexuality; after four years, it recommended that the denomination stop describing homosexuality as "incompatible with Christian teaching." When the Methodist Church's ruling assembly rejected this proposal, Foundry decided, along with 142 other Methodist churches, to become a "reconciling congregation" that welcomed the full participation of gays and lesbians.[94] Wogaman endorsed gay marriage in the mid-1990s, a step Hillary would not take publicly until more than fifteen years later. On several occasions, pro-life activists picketed Foundry, accusing Wogaman of ignoring the Bible's teaching and supporting murder.[95] On other occasions, antiabortionists targeted Hillary rather than Wogaman. In January 1997, for example, about fifty people held signs outside Foundry portraying aborted fetuses, along with a banner proclaiming "The Children of Hillary's Village."[96]

Evangelical columnist Cal Thomas, former vice-president of the Moral Majority, accused Wogaman of denying numerous scriptural teachings, including the virgin birth. Thomas argued that Wogaman had preached that the Bible, like the *Washington Post*, contained "both truth and error," a position that John

Wesley would have repudiated. Wogaman's sermons, Thomas complained, frequently provided theological support for the Clintons' liberal political positions.[97]

Some evangelicals left Foundry because of Wogaman's stances on homosexuality or abortion or because they objected that he stressed the social gospel more than personal salvation and faith formation. The congregation, however, retained some conservatives such as journalist Wesley Pippert, a Wheaton graduate and a leading analyst of the relationship between the Bible and the mass media. It also included openly gay couples and held an evening healing service. A longtime parishioner described Foundry in 1994 as a socially active church with a diverse membership that included many military personnel and homosexuals and numerous socioeconomic and ethnic groups.[98] Wogaman explained that young singles and married couples, gays, African Americans, and older white congregants worshipped together at Foundry.[99] Hillary insisted that the church ministered to the social and material needs of Washington's inner-city residents and strove to meet its parishioners' personal and spiritual needs connected with their "search for salvation."[100]

Wogaman claimed that he avoided taking political positions in the pulpit, but on the last Sunday Robert and Elizabeth Dole attended, the pastor praised the United States for intervening in Haiti to restore the democratically elected Jean-Bertrand Aristide to power, an action Bob Dole fiercely opposed. The Doles left Foundry for the theologically conservative National Presbyterian Church in 1995 shortly before the senator began his successful quest for the Republican presidential nomination. The Doles were prompted to do so in part by blistering denunciations of Wogaman's liberal theology by Cal Thomas and the Institute on Religion and Democracy.[101]

Wogaman insisted that he sought to preach prophetically "without embarrassing the president." He carefully considered how his sermons might affect the first family, but Wogaman strove not to draw attention to their presence at Foundry. The minister maintained that he went "to extraordinary lengths" to keep the services unaffected by their participation. After congregants flocked to greet the first family during the exchanging of the peace on one Sunday during Bill's first year in office, the minister requested everyone to remain in their pews thereafter and share Christ's peace only with those sitting close to them.[102] Whenever the Clintons attended, Wogaman asked the five hundred or so worshippers to remain in their seats for a couple of minutes after the benediction, enabling the Clintons to leave quietly. Having the Clintons worshipping with them, Wogaman argued, reminded congregants that political "power is exercised by real human beings" who sang hymns and prayed.[103] Wogaman did not, however, always ignore the president's presence, although his statements and prayers were similar to those of other churches regarding elected officials. In an April 1994 service, he noted that no matter what the United States did in Bosnia, Rwanda, Burundi, Northern Ireland, and other hotspots, many would denounce the nation's actions, and he exhorted worshippers to pray for the president.[104] One of the unison prayers on a Sunday in January 1997 asked the Lord to give the president "courage, wisdom, and a firm sense of your will in all that he does for the good of our country, for the good of your world."[105]

On the day of Bill's second inauguration, the Clintons held a service at 8:30 a.m. at the Columbia Baptist Church in Falls Church, Virginia, where eight hundred worshippers heard Bill's pastor in Little Rock, Rex Horne, preach. At 11:00 a.m., the couple attended a second service at Foundry Methodist, led by Wogaman, who celebrated Martin Luther King Jr.'s birthday and prayed for the reelected president.[106]

Newspapers occasionally carried accounts of the first family worshipping at Foundry. The *Washington Post* reported, during the week after the Monica Lewinsky scandal began, that the Clintons had found "solace from the unrelenting barrage of special counsels, spin doctors and television talking heads" in the warm smiles and hugs of Foundry members. Wogaman, who preached that day on "Taking the Bible Seriously," also read 1 Corinthians 13 to the congregation and urged all Americans to focus on love and forgiveness. After the sermon, the choir sang a spiritual that included the words "My God is a rock in a weary land, a shelter in the time of storm." One Foundry member expressed hope that this song provided comfort for the Clintons "after what was undoubtedly a difficult week for both of them." As they left the church, worshippers were confronted by pro-life advocates holding graphic posters of aborted fetuses.[107]

Spiritual Support and Solace

When the Clintons arrived in Washington, their relationship with evangelicals was strained because of the couple's support for abortion rights, Bill's pledge to permit gays and lesbians to serve in the military (the "don't ask, don't tell" policy), and Hillary's alleged contempt for traditional family roles.[108] Nevertheless, in late February 1993, three weeks before Hillary's father had a stroke, Linda Lader, who along with her husband had hosted the Renaissance Weekends the Clintons had attended since 1983, invited the first lady and

Tipper Gore to a bipartisan Christian women's prayer group, which included numerous evangelicals. The women met that day for lunch at the Cedars, a posh estate on the Potomac owned by The Fellowship, which sponsored the National Prayer Breakfast and dozens of other prayer groups. For the next eight years, this women's prayer group would be a major source of Christian fellowship, comfort, and support for Hillary, and several of its participants became her close friends. The group included Joanne Kemp, wife of former congressman Jack Kemp, the Republican candidate for vice president in 1996; Susan Baker, the wife of James Baker, the secretary of state under George H. W. Bush; Grace Nelson, wife of Democratic senator Bill Nelson of Florida; Eileen Bakke, wife of prominent entrepreneur Dennis Bakke; and Holly Leachman, a lay minister at the McLean Bible Church in Virginia, the home church of numerous Republican senators. Clinton especially valued the friendship of Leachman, who, the first lady wrote, "was the spiritual spark plug who kept it all going for me." During her White House years, Leachman faxed Clinton a daily scripture reading or faith message and often prayed with her.[109] Bakke gave her a copy of Nouwen's *The Return of the Prodigal Son*, which had a profound impact on the first lady, especially during the Lewinsky scandal.

Clinton thanked the women in her prayer group for praying for her. They often knew precisely "the right moment to call or to drop a note, to send a book, to let me know that they were thinking about me." Their fellowship and friendship had kept her going, had "served as both balm and spur," and had enriched her spiritual life. Her prayer group friends taught her to not rely on "her own reserves, but to draw freely and regularly from the One whose storehouse is always full." They had encouraged her "to stand strong in the midst of criticism, to give in when necessary, to take a risk when it's right, and, above all, to fear God alone, for the fear of the Lord is the beginning of knowledge."[110]

"Without the courage that comes from God alone," Clinton declared, she would not have been able to meet the challenges confronting her. The first lady insisted that she took faith "very seriously," although she confessed that "I do not believe I am a very good Christian. It is extremely hard to be a Christian," she added. Every day, her Christianity was being challenged, but she was growing in her faith as it became "stronger and deeper and bigger" and opened her "eyes to greater possibilities." "One's faith journey," Clinton argued was "a continuing effort to grow in both wisdom and stature as a Christian." "The greatest gift" people had, she averred, "is Christ's life and his example," which should guide us, challenge us, [and] support us." When people inspired others to envision "what is possible through Christ," she contended, they helped inspire actions to accomplish God's goals. "Of all the thousands of gifts I received in my eight years in the White House, few were more welcome and needed than these 12 intangible gifts of discernment, peace, compassion, faith, fellowship, vision, forgiveness, grace, wisdom, love, joy and courage" her Bible study partners provided. Her prayer group friends also gave Clinton a book filled with messages, religious quotations, and scripture.[111] Later, as a US senator from New York, Clinton was accused of trying to appear religious to advance her political prospects, but she never publicized her participation in this prayer group as first lady.[112]

The roots of The Fellowship lay in the work of Abraham Vereide, who organized small groups in the Senate and the House in the 1940s to enable their members to pray, discuss spiritual concerns, and support one another. Sen. Frank Carlson (R-KS) and Sen. Walter Judd (R-MN) were early leaders of these prayer groups, and Richard Halverson, chaplain of the Senate, played a major role from the 1950s until the 1990s.[113] In 1969, Doug Coe, who had previously served with The Navigators, an international, interdenominational Christian ministry, became the head of The Fellowship. In *Time*'s list of the nation's twenty-five most influential evangelical leaders in 2005, Coe was dubbed "The Stealth Persuader" because of his work behind the scenes with politicians in the capital.[114] Hillary called Coe "a unique presence in Washington: a genuinely loving spiritual mentor and guide to anyone, regardless of party or faith, who wants to deepen his or her relationship with God."[115] Throughout her tenure as first lady, Coe constantly assured Clinton that she was where God wanted her to be and that God was using her to achieve his purposes.[116]

The New Age Controversy

From the 1950s to the early 1990s, the White House welcomed numerous pastors, priests, and evangelists who were part of the respected religious establishment, such as Norman Vincent Peale, Francis Cardinal Spellman, and Billy Graham. Their visits, relationships with presidents, and (at Nixon's White House religious services) sermons had provided a white male Christian blessing and seal of approval for both Republican and Democratic administrations. The Clinton White House welcomed a much broader array of religious and spiritual leaders that included both mainline and evangelical clergy, theologians, gurus, and new-age spiritualists and sages. Carl Bernstein insists that the Clintons were open to new ideas and spiritual directions that had emerged since the

1960s from the black church and "the psychospiritual pseudosciences derived from twelve-step philosophy and theories of co-dependence."[117] Although Bernstein is correct, the Clintons were much less interested in non-Christian philosophies than in orthodox Christianity. They worshipped in Christian churches, primarily read the Bible and Christian literature, prayed to God, fellowshipped with Christians, and sought the counsel of Christian ministers.

Some pundits and political liberals criticized Hillary Clinton's emphasis on spirituality and religious values, whereas some theological conservatives complained about her social gospel liberalism. The greatest religious controversy of her tenure as first lady, however, resulted from her decision to invite new-age leaders Jean Houston and Marianne Williamson to meet with her for three days as 1994 ended and 1995 began. Frustrated by the failure of her health care reform campaign and the results of the midterm election, concerned about Bill's dysfunction and depression, worried about their political future, and searching for personal direction and fulfillment, Clinton also invited several self-help and motivational speakers to Camp David, including Anthony Robbins, author of *Awaken the Giant Within*, and Stephen Covey, author of *The Seven Habits of Highly Effective People*.[118]

Houston, Williamson, and other new-age proponents exhorted individuals to go deep within themselves to find the personal strength to overcome adversity. Houston, who had earned two PhD degrees and authored fifteen books, was highly respected by devotees of new-age mysticism and the human potential movement. She had held seminars for corporate executives, lectured at Harvard, and collaborated with renowned anthropologist Margaret Mead. She and her husband, Robert Masters, codirected the Foundation for Mind Research in Pomona, New York, which studied psychedelic drugs, sexual behavior, hypnosis, and humanistic psychology. Dubbed the "guru to the glitterati" after being endorsed by Oprah Winfrey and officiating at the seventh wedding of Elizabeth Taylor in 1991, Williamson encouraged women to find God by focusing on the love inside themselves. A final leader at this weekend retreat was Mary Catherine Bateson, daughter of Margaret Mead and herself a highly respected cultural anthropologist. Williamson told invited guests that the first lady was at a "low point" and wanted to discuss how to explain the administration's message more effectively to the public.[119]

"Both Bateson and Houston were shocked at how fragile and confused Hillary seemed." Houston described her as "battered" and "tormented." She did not display her typical self-confidence and appeared exhausted. Clinton sought spiritual help and planned to regain her equilibrium by praying, traveling, and writing. Bateson and Houston counseled her to love and forgive her enemies in politics and the media who had made her life so difficult. They insisted that the claims of critics such as Newt Gingrich and radio commentator Rush Limbaugh could be effectively countered as she did good works and relied on God. Bateson and Houston strove to help Clinton approach life more positively and abandon her warrior mentality.[120]

The most controversial aspect of Clinton's encounter with Houston was her "channeling" of Eleanor Roosevelt. Clinton called Roosevelt "one of my great heroines" and reported that she had read her autobiography, her newspaper columns, and many biographies about her. Clinton described these sessions as imaginary conversations or "intellectual exercises," but she was accused of holding a "séance" with Eleanor's ghost, which both Clinton and her staff fervently denied.[121] Clinton was the butt of jokes by late-night comedians and barbs from conservative radio talk-show hosts. The first lady declared, "I have no spiritual advisers or any other alternatives to my deeply held Methodist faith and traditions on which I have relied since childhood." Clinton added that Williamson "is neither my guru nor my spiritual adviser."[122] Houston contended that Clinton "never made any séance-like effort to contact the spirits of Mrs. Roosevelt or [Mahatma] Gandhi but simply engaged in an intellectual role-playing exercise." She added that the first lady would never engage in spiritualist activities because she is "a very committed Christian" and a "serious, reflective and prayerful" woman.[123] Clinton's friends and colleagues agreed that these sessions were only imaginative exercises. "No doubt she admired Eleanor Roosevelt's courage and commitments, but to say that Hillary was having séances or communing with her is just crazy," declared Melanne Verveer.[124]

The controversy over her relationship with Houston and alleged channeling of Roosevelt continued to plague Clinton throughout 1995 and 1996, in large part because of Bob Woodward's discussion of her sessions in his 1996 book *The Choice. Newsweek* characterized Clinton's imagined conversations with Roosevelt as "séances," and *New York Times* columnist Maureen Dowd joked that the first lady was "so desperate for friends that she's hanging out with the quack and the dead."[125] Limbaugh told his estimated twenty million listeners that Clinton's sessions with Roosevelt were "just flat-out weird," and a *Washington Times* headline proclaimed, "Methodists Question Hillary's Mind Games."[126] Stephen Hess, a presidential scholar at the Brookings Institution, argued that the average American considered Clinton's conversations with Roosevelt "a bit peculiar" and something a typical Yale Law School graduate would not do.[127] Dowd argued that the first lady's sessions were a sad illustration of the nation's obsession with self-esteem and personal fulfillment, as reflected by the many best-selling books on the topic. Even though the Clintons had reached the pinnacle of power, they were still searching for fulfillment. "They are so unfinished, so intellectually unstable . . . so desperate to win the love of everybody" that they constantly "take on different identities and gurus." Why was "the brainy, no-nonsense Methodist lawyer" consulting these "motivational mountebanks" who were the "spiritual equivalent of her hairstyles"? If the "uncentered" Clinton did manage to contact Eleanor Roosevelt, Dowd avowed, she would tell the first lady to "fight for some really good causes and stop worrying about who agrees with her."[128]

Others defended Clinton. Some psychiatrists emphasized that this channeling technique was often used in therapy. Sociologist Andrew Greeley insisted that "the paranormal is normal and ecstasy is good for you." He also stressed that many athletes engaged in "imaging and visualization" to prepare for their contests. Bateson called the sessions "a kind of meditation, reflection or even prayer."[129] Historian Doris Kearns Goodwin maintained that the sessions simply sounded "like a role-playing exercise" and were not weird.[130] Don Jones was unconcerned about the first lady "being tainted spiritually" by these exercises. He praised Clinton's commitment to Christ and complained that the secular Washington press corps was misleading the public about Clinton's faith. Prone to caricaturing televangelists, new-age gurus, and other spiritual leaders, many journalists did not comprehend mainline Protestant faith and disbelieved the first lady's claims as to how her faith motivated and guided her.[131]

Others provided historical and political context. One journalist stressed that Mary Todd Lincoln held séances to contact her dead son, Florence Harding sneaked her seer into the White House, and Nancy Reagan consulted an astrologer to determine her husband's travel schedule. Michael Deaver, a former Reagan aide, insisted that Hillary's actions simply provided fodder for David Letterman and Jay Leno; if the president himself were talking to Abraham Lincoln or Harry Truman, it would be much more significant. A UCLA professor of psychiatry argued that Americans expected their presidents to be saviors who could handle governing on their own. In the past, their wives played only minor political roles, but Hillary Clinton did not follow the long-standing norms and thus the public was more concerned about her mind-set and activities.[132] Wanting to evade the derision Nancy Reagan endured after consulting an astrologer and to avoid negative publicity as her husband campaigned for reelection, Clinton once again emphasized that these sessions were simply exercises designed to help reevaluate her life and deal with the challenges confronting her. She labeled them as play acting with "no psychic or religious overtones" and reiterated her loyalty to Methodist doctrine. Administration spokespersons leaped to Clinton's defense. For example, Leon Panetta, Bill's chief of staff, explained on CBS's *Face the Nation* that Hillary often consulted with friends and counselors to deal more effectively with the pressures of the White House. He added, "I can't tell you how many Hail Marys I've said since I've taken this job."[133]

An Investigation and a Book

Hillary's role in the Whitewater scandal also provoked considerable criticism during Bill's first term and contributed to making her America's most controversial first lady. Since the Clintons' days in Arkansas, rumors had circulated that she had engaged in illegal acts connected with the Whitewater land deal. In 1978, the Clintons partnered with their friends James and Susan McDougal to purchase 220 acres of riverfront property on the White River and form the Whitewater Development Corporation. Their plan to sell vacation homes went poorly, and the Clintons reported losing $40,000 on this venture. Meanwhile, Hillary did legal work for a savings and loan association that James McDougal owned. It supplied many fraudulent loans, and the McDougals were found guilty of fraud in 1995.

The resulting investigation came to include additional financial and legal activities in which the Clintons engaged in Arkansas. Bill Clinton biographer David Maraniss contended that during her husband's first term, Hillary repeatedly avoided making "full disclosure, occasionally forgetting places and events that might embarrass her, and revising her story as documents emerge and the knowledge of her questioners deepens."[134] In January 1996, independent counsel Kenneth Starr, who was investigating whether any White House staff had obstructed justice in handling records from Clinton's law firm, subpoenaed Hillary to appear before a federal grand jury. Although she believed she had done nothing wrong, having a spotlight shone on her personal life made Clinton feel "discouraged and embarrassed." She worried that "events might destroy whatever credibility I retained" and damage Bill's presidency. "I couldn't sleep for a week before my appearance, and I lost ten pounds," she reported. She believed that Starr may have wanted "to humiliate me publicly, but I was determined not to let him break my spirit." She sought to prepare herself mentally and spiritually and prayed for God's help.[135]

Clinton's subpoena came as she was beginning a tour to promote her first book, *It Takes a Village: And Other Lessons Children Teach Us.* In some ways, the book expanded upon her "politics of meaning" speech by discussing her own faith, the spiritual nature of children, and traditional moral values. Clinton argued that everyone, not only religious and political leaders, must help Americans overcome their spiritual emptiness by renewing their "own sense of spirituality."[136] The book quickly topped the *New York Times* nonfiction best-seller list, although critics argued that its popularity resulted from Clinton's notoriety, not its message or readability. Eager to avoid controversy, a *New York Times* reviewer protested, Clinton had dodged the tough issues and instead supplied "smallish recommendations, heartwarming personal anecdotes and, above all, civics-lesson platitudes."[137] The book, which Carl Bernstein assessed as combining feminism, folklore, new-age concepts, traditional religion, psychology, and psychobabble, "is often banal" and expresses commonly accepted truisms.[138] Others praised the book. An unidentified reviewer in the *Palm Beach Post* asserted that Clinton's opponents would denounce the book as too liberal (even though she opposed premarital sex and divorce) and idealistic. She lauded Clinton, however, for reminding families to spend time together and exhorting parents "to raise strong, healthy, smart, safe children." The reviewer declared that the book had inspired her to resume attending church so as to help expand the village that cared for her children.[139] A review in the *Los Angeles Times* praised Clinton's Methodist "infusion of social justice with spiritual values." The journalist highlighted Clinton's focus on people's "struggle to live up to the spiritual values" they professed and her argument that groups and nations "can suffer from an absence or misuse of spirituality."[140]

Faith and Politics

Clinton's most forthright declaration of how her faith inspired her public service, especially her advocacy for women and children, was her speech to one thousand delegates at the April 1996 General Conference of the United Methodist Church. Methodism, she professed, "has been important to me for as long as I can remember." It would be difficult, she declared, to "list all the ways" the Methodist Church has "influenced me, and helped me develop as a person, not only on my own faith journey, but with a sense of obligations to others." She learned that her faith obligated her to help individuals and improve society. "In the name of Jesus Christ," she proclaimed, "we are called" to exercise "patience and forbearance with one another" in both the church and society.[141]

Clinton insisted that the social principles of the Methodist Church had directed her work. Biblical teaching and the stories of John and Charles Wesley and other Christian leaders inspired her to express her faith through her actions. She noted that John Wesley had whiskey bottles thrown at him while he preached. "How many of us," she asked, "would even go into places now where we were likely to be the object of thrown whiskey bottles?"[142]

Clinton rejoiced that Methodists had long answered "John Wesley's call to provide for the educational health and spiritual needs of children." Methodists had helped lead "the fight to improve the quality of education, promote parental responsibility, curb smoking among young people, expand comprehensive health care, strengthen marriages," and help the destitute. She praised the denomination's Shalom Initiative through which many congregations worked to transform America's inner cities. The church's proclamation of the gospel and good works, she asserted, would "do more to change lives than any program" a legislative body passed. Churches whose members lived out the gospel and served the needy, she claimed, "would continue to grow." Clinton thanked delegates for keeping Methodist traditions and teachings alive and "for helping to awaken and strengthen the spirit and faith of men, women, and children." She exhorted Methodists "to make common cause" with other Christians to save souls and engage in social action.[143]

Paul Kengor asserted that it is unclear whether Clinton's speech "was the result of a genuine reevaluation of her faith" or an effort to help her husband win the votes of religiously devout Americans in November. Very likely, it was both. Kengor contends that Clinton's conversations with new-age and self-help proponents appeared to be "a temporary detour, a spiritual misstep along an otherwise conventional road of faith." In my judgment, Clinton was simply seeking advice from these individuals to help her deal with personal and political struggles. She did not embrace their ideas of spirituality even temporarily; given the negative response to her relationship with Houston, Williamson, Covey, and others, her misstep was political rather than spiritual.[144]

The First Lady as a Social Activist

In publicizing and promoting social causes, Clinton followed in the steps of other first ladies. Dolley Madison supported an orphanage in Washington, and Ellen Wilson strove to improve housing in the city. Jacqueline Kennedy championed the arts, and Lady Bird Johnson backed efforts to "beautify" the nation's capital by cleaning parks and providing playgrounds for inner-city neighborhoods. Most notably, Eleanor Roosevelt worked to upgrade Washington's substandard schools, nursing homes, and psychiatric hospitals. She also took the wives of cabinet members and members of Congress to inspect inadequate housing and sanitation.[145] Clinton led a health care initiative, worked to enhance the lives of women and children, and supported the Washington Interfaith Network, an organization founded by African American ministers to improve housing, establish after-school programs, and decrease crime. She also worked with Mother Teresa to open a home for pregnant teenagers who planned to give up their babies and for infants waiting to be adopted.

Health Care Reform

Clinton's Methodist faith was on display as she tackled health care reform. Her numerous speeches advocating universal health care coverage, Kenneth Woodward avowed, "resonated with the moral rhetoric of resolutions adopted by the church's governing General Conference."[146] To promote her and Bill's proposals, Clinton traveled thousands of miles, met with dozens of groups, and testified several times before Congress. In a September 1993 *USA Today* article, she stressed that her husband's administration wanted to provide "affordable, high-quality health care for every citizen" because good health was "the foundation of individual happiness and prosperity as well as a source of strength and well being for our nation."[147]

Catholic leaders felt conflicted about the health care reform initiative. They strongly endorsed universal access to health care, improved delivery of health services, and effective cost containment. They objected, however, to proposals to have Medicaid pay for abortions and insisted it "would be a moral tragedy and serious mistake to burden health care reform with abortion coverage that most Americans oppose."[148] Clinton met with Cardinal James Hickey, archbishop of Washington, and other Catholic leaders to discuss their concerns about her plan in late April 1993.

By holding closed-door meetings and granting few interviews, Clinton alienated many members of the Washington press corps.[149] Her arrogance, truculence, and unwillingness to compromise helped defeat health care reform.[150] So did the massive lobbying efforts by the health care industry. Moreover, her 1,342-page plan was so complicated, convoluted, and costly that even most Democrats did not support it. The failure of health reform caused Clinton to lose "her reputation as a savvy political player."[151] Polls after the 1994 midterm elections revealed that most Americans opposed the health care reform plan, viewing it as an ill-advised social program that gave the government too much

power. Some Democratic congressmen complained that the plan was not at-
tuned to marketplace forces and diverted attention from more important
reforms such as improving the welfare system.[152]

Affordable Housing

Clinton's concern about housing costs in Washington led her to collaborate
with the Washington Interfaith Network (WIN). This association of fifty-
five Black congregations worked to build affordable housing for low-income
residents, establish after-school programs for inner-city youth, and decrease
crime. Clinton joined more than 2,000 Black, Asian, Latino, and white churchgoers at the organization's first public meeting in 1996, and WIN quickly raised
$2.5 million. Insisting that WIN's activities had "tremendous potential" to
improve life in some Washington neighborhoods, Clinton pledged to support
it as part of her campaign to reduce crime, poverty, and unemployment and
help poorly performing schools in the nation's capital. She asked some major
foundations to help fund WIN's program.[153]

Children: Our Greatest Gift, Responsibility, and Test

As first lady, Clinton especially strove to improve the lives of children, a cause
to which she had been committed since high school. She argued that "our
children are our greatest gift, our greatest responsibility, our greatest test."[154]
"The primary obligation of both parents is to take" the gifts God gave them
in their children and help them "to flourish."[155] Several factors, especially her
mother's struggles as a girl, made the first lady an advocate for children. "Essentially abandoned" by her parents and treated coldly by her grandparents
who raised her, Clinton's mother began working as a housekeeper for another
family at age thirteen to find safety. Clinton recognized that had her mother
been born later, she would have been placed in a foster home. Her mother's
problems contributed to Clinton's "passionate commitment" to "give every
child the chance to live up to his or her God-given potential."[156]

Clinton hosted the first White House conference on early learning and brain
development and helped create the Early Head Start program to enhance the
physical, cognitive, social, and emotional development of low-income children
from birth to age three and to assist pregnant mothers.[157] In a January 1995
article in *Newsweek*, Clinton declared that she had been working diligently for
twenty-five years "to strengthen families and help children." To aid children,
she had volunteered in homeless shelters, group homes, hospitals, and schools.
In Arkansas, she had created programs to "teach parenting skills to welfare

recipients and worked with advocacy groups to improve education, health care and child care." Clinton was "deeply disturbed by the outrageous rates of out-of-wedlock births and the welfare dependency they bring" and heartbroken about the frequent neglect and abuse of children. She rejoiced that the well-being of children and families was becoming a higher national priority as increasing numbers of Americans deplored "the failings of the welfare system, high rates of illegitimacy, irresponsible parenting, poor schooling, drugs and violence."[158]

Clinton insisted that four bedrock principles helped safeguard the well-being of children. First, children "are almost always best off with their families." Second, being poor did not prevent people from being good parents; most low-income parents tried to provide "a secure home, strong values, consistency and love." Third, society must help families with special problems, including poverty, rather than give up on them. She praised her husband's administration for achieving passage of a family and medical leave bill, advocating a tax cut for low-income families, and creating government programs to preserve families, often in partnership with religious organizations. Fourth, children living in dangerous circumstances must be moved into alternative settings. This, however, must be the last resort. Children should be separated from their parents only to ensure their safety and well-being. Children should never be removed from their families simply because their parents were destitute, unmarried, or poorly educated.[159]

Clinton urged Americans to prioritize "responsible parenting," helping people gain independence from welfare and creating conditions that enabled children to thrive. She called for a national campaign to reduce teenage pregnancies and "to require fathers to take responsibility for their children and pay child support" in cases of out-of-wedlock births and divorce. This campaign would also help mothers receiving welfare acquire the skills they needed to support themselves and their children, and it would increase the adoption of children whose parents could not properly provide for them. Parents, national policies, and personal values, Clinton contended, all had important roles to play in raising children. She affirmed the 1992 pastoral letter of the National Conference of Catholic Bishops titled "Putting Families First," which declared, "No government can love a child, and no policy can substitute for a family's care. But government can either support or undermine families. There has been an unfortunate, unnecessary and unreal polarization in discussion [about] how best to help families. The undeniable fact is that our children's future is shaped both by the values of their parents and the policies of our nation."

"Taking responsibility for the children in our own lives and all children," Clinton concluded, "is the most sacred duty we have."[160]

Two months later, Clinton lamented that 23 percent of American children lived in poverty; countless children went hungry every day; thousands of children died from drugs, violence, and abuse; and increasing numbers of children were giving birth. She protested that Congress was waging war against children by proposing to cut children's programs by $40 billion during the next five years. Clinton agreed with Republicans that the federal government needed to "be leaner and more efficient," but she insisted that it had a responsibility to provide "a safety net for our neediest children and families" and opportunities for poor parents to "lift themselves up." She called for supplying free school lunches, assisting pregnant women, helping low-income families pay for daycare and heat, supplying grants to encourage adoption and foster care, and funding health and nutrition programs. Clinton argued that many middle-class American parents projected their guilt about their inadequate parenting resulting from "longer work hours, divorce, [and] shrinking resources" onto the parents of the poor. This tendency, coupled with concerns that "welfare queens" were squandering federal resources, often "overpowered feelings of charity" and kept many Americans from recognizing how corporations, the media, and state and local governments had failed to sufficiently help indigent families. Clinton again quoted "Putting Families First," which argued that many families are poor "because of economic forces beyond their control: recession, industrial restructuring, erosion of real wages, unemployment and discrimination in hiring and promotion." She urged Congress to evaluate every proposal pertaining to "welfare, nutrition, education or health by its impact on children." Clinton noted that Congress prepared environmental impact statements when considering bills affecting areas where endangered species lived. Endangered children, she argued, deserved "at least the same care we give our physical environment."[161]

Clinton quoted this pastoral letter a third time in June 1995 when she met with thirty journalists. She contended that corporate downsizing and some other business practices were negatively affecting families, repudiated claims that the government was responsible for everything that was ailing families, and discussed the tendency of teenagers "to test the limits of parental authority" and the problems of inadequate daycare. "Children's issues are marginalized," she sarcastically observed, because children cannot vote and "they can't take legislators duck hunting." During the 1980s, Clinton complained, federal funds given to the states as block grants to aid families and children were used instead to build bridges, prisons, and nursing homes. She called for promoting fatherhood and criticized the media's frequent denigration of fathers. Clinton also insisted that "the rights of children should sometimes supersede those of their parents." When children were bounced from one foster home to another or were living in abandoned cars with a single parent, she explained, "certain parental rights should be terminated."[162] Some critics complained, as they had earlier, that Clinton was trying to enlarge "the paternalistic role of state agencies and trained experts" in the lives of children. Her approach, they argued, was not that of a Marxist but of "a Swedish-style technocratic socialist."[163]

As noted, Clinton published *It Takes a Village* in early 1996 to promote the welfare of children. She argued that children are born with the capacity to exercise "faith, hope, and love, and with a deep intuition into God's creative, intelligent, and unifying force." "This inclination toward spirituality," however, needed to be nurtured and encouraged to bloom. A principal way to do this, she avowed, was by teaching children how to translate their spiritual impulses into a "shared form of expression" by using "words and rituals" that religion furnished. "If more parents introduced their children to faith and prayer at home," Clinton insisted, "there would be fewer calls for prayer in schools." She prayed for and worked to provide "a world in which all children are loved and cared for" by their own families and their communities.[164]

In her 1996 address to the United Methodist Church's General Conference, Clinton protested that too many children and women of color around the globe were "unloved, unfed, unhealthy, and unschooled." Many African and Asian women were marginalized and denied opportunities to fully participate in their societies. However, Clinton rejoiced that churches and communities throughout the world were working to solve these problems. She was encouraged that the Methodist Council of Bishops had made "the welfare of children a top priority," as reflected in its Episcopal Initiative on Children and Poverty. Although Republicans and Democrats debated how best to help children and families, Clinton contended, they could agree that children needed the nurture and care that stable families provided and that children were influenced by the values of both their parents and their societies. She stressed that the Bible admonished people to care for one another and cited Jesus's words, "Whoever welcomes one such child in my name, welcomes me, and whoever welcomes me, welcomes not me, but the one who sends me" (Mark 9:37). She challenged listeners to transpose the face of Jesus "onto the face of every child" they saw and then ask, "Would I turn that child away from the health care that child needs?" She urged Christians to heed "the church's call to strengthen families and renew our schools and encourage policies that enable each child to have a chance to fulfill his or her God-given potential." Clinton exhorted congregations to help parents to perform their crucial role to the best of their ability by encouraging and equipping them and providing the "love, attention and discipline every child needs." Clinton urged businesses to give their employees time off to meet with their children's teachers and beseeched churches to allow inner-city youth to use their facilities after school. She declared that the words of the hymn "Jesus Loves the Little Children" had impacted her more than "many earnest lectures on race relations" and reminded her that Christ loves children of all colors.[165]

In August 1997, Clinton exulted that the new federal budget would provide the largest expansion in children's health coverage since Medicaid was created thirty years earlier. It would provide checkups, antibiotics, surgeries, and other health care services for as many as five million uninsured children. She contended that her husband's administration had also aided children by ensuring that families kept their health insurance when parents changed or lost their jobs, increasing immunizations, protecting Medicaid, restricting tobacco advertising and sales to minors, extending hospital stays for mothers and their newborns, and boosting funds for nutrition and education programs for low-income women and their children.[166]

Abortion and Mother Teresa

Abortion caused more problems in Clinton's relationship with religious conservatives than any other issue. She became a strong prochoice proponent shortly after the Supreme Court's *Roe v. Wade* ruling in 1973. William Harrison, her gynecologist in Fayetteville, Arkansas, argued that Clinton adopted a prochoice stance in large part because some of her friends had had illegal abortions and the Methodist Church supported having abortions under some difficult circumstances.[167] In his first day as president, Bill signed five executive orders that substantially increased federal funding for elective abortions. This sparked a battle with Pope John Paul II that continued throughout Clinton's presidency. Four days after Clinton signed these executive orders, the Vatican newspaper, *L'Osservatore Romano*, protested that Clinton's policies would further the "way of death" and promoted "violence against innocent human beings."[168] This was the first salvo in "the most serious confrontation ever" between the US government and the Vatican.[169] During their meeting in August 1993, Pope John Paul II warned President Clinton that American greatness depended on how it treated its "weakest and most defenseless" members. To provide equal justice for all, true freedom, and lasting peace, the United States must defend innocent life.[170]

In October 1993, Hillary stated that under the national health care plan she was devising, abortion services "would be widely available." She insisted, however, that physicians and hospitals would have a "conscience exemption" and would not be forced to perform abortions.[171] Hillary's prochoice position brought her into conflict with Mother Teresa. Speaking at the 1994 National Prayer Breakfast, which Bill and Hillary attended, the celebrated Catholic nun declared, "The greatest destroyer of peace today is abortion, because Jesus said, 'If you receive a little child, you receive me.' So every abortion is the denial of receiving Jesus."[172] Attendees clapped for five minutes, but the Clintons did not join in, even though they had argued that abortion was regrettable and should be limited and Mother Teresa had not called for repealing laws permitting abortion. After her talk, the champion of Calcutta told Hillary privately that she disagreed with her "views on a woman's right to choose."[173]

In March 1995, as part of a tour of South Asia, Clinton visited Mother Teresa's orphanage in Calcutta. Determined to establish a home in Washington for women to care for their babies until they could be adopted or placed in foster homes, the nun enlisted Clinton's help. Describing her request for help, Clinton told the National Prayer Breakfast audience in 2010, "That day, I felt like I had been ordered, and that the message was coming not just through this diminutive woman but from someplace far beyond." Mother Teresa, "the most relentless lobbyist" Clinton ever encountered, called her from India and wrote her numerous letters asking how they could speed up the process to open the home.[174]

Clinton worked diligently to establish this home. She recruited lawyers to work pro bono, battled with the District of Columbia bureaucracy, and spoke with dozens of community leaders, Protestant pastors, and Catholic priests.[175] Cutting through all the red tape was harder than she had imagined, but on June 19, 1995, the Mother Teresa Home for Infant Children opened, and newspapers carried a photo of Clinton and Mother Teresa clasping hands in its nursery. During the last two years of her life, the Catholic nun strove mightily to change Clinton's views on abortion. She sent the first lady dozens of notes and messages gently entreating her to adopt a pro-life position. "Mother Teresa never lectured or scolded me; her admonitions were always loving and heartfelt," wrote Clinton, adding that she had "the greatest respect for her opposition to abortion."[176]

The Lewinsky Affair

As first lady, Hillary endured many criticisms of her character and actions, but her biggest challenge arose from Bill's sexual indiscretions with Monica Lewinsky, which came to light in 1998. Rumors began to circulate about Bill's tryst with Lewinsky in mid-January, and it quickly became one of the hottest stories in American political history. Late-night comedians parodied Bill's sex drive and the Clintons' marriage. Jay Leno quipped that the title of Hillary's next book should be *It Takes a Village to Keep an Eye on My Husband*.[177] By February 1999, more than twenty books entirely or substantially devoted to their affair were in print, near publication, or under contract. Hillary's faith helped her retain her composure, survive the pain, forgive her husband, and remain committed to their marriage as she dealt with what she called "the most devastating, shocking and hurtful experience of my life."[178] Polls indicated that her response to Bill's infidelity made her widely admired and helped prepare the way for her 2000 campaign for the US Senate. Marsha Berry, Clinton's press secretary, declared that Hillary was relying on "her strong religious faith" to deal with the crisis. Clinton later insisted that "my faith was crucial to the challenges I faced."[179]

When rumors about the affair first surfaced, Hillary believed Bill's claims that he and Lewinsky had not had sexual relations. Bill's political enemies had often falsely accused him, the first lady argued, and his right-wing opponents were again trying to discredit and destroy him. Moreover, she could not imagine Bill risking his reputation and their life's work to have a fling with an intern only a "few years older than their daughter." Hillary also believed "he loved her enough not to humiliate her."[180] She would soon be deeply disappointed. Hillary argued in mid-February that the allegations of the affair would "slowly dissipate over time under the weight" of their "own insubstantiality."[181] "It is difficult and painful," Hillary confessed, "anytime someone you care about, you love and you admire is attacked and subjected to such relentless accusations as my husband has been." Longtime friend and University of Arkansas political science professor Diane Blair stressed in January 1998 that the Clintons had "been living for five years now with unending allegations" and investigations. Hillary naturally wished that life could be different, "but she is not bent or broken. She is a very strong, grounded woman who will get through this."[182]

In March, Philip Wogaman argued that engaging in sexual misconduct did not automatically make a political leader immoral. He insisted that the morality of politicians was demonstrated by their "courage, concern for the poor, fostering world peace, running the economy responsibly and furthering racial equality." Like Hillary, he believed the president's resolute repudiation of the charges of sexual impropriety and perjury. Even if the accusations proved to be true, he pointed out, there was also credible evidence about moral lapses by Martin Luther King Jr., yet defining him by those "moral failings would be to miss the point" about his life and influence.[183] Many Americans would adopt this perspective about Bill Clinton.

On August 16, the Clintons attended Foundry Methodist Church. In his sermon that morning, associate pastor Walter Shropshire Jr. declared, "When we have opposition and hopeless situations, God bears us up on eagles' wings."[184] The next day, the president testified before a grand jury investigating his conduct and later spoke on national television. In both settings, Clinton admitted that his relationship with Lewinsky had been "inappropriate," but he refused to answer questions about what kind of physical contact they had.

When Bill finally confessed to his wife privately and then publicly admitted in late August that he had indeed engaged in sexual acts with Lewinsky, it was the worst experience of Hillary's life. As one journalist wrote, Bill had cheated on Hillary "when she was out of town, when she was out of the country, when she was upstairs, and when she had just come home from church on Easter Sunday."[185] During their twenty-three-year marriage, Hillary had repeatedly forgiven her husband for infidelities and ignominies few wives would accept. But Bill's dalliance with Lewinsky was far more humiliating than his earlier adulteries because of their age difference and because it became a public spectacle. His betrayal was much "deeper, more terrifying, more scandalous" than his earlier sexual escapades.[186] Lewinsky, who was twenty-four in 1998, claimed that she and Clinton had sexual encounters nine times between November 1995 and March 1997. "I was furious with him," Hillary explained in her 2003 autobiography. "Bill's standing in public opinion polls remained high [but] his standing with me had hit rock bottom." She experienced "profound sadness, disappointment and unresolved anger. I could barely speak to Bill, and when I did, it was a tirade." Bill kept trying to apologize, but she was not ready to forgive him. "I would have to go deep inside myself and my faith," she concluded, "to discover any remaining belief in our marriage."[187] She wished that W. O. Vaught, Bill's pastor at Immanuel Baptist Church in Little Rock in the 1980s, had still been alive to confront and counsel him. But she was "deeply appreciative" of the three ministers who did provide guidance—Wogaman, Baptist professor and evangelist Tony Campolo, and Gordon MacDonald, pastor of Grace Chapel, an evangelical congregation near Boston, who had been restored to the ministry after confessing to adultery. They "prayed with him regularly as he sought understanding and forgiveness." After Bill's confession, Hillary "spent a lot of time alone, praying and reading," and received comfort and counsel from several ministers and the women in her prayer group.[188]

Don Jones, Ed Matthews, and Billy Graham all exhorted Hillary to forgive Bill. Jones sent her a copy of theologian Paul Tillich's sermon "You Are Accepted," which emphasizes God's grace and forgiveness; Tillich argued that the essence of Christianity is unconditional love. Jones advised Hillary to choose grace in dealing with Bill's sin.[189] Reflecting on this sermon, Hillary wrote, Tillich teaches that "sin and grace exist in life in constant interplay; neither is possible without the other. The mystery—and paradox—of grace is that you cannot find it on your own; it finds you, often when you are most pained and restless."[190] "Forgiveness has nothing to do with human logic," Matthews told Clinton. "Forgiveness has strictly to do with grace. And that's God's gift," Matthews added. "I'm praying that you [recognize that truth]." Clinton responded, "I think I'm getting there."[191] She and Graham developed a warm relationship shortly before the Lewinsky crisis. The evangelist forgave Bill as readily as he had Richard Nixon two decades earlier and urged Hillary to pardon her husband.[192]

At a 1994 prayer luncheon, Clinton had argued that "forgiveness is the most powerful expression of love we can give or experience. It is also the most costly. For the Lord, it was the cross; for me, it cost my pride. . . . It is hard to forgive. But it is also essential, not only to live, but to grow in Christ."[193] The first lady reread Henri Nouwen's teaching on forgiveness. The Dutch Catholic priest exhorted people to welcome others home as the father of the prodigal son did and to offer compassion to the penitent. In *The Return of the Prodigal Son*, Nouwen analyzed the well-known biblical story from several perspectives—that of the father who pardons his defiant son, the son who returns home after squandering his inheritance, and the compliant, irate son who had remained at home. Moved by Nouwen's focus on gratitude and forgiveness, Clinton tried to practice the "daily discipline of gratitude" and extend forgiveness as he prescribed.[194] She also remembered a Sunday school lesson she had taught in Little Rock, which focused on how the concept of the new covenant provides "a new relationship with God." This covenant, she recalled, promised that "we could be forgiven, that we could seek both personally and through our relationships with others that gift of forgiveness."[195] She still struggled, however, to forgive her husband for betraying and publicly humiliating her.

Bill apologized privately and publicly to Hillary and begged for her forgiveness. On September 11, 1998, Bill told a group of ministers at a prayer breakfast, "I don't think there's a fancy way to say that I have sinned." He asserted that he had asked his family, friends, staff, and cabinet members, Monica Lewinsky and her family, and the American people for their forgiveness. "To be forgiven," he contended, two things are required in addition to sorrow. One is "genuine repentance, a determination to change and to repair breaches of my own making. I have repented." The second is the recognition "that I must have God's help to be the person that I want to be" and a refusal "to excuse and compare and to blame and complain."[196]

Bill's repentance, the counsel of respected ministers, and her own reflection and prayers led Hillary eventually to forgive her husband's "sins of weakness." When she told ABC's Barbara Walters about her decision, Walters replied, "I don't think people know how strong your faith is. It must have helped you." "I've relied on prayer," Hillary explained; "ultimately I had to get down on my knees and I had to pray" to be able to forgive Bill.[197] Her faith, Wogaman declared in mid-September, is "at the root of her life" and supplied her resilience, commitment, and fortitude. "I know she is deeply committed to her marriage and to seeing this whole thing through."[198] Mike McCurry, who served as Bill Clinton's press secretary during this period and later taught at Wesley Theological Seminary, maintained that Hillary's faith "was a very, very important part of how she dealt with that family crisis." He added that a well-worn Bible always lay on the Clinton family's dining room table during the crisis.[199]

Another minister who counseled the first lady during this troubled time was civil rights activist Jesse Jackson, whose own marital difficulties were widely known. He told Hillary and Chelsea that their situation reminded him of "another First Family in crisis, in the very first Rose Garden." When Adam and Eve disobeyed God's commandment, they immediately put on clothes to cover their humiliation and embarrassment. Sin and shame, he insisted, often led people to lie, as Bill had done. The president, Jackson argued, was like King David. Both men were extremely talented but had succumbed to sexual temptation. So had "some of the greatest American leaders in history." Jackson advised Hillary and Chelsea to practice their faith and "stand together until the storm passes."[200]

Journalist Bob Woodward argued that Bill's affair caused Hillary to retreat "to her religious and spiritual convictions." "I have to take this punishment," she confided to a friend. "I don't know why God has chosen this for me. But He has, and it will be revealed to me. God is doing this, and He knows the reason."[201] In her 2017 memoir, Hillary explained, "We've certainly had dark days in our marriage." Consider "what it would be like for the whole world to know about the worst moments in your relationship." She asked herself, "Do I still love him? And can I still be in this marriage without becoming unrecognizable to myself—twisted by anger, resentment, or remoteness? The answers were always yes. So I kept going."[202] At the 2007 Sojourners faith forum, Clinton explained, "I have been tested in ways that are both publicly known and those that are not so well known or not known at all."[203] She added, "I am very grateful that I had a grounding in faith that gave me the courage and the strength to do what I thought was right, regardless of what the world thought." Gordon MacDonald reported that the Clintons often prayed together during the period when everyone was waiting for Hillary to leave Bill.[204]

After the Lewinsky affair became public, biographer William Chafe argued, Hillary no longer helped shape the Clinton administration's policies. Withdrawing from active political engagement enabled Hillary to focus on her lifelong "spiritual quest," which was more intense at some times than others. Clinton pondered "the most fundamental questions of human existence." She was sometimes distracted by various crises from Gennifer Flowers to Monica Lewinsky, "but her search for a life of faith and meaning remained central to her personal journey."[205]

Despite his betrayal, Hillary staunchly supported Bill during his impeachment hearings, which she viewed as a right-wing crusade to sabotage everything Democrats sought to accomplish "on the economy, education, Social Security, health care, the environment, and the search for peace in Northern Ireland, the Balkans and the Middle East."[206] Pundits proffered various explanations for why Hillary stayed with Bill: she wanted to ensure the success of his presidency, she sought to further her own future political goals, and she was following her mother's example of remaining in a difficult marriage. One presidential staffer argued that Hillary remained with Bill because she believed she had a biblical duty to "love the sinner, and help him to try to overcome his defects of character."[207] Money, power, and political prestige may have played a minor role in Hillary's decision, Ed Matthews insisted, but her faith was the most important reason.[208] Although many Americans viewed Hillary as too unconventional, controversial, and close to power for their comfort, her performance as a "wounded wife," featuring her "dignified suffering" and "partisan politicking," helped save his presidency.[209]

In an August 1999 interview, Hillary argued that Bill's marital infidelities had been caused by psychological "abuse" he suffered as a young boy; his affairs were "a sin of weakness," not a sin "of malice." Although her husband had caused her "enormous pain" and anger, she resolved that people should help rather than abandon those they loved. Hillary reiterated that she had survived the Lewinsky scandal and her husband's impeachment through "soul-searching, friends, religious faith and long, hard discussions."[210]

Clinton's Critics

As first lady, Clinton was accused of having an affair with Vince Foster, verbally abusing staff, holding grudges, belittling anyone who challenged her, and using her faith "as a cover for her faults."[211] She was also criticized for trying to destroy the women with whom Bill had sex, demonizing the Clintons' opponents, and ignoring helpful advice from White House staff.[212] Gargantuan ambition was Clinton's major sin, according to biographer Joyce Milton.[213] She was widely seen as a wife who called the shots—who was steelier, smarter, and scarier than her husband. Maureen Dowd asserted that if Eleanor Roosevelt was a Bolshevik and Nancy Reagan was Marie Antoinette, Clinton was Lady Macbeth.[214]

Bernstein argued that Hillary tended to view "people and events with almost biblical judgment." Dick Atkinson, a friend from Arkansas, commented, "She often weighed matters in terms of good and evil." He added that Clinton often suspected conspiracies and demonized her opponents. An aide averred that Clinton saw life as "a series of battles," with herself as an "epic character" leading the charge against the enemy. She was happiest when attacking the women who seduced Bill, the press who maligned them, and the Republicans who thwarted their plans. Clinton, the aide asserted, often succumbed to victimization. She saw herself as "a martyr in the tradition of Joan of Arc."[215] Dick Morris, the Clintons' most important political consultant for two decades, declared that Hillary had a ruthlessness and aggressiveness that Bill lacked, "a killer instinct."[216] Another administration official claimed that Hillary was "addicted to power." He added, "She is probably the most self-righteous person I've ever known, or worked with. . . . [W]hat she says is right. And if you disagree with her . . . she holds a grudge."[217] "From childhood onward," William Chafe asserted, Clinton "thought of herself as moral, virtuous, beyond reproach."[218] Yet although she often declared her moral superiority over her opponents, she also frequently admitted her flaws. "Do I think I have faults?" she asked. "Absolutely. . . . Do I try to do better every day? Yes, I do." Like other people, Hillary declared, she was both a sinner and a saint.[219]

Hillary Clinton's faith helped motivate, guide, and sustain her during her tenure as first lady. It would play an equally important role in the next phase of her life, as a US senator from 2000 to 2009 and as a presidential candidate in 2008.

4

"Be Rigorous in Judging Ourselves and Gracious in Judging Others"

New York Senator and 2008 Presidential Candidate

As Hillary Rodham Clinton contemplated running for the US Senate in 1999, a journalist noted that conflicting interpretations and images of her abounded. To some, she was "the ultimate do-good liberal" who wanted government to do "everything from setting corporate profits to letting teenagers sue their parents." To others, she was, like her husband, a New Democrat moderate who accepted the principles of the market economy and wanted a lean and efficient federal government. Some Americans viewed the first lady as a "canny pragmatist" whose views were evolving as she gained experience and maturity, whereas others saw Clinton as an opportunist who adapted her political stances to fit her ambitions.[1]

In July 1999, the longtime Cubs fan proclaimed that she had switched her allegiance to the Yankees and announced her candidacy for a US Senate seat from New York. It was an unprecedented move; no first lady had ever run for political office. Religion played a significant factor in her campaign. Clinton discussed her political positions and promises in many churches and appealed for their members' support. An anti-Semitic slur Clinton allegedly made in 1974 against Paul Fray, her husband's campaign manager during his unsuccessful quest for the US Congress, caused controversy during her campaign.

Describing her decision to run for the Senate, Clinton wrote in her 2003 autobiography, "Most of us live with nagging voices questioning the choices we make and with loads of guilt, whatever our choice. In my own life, I have been a wife, mother, daughter, sister, in-law, student, lawyer, children's rights activist, law professor, Methodist, political advisor, citizen and so much else. Now I was a symbol," which was a new experience. She added, "Some people still felt deep ambivalence about women in positions of public leadership and power. In this era of changing gender roles, I was America's Exhibit A. The scrutiny was overwhelming."[2]

This scrutiny would increase even more in 2008 as Clinton sought to become the first woman nominated for president by a major political party. During the primaries, Clinton frequently appealed to religiously devout citizens, spoke openly about her faith, and stressed the religious aspects of and biblical basis for some of her key policies.

The 2000 Senate Campaign

As Clinton considered running for the Senate, some pundits and politicians offered conflicting advice about whether she should do so and her prospects for winning, while others provided competing perspectives regarding the first lady. Clinton "would have to be nuts to run for the Senate," declared a *Boston Globe* syndicated columnist. Former New York City Mayor Ed Koch warned that Rudy Giuliani, the presumptive Republican nominee, would conduct a "ruthless, vile, loathsome defamatory campaign." Every stop would feature a Whitewater map and a gnome wearing a Monica mask. How had "this self-described feminist, this amalgam of Princess Diana, Eleanor Roosevelt, and Evita," another journalist wondered, "emerged as an icon of persevering womanhood" and as "the hot hope" of New York's liberal Democrats? While some of the state's Democratic politicians viewed her "as the immaculate candidate, a woman sprung from the Democratic National Committee's forehead," pundits predicted that Robert Kennedy's carpetbagger example would be difficult to emulate. He was the brother of an assassinated president; she was the wife of an impeached president.[3] Others stressed that Hillary's negative ratings were "extraordinarily high"; in late November 1999, 48 percent of New Yorkers viewed her unfavorably.[4] Highly derogatory assessments would also plague Clinton in her two campaigns for the presidency.

A *Philadelphia Inquirer* columnist argued that Clinton had the celebrity status to amass a large campaign war chest and that she had championed many issues that were popular in New York, including improving childcare and providing family leave. On the other hand, the Clinton administration's failed health care initiative, which she spearheaded, was a political liability, and her endorsement of a Palestinian state might hurt her with Jewish voters. Moreover, her reputation was tarnished, fairly or unfairly, by Whitewater, Travelgate, FBI Filegate, and the Rose Law Firm billing records fiasco.[5] In addition, some of Clinton's religious values and political positions troubled New York's secular Democrats. Perhaps most problematic was that although she backed "domestic-partnership measures" to enable homosexual couples to receive the same health and financial benefits as married heterosexuals, Clinton supported the 1996 Defense of Marriage Act, prohibiting federal recognition of gay marriage and permitting states to ignore same-sex unions contracted elsewhere. This put her at odds not only with secular Democrats but with many other New York Democratic Party members.[6] Despite these potential problems, former White House aide Paul Begala predicted that Clinton might run because "at her core, she is still very much the true-believing, idealistic . . . Methodist who believes . . . that service is the rent you pay for living on this planet."[7]

Perceptions of Clinton differed greatly as she considered a US Senate campaign. She was viewed alternately as her husband's victim and his consigliere. The first lady was seen as a mother who loved to talk civics at the kitchen table, an astute lawyer who had made quick money on the futures market, and a Machiavelli who had persuaded Bill to sign the 1996 welfare bill, thereby saving his presidency. Many pundits insisted that she was her husband's equal as a politician.[8] Former Reagan speechwriter Peggy Noonan argued that Clinton offered "something for everyone." Women who had been abused and humiliated by men viewed her as a "fellow survivor." Many feminists saw her as a woman fighting "against the odds"; her triumph would be theirs. Numerous baby boomers viewed her "as representing their era."[9]

Another journalist noted that to some, Clinton was Saint Hillary, the principal "liberal voice in the Clinton White House, the patron of universal health care and the ardent advocate for children's education and welfare." David Corn, the Washington editor of The Nation, averred that many considered Clinton "a strong, assertive, intelligent woman" who promoted progressive aims. Clinton's reputation as a Methodist reformer, biographer Gail Sheehy contended, made her beloved by those who agreed with her and loathed by those who did not. Her supporters applauded her determination and "do-good reformism," whereas her detractors complained that "Clinton's iron will, fortified by her moral absolutism," made her arrogant, sanctimonious, and overbearing. Some viewed the first lady as a dangerous, demonic ideologue. Clinton "mocked

Tammy Wynette for standing by her man, then did just that during the humiliating impeachment drama." Conservative political activist Paul Weyrich denounced Clinton's "holier-than-thou attitude," while pundit Ann Coulter quipped that Hillary was "the political genius behind Whitewater, 'Filegate,' Clinton's health-care fiasco, [and] the lunatic 'vast right-wing conspiracy' charge."[10]

Two respondents to an *Atlanta Constitution* forum on whether Clinton should run for the Senate expressed views that many others undoubtedly shared. If New Yorkers "want this flaming liberal, self aggrandizing, opportunistic, elitist, sophisticated fake representing them," one wrote, it is their choice. Using the White House as her power base as she ran for the Senate, a second man declared, "is unethical." Worse yet, Clinton had "accomplished nothing concrete and positive in her adult life." Her resume consisted only of being her husband's "victim," although some would call her his enabler.[11]

Campaigning for the Senate

Clinton decided to run, but when New York's Democratic Senator Daniel Patrick Moynihan introduced her in July 1999 as his prospective replacement, her candidacy appeared to be a long shot. The Methodist outsider from a white Chicago suburb would probably be facing New York City's formidable Republican mayor, Rudy Giuliani, a Brooklyn-born Italian American and pro-choice Catholic known for his bluntness. Few US Senate races have attracted more national attention or involved more mudslinging than Clinton's 2000 campaign. The first lady's opponents launched direct-mail campaigns, issued email alerts, created websites, wrote books, and devised inventive strategies to defeat her. Although these endeavors ultimately failed, the assault on Clinton's character helped raise a large amount of money for right-wing organizations. Her opponents derided her as "the ice-cold, calculating queen of mean" who had botched health care reform, masterminded Whitewater, and accepted a Faustian bargain to save her husband's presidency. She "would sell the Lincoln Bedroom and sell out Israel" to maintain their power.[12]

The most scathing attack was perhaps Peggy Noonan's *The Case against Hillary Clinton* (2000). The former Reagan speechwriter insisted that the first lady possessed "average insights, above-average intelligence, and below-average character." Although Hillary's and Bill's impulses, assumptions, and beliefs were all left-wing, the couple had displayed "no consistent loyalty to any political philosophy, party, person, or ideology." Their only priority, Noonan

maintained, was attaining "maximum and uninterrupted power" for themselves. The Clintons were willing to use any tactics to obtain their goals; they
misled Americans on crucial issues, evaded responsibility for their mistakes
and scandals, smeared their opponents and critics, lied repeatedly, and tried
to ruin the lives of their perceived enemies. In their Manichean world, they
were good and their opponents were evil.[13]

Noonan argued that Hillary and Bill were narcissists who lowered "both
standards and expectations for our leaders." The Clintons had damaged the
nation, repudiated its long-standing idealism, created a country that was
"coarser and more dangerous" for children, and devalued political life. Hillary, she added, was a "highly credentialed rube," a "mere operator" who never
pondered what is right and assumed that her opponents had immoral motives.
She was quick to fight and "too corrupt for New York."[14]

Others discussed Clinton's political strengths and weaknesses in a more
balanced fashion. A *Washington Post* columnist praised her for providing child
nutrition and health programs in Arkansas and zealously striving to pass
health care reform at home and improve women's health and increase human
rights abroad. Her advocacy of abortion rights helped make Clinton popular
in New York City and its suburbs, but she was a Midwestern Methodist, a
WASP outsider in a state where 40 percent of residents were Catholic and 10
percent were Jewish. Moreover, the columnist claimed, her speeches had little
substance. In *Hillary's Turn: Inside Her Improbable, Victorious Senate Campaign*
(2001), the definitive account of her campaign, Michael Tomasky called Clinton
"The Laundry Lady" because her speeches consisted primarily of a long list of
"modest, unobjectionable policies."[15]

In addition to the carpetbagger accusation, Clinton dealt with other problems, some of which she created. During her husband's impeachment hearings,
her popularity skyrocketed, as two-thirds of Americans expressed admiration
for the courageous way she coped with adversity. By 2000, as she campaigned
for the Senate, her popularity had waned as her "wounded wife image faded,"
and polls showed that she and Giuliani had equal support. Clinton was criticized for not immediately denouncing a claim by Yasser Arafat's wife Suha that
the Israelis had deliberately poisoned Palestinians and for promising to march
in New York City's St. Patrick Day parade, apparently not realizing that most
Democratic Party leaders had refused to participate because homosexuals were
excluded.[16]

To help overcome these liabilities, Clinton campaigned vigorously, visiting all of New York's sixty-two counties and listening carefully to residents'

concerns. She traveled thousands of miles in a minivan, held two or three events a day, and attended scores of house parties hosted by locals. She learned what residents of small towns and rural areas were thinking and "studied their issues in numbingly minute detail."[17] As she had done as first lady, Clinton focused during her campaign on improving education, health care, and the lives of children. She highlighted her faith-based activism in numerous rallies. Her frequent challenge to "Be ye doers and not just hearers of the word" prompted one of her hosts to respond, "Thank you, Rev. Clinton!"[18]

In February 2000, a Giuliani fundraising letter accused Clinton of expressing "hostility toward America's religious traditions" because she had opposed his attempt to shut down an exhibit at the Brooklyn Museum that depicted the Virgin Mary covered with elephant dung and because she had allegedly attacked George W. Bush's efforts to use faith-based organizations rather than government programs to solve some social problems. Giuliani's letter referred to the Brooklyn Museum battle as "the latest example of a relentless 30-year war the left-wing elite has waged against America's religious heritage." An outraged Clinton responded, "As a person of faith, I am appalled that he would make false statements about me and my respect for religion in order to raise money for his campaign."[19] Clinton added, "I have worked hard . . . to support our fundamental religious values in my own life and our public life."[20] In the same month, Rob Schenck, general secretary of the theologically conservative National Clergy Council in Washington, charged that the first lady had displayed contempt for traditional religion and that the Clinton administration had engaged in numerous immoral activities.[21]

In May, Rudy Giuliani dropped out of the race because of a prostate cancer diagnosis, his impending divorce, and his wife's claims that he had had an affair three years earlier with his press secretary. US Representative Rick Lazio from Long Island replaced Giuliani. In August, polls showed that Clinton and Lazio were running neck and neck, in large part because white women favored Lazio by five to nine percentage points. Many women expressed uneasiness or antipathy toward Clinton, viewing her as an ambitious, opportunistic, and presumptuous politician who allegedly believed that her intelligence, connections, and tenure as first lady entitled her to represent New York in the Senate. "Women either identify with Hillary or judge her," explained Valerie Ross Homan, a clinical therapist in White Plains. In June, the African Methodist Episcopal Church, which had 105,000 members in New York, endorsed Clinton because of her experience and promises to improve the quality of life for all the state's residents.[22]

An Alleged Anti-Semitic Slur

Controversy erupted in July 2000 when two long-estranged Arkansas associates, Paul and Mary Lee Fray, claimed Hillary had used an anti-Semitic
insult against Paul during a heated argument on the night when Bill lost his
campaign for Congress in 1974. The allegation, reported in *State of a Union:
Inside the Complex Marriage of Bill and Hillary Clinton* (2000) by former *National
Enquirer* reporter Jerry Oppenheimer, intensified Clinton's struggle to win
the support of Jewish voters. Clinton vehemently denied that she had called
Fray a "[f-ing] Jewish bastard." Although others had testified that Clinton
sometimes used "salty language" and she admitted that she had occasionally
called people names, she labeled Oppenheimer's claim "absolutely false." The
first lady insisted that "I have never used ethnic, racial, anti-Semitic, bigoted,
discriminatory, prejudicial language against anybody."[23] In a statement released
by her campaign, President Clinton declared, "I was there on election night in
1974 and this charge is simply not true. . . . My wife has stood for social justice
and tolerance and against racial and religious hatred and bigotry for as long
as I have known her." The Clinton campaign also released a handwritten letter from Fray to Hillary, dated July 1, 1997, in which he stated, "I ask for your
forgiveness because I did say things against you, and called you names, not
only to your face—but behind your back." Fray also admitted, "At one time in
my life, I would say things without thinking, without factual foundation."[24]

At a press conference called to discuss this alleged incident, US Representative Nita Lowey, a Jewish Democrat, told reporters, "There's no way Hillary
could make a statement like that."[25] In her remarks to the press, Clinton accentuated her Methodist upbringing, her trips to Israel, and the peace talks
occurring at Camp David that weekend between PLO leader Yasser Arafat
and Israeli Prime Minister Ehud Barak. Strikingly, both Giuliani and GOP
presidential candidate George W. Bush defended Clinton against the charges
of anti-Semitism. After the story broke, Karen Adler, who advised Clinton's
campaign on Jewish matters, asked some Jewish supporters to call reporters
from the *Forward* and *Jewish Week* to underscore the first lady's love for the
Jewish people. This endeavor backfired when the Associated Press reported
that Clinton's campaign had asked her Jewish supporters to "lie" for her.[26] As
this traumatic week ended, rabbi Marc Schneier invited Clinton to speak at
his Orthodox synagogue in Westhampton Beach. An overflow crowd of five
hundred warmly welcomed the first lady and listened as she drew from the
Torah and Methodist teachings to call for opposing "bigotry, prejudice, racism

and anti-Semitism," and to express hope that the discussions at Camp David between Israelis and Palestinians would produce a peace settlement.[27]

The Importance of Religion and Campaigning in Churches

In her second debate with Lazio on October 8, Hillary claimed that her choices, including staying with Bill, "are rooted in my religious faith, in my strong sense of family, and in what I believe is right and important. I want to go to the Senate to stand up for women's choices and women's rights." Clinton declared that she had repeatedly insisted that she could "support a ban on late-term abortions, including partial-birth abortions," if the health and lives of pregnant women were protected. She argued that abortion was "a horrible procedure." But if someone's life, health, or potential for having any more children is at stake, abortion "must be a woman's choice."[28]

From Labor Day to election day, Clinton campaigned vigorously in churches, primarily Black ones, from storefront congregations in impoverished neighborhoods where few white politicians visited to prominent churches such as Abyssinian Baptist in Harlem, led by pastor Calvin Butts, a respected political activist. Altogether, she spoke in twenty-seven churches, visiting seven on a single Sunday. Paul Kengor accused Clinton of employing her faith to achieve political purposes and noted that "the intensely secular, religiously hostile New York press" did not object.[29]

Beth Harpaz, who accompanied Clinton on her church visits, described some of them in *The Girls in the Van: Covering Hillary* (2001). Harpaz reported that Clinton "always seemed at home in places of worship." The first lady could quote chapter and verse from the Bible and expound on the assigned scriptural readings in various churches with "unpretentious ease." At a service at the Metropolitan AME Church in Harlem, the prescribed reading was about God choosing Joshua to lead the Jews after Moses died. Clinton argued that, like Joshua, Christians had a choice—to get involved politically or do nothing. After she spoke, pastor Robert Bailey told his flock that God had given them the opportunity to elect a second Clinton. Hillary, he asserted, "was their Joshua."[30]

In introducing the first lady to five hundred worshippers at First Baptist Church in Crown Heights, US Representative Major Owens (D-Brooklyn) noted that many African Americans viewed the Clintons with adoration or adulation. After the reactionary policies of Ronald Reagan and George H. W. Bush and Congress's assaults on Black civil rights led by Newt Gingrich, Owens contended, the Clintons had been the only "line of defense" preventing a return to the Reconstruction era. The first lady thanked congregants for their prayers for her family. "Those prayers," she declared, "have sustained us, uplifted us and protected us." In her twenty-minute speech, Clinton discussed the inspirational life of Sojourner Truth and her own campaign, encouraging worshippers to support Al Gore's bid for the presidency. She promised to fight to reduce class sizes in public schools, give children affordable, quality health care, and help New Yorkers of different ethnicities and races better understand each other and work together.[31]

At St. Luke's African Methodist Episcopal Church, the third congregation she visited in Harlem on the first Sunday of October, Clinton, accompanied by US Representative Charles Rangel (D-Manhattan) and former mayor David Dinkins, quoted Isaiah, lauded the record low unemployment of Blacks during her husband's administration, and argued that those who did not vote were turning their backs on such Black heroes as Harriet Tubman, Frederick Douglass, and Martin Luther King Jr. The church's pastor, Melvin Wilson, told his parishioners that he could not endorse a candidate in the Senate race, but he would be voting for Clinton who "knows all about us."[32] At Emmanuel Baptist Church in the Bronx, copastor Darlene McGuire proclaimed that "for me and my house, she's the next senator of the United States." She led her congregation in singing a hymn in which she changed the words from "I told Satan, get thee behind" to "I told Lazio, get thee behind."[33]

At an Episcopal church, Harpaz explained, Clinton evoked laughter from its well-heeled white congregants by sharing one of her common "church-shticks" that went something like this: "Someone asked me the other day if I prayed. I said, yes, I do pray. I was fortunate enough to be brought up in a home where the power of prayers was understood. But . . . if I hadn't prayed before I got to the White House, I would have started after I arrived."[34]

Describing her last Sunday of campaigning, the *New York Times* reported that combining the gospel and politics, Clinton, accompanied by her daughter Chelsea, "preached and prayed her way through seven churches in seven hours yesterday," exhorting Blacks to support her. From the Bronx to Brooklyn, in congregations large and small, the first lady pleaded with and "cajoled churchgoers—almost all of them black—to vote the Democratic line."[35] Clinton's most important stop that day was at the AME Church in Queens. Pastored for more than three decades by Floyd Flake, a former US Representative (D-Queens), and his wife Elaine, the congregation had 23,000 members, making it one of the nation's largest churches. Clinton told more than 2,000 worshippers there that morning that "if you don't vote, you don't have the right to complain." With polls showing her having a slight lead, she praised her husband's administration, which was popular in the Black community. At Morning Star Missionary Baptist Church in Queens, pastor Charles Betts told his flock, "This is Sister Hillary's . . . season." Her husband's season was almost ending, but "God is raising up another woman of God."[36]

Analyzing the Election

As she campaigned for the Senate, Clinton had problems with two different groups of women. Many professional baby boomers complained that Clinton had betrayed them by staying with Bill, covering up his sexual infidelities, and failing to advance feminist ideals. On the other hand, many suburban housewives who did not espouse feminism viewed Clinton as "cold, unwomanly and pushy."[37]

In the end, the election was not close; Clinton defeated Lazio by 55 to 43 percent. Clinton received slightly more than 50 percent of the Jewish vote. "Her repeated attempts to portray herself as a great lover of all things Jewish, and her enemies' attempts to portray her as an anti-Semite, had canceled each other out."[38] Although many women had negative perceptions of her, Clinton won the women's vote in New York by more than twenty percentage points. Despite the status of Giuliani, her first opponent, the race had always been about Clinton; she was "Saint Hillary," to some and "Hell to Pay Hillary" to others. By winning this referendum on her character and platform, she had risen from a supporting character role to center stage. The "fierce hurricane" who had demolished social convention as the initial first lady to win public office would soon smash more traditions.[39]

The Empire State Senator

During her eight years in the US Senate, Clinton frequently crossed the aisle and worked with Republicans. Although she did not sponsor any major pieces of legislation, she developed a positive reputation that helped pave the way for her 2008 campaign to capture the Democratic nomination for president. Several issues that had religious dimensions arose during her tenure in the Senate, most notably faith-based initiatives, abortion, and immigration.

Despite her fame, Clinton pledged to be "a workhorse, not a show horse." According to one advisor, Clinton strove to be a mixture of Al D'Amato, New York's "Pothole Senator" who stressed local issues and constituents, and her predecessor Daniel Patrick Moynihan, who received national attention whenever he addressed domestic issues.[40] The September 2001 attacks on the World Trade Center gave New York's junior senator an even greater role to play on the national stage, and they helped convince many Americans, Clinton contended in January 2002, that only the government could address "certain common needs."[41] She moved toward the political center, worked with Republicans on numerous measures, and supported many "modest, consensus-oriented initiatives," while trying to persuade her Republican colleagues to take small steps toward more liberal positions.[42] She cosponsored a bill with Pat Roberts (R-KS) to distribute flu vaccines more effectively and teamed with Orrin Hatch (R-UT) on a bill to accelerate payments to families of public safety officers killed or injured in the September 2001 terrorist attacks on New York and Washington. Clinton joined Sam Brownback (R-KS) to promote a measure to protect refugees escaping from sexual abuse and a second bill to study the effects of violent video games and television shows on children. In 2005, Clinton joined forces with Rick Santorum (R-PA) to help pass the Workplace Religious Freedom Act, which guaranteed people's right to express their religious views on the job without fear of penalty. Clinton collaborated with Thad Cochran (R-MS) and Susan Collins (R-ME) on a 2006 bill to improve respite care and partnered with Johnny Isakson (R-GA) and John McCain (R-AZ) to sponsor a 2008 auto safety law. She also traveled across the country with Brownback to publicize the horrors of human trafficking.[43]

Carl Bernstein argued that Clinton was much more D'Amato than Moynihan because few of her accomplishments had an impact beyond New York state.[44] Clinton had a much larger national constituency than any other senator, but she did not take the lead on any major national issue, except arguably a woman's right to choose abortion.[45] On the other hand, during her first seven years in office, Clinton procured more than $2.3 billion for home-state projects, and in 2008 she obtained $346 million to fund projects for her state, the ninth-highest total of any senator.[46] *Atlantic* editor Joshua Green argued similarly that as a senator Clinton never took "a politically unpopular stance or championed a big idea, like health-care reform, that might not yield immediate benefits but was the right thing to do." He insisted that she offered "no big ideas, no crusading causes" or "evidence of bravery in the service of a larger ideal." Her major achievement as a senator had been to rehabilitate her image and political career, which made "for a rather thin claim on the presidency."[47]

Many colleagues found Clinton to be "funny, warm, diligent and immensely likable."[48] Judd Gregg (R-NH) reported that Clinton was "easy to work with, smart and willing to reach agreement on complicated issues."[49] Numerous senators were surprised by Clinton's collegiality, pleasant demeanor, work ethic, and nonjudgmental approach. John McCain maintained that she was "always well-prepared" and "conducted herself admirably."[50] Clinton developed cordial relationships with numerous colleagues. Gordon Smith (R-OR) was grateful for the comfort Clinton provided after his son Garrett died by suicide in 2003. She worked with Smith to pass a law in 2004 to screen teenagers for depression.[51]

Iraq

The action that caused Clinton the most political damage and evoked her most tortured explanations was her vote for the 2002 Authorization for Use of Military Force against Iraq Resolution. In so doing, Clinton sided with theologically conservative groups and rejected the arguments by most mainline Protestant and Catholic theologians that the invasion did not satisfy the traditional criteria for a just war.[52] The senator later tried unconvincingly to explain that she did not, like most other members of Congress, see her vote as empowering the United States to invade Iraq but rather as simply approving further diplomacy. Critics pointed out that Clinton did not read the classified intelligence report by the Joint Chiefs of Staff that raised many questions about Bush's case for war. They argued that Clinton's vote was influenced by her miscalculations about the situation in Iraq and by actions undertaken by her husband's administration, which had conducted bombing raids and relied on poor intelligence about Iraq's possession of weapons of mass destruction. Detractors also faulted Clinton for defending the spurious link between Saddam Hussein and Al Qaeda.[53] The senator recognized by 2006 that her vote would be a significant liability if she sought the Democratic presidential nomination and insisted that she had consistently criticized how the United States had conducted the war.[54] Her vote did indeed hinder her quest to win the nomination. In her 2014 memoir, *Hard Choices*, Clinton finally admitted, "I got it wrong . . . plain and simple," an acknowledgment that critics charged came years late.[55]

The Senate Prayer Group and Faith and Works

During her tenure in the Senate, Clinton participated in a bipartisan Senate prayer group, which was affiliated with The Fellowship, the same umbrella organization that sponsored the women's prayer group to which she belonged as first lady. Both groups provided an intimate, nonjudgmental setting where members could discuss their faith, work, and lives. Led by Doug Coe, who enjoyed friendships with presidents of both parties and numerous world leaders, many of whom referred to him as an "ambassador of faith," the Senate prayer group included Republicans Sam Brownback, Rick Santorum, Don Nickles (OK), Jim Inhofe (OK), Mike Enzi (WY), and George Allen (VA), Democrats Mark Pryor (AR) and Chris Coons (DE), and Independent Joe Lieberman (CT), most of whom saw their faith as crucial to their work as politicians. The Fellowship avoided theological labels, but most of its key leaders, like Coe and former US Senate chaplain Richard Halverson, identified themselves as evangelicals.[56] Clinton explained that the group's meetings allowed senators to "talk openly and pray together," which had been "a real blessing" to her.[57] Coons insisted that the meetings enabled senators to "strengthen and sustain" their faith. Avoiding divisive political issues such as gay marriage and abortion, members prayed together, sang hymns, talked about their families, and shared stories. Senators could be vulnerable, admit they did not have all the answers, and discuss such "basic questions as why are we here" on earth and what they were trying to accomplish.[58] Their meetings helped repair relationships and deepen friendships. For example, praying with Clinton prompted Brownback to confess that he had despised her and made derogatory comments about her. God, he said, had led him to recognize his sin and to ask her to forgive him. Clinton accepted his apology.[59]

Speaking on a panel at Abyssinian Baptist Church in Harlem in late December 2001 on Bush's call to increase faith-based social programs, Clinton quoted the epistle of James's statement, "Faith without works is dead," as she frequently did. She then added, "but work without faith is hard." A *Washington Post* columnist exhorted readers not to "underestimate the sense of mission" Clinton, who was comfortable with "both the rituals and language of the Christian calling," brought to her public life. The New York senator insisted that her faith and upbringing had given her "a rock-solid belief in individual responsibility and hard work" and in the value of community.[60]

Criticism, a Memoir, and the 2004 Election

Despite her efforts to keep a low profile, the New York senator attracted considerable attention and animus. In March 2001, the tabloid *Globe* proclaimed, "Clintons to Divorce," while its rival, the *National Enquirer*, announced in September 2001 that "Hillary Cheats on Bill." Although she moderated many of her positions during her Senate tenure, bashing Clinton continued to help political conservatives raise money.[61]

In July 2003, Simon and Schuster published Clinton's *Living History*. In a huge gamble, the publishing house paid her an $8 million advance and printed one million copies. Only about ten books published in the United States each year in the early 2000s had sold that many copies. This decision was a bonanza for both Simon and Schuster and Clinton. In the first month alone, a million copies of *Living History* were purchased, and about fifty thousand books were sold each week for several months thereafter.[62]

During the 2004 presidential campaign, Clinton campaigned for Democratic nominees John Kerry and John Edwards, often speaking in Black churches.[63] A Duke Divinity School professor pointed out that although Methodists constituted only 3 percent of the American population, they were 12 percent of the US Congress and 75 percent of the 2004 presidential ticket—Bush, Edwards, and Dick Cheney. That the denomination considered both Bush and Hillary Clinton, who held competing political perspectives, as members in good standing was very confusing to many journalists. They represented two major impulses in Methodism. Some noted that Bush focused on personal transformation, whereas Clinton emphasized social renewal and reform.[64] Although generally true, this observation is oversimplified: Bush also promoted compassionate conservatism and faith-based initiatives to improve society, while Clinton often discussed the importance of having a personal, life-directing relationship with God.

In 2005, Ed Klein vehemently attacked Clinton in *The Truth About Hillary: What She Knew, When She Knew It, and How Far She'll Go to Become President*, insisting that she lacked the character to be the nation's chief executive. "Hillary acts," Klein claimed, "as though she has been chosen by God" to be president.[65] He asserted, presumably metaphorically, that both Clintons had "sold their souls to the devil in order to achieve power."[66] Numerous commentators, including several conservative Christians, denounced Klein's diatribe. Albert Mohler, president of Southern Baptist Theological Seminary in Louisville, urged Christians to focus on "engaging the policies, proposals, and ideological commitments" Clinton espoused rather than on "dirt-throwing contests over scandals," as Klein did. Mohler maintained that Klein supplied little proof to "justify many of his charges and 'revelations'" and exhorted Christians to "repudiate this book."[67] Peggy Noonan called the book "poorly written, poorly thought, poorly sourced and full of the kind of loaded language that is appropriate to a polemic but not an investigative work." While noting that there were many "reasons to distrust or even dislike Mrs. Clinton," the *Economist* argued that Klein had done the nearly impossible: "written a book that will make all but fire-breathing conservatives sympathetic to her cause."[68]

Speaking Out on Religion

In mid-January 2005, Clinton spoke at a dinner in Boston to raise funds for the National TenPoint Leadership Foundation and the Dorchester-based Ella J. Baker House. These youth outreach programs, both directed by Eugene Rivers, were part of a clergy-based endeavor to reduce youth violence in the city that began in the 1990s and became a model for community-police partnerships around the country. Where others saw "trouble," Clinton declared, Rivers and other faith-inspired soldiers saw "God at work in the lives of even the most hopeless and left-behind of our children" and worked in dangerous neighborhoods to help them.[69] Clinton had supported government funding of faith-based social services several years before George W. Bush championed this approach, a collaboration many other Democrats denounced. Participating in a panel at a New York City church in December 2001, she had praised the government's partnership with religious institutions to promote such public goals as feeding the hungry and sheltering the homeless. "Faith inspires those good works, to be sure," she added. "But tax dollars are properly used to channel the energies of the faithful in a direction that helps our society."[70] In her Boston speech, Clinton argued that implementing faith-based initiatives did not violate the separation of church and state.[71] They enabled religious people to "live out their faith in the public square."[72] Americans, Clinton protested, engaged in "an unnecessary debate" about how to alleviate their nation's social ills. It did not matter whether people's efforts were inspired by faith, obligation, family commitments, or threat of federal indictment; the important thing was that they collaborated to improve society. Clinton also invoked God numerous times and testified, "I've always been a praying person."[73] Her speech, one scholar quipped, sounded like "the second coming of John Wesley" and reinforced her effort to abandon "her Northeast liberal image and move to the [political] center."[74]

Despite her long involvement in the church, frequent testimony about her faith, numerous speeches to religious groups, teaching of Sunday school, and participation in prayer groups, when Clinton began discussing the role of religion in public life more overtly and often in 2004 and 2005, numerous conservatives, who distrusted Clinton and deplored many of her stances on issues, denounced her statements as disingenuous. Activist Gary Bauer called Clinton's use of religious rhetoric her "ultimate makeover."[75] New York Conservative Party leader Michael Long disbelieved Clinton's testimony that "religion had played a central role in her life" and accused her of saying what "centrist voters" wanted to hear.[76] Many Republicans viewed Clinton's speeches mentioning God, faith, and prayer and praising faith-based initiatives as part of the Democratic Party's attempt to discard its secular image that had contributed to its defeat in the 2000 and 2004 presidential elections. Rather than expressing her true convictions, they contended, Clinton was using religious rhetoric simply to woo devout voters. Moreover, Republican leaders argued, Clinton's progressive positions on social issues clashed with the religious and moral values of most Americans.[77]

Other scholars and journalists countered that Clinton's religious commitments were long-lasting, genuine, and life-shaping. John Green, a senior fellow at the Pew Forum on Religion and Public Life, declared that "although a lot of people don't think of her as religious," Clinton was "actually the real deal."[78] In his 2007 biography, Carl Bernstein insisted that Clinton's faith inspired her to participate in politics and strongly influenced her positions on numerous issues. Jeff Sharlet and Kathryn Joyce reported that year that they had interviewed scores of Clinton's friends, pastors, and mentors about the relationship between her faith and her politics. These people repudiated the media's common characterization of Clinton's supposedly new "tone and style as part of the Democrats' broader move to recapture the terrain of 'moral values'" and argued instead that her statements about religion were consistent with her long-held convictions. Sharlet and Joyce asserted that Clinton spoke thoughtfully, eloquently, and appreciatively about "'values,' the importance of prayer, and 'heart' convictions," which most political liberals, who were unfamiliar with America's religious history, mistook "for a tidy, apolitical accommodation, a personal separation of church and state."[79]

Abortion: "Safe, Legal, and Rare"

Only Clinton's support of a congressional resolution that permitted the United States to invade Iraq in 2003 caused more controversy during her tenure in the Senate than her position on abortion. Clinton had strongly supported the prochoice stance since her days at Wellesley. In 2003, she voted twice against banning partial-birth abortions. The senator contended that women should be permitted to use a morning-after pill to prevent conception. In January

2004, Clinton gave the keynote address at the National Association for the Repeal of Abortion Laws (NARAL) dinner, which Paul Kengor called her "most vitriolic, inflammatory speech" on abortion.[80] She accused pro-life activists—the "anti-choice" people—of seeking to quietly overthrow women's right to have an abortion. Moreover, they promoted policies designed to "chip away at *all* reproductive rights." Pro-lifers, she lamented, strove to overturn *Roe v. Wade* and destroy women's right to privacy. If their strategy succeeded, poorer Americans would again have to resort to "dangerous, if not illegal, procedures." In a speech at the "March for Women's Lives" in April 2004, Clinton accused Republicans of trying to demonize the abortion rights movement and castigated Bush for appointing many officials to his administration who viewed *Roe v. Wade* as "the worst abomination of constitutional law."[81] In addition, in 2005, the senator worked to block the appointment of two pro-life Catholic US Supreme Court nominees—John Roberts and Samuel Alito—who, she feared, would vote to repeal *Roe v. Wade*. Confirming Alito, she warned, would halt "the ever-expanding circle of [women's] freedom and opportunity."[82]

As Clinton began to consider running for president, she started to moderate her position. The senator stressed preventing unwanted pregnancies, encouraging adoption, promoting abstinence, and supporting "teenage celibacy." She reiterated her oft-repeated call for making abortion "safe, legal and rare," a phrase Bill coined in 1992, and expressed sympathy for those who advocated the pro-life stance. Jim Wallis, the founder of *Sojourners* magazine and the author of *God's Politics: Why the Right Gets It Wrong and the Left Doesn't Get It* (2005), counseled Democrats to focus more on deploring the tragic frequency of abortion and less on women's right to choose, and Clinton followed his advice. In a speech in January 2005, the senator expressed her desire to find common ground with pro-lifers to prevent unwanted pregnancies and reduce abortions, which she termed a "sad, even tragic choice to many, many women." Doing this, she argued, could best be accomplished by teaching abstinence based on "religious and moral values." Both prochoice and pro-life supporters agreed that "every child born in this country" should "be wanted, cherished and loved." Clinton also declared her support for parental notification laws and for banning late-term abortions as long as legislation included an exception to protect the health of pregnant women. Some pro-life proponents applauded Clinton's speech.[83] In an open letter to the senator, the Christian Defense Coalition in February 2005 praised her sympathy for its position and hoped that she sincerely desired "to reach out to people of faith and the prolife community."[84]

Clinton acknowledged in 2005 that Americans had "deeply held differences of opinion on the issue of abortion," and she proclaimed her respect for "those who believe with all their hearts and minds that there are no circumstances under which any abortion should ever be available." The senator hoped that "people of good faith" could "find common ground in this debate" as they worked to make abortion rare. Tony Perkins, president of the Family Research Council in Washington, appreciated Clinton's attempt "to adopt a values-oriented language" but protested that "her voting record on this issue" was as defective as Planned Parenthood's condoms. Michael Long contended that the senator had suddenly become "slightly pro-life," but Clinton maintained that she had long advocated this position. A *New York Post* columnist agreed with Clinton, pointing to a 1999 speech in which she had used almost identical language. Democratic strategist Hank Sheinkopf contended that the senator understood faith-based arguments. She recognized that social issues could be defined "in a manner that makes the left feel comfortable while not upsetting people on the center-right."[85]

Although Clinton moderated her position on abortion, the decision of two Catholic colleges to invite the senator to speak provoked substantial opposition and brought her negative publicity. On January 31, 2005, Clinton gave an address on the government's role in health care at Canisius College, a Catholic institution in Buffalo, New York, which generated protests from several Catholic and pro-life groups. Judie Brown, president of the American Life League, asserted that "Clinton's entire career has been characterized by complete defiance toward the Church's stance on the sanctity of innocent human life." The senator's repeated calls for *Roe v. Wade* to "remain the law of the land illustrate how fundamentally opposed she is to the Catholic Church on this most basic of civil rights." Hundreds of people called or sent e-mails to the Buffalo diocese to complain about Canisius's decision to invite Clinton to speak.[86] The national Catholic press also criticized Canisius's action, with the Catholic Exchange website dubbing Hillary an "abortion crusader."[87]

In April 2005, two weeks after Clinton voted to annul the "Mexico City Policy"—President Bush's executive order that stopped funding foreign population assistance programs promoting abortion—Marymount Manhattan College, a small Catholic school in New York City, announced that the senator would give its commencement address and be awarded an honorary degree. Irate Catholic groups again organized opposition. Patrick Reilly, president of the Cardinal Newman Society, which oversees hundreds of Newman Centers for Catholic students throughout the nation, denounced Marymount

Manhattan's invitation as scandalous given Clinton's support for partial-birth abortion and embryonic stem cell research and her proclamation that contraception was "basic health care for women."[88]

At the 2008 faith forum at Messiah College in Pennsylvania, Clinton stated, "I believe that the potential for life begins at conception." After great soul-searching over the course of many years, however, she concluded that in an ideologically pluralistic nation, individuals should have the right to make their own decisions about whether to abort a fetus without government intrusion. As noted, Clinton strove to follow the United Methodist Church's *Book of Discipline* on moral questions. The denomination supported legalized abortion and belonged to the Religious Coalition for Reproductive Choice, a "national, interfaith movement" founded in 1973 by mainline Protestants to use "the moral force of religion to protect and advance reproductive health" and personal choice.[89] The denomination's official pronouncements on abortion reinforced Clinton's prochoice position. Clinton argued at this forum that the *Book of Discipline* included contradictory perspectives on abortion and that her position was consistent with her denomination's current stance. Clinton claimed that she had worked as a private citizen, first lady, and senator to make abortion both safe and rare. She had supported adoption, foster care, and a campaign to reduce teenage pregnancy. While visiting China as first lady, she had denounced its one-child policy, which was "an intrusive, abusive, dehumanizing effort to dictate" how many children couples could have and had led to many abortions and forced sterilizations.[90] Pro-life activists accused Clinton of being inconsistent: she championed the rights of children but did not fully protect those same children when they were in the womb.[91] Abortion would again cause problems for Clinton when she ran for the presidency in 2016.

Criminalizing the Good Samaritan

In March 2006, Clinton engaged in a dispute with US Representative Tom Tancredo (R-CO) over a bill the House had passed four months earlier that made it a felony, rather than a misdemeanor, to live in the United States illegally. The bill also prescribed up to five years of imprisonment for anyone who assisted an undocumented immigrant "to reside in or remain in the United States." As the Senate prepared to debate this bill, Clinton protested that "it is certainly not in keeping with my understanding of the Scripture, because this bill would literally criminalize the Good Samaritan and probably even Jesus himself."

Tancredo accused Clinton on ABC's *This Week* of not knowing "the first thing about the Bible," saying that her "interpretation of both the law and the Bible are certainly wrong to say the least." The House bill, he insisted, had "nothing to do with criminalizing Good Samaritans." Agreeing with Tancredo, Rep. Peter King (R-NY), one of the bill's cosponsors, declared, "I hope Sen. Clinton is a better legislator than she is a theologian." He added, "I don't think Jesus would have defended alien-smuggling gangs. I don't think Jesus would favor hundreds of immigrants dying in the desert."[92]

Numerous religious leaders and groups agreed with Clinton's objections, and more than 100,000 people marched in Chicago to protest the bill. In an op-ed in the *New York Times* in March, Cardinal Roger Mahony, archbishop of Los Angeles, complained that the proposed law was "so broad that it would criminalize even minor acts of mercy like offering a meal or administering first aid." Mahony had pledged to instruct the priests in his diocese to disobey this proposed law should it pass, even though it would subject them and other church and humanitarian workers to criminal penalties. Mahony noted that the nation's laws currently did not require social service agencies to determine people's legal status before aiding them. Not assisting the needy violated a higher authority than that of Congress—God's law.[93] The Senate did not pass the bill.

The 2008 Presidential Campaign

Immediately after their defeat in the 2004 presidential race, some Democrats began calling on their party to stop running away from religion and allowing Republicans to dominate the field. Some Democratic strategists insisted that John Kerry's lack of emphasis on religion and moral values had contributed significantly to his defeat. As many as a quarter of voters had rated "values" as their principal concern, prompting them to support George W. Bush, an outspoken evangelical, rather than Kerry, a liberal Catholic who said little about his own faith or religious issues. Republican caricatures of Kerry "as antifamily and antireligion," Bill Clinton contended, had cost him many votes. Some Democrats vowed not to make this mistake again in 2008. One strategist urged the party to portray its commitment to an active federal government as based on biblical values such as Jesus's call to feed the hungry, heal the sick, and clothe the naked.[94]

After the election, Kerry admitted that he had not argued aggressively enough that "real faith" entailed denouncing unjust wars, reducing poverty, helping children, and taking care of the earth.[95] House Minority Leader Nancy Pelosi established a Democratic Faith Working Group to equip Democrats to discuss issues from a moral and religious perspective. To help candidates talk more easily and effectively about biblical themes, moral values, and their own faith, Democrats enlisted the aid of Jim Wallis. The left-leaning evangelical argued that Democrats needed to "neutralize the abortion issue" by advocating "the drastic reduction of abortion."[96] In early 2005, Wallis visited Democrats on Capitol Hill to help guide Senate press secretaries on how to "discuss the budget in terms of moral values." He urged Democrats to stop focusing on such culturally divisive issues as abortion and gay marriage and instead accentuate war and poverty, which were also religious issues.[97]

Wallis contended that behaving and talking as people of faith, as Tim Kaine did when he ran for governor of Virginia in 2005, would help religiously committed Democrats win elections. Kaine, a devout Catholic, had triumphed in a state where seven out of ten voters were Protestants by presenting his political positions in terms of his Catholic faith. Other Democrats, Wallis declared, should look to Kaine (who would become the Democratic vice-presidential nominee in 2016) for advice about how to winsomely discuss their faith to help garner the votes of religious Americans. Kaine counseled his fellow Democrats to explain their spiritual motivations for participating in politics. Wallis insisted that a religiously devout Democrat could win the presidency only if the party's liberal base moved to the center on abortion, became more comfortable with its members speaking about religion in the public sphere, and recognized that most Americans rejected moral relativism. To gain the White House in 2008, Wallis asserted, Democrats must nominate a candidate who understood faith-oriented voters and could cogently discuss issues such as poverty, the environment, and abortion in moral terms.[98]

Soon after the 2004 election, Mara Vanderslice and Eric Sapp created a consulting firm called Common Good Strategies to help Democratic candidates speak more openly and effectively about their faith and win the votes of faith-driven Americans. The twenty-seven-year-old Vanderslice was a graduate of Earlham College, a Quaker institution in Indiana, and worked for *Sojourners* before serving as Kerry's director of religious outreach during his 2004 campaign. Sapp was a twenty-eight-year-old graduate of Duke Divinity School who had previously worked for Sen. Edward Kennedy (D-MA). Frustrated that Kerry had largely ignored her advice, Vanderslice partnered with Sapp to advise Democratic candidates in 2006. All seven of their clients won their races, including US Senate seats in Ohio and Pennsylvania and the governorships of Michigan, Ohio, and Kansas. The two evangelicals convinced these candidates to advertise on Christian radio stations, give talks at religious schools, and meet privately with theologically conservative and moderate clergy. Vanderslice and Sapp helped Michigan's Democratic Party incorporate biblical language into its platform and enlisted nuns in Michigan and Ohio to phone Catholic and Protestant pro-lifers, urging them to support Democratic candidates. They counseled their prochoice clients to emphasize reducing the demand for abortion and cautioned them not to argue, as many liberal Christians did, that Jesus was interested in social justice but not sexual morality. Two of their clients—Sen. Bob Casey of Pennsylvania and Gov. Ted Strickland of Ohio—had already spoken candidly about their faith, but others, including Sen. Sherrod Brown of Ohio, Gov. Jennifer Granholm of Michigan, and Gov. Kathleen Sebelius of Kansas, had not.[99]

The Role of Religion in the 2008 Campaign

As the battle for the 2008 Democratic nomination began, some pundits asked whether Clinton could win a significant portion of religious voters. Clinton's Christian convictions, frequent emphasis on spirituality, and persistent promotion of moral causes, they asserted, might make her attractive to many religious voters. Her firm support of religious freedom in the schools and the workplace and of providing government funds for faith-based organizations that supplied social services, her denunciation of the destructive impact popular culture had on children, and her diligent efforts to stop human trafficking and improve the lives of women and children were also potentially appealing to religiously active Americans.[100]

Nevertheless, Clinton faced powerful obstacles in her quest to win the votes of religiously committed voters. A 2000 *Wall Street Journal* / NBC News poll had reported that only 12 percent of the public viewed her as "extremely/very religious," and the percentage had not increased appreciably during Clinton's years as a senator. Another impediment was the widespread perception that most Democrats were secularists or at least not religiously minded; they had allegedly restricted their faith, if they had any, to private matters and had ceded public discussion of religious issues to Republicans. Moreover, many Americans viewed Clinton's professions of personal faith as disingenuous, incompatible with some of her actions, or politically opportunistic. An even greater hurdle was Clinton's strong support of abortion rights. Despite her efforts to moderate her public statements about abortion beginning in 2005,

Clinton was still arguably the most resolutely prochoice presidential candidate in American history.[101] As *Christianity Today* put it, "Clinton's consistently pro-choice stance on abortion clashes with most evangelicals' deeply held belief that life begins in the womb and should be protected at great cost."[102] While many mainline Protestants, liberal Catholics, and some evangelicals cared about the social-justice issues Clinton promoted, most religiously committed Americans took politically conservative stances on social issues.

Several polls conducted in February 2008 produced conflicting results about which presidential candidates religious voters favored. A Gallup poll reported that those who attended church weekly preferred Clinton over Obama by 46 to 43 percent. A Barna Group poll indicated that 40 percent of the religiously devout planned to support the Democratic candidate in November, whereas only 29 percent would vote for the Republican nominee. Both Clinton and Obama were seen as more personally religious and addressing more religious issues than any Republican candidate except Mike Huckabee. This poll found that 20 percent of evangelicals would vote for Clinton and 18 percent would cast ballots for Obama against a Republican in the general election. Prospective voters were impressed by Clinton's work to alleviate poverty, provide health care for children, and reduce abortion, while they liked Obama's upbeat message and emphasis on reducing political division. Other polls conducted in February, however, gave Obama a significant lead over Clinton among the religiously committed. When asked by *Relevant* magazine "Who would Jesus vote for?," 29 percent chose Obama and only 2 percent selected Clinton. A poll conducted by GodTube reported that 20 percent of respondents supported Obama while only 8 percent backed Clinton when asked to choose among all Democratic and Republican candidates. Finally, a *Christianity Today* poll reported that 31 percent of prospective voters supported Huckabee, 24 percent Obama, 17 percent John McCain, and a mere 6 percent favored Clinton.[103]

Recognizing how important winning the votes of religious groups was to their electoral success, Clinton, Obama, and John Edwards, the three leading candidates for the Democratic nomination, all hired coordinators to direct their outreach to this constituency. In her speech at Tufts University near Boston shortly after the 2004 election, Clinton faulted Democrats for failing to engage evangelical Christians, thereby "essentially ceding the vote to President Bush."[104] Trying to avoid Kerry's flawed strategy, in December 2006, Clinton enlisted Burns Strider, a Southern Baptist who had previously headed the religious outreach efforts of several Democratic congressmen, to help her to win the votes of religious groups. During the primaries, Strider highlighted

Clinton's ardent efforts to bring religious values into public life, including her support for faith-based initiatives, cosponsorship of a law to prohibit religious discrimination, and energetic work to help children, the indigent, and people without health care. Clinton strove to woo mainline churchgoers as well as many pro-life Catholics, Latino evangelicals, and Black Protestants who were deeply concerned about social justice and repulsed by many aspects of Republicans' domestic policies but disliked Democratic candidates who staunchly advocated abortion rights, gay rights, and strict church-state separation. In making this appeal, a journalist argued, Clinton was "reclaiming her moral roots. She hasn't found religion in order to make a presidential run—it's more like she's finally coming clean."[105]

As she campaigned for the Democratic nomination, Clinton spoke frequently and fervently about her faith. She participated in two faith forums (one sponsored by *Sojourners* magazine in June 2007 and one hosted by Messiah College in April 2008), discussed her religious convictions and practices in several interviews, and addressed numerous religious groups. Speaking at a commemoration of the 1965 Selma voting rights march in March 2007 at the city's First Baptist Church, Clinton asked attendees to pray for the families of those who had died when tornadoes swept through Alabama. She quoted Paul's admonition to the Galatians, "Let us not grow weary in doing good, for in due seasons we shall reap, if we do not lose heart," to implore the audience to continue the marchers' quest to ensure "freedom, justice, opportunity" for all Americans.[106] "I have been enveloped and protected by my faith, and I have been sustained by the prayers and the faith of so many," Clinton told the National Hispanic Prayer Breakfast in June 2007. She exhorted attendees to put on their armor, "rooted in the reality" of a "relationship with God," to aid "those who are hurting, those who feel lost and left behind." Clinton added, "I'm a Methodist, and 'Faith in action' was the rallying cry of my Methodist upbringing. . . . I know faith without works is dead. But work without faith is too hard." The senator praised Hispanic pastors for helping people experience the "hope that comes" from having a "personal relationship with Christ" and for supporting government efforts to aid the economically and spiritually impoverished.[107]

At the *Sojourners* forum, Clinton declared, "I take my faith very seriously and very personally," and she insisted that it guided her every day. She explained, however, that both the Methodist tradition, which was "suspicious of people who wear their faith on their sleeves," and Christ's condemnation of the Pharisees' ostentatious displays of piety had made her reluctant to discuss her faith. People's trials, Clinton contended, could lead them to or away from faith. The prayers of friends and of thousands of other Americans had sustained her during very difficult times. Her faith had given her the courage and strength to do what she "thought was right, regardless of what the world thought." The senator prayed for discernment, wisdom, and fortitude. She prayed for her family and friends and for people who faced daunting challenges, such as a Congolese man she met while campaigning in Iowa. In his native country, he had been beaten, jailed, hung on a tree, and left to die, but was rescued by Christians. Clinton argued that having more than forty-five million uninsured Americans, nine million of whom were children, "is a moral wrong," and she implored the United States to combat the threat global warming posed "to God's creation."[108]

Clinton discussed her faith at length in a July 2007 interview with the *New York Times*. The front-page story included pictures of her in a Sunday school class as a young girl, her praying as an adult, and two ministers who had influenced her views of "faith and social responsibility." The senator testified that she had long "had a deep personal faith that was rooted in the Methodist church." She believed in the Trinity—Father, Son, and Holy Spirit—and had often felt the presence of the Holy Spirit in her life. Clinton fed her faith by praying and reading the Bible, commentaries on Scripture, and other Christians' faith journeys. She found the Psalms "both comforting and challenging" and Isaiah "very intriguing and provocative," but she primarily read the New Testament. For some individuals, having "a personal relationship with God, a sense that you're saved," Clinton noted, "is incredibly both moving and comforting." She sought to balance the personal gospel with the social gospel—nurturing her own soul and also serving God in the world. Her faith, Clinton explained, directed how "I live my life and who I am." She sought God's guidance and wisdom and tried to live morally. Clinton added, "I have tried through my works to demonstrate [the] commitment and compassion that flow from my faith." Her faith was like "background music. It's there all the time. It's not something you have to think about, you [simply] believe it." Her faith motivated and energized her to serve others.[109]

Clinton affirmed the bodily resurrection of Jesus but was unsure about whether individuals needed to accept Christ as their Savior to go to heaven. The numerous Sunday school teachers and theologians she had asked about this issue offered many different answers. The senator noted that many Christians believed salvation depended on having a personal relationship with Jesus and viewed the work of missionaries to convert people as essential, whereas other "deeply Christ-centered" individuals insisted that only God knew the eternal destiny of those who did not embrace Jesus as their Savior.[110]

Although Clinton usually attended liturgically oriented services, she also enjoyed lively, musically driven ones. She was fascinated by the different ways in which people expressed their faith in worship and tried to live out their religious commitments in the world. Many Democrats, Clinton complained, had unwisely concluded that it "was somehow illegitimate to express your faith in the public square."[111]

When she sinned, Clinton asked God for forgiveness. The basic idea of the new covenant, she declared, was that people could have "a new relationship with God" and experience the pardon of God and other people. Clinton had taught a Sunday school lesson on the importance of people forgiving themselves; she insisted that everyone had done things that made them feel ashamed or guilty and that many people carried enormous burdens. Faith empowered individuals to release these encumbrances; they needed to forgive themselves, make amends, and forgive others.[112]

Responding to her interview, conservative columnist Cal Thomas accused Clinton of rewriting the Good Book, especially by questioning whether "being a Christian is the only way to salvation." Thomas cited Jesus's declaration— "I am the way, the truth and the life; no one comes to the Father but by me" (John 14:6)—and asked, "if there are other ways to God than through Jesus," why did he come to Earth and "allow himself to be crucified and suffer rejection?"[113]

In November 2007, Clinton spoke at the Global Summit on AIDS at Saddleback Church in Orange County, California, a megachurch pastored by Rick Warren, author of the best-selling *The Purpose Driven Life* (2002). Forgoing her usual pattern of discussing her faith and religious matters with like-minded groups such as First Baptist Church in Selma and the *Sojourners* forum, Clinton ventured into the world of evangelical Christianity. At Saddleback, the senator testified, "My own faith journey is approaching a half a century, and I know how far I still have to go." She praised Saddleback Church for "fighting against spiritual emptiness, corrupt leadership, poverty, illiteracy, and diseases like AIDS around the world." Clinton accentuated "the sustaining power of prayer," quoted her favorite Bible passage—"faith without works is dead"—and urged Christians to minister to the sick as Jesus did. She insisted that Christians "are called to respond, with love, with mercy, and with urgency" to the AIDS crisis and pledged that if elected president she would ask Congress for $50 billion over five years to combat AIDS/HIV. Clinton praised the faith community for denouncing racial discrimination, supporting debt relief for the world's poorest countries, protesting genocide in Darfur, and working to reduce global warming.[114]

Campaigning in South Carolina in December 2007, Clinton used the theme "For Such a Time as This," based on a verse from the Old Testament book of Esther. Sixty African American ministers sat on the stage behind Clinton as she spoke in Spartanburg. "The senator's faith is . . . very personal and dear to her," the spokesperson for her South Carolina campaign declared, and is reflected in "all aspects of [her] life, so it's a natural part of the campaign." Richard Land, head of the public-policy arm of the Southern Baptist Convention, asserted that Clinton and Obama shared a social gospel background that was "authentic with both of them."[115]

At the Compassion Forum at Messiah College, Clinton fielded questions about the nature and importance of her faith, abortion, euthanasia, the problem of evil, US humanitarian foreign aid, and whether God wanted her to be president. She asserted that faith was a spur, an anchor that kept people stable during the storms of life, and a resource that guided individuals in daily life. The senator had "felt the enveloping support and love of God" and the power of the Holy Spirit throughout her life. God's grace had been "incredibly sustaining." Without God's unconditional love and forgiveness, Clinton declared, she could not cope with the challenges she confronted. Faith involved grace, love, mystery, and provocation. It made life meaningful. She had met many people in her travels around the nation whose faith astounded her, such as a woman in Philadelphia whose son and grandson had recently been murdered. Despite these tragedies, God had given this woman the strength to operate a daycare center and care for other people's children. Repudiating the view that religion had too much influence in public life, Clinton contended that people of faith had a right and even an obligation to participate in public debates about issues, though they must do so respectfully and recognize America's ideological diversity. Clinton admitted that she could not explain why "a loving God allows innocent people to suffer." She had pondered this question endlessly and would someday ask God about it. She was convinced, however, that God expected people to help the hurting and alleviate poverty.[116]

Clinton argued that the United States should play a leading role in educating children, promoting women's rights, improving health care around the world, and reducing malaria, tuberculosis, and HIV/AIDS. She wanted the US government, NGOs, and faith communities to partner with foreign governments to tackle these issues and to aid the world's "poor, disenfranchised, [and] disempowered." She pledged to "rebuild America's moral authority and demonstrate our commitment to compassionate humanitarianism."[117]

When asked "Do you believe God wants you to be president?," Clinton declared that "Abraham Lincoln was right in admonishing us not to act as though we knew God was on our side." Instead, Christian politicians should strive to "be on God's side." Echoing the apostle Paul, the senator insisted that people saw "through a glass darkly." Christians could not know definitively what God's will was, but by praying and reading the Bible and commentaries, they could gain God's guidance. Christians must not become complacent or conclude that they knew the mind of God. Rather, she averred, they should strive to "make a difference in people's lives." She had done that throughout her life and would continue to do so if elected president.[118]

On Easter Sunday in 2008, William Curtis, pastor of the large Mount Ararat Baptist Church in Pittsburgh, declared, "The resurrection of Jesus Christ makes it possible for even an African-American and a female to articulate the hopes and dreams of America, and do so with the hope of becoming president."[119] During the next three weeks, two matters relating to religion caused controversy in the Democratic primaries. In April, Clinton criticized Barack Obama for denigrating the faith of ordinary Americans and for continuing to affiliate with Trinity United Church of Christ in Chicago after its head pastor, Jeremiah Wright, accused the federal government of inflicting AIDS on African Americans and argued that the United States deserved the terrorist attacks of September 11 because of its racist practices. At a private fundraising event in San Francisco in April 2008, Obama asserted that many residents of small Pennsylvania towns were clinging "to their guns and religion" because they were frustrated with economic conditions. Numerous Democrats criticized Obama's statement, including Pennsylvania Governor Ed Rendell. Obama's comment, Clinton charged, did not reflect "the values and beliefs of Americans."[120] African American editor George Curry accused Clinton of trying to exploit Obama's statement for political ends.[121]

During a debate in Philadelphia in mid-April, Clinton again faulted Obama for remaining at Trinity Church after Wright's scathing attack on the United States. She stressed that individuals chose the churches they attended and claimed that she would have left Trinity after Wright's incendiary remarks. Curry objected that Clinton was using "Wright's words for political gain." Curry was pleased that many Black and some white ministers were defending

Wright's prophetic denunciations of American actions. Dean Snyder, the senior pastor of Foundry United Methodist Church, where the Clintons had worshipped in the 1990s, declared that Wright had "served for decades as a profound voice for justice and inclusion in our society." Evaluating "his dynamic ministry on the basis of two or three sound bites does a grave injustice to Dr. Wright, the members of his congregation, and the African American church which has been the spiritual refuge of a people that has suffered from discrimination, disadvantage, and violence." Snyder admitted that he had made statements similar to Wright's in some of his own sermons. Ed Matthews, one of Clinton's pastors in Little Rock, insisted that some of his antiwar sermons during the 1960s, like the recent ones by Wright, demanded that the United States change its policies. He chastised citizens who said, "America right or wrong." Matthews added that Clinton had disagreed with his support of gay marriage and opposition to the death penalty but had not left his church.[122]

Throughout the primaries, Hillary and Bill Clinton spoke to clergy groups and campaigned in churches. In August 2007, Clinton met with a group of African American pastors and community leaders in San Francisco. She discussed several of her major initiatives, including her programs to provide pre-kindergarten for all children, universal health care, and good-paying jobs. Harold Mayberry, senior pastor of First African Methodist Episcopal Church in Oakland, praised her partnership with leaders in New York to establish a charter school for Black male teenagers and her focus on reducing crime and violence in African American communities.[123] Although most Black pastors backed Obama, many African Americans supported Clinton. In October 2007, she spoke at Abyssinian Baptist Church in Harlem, a congregation pastored from 1937 to 1972 by Adam Clayton Powell Jr., who also represented Harlem in the US House of Representatives from 1945 to 1971. The church's current pastor, Calvin Butts, argued that Clinton's candidacy could open new doors for women. Clinton promised to end Bush and Cheney's "cowboy diplomacy" and restore the nation's image abroad. She also pledged to improve the lives of ordinary Americans by working to provide universal health care and affordable housing, rebuild America's aging infrastructure, and pass a new GI Bill to fund post–high school education for soldiers who served in Iraq and Afghanistan.[124]

In mid-January 2008, Clinton discussed her plans for reforming immigration, prisons, and health care, saving energy, reducing unemployment, and solving the nation's mortgage crisis with the Ministers Coalition of Compton,

California. She stressed to this audience that the Bible taught Christians "we just can't be hearers but we must be doers of the word."[125] On the first Sunday of February 2008, Bill visited three African American churches in the Los Angeles area to solicit votes for his wife, two days before the California primary.[126] The next Sunday, Bill campaigned for Hillary at two Black churches—Temple of Praise in Washington and the Greater Mt. Nebo African Methodist Episcopal Church in Bowie, Maryland. Bill emphasized his wife's work to resolve the mortgage crisis, plans to provide universal and affordable health care, proposals to create an "independent clean energy future," initiative to help students pay off their college debts, and pledge to withdraw US troops from Iraq.[127]

During the campaign, both Clinton and Obama worked to woo Catholics, who had been a major part of the Democratic coalition since the New Deal. Both candidates hired Catholic outreach directors, recruited prominent Catholics to speak on their behalf, and crafted mailings highlighting their support of Catholic social teachings on economic justice.[128]

As Clinton spoke more openly about her faith, discussing her prayer life and including biblical references in her speeches, many political conservatives objected either that her focus on faith was politically motivated or disingenuous or that her religious views were theologically liberal. Meanwhile, some political liberals faulted her for talking too much about the importance of religion in public life. Andrew Ferguson, editor of the *Weekly Standard*, claimed that Clinton espoused a very liberal Protestant perspective that believed "in everything but God." Spokespersons for the Institute of Progressive Christianity condemned Ferguson's statement as "gutter politics," an attempt to demonize Christians who espouse the social gospel tradition, and a "malicious denigration" of Clinton's faith.[129] Whereas many Americans said they would not vote for Clinton because she was godless, perhaps speaking for many others, a Black woman said she refused to vote for the New York senator because she was too religious. She did not like Clinton's "religious tone," protested that the senator frequently implied that "God wants me in politics," and feared that Clinton's religious views negatively affected her decision-making.[130]

During the campaign, Clinton highlighted her efforts to help children and promised to do more to improve their lives. As a senator, she advocated a national pre-K initiative to supply funds to states that would enable them to create high-quality pre-K programs.[131] She promised to quadruple the subsidies for Early Head Start, which she had helped establish as first lady, and to substantially increase the funding of Head Start.[132]

The Conservative Quest to Deny Clinton
the Nomination, and Sexism

Some political conservatives worked vigorously to help deny Clinton the Democratic nomination. Richard Collins oversaw the Washington, DC–based "Stop Her Now," which claimed to be "rescuing America from the radical ideas of Hillary Clinton." He denounced the senator as an arrogant, vicious, big-government liberal. In *Whitewash: What the Media Won't Tell You about Hillary Clinton but Conservatives Will* (2007), Brent Bozell, the head of a conservative media watchdog group, and Tim Graham argued that the wife of "a disgraced, impeached president" had become a presidential frontrunner despite "her staggering number of personal, political, and financial scandals," never holding an elective office before 2001, and "her leftist political agenda," all because the national media had shamelessly promoted her aspirations for two decades.[133] In her 2007 book, *The Extreme Makeover of Hillary Rodham Clinton*, Bay Buchanan, sister of conservative pundit Pat Buchanan, censured Clinton's record on health care, the war in Iraq, and same-sex partnerships.

Sexism played a role in Clinton losing the nomination to Obama. In 2005, former Clinton advisors Dick Morris and Eileen McCann argued in *Condi vs. Hillary: The Next Great Presidential Race* that Clinton was "on a virtually uncontested trajectory to win the Democratic nomination and, very likely, the 2008 presidential election." Political strategist Susan Estrich contended that same year in *The Case for Hillary Clinton* that she had "the most money, the best organization, and the most loyal staff" among all potential candidates, and that she was "also young enough, old enough, smart enough, bold enough, and for all those reasons beloved enough by the voters of the Democratic Party" to secure both the Democratic nomination and the executive office.[134] So what went wrong? The primary factor was Obama's charisma, eloquence, and shrewd campaigning, but sexism also contributed.

The media have frequently trivialized the campaigns of women candidates by focusing on their physical appearance and clothing. Clinton's pantsuits and changing hairstyles were often mocked. The *New York Times* referred to Clinton's "cackle," while the *Washington Post* commented on her cleavage. Women have often been held to a different standard than male candidates and ridiculed in ways that their male counterparts rarely are. When "Clinton declared her candidacy" in 2008, argued Amanda Fortini, "the sexism in America, long lying dormant, like some feral, tranquilized animal, yawned and revealed itself."[135]

Throughout the campaign, Clinton was frequently portrayed as a mother, a pet, and an iron maiden, three common stereotypes of professional women. Clinton was more often criticized, however, as not feminine enough. She was the antiseductress who reminded men of affairs that went horribly bad.[136] Clinton was continually described as "overly ambitious," "calculating," "cold," "scary," and "intimidating."[137] On the other hand, the media widely reported that she had almost cried while campaigning in New Hampshire, because it contradicted the tough image Clinton projected.[138]

At times, media analysis of Clinton was blatantly sexist. Chris Matthews called Clinton a "she-devil" in a broadcast on MSNBC; he also referred to her as "Nurse Ratched . . . who takes pleasure in inflicting psychic pain on her patients." An editor at National Public Radio equated Clinton with actress Glenn Close's knife-wielding character in *Fatal Attraction*. A Republican strategist contended on ABC's *Nightline* that Clinton was "tough," "mean," and "ruthless," and could not be trusted.[139] Facebook groups were named "Stop Running for President and Make Me a Sandwich" and "Life's a Bitch So Don't Vote for One." A YouTube video featuring a KFC bucket read, "Hillary's Deal: 2 Fat Thighs, 2 Small Breasts, and a Bunch of Left Wings." The words "slut" and "cuntbag" frequently defaced her Wikipedia page. Rush Limbaugh asked, "Will this country want to actually watch a woman get older before their eyes on a daily basis?"[140]

Infuriated by what they denounced as sexist news coverage of her campaign, many Clinton supporters proposed boycotting the cable networks, displaying videos on a "Media Hall of Shame," and prodding the candidates to address this issue.[141] These complaints elicited more ridicule than sympathy or indignation. Charles Krauthammer pointed out that Obama was facing racial discrimination and John McCain was dealing with age discrimination; he argued that Clinton needed to grow up and "take it like a man."[142]

Based on their extensive analysis of media coverage during the 2008 primaries, Diana Carlin and Kelly Winfrey conclude that sexism was not just "in the minds and hearts of right-wing crackpots and Internet nut-jobs, but it . . . flourished among members of the news media." Many media figures argued that women were not as competent as men and were unsuited for the top political offices, even if they had outstanding qualifications. While numerous voters viewed Clinton or Sarah Palin, the Republican vice-presidential nominee, favorably as supermoms who understood the concerns of ordinary people, many media depictions helped undermine both women's credibility.[143] Other scholars argue that media treatment of female political candidates improved significantly in the decade before Clinton's 2008 campaign, but that this improvement did not apply to the presidency, which continued to be viewed as a male prerogative, especially because of public concerns about defending national security and thwarting terrorists.[144] Meanwhile, numerous men and women believed that a woman's place was in the home, not in government, and that they could not serve effectively because they were "too soft, flighty, and inconsistent."[145] Some men felt threatened by Clinton's presidential bid. She challenged the still widespread assumption that men should dominate government, business, and the church.[146]

When she suspended her quest to obtain the Democratic nomination, Clinton declared, "Although we weren't able to shatter that highest, hardest glass ceiling this time, thanks to you, it's got about 18 million cracks in it and the light is shining through like never before, filling us all with the hope and the sure knowledge that the path will be a little easier next time." She added, "If we can blast 50 women into space, we will someday launch a woman into the White House."[147]

Clinton's faith helped guide and sustain her in her work as a senator; as she campaigned for president, it was front and center in the faith forums held by *Sojourners* and at Messiah College and in her 2007 *New York Times* interview. Her faith helped her cope with her very disappointing loss of the 2008 Democratic presidential nomination and would motivate and direct her as she faced the challenges of the next chapter in her life as the nation's third female secretary of state.

5

"I Look upon All the World as My Parish"
Secretary of State and Seeking the Oval Office

In January 2009, Hillary Clinton became the nation's third female secretary of
state and the first elected official to hold this position since Edmund Muskie
occupied it in 1980–81. Some friends marveled at how graciously and calmly
Clinton accepted her loss to Barack Obama and were amazed by her willingness
to serve as his chief diplomat. Clinton was persuaded to take this position by
Obama's argument that he needed someone who possessed immense stature
and respect to oversee foreign policy. Her longtime policy chief, Neera Tan-
den, explained that Clinton accepted the position because she felt "a sense of
obligation, duty, responsibility, as part of her general outlook; perhaps it is
her Methodism." One of her colleagues pointed out that Clinton had avoided
the "deep funks" into which three other recently defeated presidential candidates—Al Gore, John Kerry, and John McCain—had descended.[1]

Traveling almost one million miles and visiting 112 countries in four years,
Clinton energetically served her country. Like John Wesley, she saw the world
as her parish, her field of ministry. Clinton contended that her optimistic perspective on life springing from her Methodist upbringing and theology made
her foreign-policy philosophy "inclusive and outward-looking." She explained
in her 2014 memoir, *Hard Choices*, "I worked to reorient American foreign
policy around what I call 'smart power.'" This entailed using "the traditional
tools of foreign policy—diplomacy, development assistance, and military
force—while also tapping the energy and ideas of the private sector and empowering citizens, especially the activists, organizers, and problem-solvers."

Clinton testified that her Methodist faith also inspired her to promote several humanitarian causes—reducing human trafficking, providing clean, efficient cookstoves, promoting maternal health care in developing nations, and, most notably, striving diligently to advance women's rights.[2]

Foreign-policy analyst Walter Russell Mead argued that the spirit of nineteenth-century missionaries who spread the gospel, promoted human rights, and helped reform economic and social conditions throughout the world dwelt in Clinton and shaped her key convictions about the United States' global role. Whereas some realists saw "global meliorism"—the concept that American foreign policy should strive to create a better world—as a derogatory phrase, for Clinton it was a bedrock principle.[3] The United States is "indispensable," she declared in a speech at the Council on Foreign Relations in February 2013; it is "the force for progress, prosperity and peace."[4] During her tenure as secretary of state, Clinton promoted what some pundits referred to as the "Hillary Doctrine"—the policy that enhancing women's rights furthered global stability and strengthened American security. Clinton's passion for helping women and children began early in her life and helped guide her work as first lady. Describing Clinton's priorities as secretary of state, human rights activist Theresa Loar opined, "I honestly think Hillary Clinton wakes up every day thinking about how to improve the lives of women and girls. And I don't know another world leader who is doing that."[5]

During President Obama's first term, he and Clinton worked to strengthen American alliances, end wars in Afghanistan and Iraq, and halt a global financial crisis. They dealt with increased economic and political competition from China, intensifying threats from Iran and North Korea, and revolutions throughout the Middle East. The nation's "most globe-trotting secretary of state" was also its most popular politician. Her approval ratings were consistently in the high 60 percent range, and she was the only chief diplomat in history who had to avoid the paparazzi. After more than twenty years in the limelight, Clinton managed once again to reinvent herself—from a "losing presidential aspirant" to a "world-class problem-solver."[6] When she left the office in 2013, Michael O'Hanlon, a foreign-policy expert, rated her State Department record as "more solid than spectacular," an assessment many other analysts share.[7] Her work as secretary of state, coupled with her prominence as first lady and a US senator, helped her capture the 2016 Democratic nomination for president.

After resigning as secretary of state on February 1, 2013, Clinton continued her work on behalf of women around the globe through the Clinton

Foundation. She also began to campaign for the 2016 Democratic nomination for president. Her Methodist faith played a major role in all three enterprises.

The Hillary Doctrine

Before becoming secretary of state, Clinton had long worked to increase the rights and elevate the status of women. Although Clinton rarely quoted the Bible or used distinctively religious language in her quest to halt the maltreatment of women and help them overcome many impediments to full human rights, it clearly rested on a moral foundation derived from her Methodist faith and heritage. As chair of the American Bar Association's Commission on Women in the Profession in the 1980s, she strove to expand the opportunities of and respect for female attorneys. As first lady of Arkansas, Clinton helped produce a *Handbook on Legal Rights for Arkansas Women*. Her work to reform health care as the nation's first lady was motivated in large part by her desire to give women and children greater access to physicians and medical facilities.

In her travels abroad as first lady, Clinton often highlighted the problems women faced and met with women from all walks of life to discuss how to improve their living and working conditions and increase their political influence. Celebrating International Women's Day in March 1995 in Copenhagen, Denmark, Clinton argued that women could significantly help their nations meet great challenges, but only if they were "empowered through education, legal rights and protection from violence" and received "access to adequate social services, employment opportunities, political institutions, and decision making." Educating girls and women, she contended, contributed to the health and prosperity of developing nations more than any other factor. It led to "higher economic productivity, greater participation of women in the modern labor sector, lower infant and maternal mortality rates, improved child nutrition and family health, longer life expectancy, lower birth rates, and stronger families and communities." Clinton announced in her speech that the United States would allocate $100 million over the next ten years to expand educational opportunities for hundreds of thousands of impoverished girls and women in Latin America, Africa, and Asia.[8]

While visiting Asia in April 1995, Clinton met with untouchables and ragpickers in India, the prime minister of Pakistan, and the president of Sri Lanka. Denying girls education, basic health care, and employment opportunities, she insisted, "is a human rights issue."[9] This trip reinforced her commitment to continue to work to reform American health care, provide family leave and an earned income tax credit, and end the gag rule on abortion to help empower women.[10] For the remainder of her tenure as first lady, Clinton met frequently while abroad with women from outside the halls of power. She visited families, schools, government officials, health clinics, hospitals, and one of Mother Teresa's orphanages in Calcutta.[11] In August 1995, Clinton helped create the President's Interagency Task Force on Women, which she and Donna Shalala cochaired, and the President's Interagency Council on Women, led by Theresa Loar, to help coordinate domestic and foreign policies pertaining to women's issues.

"20 Minutes That Changed the World"

In September 1995, Clinton made headlines around the world by condemning domestic violence, rape, prostitution, and sex slavery in an address at a United Nations women's conference in Beijing. She censured drowning, suffocating, or denying food to female babies and burning women to death because their dowries were meager. Clinton also denounced physical violence against women (a principal cause of the death of women between ages fourteen and forty-four in many nations), genital mutilation, and forced abortions and sterilization. In addition, the first lady sought to focus the world's attention on the issues that would make the greatest difference for women and their families: "access to education, health care, jobs, and credit" and the ability "to enjoy basic legal and human rights and participate fully in the political life of their countries." When women were healthy, educated, and safe from violence and could work as "full and equal partners in society," she told the 17,000 conferees, their families flourished. Clinton stressed that women represented 70 percent of the world's destitute and two-thirds of those who could not read or write. Women and children were also a large percentage of the world's refugees. Much of the work women did, including taking care of children and the elderly, was not valued by economists, historians, or government leaders. Many women, she protested, were "dying from diseases that could have been prevented or treated," watching their children suffer from malnutrition, and being prohibited from attending school by their fathers, forced into prostitution, and excluded from voting and receiving loans.[12]

Every woman, Clinton told this diverse gathering, "deserves the chance to realize her God-given potential." Women could not achieve "full dignity until their human rights are respected and protected." Most nations had long acknowledged that women were entitled to personal security and to determine how many children they would have, she asserted, but scores of governments were not guaranteeing these protections and personal freedoms. Tragically, the rape of women continued to be "an instrument of armed conflict," millions of young girls were "brutalized by the painful and degrading practice of genital mutilation," and many women were forced to undergo abortions or submit to sterilization. "As long as discrimination and inequities" remained so common around the world and women and girls were "valued less, fed less, fed last, overworked, underpaid, not schooled and subjected to violence" in their homes and society, "a peaceful, prosperous world" could not be created, Clinton told conferees. "God's blessings on you, your work and all who will benefit from it," she concluded.[13]

Valerie Hudson and Patricia Leidl called Clinton's address in Beijing "electrifying" and "a watershed event for the United States and arguably the entire world." It helped shape how the United States responded to the Taliban's oppression of women in Afghanistan beginning in 1996.[14] Kate Grant, a journalist who attended the conference, dubbed Clinton's address "20 Minutes That Changed the World." The first lady, she argued, had been dazzling, forceful, and brave. "In the capital of a brutal communist regime" that had often turned "a blind eye to female infanticide, forced abortions and other assaults on women's rights," Clinton "proclaimed eleven earth shaking words: 'Women's rights are human rights and human rights are women's rights.'"[15] The speech was also a pivotal moment for Clinton; the fervent response to her words showed her that "she had a voice," which she could use to "help those who had no power."[16] Clinton reported that thereafter, when she traveled overseas, women quoted parts of her speech or gave her copies to autograph.[17] At the conference, delegates from 189 nations endorsed a Platform for Action that called for the "full and equal participation of women in political, civil, economic, social and cultural life."[18] Among the many women inspired by Clinton's address in Beijing was Theresa Loar, who in 1999 cofounded Vital Voices Global Partnership, a global NGO that invested in women's lives to improve the world.

Speaking in Tunis, Tunisia, in 1999, Clinton continued her assault on the exploitation of women by excoriating Islamic fundamentalists in Algeria and Afghanistan who brutalized women. She denounced them for raping teenage girls, denying jobs to professionally trained women, and burning girls' legs with acid because they had ventured into public with uncovered ankles. Those who committed "these hateful deeds," Clinton declared, "pervert the great religion in whose name they claim to act." Noting that Tunisian women enjoyed numerous rights, Clinton implored them to condemn the Taliban for misusing Islam to abuse Afghan women. Clinton also toured one of Tunisia's twenty-three family planning clinics, which, she argued, had "played an important role in advancing the status of women."[19]

Empowering Women

In a 2001 article in *Time* magazine, Senator Clinton previewed what later became known as the Hillary Doctrine. She praised President George W. Bush and his wife Laura for denouncing the Taliban's mistreatment of women and insisting that women must be permitted to help determine Afghanistan's new government and shape its society. She urged Congress to provide funds to improve education and health care for Afghan women and children and to equip women to participate in developing democratic practices and civil organizations. Women's rights, she proclaimed, were not simply American or Western rights; they were human rights, universal values that should be promoted throughout the world. The Taliban had prohibited girls from attending school and had prevented women from accessing health care, working outside the home, or even appearing in public unless covered by a burqa from head to toe. If Afghan women gained the freedom to determine their future, Clinton concluded, that could help prod other countries to grant women full civil rights. Americans must promote values that would act like antibodies to destroy "the virus of evil" that dwelt in many hearts around the globe and contributed to the oppression of women.[20]

As a senator, Clinton prioritized protecting and enhancing women's rights. She denounced teen date rape, opposed cutting survivors' benefits under Social Security, and supported the Paycheck Fairness Act, which strove to end wage discrimination based on sex.[21] As she struggled to break the glass ceiling, her 2008 presidential campaign denounced sexism and highlighted her political experience, achievements, and ability to govern the nation effectively and advance the public good. As a presidential candidate, Clinton became the target of sexist attacks such as those discussed in the previous chapter, further intensifying her determination to advance women's rights.[22]

Hudson and Leidl argue that Clinton's "signature issue during her tenure as secretary of state was women's empowerment."[23] As the nation's principal diplomat, Clinton continued to contend, as she had done as first lady, that the best way to provide peace and social stability throughout the world was by empowering women and minorities and increasing their economic opportunities. During her US Senate confirmation hearing, Clinton pledged that as secretary of state she would treat women's issues "as central to our foreign policy, not as adjunct or auxiliary or in any way lesser" than other challenges confronting the nation.[24] Speaking to an international women's conference at the United Nations headquarters in March 2010, she asserted that "the subjugation of women is a direct threat to the security of the United States." Granting rights to women, Clinton added, was essential to ensuring "the peace and progress of the 21st century." The United States, she explained, had created a Women's Action Plan to help women gain leadership roles in the public and private sectors, create jobs for women, increase women's access to education and health care, and promote social justice.[25] In a December 2010 address, Clinton declared that "the United States has made empowering women and girls a cornerstone of our foreign policy," calling women's equality a moral, humanitarian, and national security issue. "Give women equal rights, and entire nations are more stable and secure," she proclaimed. "Deny women equal rights, and the instability of nations is almost certain."[26]

In a March 2011 cover story, *Newsweek* introduced the moniker of the "Hillary Doctrine" to describe the belief that "the subjugation of women is a direct threat to the security of the United States."[27] Other commentators offered different versions of the Hillary Doctrine. John Cassidy defined it in the *New Yorker* as "a sustained global campaign targeting radical Islam" that involved "military, diplomatic, economic, political, and rhetorical" options employed by the United States and its advocates.[28] Diplomat James Goldgeier called the Hillary Doctrine a worldview that "appreciates the limitations of U.S. power and yet still maintains the resolve to identify opportunities to lead the world."[29]

Although Clinton never spoke of herself as promulgating a "Hillary Doctrine," she called procuring the full human rights of women and girls "the unfinished business of the 21st century." Throughout the world, women and girls were demeaned, degraded, and denied basic human rights. Anywhere women were "disempowered and dehumanized," antidemocratic forces and political extremists who threatened American security were likely to flourish.[30]

In the State Department's 2010 Quadrennial Diplomacy and Development Review (QDDR), Clinton outlined a plan to foster "sustainable economic growth, food security, global health, climate change, democracy and governance, and humanitarian assistance." The plan called for investments to advance the welfare of women and girls in each of these areas.[31] Echoing Clinton's own words, the QDDR asserted that "women are critical to solving virtually every challenge we face as individual nations and a community of nations." The review declared, "Women are at the center of our diplomacy and development efforts—not simply as beneficiaries, but also as agents of peace, reconciliation, development, growth, and stability."[32]

As secretary of state, Clinton prodded the Obama administration to create an ambassador at large for global women's issues, a position filled by Melanne Verveer, her former chief of staff. In a 2009 interview, Clinton complained that cultural resistance to providing gender equality was deep-seated. Ending discrimination against women was "the last great impediment to universal progress." Unless women had greater rights and responsibilities, Clinton argued, many of America's foreign policy goals could not be achieved. The secretary of state praised the power of microlending to improve women's economic situation, stating that the "wanton, senseless, brutal violence perpetrated against girls and women" must be halted. Studies by the World Bank and other groups, Clinton pointed out, had proved that countries where women were mistreated and denied equal rights were unstable and potential incubators for political extremism. Moreover, women who could provide for their own financial needs and whose children attended school would have fewer children, reducing environmental pressure on and battles over water and land.[33]

Clinton drew attention to women's issues almost everywhere she traveled, including some of the most conflict-riddled places on the planet. During an eleven-day trip to Africa in the summer of 2009, she visited the Democratic Republic of Congo, where 5.4 million people had been slaughtered in the world's "most deadly conflict since World War II, where 1,100 women and girls are raped every month" and "where poverty, starvation, and all of the ills that stalk the human race are in abundance." She saw "the best and the worst of humanity" as she met "women who had been savaged and brutalized physically and emotionally," courageous women of faith who had gone into the jungle to rescue other victims of attacks, and Christian doctors and nurses who cared for the wounded.[34] Clinton met with women trying to organize unions in hotels and textile factories in Cambodia. In January 2011, she traveled to Yemen, a nation infiltrated by Al Qaeda that permitted men to marry girls as young as age nine. She discussed security and development issues with President Ali Abdullah Saleh and talked with individuals who rarely met US secretaries of state—community activists, students, and women.[35]

Clinton's emphasis on women's rights had numerous consequences. In 2012, the State Department requested $1.2 billion for programs designed to assist women, undoubtedly much more than previous administrations used for such purposes, but the department only began to track expenditures targeting women in 2010.[36] Her policies helped prompt many nations to appoint women to important diplomatic positions, including ambassadors to the United States (at least twenty-five women served in this capacity during Clinton's tenure, an all-time high).[37] Many women testified that they were alive or could experience better lives because Clinton had come to their villages, been photographed with them, discussed their work on television, or talked with their leaders.[38] However, critics questioned how Clinton "could be a credible voice for women if her own country has not ratified" the Convention on the Elimination of All Forms of Discrimination Against Women and the United States espoused "militarist values that put women's lives in danger and set back the cause of women by fanning ethnic hatred."[39] They also complained that strategic needs drove the Obama administration's policy decisions and that the State Department sometimes failed to condemn abuses of women and girls. The most blatant example was the United States' "conspicuous silence" about how Saudi Arabia mistreated its female citizens.[40]

Clinton's Promotion of Other Humanitarian Causes

Haiti

In addition to her emphasis on women's rights, Clinton championed several other humanitarian causes, including aiding Haiti after the devastating earthquake in January 2010, reducing human trafficking, and supplying cleaner and more efficient cooking stoves. Clinton directed the Obama administration's response to the calamity in Haiti and persuaded the president to use the US military to provide relief. While in Haiti in late 1975, Clinton had visited the Cathedral of Our Lady of the Assumption in Port-au-Prince, which had "served as a beacon of hope and faith" in the midst of Haiti's political repression and poverty. Seeing pictures of the magnificent cathedral largely reduced to rubble by the earthquake broke her heart. But she also witnessed Haitians dancing and singing as they helped each other and built makeshift communities. These scenes reminded her of Isaiah 54:10: "Though the mountains be shaken and the hills be removed, yet my unfailing love for you will not be shaken nor my covenant of peace be removed." Clinton rejoiced that people of faith from around the world were aiding the Haitian people. She urged those attending the National Prayer Breakfast in February to continue to remember their plight after the news cameras moved on to the next tragedy. "Let us pray," she proclaimed, "that we will all continue to be our brothers' and sisters' keepers." She also urged people to pray that the power of faith would make them "whole as individuals" by providing "personal salvation" and make them "a greater force for good on behalf of all creation" so as to fulfill John Wesley's rule: "let us do all the good we can, by all the means we can, in all the ways we can, in all the places we can, to all the people we can, as long as ever we can." The outpouring of generosity in Haiti reminded Clinton of the story of Elijah in 1 Kings 19. The prophet had experienced God not in a strong wind, an earthquake, or a fire, but in "a still small voice." She exhorted attendees to be quiet periodically and listen to the Lord, rather than responding only when a natural disaster or human-produced catastrophe occurred.[41]

Human Trafficking

Under Clinton's leadership, the State Department also worked to reduce human trafficking. Clinton told the United Methodist Women in 2014 that fighting human trafficking had been one of her personal priorities since the late 1990s. She explained that the State Department had taken several steps to stop human trafficking, which by 2010 had become an epidemic. In that year, Clinton instructed the department to report on trafficking in the United States, not only in foreign countries. Many American states were developing shelters for victims and passing safe harbor laws that provided social services for children forced into prostitution instead of treating them as juvenile delinquents. In 2011, the Clinton Global Initiative launched a program, supported by the State Department and with an accompanying website (http://www.theslaveryfootprint.org), to help Americans understand how their lifestyles, consumption, and possessions affected human trafficking, forced labor, and modern slavery. In addition, the State Department sought to help faith communities collaborate to combat these evils. Clinton praised Methodist women for forming dozens of grassroots networks to rescue enslaved individuals, help them reconstruct their lives, and publicize this evil. She implored Christians not to ignore people's physical and material problems. Jesus, she said, told his disciples to feed, rescue, heal, and love the needy, which included trafficked individuals.[42] While visiting Cambodia in 2011, Clinton stopped at a women's shelter operated by Somaly Mam, making Mam's efforts to rescue young female victims respectable to government officials.[43]

Cookstoves

In the early 2010s, poorly ventilated stoves and open fires, the principal source of cooking and heating for three billion people in developing nations, produced smoke that killed almost two million people a year—more than the number who died from malaria. This smoke also contributed to numerous chronic illnesses and various acute health problems, including low birth weight, lung cancer, emphysema, bronchitis, and cardiovascular disease. Women and children spent countless hours foraging for wood, making them vulnerable to attack. In addition, conventional stoves generated substantial amounts of black carbon, contributing to climate change.

In September 2010, Clinton announced the formation of the Global Alliance for Clean Cookstoves, a $60 million partnership designed to save lives, improve people's well-being, empower women, and prevent climate change by supplying 100 million cookstoves by 2020. The alliance, led by the United Nations Foundation, strove to create a global market for clean cookstoves.[44] Clinton frequently beseeched world leaders to encourage their citizens to purchase these products. "People roll their eyes when she talks about clean cookstoves," declared Anne-Marie Slaughter, Clinton's former policy planning chief. But if the alliance succeeds, "we will have reduced carbon, improved women's security and saved millions of lives, and that is enormous."[45]

Clinton's Continuing Quest to Help Women

After resigning as secretary of state at the end of Obama's first term, Clinton continued her efforts to empower women. In September 2013, she announced that the Clinton Foundation would lead "a broad effort to evaluate the progress women and girls had made since Beijing and to chart the path forward to achieve full and equal participation for women and girls." This initiative, soon called the No Ceilings project, undertaken in partnership with the Bill and Melinda Gates Foundation, strove to advance the rights and opportunities of women and girls. Clinton declared that women still faced many "ceilings that held back their ambitions and aspirations and made it harder, if not impossible, for them to pursue their dreams."[46] The project focused on providing family planning, education, and employment for women; improving maternal health; increasing internet access, paid maternity leave, and the number of female entrepreneurs and executives; ending violence against women; and preventing child marriage.[47]

In her 2014 address to the United Methodist Women, Clinton argued that "women can drive economic recovery and growth." If nations raised the minimum wage, gave parents flexible hours at their jobs and paid family leave, invested in early childhood development, provided affordable, quality childcare, and enabled girls to receive STEM education and mentoring in science and mathematics, women could lift up themselves, their families, and their countries. She insisted that contemporary women, like their indomitable female Methodist predecessors, could take the "social Gospel out into the world" and aid the multitudes, even when they had meager resources like the mere five loaves and two fish in Jesus's famous feeding miracle in the gospels.[48]

In her 2014 memoir, Clinton contended that most men who worked in Washington's foreign-policy establishment failed to understand that "the places where women's lives were most undervalued" were "most plagued by instability, conflict, extremism, and poverty." Helping women and girls receive their rights, she declared, was not only the morally correct policy but "smart and strategic." Many scholarly studies, Clinton noted, showed that "improving conditions for women helped resolve conflicts and stabilize societies." She had worked to move "women's issues" from the periphery to the center of American foreign policy and international diplomacy because it was at "the heart of our national security."[49]

Gay Rights, Religious Liberty, and the Power of Religion

Clinton's understanding of Scripture and human dignity led the secretary of state to support gay rights around the globe. In a December 6, 2011 speech in Geneva, Switzerland, Clinton announced that the US government would use varied diplomatic means to procure and protect gay rights throughout the world.[50] Clinton strove to "firmly place LGBT rights within the international community's framework of human rights." In this speech, she sought to refute myths of "antigay zealots": "that gay people were mentally ill child abusers; that God wanted us to reject and isolate them; that poor countries couldn't afford to care about human rights; [and] that these countries didn't have any LGBT people." Like being a woman or part of a racial, religious, or tribal minority, she argued, being LGBT did not make a person less human.[51] Clinton also protested the harassment of and attacks on gay people in various countries, including Uganda, sometimes directly to the leaders of these nations.[52]

As secretary of state, Clinton also strongly promoted religious freedom. At the swearing-in ceremony for Suzan Johnson Cook as the Ambassador-at-Large for International Religious Freedom, Clinton promised that she and Cook, the first Black woman to serve as a senior pastor in the two hundred–year history of the American Baptist Church, would work closely together to defend the values they held so dearly. Their work would be demanding because many authoritarian regimes were abusing their citizens, violent extremists were attempting to exploit sectarian tensions, and religious freedom was being threatened by "both quiet intolerance and violent attacks."[53]

Clinton also worked with the Organization of Islamic Cooperation, which represented almost sixty nations, to promote "freedom of expression and worship" and combat "discrimination and violence based upon religion or belief." She argued that religious freedom was closely connected with the right to think for oneself, say what one thinks, and peacefully assemble with others. Clinton actively strove to preserve the statement in the United Nations' Universal Declaration of Human Rights that everyone has the right to "practice any religion, to change our religion, or to have none at all." On her first trip to China as secretary of state in February 2009, she attended a service at a house church to support these places of worship as the Chinese government was cracking down on them. Clinton told Egyptian leaders in the summer of 2012 that "all citizens should have the right to live, work, and worship as they choose," whether they were Muslims, Christians, or part of any other religious body. She avowed that no political leaders or religious group could properly impose their "authority, ideology, or religion" on others.[54]

Clinton also encouraged State Department diplomats to engage in dialogue with religious leaders in other nations to promote greater understanding. After the 2012 attack on the US compound in Benghazi, Libya, that killed four Americans, including Ambassador Chris Stevens, Clinton condemned using violence in the name of religion. Ensuring religious freedom, she insisted, was essential to preserving national stability. "All people of faith and good will," the chief diplomat declared, "know that the actions of a small and savage group in Benghazi do not honor religion or God in any way. Nor do they speak for the more than one billion Muslims around the world." She added, "When all of us who are people of faith—and I am one—feel the pain of insults, of misunderstanding, of denigration to what we cherish," whether individuals are Christians, Jews, Hindus, Buddhists, or Muslims, "we must . . . not . . . resort to violence." Clinton insisted that "the great religions of the world are stronger than any insults. They have withstood offense for centuries. Refraining from violence, then, is not a sign of weakness in one's faith"; rather, it is "a sign that one's faith is unshakable." "In my tradition, like all traditions," Clinton concluded, "we are expected to love one another. And together, we have to translate that into better understanding and cooperation."[55]

Clinton insisted that religion could be either a "force that drives and sustains division" or a "healing balm." In Northern Ireland, Christianity had long

promoted hatred, isolation, and insularity instead of cooperation and collaboration, but thankfully, since the signing of the Good Friday Agreement in
1999, "the bonds of common humanity" had become "more powerful than the
differences fueled by ancient wrongs," as ballots replaced bullets. As the people
of Northern Ireland continued to work to resolve disputed issues, they were
experiencing anew the fruit of the scriptural admonition "Let us not become
weary in doing good, for at the proper time we will reap a harvest if we don't
give up" (Galatians 6:9). Even where God's presence and promises seemed
"fleeting and unfulfilled or completely absent," Clinton argued, the power of
faith and "the determination to act can help lead a nation out of darkness."[56]

Clinton cited Liberia as an example of how faith, prayer, and zealous striving could bring peace. In 2010, she had been deeply moved by watching the
film *Pray the Devil Back to Hell*, which portrayed the story of Leymah Gbowee.
Devastated by the murders and widespread fear that had gripped Liberia for
years, Gbowee organized women in churches and mosques to pray for an end
to the violence. The prayers for peace by members of this mass movement were
answered, and the conflict and carnage finally stopped when Ellen Johnson
Sirleaf was elected president in 2006.[57]

Clinton insisted that every world religion had "the same marching orders." They all taught their followers to care for the destitute, visit orphans,
widows, and prisoners, be charitable, relieve suffering, love neighbors, and
welcome strangers. The sacred texts of all these faiths commanded people
to act lovingly, but people often failed to do so. Sadly, organized religions
often inhibited the exercise of faith, perverted love, and undermined the
teachings of their own scriptures. She protested that religion was being used
"to justify horrific violence, attacks on homes, markets, schools, volleyball
games, churches, mosques, synagogues, [and] temples" and "to deny the
human rights of girls and women." Throughout the Middle East, Africa, and
Asia, religion was being employed to discriminate against and even justify
the execution of gays and lesbians, as well as to stifle free expression and
prevent peaceful protests.[58]

Clinton argued that the Obama administration was working to stop human
rights violations "perpetrated in the name of religion." It was supporting peace
negotiations from Northern Ireland to the Middle East, promoting interfaith
dialogue with Muslims, and condemning religious repression in Iran. The administration was also working to help girls, women, gay men, and lesbians
obtain their basic human rights, which were often denied to them on religious
grounds. In addition, the State Department was exhorting Muslim nations

to end religious intolerance. In a 2016 op-ed, Clinton asserted, "As secretary of state, I made it a cornerstone of our foreign policy to protect the rights of religious minorities around the world." She argued that the State Department had stood up for oppressed religious groups in Egypt, China, and Tibet because when democracy ceases to exist, "a leader or ruling faction can impose a particular faith on everyone else." Critics argued that Clinton's defense of religious freedom was not as robust as she claimed. Some politicians and academicians contended that the State Department's implementation of the International Religious Freedom Act of 1998 did little to challenge Egypt, China, and other nations that repeatedly denied their citizens religious freedom.[59]

Faith and Diplomacy

Clinton's keynote address at the 2010 National Prayer Breakfast highlights her religious convictions and struggles during her tenure as secretary of state. Clinton reported that she had attended every annual prayer breakfast since 1993. She had heard many "heartfelt descriptions of personal faith journeys . . . impassioned pleas for feeding the hungry," aiding the destitute, and caring for the sick, and "speeches about promoting understanding among people of different faiths." She had listened to three presidents, all men of faith, discuss how their burdens were almost impossible to bear and appeal for an end to "the smallness, irrelevancy, even meanness, of our own political culture." Her heart had "been touched and occasionally pierced" and her spirit had often "been lifted by the musicians and the singers" who had "shared their gifts in praising the Lord." And "during difficult and painful times," the personal connections she developed with people who did not share her party or political perspective strengthened her faith. Clinton confessed that she had often tried "to figure out how to close the gap of what I am feeling and doing with what I know I should be feeling and doing. As a person of faith, it is a constant struggle, particularly in the political arena, to close that gap."[60]

In her speech, Clinton also shared her own faith journey. Methodism, she declared, "was a particularly good religion" for her because of its emphasis on the connection between faith and works. Fulfilling Wesley's dictum to "Do all the good you can" was "a tall order." Clinton explained that following it involved several "interpretive problems": "Who defines good? What are we actually called to do, and how do we stay humble enough, obedient enough, to ask ourselves, 'Am I really doing what I'm called to do?'" She exhorted Christians not to sit on the sidelines but to participate in the public arena.[61]

Clinton asserted again in 2012 that her faith guided her public service. "It is very much fundamental as to who I am and how I see myself," she declared.[62]

During her years as secretary of state, Clinton's friends argued that she continued to be "a deeply optimistic Methodist who believes that government can advance human progress." Although she was a policy wonk and a "shrewd political operator," friends added, "she is never more energized or relentless as when she is pursuing a cause that she believes will improve people's lives." Her admirers praised her dogged determinism to accomplish her agenda, whereas detractors complained about her self-righteousness and support for big-government liberalism. Betsy Ebeling asserted that being secretary of state gave Clinton "a great stage" to pursue "many things she's always cared about."[63]

Impressed by her work as secretary of state and personal popularity, columnist Bill Keller argued in January 2012 that the Democratic Party should replace Joe Biden with Hillary Clinton as its vice-presidential candidate. Clinton, he asserted, had "a Calvinist work ethic, the stamina of an Olympian, an E.Q. to match her I.Q.," and great political instincts. She could "imagine how the world looks to an ally or adversary"; she listens and "learns from her mistakes." She had been a strong contender for the presidency four years earlier, Keller stressed, and as secretary of state, she had dealt effectively with both the Obama White House and foreign nations. According to Gallup, she was the nation's most admired woman for the tenth consecutive year, far ahead of Michelle Obama, Oprah Winfrey, Sarah Palin, and Condoleezza Rice. Her 64 percent approval rating was the highest of any American politician.[64]

A Rock-Star Diplomat?

Clinton's work as secretary of state has been both commended and censured. She was dubbed a "rock-star diplomat," and one commentator asserted that her legacy would be as great as George Marshall's. Another contended that she had refashioned American diplomacy, shaping it "as much by her own personality and fame as by a guiding philosophy." Eric Schmidt, the chair of Google, argued that Clinton was "perhaps the most significant secretary of state since Dean Acheson, who helped unify the relationship between modern Europe and the United States." Sen. Lindsey Graham (R-SC) insisted that Clinton "is extremely well respected throughout the world, handles herself in a very classy way and has a work ethic second to none."[65]

In *The Secretary: A Journey with Hillary Clinton from Beirut to the Heart of American Power* (2013), Kim Ghattas maintained that Clinton helped elevate the status of the United States and made it a desirable partner again. Hudson and Leidl called Clinton "the world's most influential and eloquent exponent of the proposition that the situation of women and the destiny of nations are integrally related" and lauded her for making that conviction an integral part of US foreign policy.[66] The Obama-Clinton national security team, one journalist maintained, was the most harmonious one in decades, despite facing colossal challenges on many fronts. Its members had supported democratic rights in Libya and other nations and had dealt effectively with regimes that challenged "American security interests (Egypt and Bahrain)" or American power (Syria).[67] Clinton and Obama had ended the war in Iraq, killed Osama bin Laden, and helped overthrow Libyan dictator Muammar al-Qaddafi. Clinton promoted Obama's 2011 shrewd "pivot" to focus strategically and economically on Asia and the Pacific Rim. Many scholars credited Clinton with overseeing the negotiations with Russia that produced the 2010 New START Treaty, which reduced strategic offensive nuclear weapons. She also made women's rights and climate change high priorities of the Obama administration.[68] Others contended that Clinton helped reestablish the United States' reputation abroad. Her diplomatic efforts had helped end fighting between Israel and Hamas; played a major role in convincing China to reduce its carbon emissions; rallied nations to support sanctions that forced Iran to curb its nuclear ambitions; and passionately promoted the rights of religious minorities, women, and children throughout the world.[69] Many extolled Clinton's ability to establish cordial relationships with both her staff and world leaders. "I think that she is brilliant at connecting with people on a political level," declared Madeleine Albright, the nation's first female secretary of state.[70]

Swanee Hunt, a social activist, professor, and ambassador to Austria during the Clinton administration, argued that like George Marshall, whose 1947 plan supplied indispensable aid to rebuild Europe after World War II, Clinton had helped make the world more stable. Like the general, Hunt asserted, Clinton had expanded the concept of security far "beyond bombs and bullets," primarily by getting more women involved in diplomacy, peace talks, and decision-making. Clinton had helped raise the number of women involved in peace negotiations from a paltry 5 percent of all participants to about 30 percent, the critical mass researchers argued was necessary to "build bridges across political and ethnic divides"; provide "fresh ideas and perspectives"; shift budgets from procuring military hardware to improving education, health, and the environment; "create a more civil political sphere; and govern with greater transparency and less corruption." Clinton implored emerging democracies to appoint women to constitutional commissions and ministerial posts. In addition, she created the Women in Public Service Institute in 2012 to enable outstanding young women leaders from around the world to learn from distinguished scholars and political leaders and from one another.[71]

Walter Russell Mead praised Clinton's energetic efforts to empower women around the world and to push foreign governments to engage more with civic organizations. The roots of interest in women's rights abroad, he argued, lay with American missionaries who had censured foot-binding in China and created programs to educate women and girls throughout the Middle East. State Department attempts to develop a broader social and political agenda, he asserted, had begun with Condoleezza Rice, who served as secretary of state under President George W. Bush. Clinton, however, had increased the department's activities in these areas with beneficial results.[72]

On the other hand, Mead insisted that American attempts to promote democracy in conjunction with the Arab Spring movements had generally been unsuccessful except in Tunisia. Egypt and Libya were abject failures. The debacle in Libya led to the Benghazi attack that ensnared Clinton in congressional investigations. The fiasco also increased public resistance to using greater American military power overseas.[73]

Other criticisms of Clinton's work, including her signature policy, abounded. The Hillary Doctrine, Hudson and Leidl averred, provided a new basis for analyzing America's national interest: How did other nations treat women? However, the "scorecard for the Hillary Doctrine is mixed"; it involved some victories and some "troubling inconsistencies and lapses." They added, "The issue of proper implementation dogged the Hillary Doctrine from the very beginning." Was the focus on women, they asked, driven by operational realities or simply rhetoric? It would last only if propelled by the former.[74] More damning was the assessment by American Enterprise Institute scholar Michael Rubin, who predicted that Clinton "will be remembered not for women's empowerment, but rather for their betrayal. . . . Largely because of her policies and silence," Rubin alleged, "women in the Islamic world have suffered their worst setbacks in generations."[75]

Critics offered many other complaints. Clinton had supported the Obama administration's increased use of drone strikes, mishandling of Libyan and Syrian regime change, expansion of the surveillance power of the state, and ineffective peace talks with the Taliban.[76] Despite her attempts to improve the United States' problematic relationship with Pakistan, anti-Americanism remained powerful there.[77] Most significantly, Clinton was sharply criticized, although exonerated of alleged misconduct, in the 2012 attack on a US outpost in Benghazi, Libya. During the 2016 presidential campaign, she was lambasted for using a private e-mail server while secretary of state. FBI Director James Comey judged her action to have been "extremely careless" but not criminally culpable, and Republicans hammered away at her poor judgment, which contributed to her loss to Donald Trump.[78]

Others broadened their negative appraisals of Clinton's performance as secretary of state still further. Republican strategist Karl Rove insisted that her single achievement was breaking the record for most countries visited by an American chief diplomat.[79] *Wall Street Journal* columnist Bret Stephens argued that Clinton might have deserved to be considered a great secretary of state if she had produced a significant diplomatic advance as Henry Kissinger did, "dominated the administration's foreign policy" as James Baker did, assembled a major alliance as Dean Acheson did, created a great doctrine as John Quincy Adams did, developed an influential plan as George Marshall did, or laid the foundation for an impressive victory as George Shultz did. But Clinton had done none of these things. Moreover, under her watch, Russia's behavior in Syria had worsened, and China had become more aggressive in the South China Sea. Clinton, Stephens concluded, should not be "held accountable for [all] the failures of a president she understood (earlier and better than most) as a lightweight." But she had chosen to serve as his secretary of state and shared the blame for his foreign-policy failures.[80] Gil Troy agreed that as secretary of state, Clinton "left no defining doctrine or legendary legacy," but he maintained that by "crusading for women's rights, she helped Obama make America's foreign policy more global and less confrontational."[81]

Clinton spent four years directing US foreign policy, accomplishing some of her goals and failing to attain others. Her faith, coupled with her life experiences, motivated her to strive mightily to increase the rights of women around the globe and improve their opportunities to realize their God-given potential. Few analysts, regardless of their overall assessment of Clinton's record as secretary of state, could fault her passion, work ethic, or humanitarian achievements.

After leaving the State Department in February 2013, she worked at the Clinton Foundation in New York. In a tweet in June 2013, Clinton identified herself by numerous titles, including "women and kids advocate." This, wrote columnist Sally Quinn, "has always been her true passion." Clinton underscored the point by enjoining the foundation to "champion children's and women's issues."[82] For the first time in twenty years, Clinton had no role, informal or formal, in the federal government.

The Second Presidential Campaign Begins

In June 2013, Clinton tweeted that she was a "Wife, mom, lawyer, women and kids advocate, FLOAR, FLOTUS, US Senator, SecState, author, dog owner, hair icon, pantsuit aficionado, glass ceiling cracker, [and] TBD." Many pundits saw this tweet as launching her campaign to secure the 2016 Democratic nomination for president. Columnist Sally Quinn expressed surprise that Clinton did not mention that she was a Christian, a Methodist, or a person of faith. After all, Quinn asserted, "Clinton is well known for her faith." Those who wanted to understand Clinton, Quinn quipped, should "follow the faith." She reminded Clinton that candidates who openly discussed their personal faith were "more likely to appeal to the American public," while lamenting that many politicians had "shamelessly exploit[ed] religion for their own political purposes."[83]

In November 2013, Clinton was the keynote speaker for the United Methodist City Society's celebration of the 175th anniversary of its work in New York City. She praised the society's efforts to end injustices and asserted that its proponents had been "motivated by a vision of what could be." Clinton exhorted participants to increase their efforts to bring the gospel to those who had not yet "had the chance to believe." Through their theological beliefs, discipline, and ministry to the needy, Methodists had "a great gift to offer" Americans who felt disconnected and insecure. In introducing her mother, Chelsea declared that the Methodist women who worked in the tenement slums of lower Manhattan reminded her of Hillary's work to empower women and children.[84]

Recognizing the importance of faith in the lives of many Americans and the need to describe how her faith had impacted her life and policies, Clinton began to speak more openly and frequently about religious matters as she began her quest for the presidency in 2014, as she had done during her 2008 campaign. But how to discuss her faith on the campaign trail was a dicey issue for Clinton. In 2014, surveys revealed that almost half of Americans wanted religion to play a larger role in politics. More than 40 percent of Americans, including nearly one-third of Democrats, insisted that political leaders said too little about their faith.[85] On the other hand, however, voters often are skeptical when politicians talk about their faith, suspecting that they have ulterior motives. This was especially the case with Clinton. Many expressed surprise and suspicion about Clinton's professions of faith, with some denouncing them as disingenuous, even though her faith, as we have seen, had been very consistent throughout most of her life. A 2014 *Washington Post*–ABC News poll reported that more than half of Americans did not trust Clinton. During her Senate and first presidential campaigns, she had struggled to be personable and appear authentic.[86] Despite these issues, polls in mid-2014 showed that Clinton was running strongly among mainline Protestants, competitively among white Catholics, and trailing prospective Republican candidates only with evangelicals.[87]

To highlight her faith, Clinton spoke to several religious groups, most notably the 2014 gathering of Methodist women and the 200th anniversary of Foundry United Methodist Church in Washington in 2015, and discussed the Bible and religious themes on campaign stops and in interviews. Meanwhile, some supporters worked to publicize Clinton's faith. In April 2014, Burns Strider, a Southern Baptist who headed Clinton's 2008 outreach to faith communities, and Nashville businessman Rick Hendrix launched a website called Faith Voters for Hillary. The site declared, "The teachings of her faith, the principles of the Methodist church, and the examples of her family have been the guiding light throughout her life." It also highlighted how Clinton would serve religious communities if elected president. The site complemented the Twitter account @Faith4Hillary, which had gone live more than a year earlier and had more than 38,000 followers.[88]

As Clinton began her campaign, numerous friends, associates, and commentators hailed her faith as genuine, life-directing, and empowering. A journalist noted that many people questioned the authenticity of Clinton's faith and her motives for quoting the Bible, but those who knew her well avowed that she truly believed what she professed. Lissa Muscatine, Clinton's friend and former speechwriter, insisted that Clinton was a "very religious" Methodist whose faith inspired her commitment to social justice. Her desire to study Scripture more deeply, Burns Strider explained, prompted Clinton to teach a Sunday school class at First Methodist Church in Little Rock. Clinton also sent people "grace notes," as she called them—gifts that people did not deserve but that sprang from "the everyday joys, beauties, kindnesses, pleasures of life that can strike a deep chord of connection between us and the divine." She had greatly comforted Strider when his mother died in 2012.[89]

In April 2014, Clinton went to Louisville, Kentucky, to address a gathering of 7,000 of the nation's 800,000 members of United Methodist Women, an organization that focused on improving education, abolishing human trafficking, and other social-justice issues. She presented moral arguments drawn from Scripture and the Methodist social gospel tradition for several of her policies: increasing the minimum wage, equalizing pay for men and women, providing more opportunities for disadvantaged Americans, reducing the number of women who died while pregnant or giving birth, and helping victims of human trafficking. Clinton lauded the Methodist church for giving people both "the great gift of personal salvation" and "the great obligation of the social gospel." In working to aid families, children, and the oppressed and persecuted around the world, Clinton asserted, she had been guided by the biblical triad of faith, hope, and love.[90]

The story of Jesus feeding a multitude with five loaves and two fish, Clinton explained, motivated her political work. In thinking about this episode, she was struck by what happened before Jesus performed the miracle. As it grew late and the crowd became hungry, the disciples prodded Jesus to send people to find their own food, but Jesus told them to feed the throng. In so doing, he was teaching the disciples about "the responsibility we all share" to serve the community, especially people "with the greatest need and the fewest resources." His admonition had inspired the Methodist social-justice mission from the denomination's inception. "Like the disciples of Jesus," Clinton argued, "we cannot look away, we cannot tell those in need to fend for themselves and live with ourselves." Christians must instead rescue, heal, and love the needy. She commended Methodist women for "fighting to end the scourges of human trafficking and domestic violence" and "advocating for social, economic and environmental justice" at home and abroad. She then implored them to continue to put their "faith into action."[91] Commenting on Clinton's address, Strider declared that "she's been out and about the planet working and doing things and speaking out, especially on things that Methodists would categorize as social justice issues."[92]

Conservative columnist Cal Thomas, who rarely missed an opportunity to denigrate Clinton's religious perspective, noted that she had explained that as secretary of state her faith had inspired her to launch "initiatives to combat human trafficking, promote maternal health care in developing countries and fight for women's rights." He insisted, however, that secularists also supported these causes. Moreover, the same Bible that provided the mandates for these social reform initiatives taught that life began at conception and expressed a traditional view of marriage, whereas Clinton endorsed abortion and alternative family arrangements. Clinton, Thomas protested, believed in the "social gospel," which actually "is more social than gospel." Inspired by the social gospel, Clinton and other liberal Democrats, Thomas claimed, had created numerous unsuccessful social programs, piling new programs on ineffective old ones and "hoping the new ones will miraculously work better." Why not instead follow the scriptural admonition that those who did not work should not eat (2 Thessalonians 3:10)? Thomas further criticized Clinton's use of the feeding of the five thousand to defend her argument that Christians had a responsibility to improve the world. Christ performed this miracle, he insisted, to authenticate his divinity, not to provide an early example of a food bank or food stamps program. Clinton, he concluded, "is more comfortable with religious language than some of her [Democratic] predecessors . . . but her policies" differed little from those of liberal skeptics.[93]

Defending Clinton, one Methodist women's conference participant denounced Thomas's "rigid fundamental[ist] approach to his faith" and exhorted him to "have more respect for what people do instead of what they profess." By dedicating her life to helping women and children around the world and serving the "least of our brothers and sisters," Clinton, she argued, was emulating Jesus.[94]

At Foundry's bicentennial celebration in September 2015, Clinton used the children's song "This Little Light of Mine" to describe her understanding of Christian witness in the world. "Too many people," she declared, "want to let their light shine, but they can't get out from under that bushel basket." God's mandate is too great to accomplish alone, she added; a village is needed to achieve it. Clinton's village was the Methodist Church, which had long "been a source of support, honest reflection and candid critique."[95] She also argued that God had given everyone, regardless of their age, gender, income, race, or religion, gifts that enhanced their value and dignity. The apostle Paul exhorted Christians to use their gifts, "especially in the service of others," and to create "a better, fairer and more peaceful world." She concluded, "We should be, in Paul's words, generous and diligent and cheerful in our service. That's how we honor God, who gave us these gifts in the first place."[96]

Some of Clinton's encounters and interviews on the early campaign trail provided insights into her faith. In late May 2015, she talked with Frederick Donnie Hunt, a Black Baptist minister, who was reading 1 Corinthians 13 in a bakery in Columbia, South Carolina. She commended him for doing the most important thing in life: studying "what the scripture says and what it means." When the pastor testified that he always learned something new when he read the Bible, Clinton responded, "Well, it's alive. It's the living Word." After their discussion of the passage, Hunt commended Clinton for knowing "that particular scripture."[97] In a September 2015 interview, Clinton praised Pope Francis for emphasizing Christ's teachings about humility, respect for one another, and helping the destitute and troubled "whether they are on the side of the road" or in prison.[98]

In 2015, leading Christians weighed in on Clinton's candidacy. Baptist professor and evangelist Tony Campolo argued in the *Washington Post* that Clinton possessed outstanding qualifications, had demonstrated great administrative ability, understood how Congress worked, and was a "brilliant negotiator." She had "modeled being a faithful wife and a loving, effective mother" during "a crisis that would have destroyed most marriages." Clinton was "a committed Christian" who faithfully engaged in "the spiritual disciplines of Bible study and prayer." To appeal to fellow evangelicals, Campolo emphasized that she had a plan to reduce abortions by 50 percent, and he offered to create an Evangelicals for Hillary committee. David French, an attorney, Iraq War veteran, and contributor to *National Review*, countered that Clinton "was a dishonest first lady, a middling senator, and a failed secretary of state" who "had no recognizable record of public accomplishment." Her record as secretary of state was "truly disastrous," as Cold War–era tension with Russia had flared again, Syria and Iraq were torn asunder by civil war, and jihadists controlled much of the Middle East. As first lady, secretary of state, and head of the Clinton Foundation, French maintained, Clinton had displayed "evasiveness and lack of integrity." Most troubling to Christians was her strong support for "abortion-on-demand, including even late-term, partial-birth abortions," and her opposition to religious freedom laws. The nation had more honest, competent politicians, both male and female. Clinton was "the wrong choice for Christians of every ideological stripe."[99]

As Clinton began her campaign, numerous commentators assessed her chances for victory and evaluated her strengths and weaknesses. "Everyone sees the Hillary they want to see," columnist Eleanor Clift asserted in June 2014. The images and interpretations Americans had projected onto Clinton over the years revealed "more about our changing culture and politics than any significant shift in how she sees the world." She had been perceived as a radical feminist, a left-wing activist, and a national security hawk. Currently she was viewed as "tougher than her husband" and "to the right of President Obama on defense and national security issues. She is the first woman who would enter the race without having to convince the voters that she could be commander in chief." Clinton had already demonstrated she could serve effectively in that capacity.[100]

Maureen Dowd, one of Clinton's most persistent liberal critics, reported in the same month that a White House aide had told her, "Hillary, though a Methodist, thinks of herself like an Episcopal bishop who deserves to live at the level of her wealthy parishioners, in return for devoting her life to God and good works." Dowd insisted that Clinton was knowledgeable and tough, but that her many political battles and personal difficulties had made her defensive, a trait that sometimes negatively affected her judgment. At the end of *Frozen*, Dowd observed, Elsa discovers that her powers could "be used for good, once her heart is filled with love. She escapes from her prison, leaves behind the negative things that held her back, and leads her kingdom to a happy and prosperous future. Can Hillary?"[101]

Many pundits and Republican activists accused Clinton of antagonism toward the media, having thin skin, and refusing to accept criticism.[102] Some commentators claimed that Clinton offered no new ideas. *Washington Post* columnist Jennifer Rubin argued that Clinton's 2014 book *Hard Choices* "was vapid" and faulted her for refusing to discuss difficult policy issues on her book tour. Because she put forth no new policy ideas, the coverage of her campaign was focusing on her gargantuan speaking fees ($200,000 or more), her prickly relationship with the media, "her limited political talents," and the "palace intrigue in Hillaryland." She refused to disassociate herself from the president or assert positions that distinguished her from him, thereby appearing to be running for a third Obama term.[103]

In running for the presidency, Clinton had to deal with the many Hillary haters who had first emerged on the national scene in 1992. Since then, she had become one of America's most polarizing figures, and bashing her had become a "national sport." Although critics had denounced Al Gore, Bill Clinton, Barack Obama, Sarah Palin, George W. Bush, and Dick Cheney, hatred of Hillary had been "particularly virulent and irrational." Negative reactions to Clinton dated back to her comments about a Tammy Wynette song and baking cookies during the 1992 presidential campaign, by which she offended many cultural traditionalists, stay-at-home mothers, and country-western fans.[104] Her testy rhetoric, Gil Troy argued, led many to cast her "as the ultimate 'feminazi,'" the "yuppie wife from hell," and "the harsh Northeastern careerist know-it-all." The Clintons' talk about a copresidency, the health care reform fiasco, and a series of scandals during Bill's first term had made matters worse. Conservative magazines, tabloid newspapers, talk radio, and sensation-seeking television news networks helped Hillary hating flourish.[105]

On the other hand, Troy contended, three shifts had helped diminish hostility to Hillary. First, after the failure of the Clinton administration's health care reform initiative, she had adopted a more passive, traditional role as first lady and was widely pitied as the victim of a philandering husband. Second, Hillary's effective service as New York's junior senator had enabled her to establish legitimate political credentials. Third, Obama ran to her left in 2008, helping make her policies seem more centrist. Amazingly, many working-class white men who had previously detested her became convinced that she would work to help them and constituted part of her base in several states. Troy advised Clinton to focus on substantive policies, not accentuate her celebrity. She needed to make a case that her presidency would significantly benefit all Americans.[106]

In 2014, television analyst Jeff Greenberg counseled Clinton to address Ralph Reed's Faith and Freedom Coalition, the Family Research Council's "Values Voter Summit," or another organization with a similar perspective and focus. Like John F. Kennedy speaking in 1960 to the Greater Houston Ministerial Association about whether a faithful Catholic could serve as president, or like Ronald Reagan appearing before the Urban League in 1980 to explain his policies, Greenberg thought Clinton could garner votes by presenting her priorities to and emphasizing her common ground with these groups. He suggested that Clinton admit that her differences with these groups on such issues as abortion, same-sex marriage, and the role of the federal government were profound. She could stress, however, that she agreed with them that the family was under assault in American culture, making the job of parents more difficult. She had argued in *It Takes a Village* that by embracing such values as honesty, responsibility, and diligence, communities helped parents raise children. Clinton could also point out that although she backed providing federal assistance to help working parents pay for childcare, she highly valued stable, two-parent families. She could remind religious conservatives that while many marriages were ending in divorce, she had worked diligently to preserve her own marriage despite her husband's infidelity. In addition, Clinton could emphasize that teenage pregnancy, the crime rate, and other social ills had declined significantly under the last two Democratic presidents.[107] Of course, there is a vast difference between the audiences Kennedy and Reagan addressed, which were not overtly hostile to them, and the people Clinton would have encountered at a Faith and Freedom Coalition or Values Voter

Summit meeting. Had Clinton spoken to these groups, she probably would have faced antagonistic questions, and the audience's negative reaction to her policies might have created an embarrassing situation. On the other hand, had Clinton reached out to conservative religious groups whose members were more receptive to her views—such as Rick Warren's Saddleback Church in California—where, as discussed in chapter 4, she received a standing ovation in 2007 when she spoke on the church's response to AIDS, it could have helped her win the presidency in 2016. As we will see, religious issues were a significant factor in the election, and Donald Trump appealed to religious constituencies, especially evangelicals, more effectively than Clinton did.

6

"Be Not Weary of Well Doing"

The 2016 Presidential Campaign

The 2016 election featured what one pundit called "the two most unpopular presidential candidates in the modern era."[1] Although this statement may be true, both Clinton and Trump had many diehard supporters who worked zealously to win votes for them. Religious issues played a major role in the 2016 campaign. Clinton adopted a Methodist maxim as her unofficial campaign slogan: "Do all the good you can, for all the people you can, in all the ways you can, as long as you ever can."

For the first time in several presidential election cycles, Democrats had a good chance to reduce or perhaps even eliminate the so-called God gap, whereby people who attended church regularly voted for Republican candidates far more than Democrats. The Clinton campaign took several steps to achieve this outcome. The challenge was great because in January 2016, Pew reported that the percentage of Americans who viewed Clinton as "not too" or "not at all" religious had risen substantially since 2007. That year only 24 percent of adults placed Clinton in one of these categories; in 2016, 43 percent did.[2] In January 2016, her campaign hired Sarah Bard to serve as its Jewish outreach coordinator. In July, the campaign selected John McCarthy, who had helped Barack Obama appeal to Catholic voters in 2012, to direct its faith efforts and chose Zina Pierre to oversee its efforts to reach African American voters. Because of Clinton's strong religious convictions, McCarthy claimed, outreach to people of faith had already "been at the very core of this campaign." For the last three months before the election, McCarthy promised, Clinton would frequently discuss her faith and her religious motivations for her policies. Nevertheless, Clinton and the Democratic National Committee did not actively solicit the faith-based vote as much as the Obama campaign did in 2012 or especially in 2008, according to John Green, a leading expert on religion and politics.[3]

By July, Donald Trump had solidified the white evangelical vote, but some prominent Christian conservatives opposed him, and many Jews and Muslims were deeply suspicious of him. According to a Pew Research Center survey, registered voters who attended religious services at least weekly favored Trump by 49 to 45 percent, a much smaller margin than the 55–40 edge Mitt Romney had over Obama in July 2012. Moreover, Clinton led Trump by a nineteen-point margin among Catholics who attended mass weekly, whereas Romney had held a three-point advantage over Obama with this same group in 2012. Michael Wear, Obama's evangelical faith adviser, insisted, "The bar is lower than it's ever been for Democrats just to show they're not antagonistic to people of faith." If the election was as close as some prognosticators predicted, John Green contended, a faith-based appeal by the Clinton campaign could make a major difference in the outcome. Meanwhile, Clinton held a large lead with the "nones," whose numbers had risen from 14 percent of registered voters in 2008 to 21 percent in 2016, making them a larger bloc than Catholics (20 percent), white evangelicals (20 percent), or white mainline Protestants (19 percent).[4]

During the campaign, Clinton struggled with how to present herself and her ideas and how to respond to Trump's unusual attacks. She received varied advice from pundits and Democratic strategists and politicians, including about how best to reach out to religious groups. Wear urged Clinton to reject a "far-left mandate" and instead focus on unifying the nation. She had an excellent opportunity to appeal to "discouraged, disempowered members of the conservative establishment and key Republican constituencies—like evangelicals—who have a true crisis of conscience regarding Donald Trump." Wear argued that few politicians were "better positioned to advance a truly pro-family economic agenda" than Clinton and advised her to move to the center on social issues by embracing both "LGBT rights and religious freedom, both reproductive choice and abortion reduction."[5]

Jack Jenkins of the Religious News Service argued that critics often dismissed Clinton's faith "as duplicitous and disingenuous," but her "thoughtful, conciliatory approach to religion . . . should sound familiar to millions of America's so-called 'Mainline Christians.'" Trump could not "speak coherently about the Bible, much less his own theological beliefs," prompting criticism

from an unusual assortment of religious luminaries including some evangelicals, leaders of Trump's own Presbyterian denomination, and Pope Francis.
Most Americans misunderstood how important Clinton's faith was, Jenkins
maintained, because of the reporting by the nation's media. Conservative
media outlets argued that theological liberals like Clinton were not true Christians, whereas left-wing commentators censured debate moderators for even
asking Democratic candidates about their religious practices. Clinton, Jenkins
emphasized, had been nurtured in the Methodist faith and had attended many
Pentecostal camp meetings in Arkansas, which had enabled her to "develop a
spiritual parlance" that appealed to Black and charismatic Christians. Clinton,
however, faced a difficult challenge in talking about her faith and religious
issues. Theological conservatives complained that her religious views were
too liberal, while many political liberals and "nones" counseled her not to discuss religious matters at all. Because about a quarter of liberal voters had no
religious affiliation, many leading Democrats downplayed the importance of
reaching out to religious voters. However, Jenkins argued, this was an unwise
strategy because many mainline and Black Christians were Democrats, and
a recent Pew poll found that 64 percent of African Americans wanted political
candidates to say more about their faith.[6]

Trump, Clinton, and Evangelicals

In choosing whom to vote for in the 2016 presidential election, evangelicals
and other Christians considered numerous factors: the candidates' personalities and character; their positions on abortion, religious freedom, foreign
policy, the economy, racial justice, and tax policy; and whom they were likely
to appoint as Supreme Court justices and federal judges. Many evangelicals
supported Trump first and foremost because he identified eleven judges he
would nominate for the Supreme Court. Evangelicals, author Rachel Held
Evans quipped, "would vote for a ham sandwich" if it promised to appoint
the right justices.[7] Although many younger evangelicals were committed to
alleviating poverty, promoting racial reconciliation, protecting the environment, and ending human trafficking, their parents' generation still viewed
defending traditional marriage, preventing abortion, and ensuring religious
freedom as the most important social issues. Arguing that achieving these
three goals depended on the Supreme Court, such influential evangelicals as
Liberty University president Jerry Falwell Jr., Dallas megachurch pastor Robert
Jeffress, and theologian Wayne Grudem exhorted Christians to vote for Trump

despite his abrasive personality, moral flaws, and inflammatory comments. If Clinton were elected, they asserted, she would appoint judges who would preserve *Roe v. Wade* and allow Christian organizations and churches that upheld conventional views of marriage to be persecuted. Her election might even be "a knockout punch" to the Christian right's social agenda.[8]

"Trump speaks to the profound fears animating so many white evangelicals today," stated R. Marie Griffith, director of Washington University's Center on Religion and Politics. Many of them fear that "they and their values are being displaced by foreign, immigrant and Muslim forces as well as by domestic movements" promoting Black Lives Matter, gay rights, and feminism.[9] Many evangelicals considered Clinton "personally responsible for babies being aborted," declared Deborah Fikes before she left the board of the National Association of Evangelicals to endorse the Democrat. After resigning, Fikes was repeatedly censured for "supporting a daughter of Satan" and told that she "had the blood of 60 million babies" on her hands. A *World* magazine cover depicted a grim reaper wearing an "I'm With Her" button from Clinton's campaign.[10] Numerous religious conservatives also warned that Clinton would permit LGBT rights to trump religious freedom.

Many commentators noted the irony of evangelicals supporting Trump rather than Clinton and the sexual double standard evangelicals employed in evaluating the candidates. Trump was a thrice-married, casino-owning entrepreneur well known for his bigoted remarks, name-calling, and other un-Christ-like behavior. Clinton, by contrast, attended church regularly, had taught Sunday school, had attended prayer meetings as first lady and a senator, and had long-lasting relationships with prominent evangelical leaders, including Billy Graham, megachurch pastors Rick Warren and Bill Hybels, and social activist Tony Campolo, while Trump had no such relationships. Many evangelicals ignored "Trump's affairs and bragging about his sexual conquests," asserted a *Christianity Today* editor. Meanwhile, they held Hillary responsible for her husband's affairs instead of praising her for working to rebuild her marriage.[11]

Whereas older white male religious-right leaders stood staunchly with Trump, some evangelicals, especially younger ones, females, and minorities, were repelled by his personality and inflammatory statements, and considered other social issues as important as abortion and religious liberty; accordingly, they refused to support him. These evangelicals insisted that Christians had a mandate to aid the indigent, imprisoned, immigrants, refugees, and victims of human trafficking and sexual abuse and to protect the environment.

Many of them wanted to reform the criminal justice system and supported
the goals of the Black Lives Matter movement. Like other evangelicals, they
strongly opposed abortion, but some of them accepted same-sex marriage.
Some evangelical leaders, including Samuel Rodriguez Jr., president of the
National Hispanic Christian Leadership Conference, which represented about
forty thousand congregations, declined to serve on Trump's faith advisory
board. A *Christianity Today* editor reported in October 2016 that only one of
the thirty-three influential millennial evangelicals she had profiled two years
earlier was backing Trump. Several of them were using the hashtag #never
Trump. More than a thousand students at Liberty University signed a petition
criticizing Falwell for endorsing a candidate who promoted things Christians
should oppose, thereby tarnishing the school's reputation.[12]

Although a significant percentage of evangelicals supported Trump during
the Republican primaries and as many as 80 percent of them voted for him
in the general election, some prominent evangelical leaders denounced him,
including Russell Moore, the head of the Southern Baptist Ethics and Religious
Liberty Commission; Texas author and pastor Max Lucado; *Christianity Today*
editor Andy Crouch; and Peter Wehner, a speechwriter and adviser for George
W. Bush. Moore argued that evangelicals should not demand proof that Trump
had been born again, but that they should continue to affirm, as they had done
in other elections, that character matters and strongly promote "traditional
family values." Backing Trump for the Republican nomination, Moore maintained, required evangelicals to repudiate many of their key beliefs. Trump was
not morally fit to hold office. He viewed women the way Bronze Age warlords
did. Voting for Trump, Moore avowed, would deeply hurt evangelicalism; it
would say loudly and clearly that evangelicals cared more about image, money,
power, and winning elections than about moral principles and social justice.[13]

In February 2016, Moore lamented that some evangelical leaders who had
emphasized the importance of politicians' character during the Clinton administration were now downplaying Trump's profanities, race baiting, wooing
white supremacists, bragging about adulterous affairs, and degrading public
morality through his casinos.[14] After Trump received the Republican nomination, Moore argued that his repeated "misogynistic statements," "racist invective," and "crazed conspiracy theorizing" confirmed his lack of judgment and
character. Sadly, some members of "the old-guard Religious Right establishment" were either defending or ignoring his statements. Moore feared that
evangelicals' support of Trump would do more damage to the witness of the
gospel than had the 1980s televangelist scandals.[15]

In late April, a group of Christian pastors and professors, including ethicist David Gushee, *Sojourners* founder Jim Wallis, activist Shane Claiborne, pastor Otis Moss III, and author Lisa Sharon Harper, issued a statement imploring Christians to oppose Trump because he was fueling citizens' anger, promoting racial and religious bigotry, undermining the dignity of women, damaging civil discourse, offending moral decency, and threatening basic American values and the health of the republic. Gushee was "heartened that many Americans, including many Republicans and many of my fellow evangelicals" recognized that Trump represented "a unique kind of danger," and he was hopeful that their resistance would keep the tycoon out of the White House.[16] Some evangelical leaders were disturbed by Trump's proclivity to boast about himself and belittle numerous groups, his past support of abortion and gay rights, and his pledges to prohibit Muslims from entering the United States and deport Mexican immigrants. A small number of evangelicals joined the "Never Trump" camp.

Moore's fellow Southern Baptist, Albert Mohler, president of the denomination's seminary in Louisville, was conflicted about which candidate Christians should support. The battle between Trump and Clinton, he warned, would require professing Christians to rethink "what we believe about the purpose of government and the character of political leadership."[17] Mohler protested that Trump's "entire mode of life" clashed with "American evangelical conviction and character."[18] Max Lucado, a best-selling author and copastor of a large independent Christian church in San Antonio, also lambasted Trump. In a blog post in February, Lucado argued that Trump's "insensitivities" toward various groups would not "be acceptable even for a middle school student body election." He felt compelled to criticize Trump because the Republican "repeatedly brandishes the Bible and calls himself a Christian." Americans expected their chief executive "to set a respectable standard for our nation," which Trump clearly would not do.[19]

To counter these critics and woo evangelicals, Trump established a Faith and Cultural Advisory Committee on June 21.[20] Its more than twenty-five members included some of the nation's most prominent evangelicals—Jerry Falwell Jr.; psychologist James Dobson, founder of Focus on the Family; Paula White, pastor of a megachurch near Orlando; charismatic Texas ministers and prosperity gospel preachers Kenneth and Gloria Copeland; Robert Jeffress, pastor of the eleven thousand–member First Baptist Church of Dallas; political activist Ralph Reed, founder of the Faith and Freedom Coalition; Michelle Bachmann, Minnesota's first female congresswoman; African American Harry Jackson, senior pastor at Hope Christian Church in Maryland; and Tony Suarez, executive vice president of the National Hispanic Christian Leadership Conference.[21] The faith council advised Trump's campaign on issues that were critical to Christians and helped his staff articulate positions on national defense and the economy.

That same day, Trump met with about a thousand evangelicals and conservative Catholics to discuss his policies and solicit their support. The Republican touted his Christian credentials and promised to defend religious liberty and appoint pro-life Supreme Court justices. Numerous prominent attendees endorsed Trump, including former Arkansas governor Mike Huckabee and Ben Carson, a retired neurosurgeon who had sought the 2016 Republican nomination. Carson warned that Clinton would perpetuate Obama's harmful policies, including preserving the Affordable Care Act and championing gay rights, so conservative voters must not be too picky about Trump's character and qualifications. Although not endorsing Trump, Franklin Graham, who had taken over leadership of his father Billy Graham's ministry organization, defended the presumptive Republican nominee. Evangelicals had a right to be concerned about his multiple marriages, earlier support for abortion rights, and crude language, Graham declared, but numerous biblical heroes had also committed serious sins. Moses had disobeyed God during the Israelites' wandering in the wilderness, David had committed adultery and murder, and Peter had denied three times that he knew Jesus. The only perfect person, Graham stressed, is Jesus Christ, who was not running for president. Attendees expressed alarm that lawsuits had been filed to require business owners to supply services for same-sex weddings, restrict prayer in public schools, and allow transgender individuals to use whichever restrooms they chose. Many complained that homosexuals were pushing their agenda on the nation. One participant asserted that even Clinton's initials—HRC—proclaimed that she would support the Human Rights Campaign, an LGBT rights advocacy group.[22] For many attendees and other religious conservatives, the key issue in the election was abortion. The president of an antiabortion group pointed out that Trump had promised to appoint "pro-life" justices to the Supreme Court, support legislation to prohibit abortions after a woman was five months pregnant, and end government funding of Planned Parenthood.[23]

At his meeting with conservative Christians, Trump also claimed that "we don't know anything about Hillary in terms of religion." Clinton had been in the public eye for many years, he added, and yet "there's nothing out there."[24]

Trump's assertion clashed with Clinton's life and public record; although she had been more reluctant to speak in recent years, she had discussed her faith in countless speeches, interviews, and books.[25] Ignoring this wealth of testimony, Trump warned that Clinton's lack of religiosity would produce policies that should horrify evangelicals and accused Obama and Clinton of "selling Christianity down the tube."[26]

In response, the Clinton campaign released a statement by Deborah Fikes declaring that Clinton "lives the Golden Rule in her private life and in her public policies." She added, "People of faith are praying that Sister Hillary and not Mr. Trump will be elected in November."[27] Clinton argued that Trump was attacking her faith to divert attention from his lack of political experience and substantive policy proposals. She reminded voters of her frequently repeated dictum: "As we Methodists like to say, do all the good you can for all the people you can in all the ways you can."[28] Others highlighted Clinton's frequent statements about how important her Methodist faith was to her. Politifact called Trump's statement about Clinton's religion "inaccurate and ridiculous" and rated it "Pants on Fire."[29] Other journalists noted how odd it was for a man whose connection with Christianity was so tenuous to question the faith of his opponent. Trump had often been described as not very religious, previously denied central Christian tenets including heaven and hell, and claimed that he had no need for God's forgiveness.

Political commentator Lawrence O'Donnell called Trump's public professions of religion at his June 21 meeting "the most hollow we've ever heard from a presidential candidate." Every other candidate in 2016, he asserted, was either genuinely religious or at least had done enough homework to sound religious. Michael Farris, the chancellor of Patrick Henry College, argued that Trump's worldview "is greed" and his "god is his appetites." These right-wing luminaries, Farris complained, had chosen politics over faith; they had declared themselves to be Republicans no matter what the party's presidential "candidate believes and no matter how vile and unrepentant his character."[30]

Throughout the campaign, Trump met with other evangelical groups. He continually highlighted the issues that mattered most to them—abortion, religious freedom, and conservative Supreme Court justice appointments— and attacked Clinton as either having no faith or being a theological liberal.[31] Trump also argued that Clinton did not have the temperament, judgment, or integrity to be president. He called his rival a "world-class liar" who "may be the most corrupt person ever to seek the presidency" and accused her of running "the State Department like her own personal hedge fund."[32]

Their desire to see Trump elected to promote the policies about which they cared most deeply caused many evangelicals to reverse their previous stance on the importance of politicians' character and on whether individuals who committed immoral acts in private could behave ethically in performing their public duties. In 2011, only 30 percent of white evangelicals affirmed that this was possible, whereas by 2016, 72 percent agreed with the statement. Sexual stereotypes, sexism, and dislike of feminism all played a role in evangelicals' animosity toward Clinton. As Calvin University historian Kristin Du Mez explained, to evangelicals, Clinton was not properly maternal or submissive; she had been on the wrong side of the 1990s culture wars and symbolized many things evangelicals opposed, especially abortion, gay rights, and sexual promiscuity. Many evangelicals ignored or downplayed Trump's affairs and boasting about his sexual prowess and conquests while blaming Clinton for contributing to and enabling her husband's sexual infidelity.[33]

Much of the evangelical support for Donald Trump sprang from deep distrust of and disgust with Clinton. Rachel Held Evans, like many other people raised in evangelical families, was taught to vilify the Democrat. Conservative Christians, she noted, were not allowed to say "bitch," but they made an exception for Hillary. At an apologetics conference she attended, the audience booed whenever Clinton's name was mentioned. Numerous polls revealed that many evangelicals planned to vote for Trump mainly because of their longstanding hostility toward his opponent.[34] A July 2016 survey indicated that of the 78 percent of white evangelicals who said they supported Trump, only 30 percent were principally voting for him, whereas 45 percent indicated that their decision was "mainly a vote against Clinton."[35] A Pew poll in mid-September reported similarly that three quarters of evangelicals said that their dislike of Clinton was a primary reason why they supported Trump.[36]

Evangelical disdain for Clinton had been building for a quarter century. It had begun with her dismissive answer, during Bill's 1992 presidential campaign, as to why she continued to work as a lawyer while he served as Arkansas's governor: "I suppose I could have stayed home, baked cookies and had teas." For many evangelicals who believed that women should be stay-at-home mothers, this answer had lived in infamy. Moreover, in their minds, Clinton was closely connected with evangelicals' losses in culture-war battles dating back to her husband's first presidential term in 1993. The former first lady symbolized much they despised: "abortion rights advocacy, feminism and, conversely, a rejection of biblical ideas of femininity and womanhood."[37]

Although many prominent evangelicals were critical of or at least wary toward Trump, in mid-July, 78 percent of registered white evangelicals (who constituted about 20 percent of all registered voters) said they would vote for the Republican if the election were held today, a slightly higher percentage of this constituency than had planned to vote for Mitt Romney in July 2012. Meanwhile, two-thirds of religiously unaffiliated registered voters (those who described their religion as "atheist," "agnostic," or "nothing in particular") declared they would vote for Clinton. In addition to liking his stances on abortion and Supreme Court nominees, most evangelicals preferred Trump's policies on guns, taxes, the economy, terrorism, immigration, healthcare, and foreign affairs.[38] Speaking for many religious conservatives, Ralph Benko warned in *Forbes* that Clinton would "tax the American lemon until the pips squeak."[39] These factors trumped the Republican's inconsistency over the years on many of these issues, his multiple marriages, and his lack of piety. Some influential evangelicals were pleased that Trump was actively courting them and believed that he would give them a seat at the table in his administration. The poll revealed, however, that most voters were unhappy with both candidates and thought that neither of them would be a good president.[40]

Despite their disappointment with Trump's character and actions, few prominent evangelicals publicly endorsed Clinton. Many younger evangelical women wanted to see a female president, but Clinton's ardent support for abortion was a deal breaker for most of them. The abortion issue caused great difficulty for Clinton throughout the campaign.[41] In July 2015, Planned Parenthood, which Clinton had strongly supported, was accused of selling fetal tissue, which provoked extensive controversy and censure. Clinton defended the organization, arguing that it had aided many women for more than a century by providing cancer screenings, family planning, and other health services. She reiterated her desire to make abortion "legal, safe and rare," highlighted her initiative as first lady to reduce teenage pregnancies, and pledged to ensure that women could "afford to make responsible decisions" about having children.[42]

A May 2016 decision on abortion by the United Methodist Church caused additional problems for Clinton. The denomination's general assembly voted overwhelmingly to withdraw from the Religious Coalition for Reproductive Choice, which biographer Paul Kengor called a left-wing organization whose members were convinced that Jesus approved of "their belief in a sacred 'right to choose,'" and rejected a resolution to support abortion rights. This action put

Clinton in direct opposition to her denomination. Would this self-described "old-fashioned Methodist" follow the lead of her church, "soften her fanatical position on abortion," and stop promoting unlimited "abortion rights," Kengor asked? "Not a chance," he correctly concluded.[43]

Many evangelicals and numerous conservative Catholics also deplored Clinton's support for same-sex marriage. Clinton had previously backed the 1996 Defense of Marriage Act. Running for the Senate in 2000, she declared, "Marriage has historic, religious and moral content that goes back to the beginning of time, and I think a marriage is, as a marriage has always been, between a man and a woman." In 2008, Clinton, like Barack Obama, had defended keeping marriage between heterosexuals, advocating civil unions for homosexuals and allowing the states to determine standards for marriage. In 2013, however, Clinton posted a statement supporting same-sex marriage in conjunction with the Human Rights Campaign. "LGBT Americans are our colleagues, our teachers, our soldiers, our friends, our loved ones, and they are full and equal citizens and deserve the rights of citizenship," she declared, including marriage.[44]

Gay Americans were delighted by the Democratic Party's position on LGBT issues. Bisexual activist Eliel Cruz called the Democratic platform, which was "being spearheaded by two people of faith," the most LGBT-progressive one in history. Clinton promised to push for a bill prohibiting employers from discriminating based on sexual orientation or gender identity, protect transgender rights, and stop the practice of conversion therapy. Clinton and her Catholic running mate Tim Kaine's support for LGBT rights was at odds with their denominations, Cruz contended, but it harmonized perfectly with their own faith. Emphasizing that God called all of creation "very good" and wanting to celebrate "God's beautiful diverse family," Kaine had worked for LGBT equality. For progressive Christians like Clinton and Kaine, Cruz avowed, advocating the "full spiritual and legal equality of LGBT people" was consistent with their support for Black Lives Matter, welcoming of refugees, and aiding the poor and sick.[45]

A third issue that undercut Clinton's efforts to win evangelical votes was her stance on religious freedom. As previously discussed, Clinton had long supported religious liberty. She staunchly backed the 1993 Religious Freedom Restoration Act, especially its provision protecting religious freedom in public schools. Quoting her husband, she declared in *It Takes a Village* that "nothing in the First Amendment converts our public schools into religion-free zones, or requires all religious expression to be left behind at the schoolhouse door."

Religion, she added, "is too important in our history and our heritage" to be kept out of schools. Clinton argued that students should be able to participate in individual or group prayer, student religious groups should be able to meet as readily as other extracurricular clubs, students should be able to express their religious beliefs in their assignments, and schools could teach about the Bible and other scriptures in history and literature classes.[46] As a senator, Clinton cosponsored with Rick Santorum (R-PA) the Workplace Religious Freedom Act, which guaranteed people's right to express their religion on the job without fear of negative consequences. In a 2011 speech in Istanbul, Clinton argued that the right of religious freedom was "endowed by our Creator" and not "bestowed by any government." It did not depend on a government's endorsement, but nations should ensure that people had the freedom to practice any religion they chose or to change their religion.[47]

Despite these affirmations of religious liberty, Clinton's criticism of the Supreme Court's 2014 decision to permit Hobby Lobby not to provide abortifacients as part of its health insurance provisions alarmed religious conservatives. Clinton protested that the court had ruled that "a closely held corporation has the rights of a person" regarding religious freedom, which enabled its employers to "impose their religious beliefs on their employees" and deny women the use of contraceptives as part of their health plans. Pro-life proponents countered that Hobby Lobby's plan paid for sixteen of twenty FDA-approved contraceptives.[48] Other conservatives argued that Clinton's 2015 declaration that "deep-seated cultural codes, religious beliefs and structural biases have to be changed" seriously threatened religious liberty. Marc Thiessen, a fellow with the American Enterprise Institute and a former chief speechwriter for President George W. Bush, contended that, if elected president, she would try to force religious conservatives "to change their beliefs and bend to her radical agenda favoring taxpayer-funded abortion on demand." Thiessen, like many other conservatives, feared that as president, Clinton might be able to select as many as four Supreme Court justices and would not choose jurists who respected religious liberty.[49]

Alexandra Desanctis, writing in the *National Review*, expressed similar sentiments, asserting that Clinton's "record on religious freedom is atrocious." The Democrat had actively thwarted the rights of religious minorities as she advanced "expansive access to abortion and the supremacy of LGBT rights."[50] Desanctis and other critics denounced Clinton's support for the proposed Equality Act, which called for adding protections based on "sexual orientation" and "gender identity" to the 1964 Civil Rights Act; conservatives maintained that this provision would undercut rights guaranteed by the 1993 Religious Freedom Restoration Act. They also lambasted her backing of "the HHS contraceptive mandate and pro-choice interests at the cost of religious liberty and freedom of conscience for both individuals and faith-based organizations." When citizens' beliefs and practices conflicted, conservatives contended, religious liberty should be protected, and the state should allow people to express their religious convictions even when they clashed with other major societal values. They feared that Clinton would make the rights of religious groups "subordinate to the progressive consensus on reproduction, gender, and family." The Clinton camp reacted by calling conservatives' fears greatly exaggerated. It emphasized her Methodist faith, support of religious freedom as a senator and secretary of state, and belief that faith was vital in public life.[51] Despite such assurances, fears that Clinton would undermine the religious freedom of many Americans, which Trump fueled, hurt her efforts to win the votes of evangelicals and Catholic traditionalists.

Departing from most of her evangelical colleagues, Deborah Fikes, an advisor to the World Evangelical Alliance, backed the Democrat because her stances on poverty, education, immigration, human rights, equality, and racism fit well with Fikes's own "values as a follower of Christ." A Christian attorney in San Francisco declared that Clinton's previous work with the Children's Defense Fund convinced her to vote for the Democrat. No other recent presidential candidate cared so much about women and children.[52] One hundred sixteen women under age forty, all of whom were pastors, elders, or deacons, participated in an effort directed by Methodist minister Bill Shillady to provide a daily devotional for Clinton. Some of them also created the #wepraywithher project to support the work of Clinton and other trailblazing women. One devotional writer commented on having been drawn to Clinton by how much she talked "about her faith and how real that is to her."[53]

Clinton, like theological conservatives, affirmed that Jesus was divine, that his death atoned for humanity's sins, and that his resurrection was a historical event; she prayed regularly and knew the Bible well, as evidenced by her ability to cite passages easily and accurately. Nevertheless, many evangelicals refused to acknowledge that she was a fellow believer, and some even castigated her as the devil. Many theological conservatives, Du Mez argued, either demonized Clinton or claimed that she opposed everything they valued. In numerous books and hundreds of articles and on many radio shows, conservative Christians censured the Democrat, denouncing her views on abortion and warning that she would use the power of government to undermine religious freedom.

Viewing their perspective as the only truly Christian one, Du Mez asserted that many evangelicals assumed that Clinton was lying about her faith.

Some theologically conservative Methodists, most of whom disagreed with Clinton's policies, countered that her faith appeared to be genuine. For example, Methodist Mark Tooley, president of the Institute on Religion and Democracy, a conservative research organization in Washington, faulted conservatives who dismissed her sincere religious beliefs. It was impossible to understand Clinton's "political framework," he added, "without understanding her Methodist background."[54]

Faith on the Campaign Trail

"The conventional Washington wisdom holds that Clinton is reluctant to talk about her faith," Daniel Burke observed in October 2016, "which is partly true."[55] After Clinton's 1993 speech at the University of Texas, members of the religious right refused to join her spiritual quest while "the secular left mocked her desire to embark on one." This, combined with unremitting investigations of her financial practices, made her more guarded about baring her soul.[56] For the next fifteen years, she did not frequently discuss her personal religious beliefs or practices, although she stated repeatedly that prayer and pastoral counseling had convinced her to remain with her husband after his affair with Monica Lewinsky. During her twenty-five years in the public spotlight, however, Clinton had asserted that her Methodist faith helped inspire her work, especially her efforts to help children, women, and the poor as she responded to Jesus's commandment to take care of "the least of these," much more than most analysts acknowledged.[57] During her presidential campaign, Clinton discussed her faith in many Black churches, seeming very comfortable and earning thousands of loyal supporters.[58] Throughout the campaign, Clinton insisted that her faith provided strength and guidance and that she tried to live by Wesley's injunction to "do all the good you can."[59]

Some pundits criticized Clinton for not doing more to highlight her faith or using more biblical and moral language to discuss and defend her policies during the 2016 campaign, but the Democrat spoke fairly frequently about these matters. In January, an Iowa resident asked Clinton how her policies aligned with the Ten Commandments. Clinton responded that she was "a person of faith," "a Christian," and "a Methodist." Christians, she insisted, constantly pondered "what we are called to do and how we are asked to do it." Her study of the Bible and conversations with other Christians had convinced her that "the most important commandment is to love the Lord with all your might and to love your neighbor as yourself." Christ implored his followers to do this, and the Bible was replete with calls to care for the poor, visit prisoners, welcome strangers, and lift up the downtrodden. Clinton was awed by people who consistently followed Christ's instructions to turn the other cheek, go the extra mile, and forgive others. She regretted that Christianity, "which has such great love at its core, is sometimes used to condemn so quickly and judge so harshly." Clinton insisted that she continually tried to do better and to be kinder and more loving, even toward those who treated her harshly.[60] Evangelical ethicist David Gushee commended Clinton for defending "a love and service version of Christianity congenial to mainline Protestants," affirming "strong, faith-based religious, moral, and political convictions," recognizing that "people's life experiences shape how they interpret faith," and expressing "respect for and commonality with people of other religions."[61]

In early February, Clinton met with about one hundred Black clergy at Philadelphia's Bethel African Methodist Episcopal Church. "Systemic inequities," Clinton declared, afflicted the nation's economy, laws, schools, prisons, hospitals, and even its water supply. African Americans were almost three times as likely as whites to be denied a mortgage, and the median income for white families was more than twelve times that of Black families.[62] Bethel's pastor, Mark Tyler, was impressed by Clinton's understanding of the issues the Black community cared most about—jobs, education, violence, and treatment by the police. Tyler estimated that about half of the ministers who attended the meeting expressed support for Clinton.[63] Led by Cynthia Hale, senior pastor of Hope Christian Church in Decatur, Georgia; Otis Moss Jr., pastor emeritus of Olive Institutional Baptist Church in LaGrange, Georgia; and Kirbyjon Caldwell, head pastor of Windsor Village United Methodist Church in Houston, the clergy laid hands on Clinton to anoint her for the presidency. "Until He [Christ] comes again, Secretary Clinton and President-to-be Clinton," they proclaimed in unison, "we decree and declare from the crown of your head to the soles of your feet that the favor of the Lord will surround you like a shield, in Jesus' name."[64] Responding to this anointing and undoubtedly speaking for many religious conservatives, a blogger wrote, "When a candidate idolizes Margaret Sanger and is a darling of Emily's List [a political action committee that sought to elect Democratic female candidates who supported abortion rights], conservatives need to run, not walk, in the other direction." God was displeased with Americans for slaughtering more than "one million babies per year in the womb" and embracing homosexual marriage, he added. Christians must not "remain mum about this tragic court-approved holocaust."[65]

At a town hall in February, Clinton declared, "I am a person of faith" who was raised in the church and has struggled to reconcile "ambition and humility" and "service and self-gratification." She explained that she was constantly asking how to fill a position as powerful as president of the United States without losing "track of who I am, what I believe in and what I want to do to serve." Clinton had never discovered an "absolute answer, like, 'OK, universe, here I am, watch me roar' or oh, 'my gosh, I can't do it, it's just overwhelming, I have to retreat.'" Reading the works of Dutch theologian Henri Nouwen, she testified, had helped her "practice the discipline of gratitude. So regardless of how hard the days are, how difficult the decisions are," she strove to "be grateful."[66]

In her concession speech on the night of the New Hampshire primary, Clinton again stressed that her Methodist faith had motivated her to pursue a life of service. It had impelled her to work at the Children's Defense Fund to expose racism in the schools of Alabama, reform juvenile justice in South Carolina, and aid children who went to bed hungry, were denied a quality education, or were abused or abandoned. She wanted everyone to be able to achieve their "own God-given potential."[67]

In late February 2016, Clinton spoke at three churches in the Kingstree, South Carolina, area.[68] A few days before Super Tuesday (March 1), when a large contingent of black evangelicals would be voting in southern states, Clinton appeared at the gospel music Stellar Awards, honoring African American artists. It was easy to become discouraged when facing troubles, she confessed to the audience, but when she heard a Christian song at church, on the radio, or sung by a friend, it lifted her spirits. She was especially moved by "His Eye Is on the Sparrow," which expressed what the gospel "means to so many of us." In an interview after this event, Clinton declared, "I am a person of faith . . . who finds inspiration and support and meaning in many different ways," including music.[69]

In early March, Clinton spoke at Holy Ghost Cathedral, a Pentecostal congregation in a hardscrabble Detroit neighborhood, one of three Black churches she visited that Sunday. She was introduced by the church's pastor, Corletta Vaughn, who testified that the former first lady had taught many "women how to stand [fast] in the face of adversity." Clinton testified that her faith and belief in God's saving grace had long guided and strengthened her. During difficult times in her life, she had often been struck by the story of the Prodigal Son. After his son had deeply disappointed him but then repented, the father embraced the wayward son, dressed him in his finest clothes, and prepared a banquet in his honor. This example, Clinton explained, had led her to forgive her husband for his sexual transgressions and reminded her to "practice the discipline of gratitude every day" even "when it doesn't feel" she had much for which to be thankful.[70]

In late April, the Clinton campaign released a sixty-second commercial titled "Love and Kindness." The text on the screen included her favorite Methodist maxim. The commercial trumpeted some widely accepted values—goodness, compassion, and hope. The soundtrack evoked a gospel quartet, and one columnist argued that the commercial could have been titled "Agape and Chesed"—the Greek word that describes the unconditional love of God and the Hebrew word for kindness.[71]

On the last Sunday in April, Clinton visited Trinity Baptist Church, a Southern Baptist congregation in North Philadelphia. Cathy Johnson, the church's assistant pastor, insisted that "Clinton's comfort with scripture and the nuances of the Baptist church are not something you can fake." Clinton "had a connection with her faith," Johnson added, that could not be "conjure[d] up for political opportunity." Clinton proclaimed that faith and prayer were very important to her. She admitted that "lots of days I fall short, but I get up and try again the next day."[72]

During her campaign, Clinton sometimes met with groups of clergy, usually African American ones. For example, in June 2015, she discussed her Methodist faith, regular study of the Bible, and frequent church attendance with Black pastors at Christ the King United Church of Christ in Florissant, Missouri, near Ferguson, a destitute Black community where protests against a predominately white police force had erupted in violence the previous summer.[73]

While campaigning for the presidency, Clinton continued her long quest to reconcile her head and heart, to combine the best aspects of conservativism and liberalism, that began during her high school years. In a 2014 interview, Clinton had recommended E. J. Dionne's *Our Divided Political Heart* (2012), because it described how almost everybody "has some conservative and liberal impulses." "Just as individuals have to reconcile" these instincts within themselves, she said, the political system has to do so "to function productively." During her campaign, Clinton exhorted Americans to express "more love and kindness," to search for common ground, and to listen carefully to each other.[74]

On July 8, 2016, Clinton spoke to several thousand African Methodist Epis-copal Church members in Philadelphia who were celebrating the two hundredth anniversary of their denomination's founding. She praised their commitment to following the Lord's requirement in the book of Micah "to do justice, love kind-ness, and to walk humbly with your God." She concurred with President Obama that "the church is the 'beating heart' of the African American community," the "place where people worship, study, grieve and rejoice without fear of persecution or mistreatment." Her experience as a lifelong Methodist had taught her how important the church is. She quoted Proverbs 2:2: "Incline our ears to wisdom and apply our hearts to understanding," to underscore the benefits of people listening to one another. She also quoted from 1 Corinthians 13 to argue that "love [is] the greatest virtue, necessary to keep faith and hope alive and to give us direction." She called for ending the structural racism plaguing the nation, rebuilding communities, and helping police and community residents to work cooperatively. Clinton exhorted AME Christians to "not grow weary in doing good"—"for in due season, we shall reap, if we do not lose heart" (Galatians 6:9). She concluded, "There are lost lives to redeem, bright futures to claim. Let us go forth . . . with a sense of heartfelt love and commitment."[75] At the end of July, Clinton and vice-presidential candidate Tim Kaine visited the Sunday morning service of Imani Temple Ministries, an African American congregation in Cleveland. Clinton discussed her faith, stressed the importance of improving the economy, and pledged "to lift up everybody in America."[76]

As Clinton prepared to speak to the National Baptist Convention in Kansas City, Missouri, in September, *Washington Post* columnist Jennifer Rubin ad-vised her to "send a message to a wider audience of religious Americans" about her faith. Running against a foe "who is a moral toxic waste dump" gave Clinton an opening to woo religious voters. If she presented "her religious experience in a genuine way, without hint of moral condescension, voters might see her in a different light." Rubin also counseled Clinton to emphasize the important role that religion had played in American history, from abolitionism to civil rights to environmental protection, to show evangelicals that religious liberals were willing to discuss faith in the public square.[77]

In her address to the National Baptist Convention, the nation's largest African American denomination with more than eight million members, Clinton strove to present herself as "a kinder, gentler candidate" by highlighting her Method-ist faith.[78] After admitting that talking about her faith was challenging for a "Midwestern Methodist," the Democratic nominee spent half an hour quoting the Bible, hymns, and Francis of Assisi to describe her "activist, social justice faith—a roll-up-your-sleeves-and-get-your-hands-dirty faith." Clinton declared, "I am grateful for the gift of personal salvation and for the great obligation of the social gospel to use the gift of grace wisely." Her faith, she asserted, had led her to devote her life to serving others. As a Sunday school teacher, she had taught the "hard lesson" that Jesus did not ask or urge his followers to love one another; rather, he commanded them to do so. This mandate was "at the core of our Christian faith." Saint Francis allegedly stated, "Try to preach the gospel always, and, if necessary, use words." While emulating Saint Francis, she had also long striven to follow the prophet Micah's prescription to "do justice, love kindness and walk humbly with our God." America's greatest leaders, Clinton insisted, were "often the most humble because they recognize both the awesome responsibilities of power and the frailty of human action." She admitted that she had made mistakes and invoked the well-known lyrics of the hymn "Amazing Grace": "It's grace that lifts us up, grace that leads us home."[79]

Clinton stressed that her faith would guide her as president. Her family and church had instilled in her "a deep and abiding Christian faith and practice." Scripture, she added, "tells us that faith without works is dead. The Epistle of James tells us we cannot just be hearers of the word, we must be doers. And I believe that with all my heart." She strove "to reflect the love of God and follow the example of Jesus Christ" so as to promote "the greater good of God's beloved community," leading her to spend her life "serving others, especially children." "It would have been easier and certainly more remunerative to follow many of my law school classmates to a high-powered New York law firm," she explained. "But the call to service rooted in my faith was just too powerful." Therefore, she had instead worked with the Children's Defense Fund to help children with disabilities, juvenile delinquents, and victims of racism. Every child needed "clean water to drink, clean air to breathe and good schools no matter what zip code they live in." Clinton praised the work of Triumph Baptist Church, a Black congregation in Philadelphia, which, guided by "the three E's of evangelism, education, and economic development," had established a credit union to provide loans to small businesses, built a supermarket, and aided many impoverished families. She promised to provide universal prekindergarten and make college affordable for everyone.[80]

Because of their "limitations and imperfections," Clinton told Black Baptists, Christ's followers "must reach out beyond ourselves to God and to each other." The Christian faith, she proclaimed, "is a journey that never ends. It's a constant challenge to live up to our own hopes and ideals, to love and to forgive others as we want to be loved and forgiven ourselves." Americans, Clinton argued, needed "a president who understands the powerful role that faith, and communities of faith" had long played in promoting justice.[81]

In her address, Clinton pledged to combat systemic racism, reform the criminal justice system, increase the national minimum wage, ensure that women received equal pay, restore high school vocational programs, stop efforts to limit voting rights, and support other policies that translated "love into action." Her rival, Clinton contended, had "a long history of racial discrimination" in his businesses and trafficked "in toxic conspiracy theories, like the lie that President Obama is not a true American." Clinton insisted that as secretary of state she had wrestled with many hard choices that drove her to her knees. The nation, she asserted, needed "a president who will pray with you and for you."[82] Illustrating the challenges Clinton confronted in discussing her faith, Sarah Levin, a spokesperson for the Secular Coalition, complained that "Americans do not 'need' a candidate to pray for or with them." Instead, they needed one who would "lead effectively and represent the values shared by Americans of all faiths and of no faith."[83]

Some pundits argued that Clinton was focusing too much on tearing down Trump and not enough on putting forth positive proposals. Recognizing that many prospective voters disliked and distrusted her, Clinton's aides encouraged her to show Americans that she would help solve their problems and to offer "an uplifting vision" for the nation's future. This prompted Clinton to issue in early September a 288-page policy book titled *Stronger Together*, which included dozens of distinct policy proposals.[84] Clinton also vowed to accentuate the positive—"to give Americans something to vote for, not just against."[85]

Clinton conceded in mid-September that even though she had been campaigning for eighteen months, many Americans still did not clearly understand what motivated her or what her priorities as president would be. As a result, during the last six weeks of the campaign, the Democratic nominee attempted to reintroduce herself and her key ideas to the nation. She sought both to garner support for her agenda and produce a mandate that, if she were elected, would help pressure Congress to adopt her policies. Clinton continued, however, to have trouble selling herself and her message; polls showed that only about one-third of the electorate viewed her as honest and trustworthy, about the same percentage who saw Trump as possessing these qualities.[86]

With "Do All the Good," a shortened version of Wesley's dictum, serving as a backdrop, Clinton told supporters in Fort Pierce, Florida, in early October that she wanted to conclude her campaign by highlighting ways to improve opportunities for children, aid struggling families, and promote the virtues of volunteerism.[87] Although she focused more on her faith, experience, and public-service goals and less on trying to discredit Trump, polls showed him gaining on Clinton during those last six weeks.

While discussing her faith, the Bible, and religious matters during her 2016 campaign, Clinton received emails from both Burn Strider, her 2008 faith adviser, and Bill Shillady that provided spiritual encouragement. Clinton and Shillady met in 2002, and thereafter their families often spent Easter, Christmas, and other holidays together. Shillady officiated at Chelsea's wedding in 2010 and at a memorial service for Dorothy Rodham, Clinton's mother, in 2011. Shillady began sending Clinton daily devotionals around Easter 2015 that included short scriptural passages, brief commentaries about them, and prayers. During the last several months of the 2016 campaign, Shillady assembled a team of Christians, including numerous young female pastors, to write these devotionals. Clinton insisted that these devotionals helped keep her grounded during the intense pressure of the campaign.[88]

Some Democrats urged Clinton to do more to appeal to nonreligious Americans. Hemant Mehtais, the editor of FriendlyAtheist.com, argued in July that Clinton was "missing a golden opportunity to solidify and grow her base" by not reaching out more aggressively to Americans with no religious affiliation. While the candidates considered the country's 55 million Hispanics pivotal to the election, they largely ignored its 56 million nonreligious citizens. These prospective voters were not asking Clinton to denounce her Methodist faith or change her views, he insisted. They simply wanted her to promise to prevent religious groups from using taxpayer money to discriminate against LGBT individuals and to fight to provide comprehensive sex education in schools, reproductive choice, scientific literacy, environmental protection, and greater funding for the National Institutes of Health. Unless Clinton did more to motivate religiously unaffiliated Americans to vote for her, Mehtais warned, they might cast ballots for third-party candidates or not vote at all.[89]

The Democratic National Convention

On the eve of the Democratic National Convention in Philadelphia in late July, Michael Gerson, a former speechwriter for George W. Bush, argued that Trump's "angry, secular message" provided an opening for Clinton and Kaine to appeal to religious voters. Republican senators described Kaine as "very bright" and "unfailingly courteous and positive." The deeply spiritual senator from Virginia fluently spoke "the language of Catholic social thought, in the dialect of Pope Francis." Millions of Catholics who viewed immigration positively and sought to base their political policies on moral principles might respond to religiously based appeals by the Democratic candidates. Many Latino Catholics and some theologically conservative Catholics, Gerson emphasized, were repulsed by Trump's personality, manner, and message. For example, George Weigel, a prominent Catholic conservative, called Trump "utterly unfit by experience, intellect, or character to be president of the United States." Clinton had to overcome several obstacles at the convention, Gerson asserted, most significantly her alleged dishonesty and untrustworthiness, her lackluster appeal to younger voters, and her difficulty communicating her core convictions. To do so, Clinton could employ the language of mainline Protestantism on social justice, of Catholic social thought, and of the African American civil rights tradition to stress the religious ideal of the common good.[90] DuMez similarly exhorted Clinton to speak more explicitly about her faith, especially since the religious right had "vacated all pretense of seeking a candidate who embodies Christian values."[91]

Religion played a significant role at the convention. Every session began and closed with prayer. Some sessions discussed outreach to faith communities, as mainline Protestants, Black Protestants, Muslims, and leaders of other religious groups urged the party to marry faith with public action. Signs declaring "Do All the Good" blanketed the convention hall.[92] The "Nuns on the Bus" tour ended its three-week, thirteen-state campaign to promote social justice at the convention. African Methodist Episcopal Church bishop Vashti McKenzie told delegates that Christians had a responsibility to save souls, help the needy, and alleviate social evils.[93] "Religion was everywhere at the DNC," one columnist explained, although "it rarely felt overpowering, or even explicitly Christian." Nevertheless, she observed, numerous Democrats claimed that Christian teaching provided a foundation for LGBTQ rights, a woman's right to choose abortion, and constructing "a coalition that reflects the nation's diversity."[94]

The convention elevated the language of love and the importance of faith in ways that many people belonging to various faith communities valued. Senator Cory Booker of New Jersey insisted, "We are called to be a nation of love," while William Barber II, a Protestant pastor who had led "Moral Mondays" civil rights protests in North Carolina, declared, "We must shock this nation with the power of love." The convention floor was filled with placards proclaiming "Love Trumps Hate." In numerous performances and cameo appearances, musical stars accentuated the biblical triad of faith, hope, and love. Some commentators noted that Trump's disparagement of Mexican immigrants, Muslims, the disabled, African American protesters, and women, and his popularity with white supremacists and anti-Semites opened the door for Democrats to declare themselves the party of lovingkindness. Speaking for many progressive Protestants, Otis Moss III, Jeremiah Wright's successor at Trinity United Church of Christ in Chicago, rejoiced that love had been "discussed explicitly and implicitly" at the convention. Omid Safi, the director of Duke University's Islamic Studies Center, stated that the convention's rhetoric frequently embodied one of the Qur'an's most-known verses: "God commands you to engage in love and justice" (16:90), while Sikh activist and filmmaker Valarie Kaur saw the convention as reflecting her faith's emphasis on serving God and humanity through "relentless love." A University of Notre Dame theology professor noted that some heard the Democrats' "love language" as distinctively Christian, while others heard it as a more secular form of spirituality.[95]

Gerson was disappointed by Clinton's acceptance speech at the convention. Republicans had failed "shockingly" and "disturbingly" at their convention to describe "America's unifying ideals," but so had Clinton. Her husband had labeled her a "change maker," and Obama had argued she had the "intelligence" and "judgment" to continue his administration's best policies, but Hillary had presented herself "as conventional, normal and safe, in sharp contrast to a small, unstable man 'moved by fear and pride.'" She briefly mentioned her Methodist faith, but it was disconnected from "the rest of her reasoning— more an ornament than a foundation." The nation's two principal parties, Gerson lamented, had "chosen the untrusted [to run] against the unstable, the uninspiring against the unfit."[96]

The Tim Kaine Factor

Clinton chose a running mate, Tim Kaine, who shared her robust progressive Christian faith.[97] The former governor of Virginia had attended a Jesuit high school and spent a year during his Harvard Law School studies working for a Jesuit mission in Honduras. His experience there rejuvenated his commitment to Catholicism. Jesuits are the most theologically liberal and socially engaged Catholic order, a tradition Kaine ardently embraced. For thirty years, Kaine and his wife had worshipped at a predominantly African American Catholic church in Richmond, where he cofounded and led a men's Bible study.[98] "My faith," he declared, "is central to everything I do." Like the Good Samaritan, he strove to care for others.[99] Clinton's choice of Kaine as her running mate was politically astute, since Catholics were an important constituency in several closely contested states, including Pennsylvania, Ohio, Wisconsin, and Michigan. Many prospective voters in these pivotal battleground states seemed to resonate with Kaine's Catholic background.[100]

In introducing Kaine at the Democratic National Convention, Rep. Bobby Scott of Virginia insisted that few people practiced the injunction from Micah to "act justly and to love mercy and to walk humbly with your God" as fully as the Democratic vice-presidential candidate. In his acceptance speech, Kaine declared that his Catholic faith determined his life's mission and was "the North Star" directing his actions. He stressed the importance of "faith, family and work," quoted Jesus' commandment to "love [our] neighbors as ourselves," and argued that Clinton's faith had prepared her well to be president.[101]

A *Newsweek* columnist predicted that Kaine might be "a game-changer" for the Democrats if he could attract moderate Republicans who were disenchanted with Trump's extremism. Kaine represented mainstream post–Vatican II Catholicism, with its emphasis on caring for the poor, fighting for racial justice, and opposing the death penalty. Kaine had spoken frequently about his faith—almost as much as his Republican counterpart Mike Pence.[102] Kaine insisted that Clinton's powerful spiritual experiences as a youth still drove her strong faith. Their shared faith and commitment to service intensified the bond between them.[103]

Kaine personally opposed abortion but maintained that women should have the right to make their own decisions about the matter. His view on abortion was shared by many Americans: he personally opposed it but believed the government should allow women to make their own choices rather than forcing his moral view on them. After consulting their own consciences and their partners and pastors, women should decide whether to continue their pregnancies. As Virginia's governor, he had supported parental consent requirements and a ban on "partial-birth" abortions. Accepting the position of the Roman Catholic Church, he had long opposed same-sex marriage and permitting gay adults to adopt children, but by 2013 he had changed his stance on these issues. "All people, regardless of sexual orientation," he insisted in that year, "should be guaranteed the full rights to the legal benefits and responsibilities of marriage under the Constitution."[104]

During his debate with Pence in October, Kaine described the Jesuit missionaries he had worked with in Honduras as his heroes. Like Clinton, he believed that Christians should fully and enthusiastically live by the teachings of their faith. Despite testifying strongly to their faith, neither Clinton nor Kaine could claim as Pence did to have a personal conversion experience. In words that resonated with evangelicals, Pence testified, "my Christian faith became real for me when I made a personal decision for Christ when I was a freshman in college."[105] Of course, Trump could not make such a statement either.

After the vice-presidential debate, Cal Thomas trained his guns on Kaine. He noted that the Democrat frequently mentioned his Catholic faith and called his mission trip to Honduras in 1980 a "turning point" in his life. What Kaine omitted from his narrative, Thomas complained, was that he had been exposed to liberation theology taught by Catholic priests who supported Marxist efforts to violently overthrow Latin American governments. Kaine, like Vice President Joe Biden, Secretary of State John Kerry, and House Minority Leader Nancy Pelosi, rejected the teaching of numerous popes on social issues. Kaine's argument that people should "celebrate, not challenge" the "beautiful diversity of the human family" could "legitimize a multitude of sins." Maureen Ferguson of the Catholic Association argued that Kaine's position clashed with Pope Francis's March 2016 encyclical *Amoris Laetitia*, which stated, "There are absolutely no grounds for considering homosexual unions to be in any way similar or even remotely analogous to God's plan for marriage and family." Another spokesperson for this organization protested that Kaine's claim that the Catholic Church should change its views on marriage and the family was consistent with Clinton's argument that pro-life people of faith needed to change their position about abortion. Both statements exposed "the Clinton campaign's profoundly anti-Catholic ideological agenda."[106]

Testimonies to Clinton's Faith

During the campaign, numerous friends, associates, fellow politicians, and journalists testified that Clinton's faith was very important to her life and work. Many of Clinton's closest confidants described her as "a devout Methodist" whose faith guided her actions. Bill frequently told audiences that to understand his wife, people must examine her Methodist faith. He insisted that she lived by the last line of a hymn that proclaimed, "If I can help someone as I travel on, then my living would not be in vain."[107] Democratic strategist and businessman Richard Socarides, who worshipped with the Clintons at Foundry Methodist Church in the 1990s, insisted that Hillary's "exceptionally strong faith" had shaped her political policies, especially those regarding children, families, and refugees.[108] Kaine frequently introduced Clinton at rallies as someone who, inspired by her faith, had been "battling hard for families and kids, long before she was in office."[109] Stumping for Clinton in North Carolina a few days before the election, Barack Obama declared that her "North Star" was the Methodist creed to "do all the good you can."[110] *Washington Post* columnist E. J. Dionne argued that Clinton "is authentically religious." She had "thought seriously about what the Scriptures teach" and her Christian faith deeply impacted her view of the world. Her religious views, he added, shaped "many of the choices she has made in her life."[111] Duke historian William Chafe argued that the values instilled in Clinton by her Methodist social gospel heritage served as "the anchor of her life."[112]

A political activist asserted that Clinton was at "her core a true Methodist and devout public servant" who embodied the charge in the United Methodist Church's *Book of Discipline* that church members should "live lovingly and justly as servants of Christ." Methodists were called to heal the sick, and she had promoted affordable health care; to feed the hungry, and as secretary of state, she had established the Feed the Future initiative on global hunger and poverty; to care for strangers, and she had advocated immigration reform and generous responses to humanitarian crises around the globe; to free the oppressed, and as first lady and secretary of state, she had championed human rights, especially those of women and LGBT individuals; to provide "a compassionate, caring presence," and as a senator, she had comforted and aided families who lost loved ones on 9/11; to work "to develop social structures that are consistent with the gospel," and she had cofounded Arkansas Advocates for Children and Families and helped create the Children's Health Insurance Program. If elected, Clinton would "bring this commitment to justice and service into the White House."[113]

Otis Moss Jr. endorsed Clinton because of her qualifications, preparation, and dedication. He praised her "intellect, courage under fire," and "fervent and enduring faith in God." She had been reared in "the dynamic faith of the United Methodist Church" and profoundly respected Christian, Jewish, Muslim, Hindu, Buddhist, and Sikh faith traditions. Clinton refused "to grow weary in doing what is good, right and just for all humankind." She had, Moss averred, "a long record of dedication to the great causes of history," including "the struggles for justice, equal pay, worker protection, ecology and environment, voter rights and protections." Clinton had worked for four decades to provide "excellent education for everyone" and "economic justice for the poor," to aid the marginalized and the vulnerable, and to protect children and families.[114]

E. J. Dionne argued that Clinton brought together two central components of the Methodist faith: the individual and the community. While the "upright Midwestern Methodist" focused on personal salvation as expressed in dedication to duty, determination, and diligent work, Clinton's commitment to community was evident in her policy proposals and values; her campaign slogan in 2008 was "All of Us Together," and in 2016 it was "Stronger Together."[115] Some Americans accused Clinton of relentlessly pursuing power, humorist Garrison Keillor maintained, but she was instead practicing "the good habits of a serious Methodist. Be steady. Don't give up. It's not about you. Work for the night is coming."[116]

Journalist Bill Moyers and historian Michael Winship objected to this portrait. They contended that Clinton had indeed been "weaned on the social ethics of John Wesley," who was a "courageous champion of the poor and needy," but her years in Washington had led the Democrat to focus on doing well rather than doing good. She had marinated for so long "in the culture of wealth, influence, and power" as to conclude that a person's "own power in democracy is more important than democracy itself"; now it would require "a conversion worthy of John Wesley" for her to reject that mind-set.[117]

Clinton's Image Problem

As she campaigned, Clinton dealt with an image problem. As one pundit put it, "Clinton is the living embodiment of a Rorschach test—a perfect reflection of every negative and positive attribute cast upon her." Questions about her authenticity had dogged Clinton for twenty-five years. To win the election, she needed to convince many skeptical voters, especially independent ones, that her frequent citing of the works of Henri Nouwen was not "a premeditated ploy" but rather "a window into her soul"—that she truly was "a pragmatic, yet tireless fighter for the least of these."[118]

Clinton had great difficulty displaying "the funny, kind, passionate woman her friends and colleagues insist actually exists." Many maintained that she hid "her true personality behind a hard, defensive shell of anodyne comments and legalistic language." Clinton feared that if she revealed her true feelings, she would be attacked even more ferociously. Since Michael Kelly's 1993 "Saint Hillary" article, Clinton complained, she had often been viewed "as a moralistic, know-it-all crusader" who reminded people of their boss or mother-in-law. Her political opponents and much of the news media depicted her as "deceitful, cold and distant," but her personality, life experiences, and personal philosophy made it difficult to discuss her feelings. One friend explained that Clinton's stubbornness bordered on self-righteousness. She resisted talking about herself because she believed politicians should focus on issues and policies.[119] Chafe contended that if Clinton wanted "to earn the trust and respect of the American electorate" and prevent people from seeing her principally as a Wall Street insider who strove to line her own pockets and accrue power, "she must talk a lot more about who she really is and how her character was shaped." She needed to discuss how the values she learned from her dedicated mother and her passionate youth minister had "guided virtually all of her political activities," especially her efforts to advance women's rights, improve the health and education of children, and promote racial equality.[120]

Entering the final phase of the campaign, Clinton continued to confront questions about her trustworthiness. The debate over which Hillary was the real one raged on. Many friends and coworkers argued that she had spent her life fulfilling her Methodist calling to "do all the good you can," while many prospective voters continued to believe that she was "willing to do anything or change any position to accomplish her ambitions."[121]

Mendacity and Money

Two issues especially tarnished Clinton's image: her alleged lying and financial improprieties. Few politicians have had to deal with more charges that they engaged in unsavory, immoral, and illegal activities than Hillary Clinton. By 2016, the Clintons had been the subject of more than twenty official investigations concerning Whitewater, the windfall profits Hillary earned by trading cattle futures, the White House travel office "scandal," the suicide of Vince Foster, and Filegate (in which a low-level White House staff member improperly requested the FBI files of some politicians), but they had produced little damning evidence of wrongdoing.

"From the firings of White House travel office employees in 1993 to the 2015 email scandal that still haunts this campaign," Ron Fournier argued in

The Atlantic, "Clinton has a history of deflections, deception, and untruths." Clinton had knowingly misled the public on some matters. Her supporters' claim that she had been the victim of despicable attacks by Republican extremists had some merit, Fournier acknowledged, but they did not give Clinton a "free pass" to distort the truth. Even her admirers admitted that she had a "credibility deficit." During the Democratic primaries, people who wanted to support an honest, trustworthy candidate had voted overwhelmingly for Bernie Sanders, according to exit polls. Since she could not persuade many voters that she had always been honest, Fournier advised her to try to convince them that "she's *their* liar—she's on *their* side" and that Trump lied as much or more.[122] A Fox News survey in early August revealed that both Clinton and Trump were considered "honest and trustworthy" by only 36 percent of prospective voters.[123]

Trump repeatedly decried Clinton as "Crooked Hillary," and her actions, especially her use of a private email server as secretary of state, her mishandling of the 2012 assault on the US diplomatic compound in Benghazi, Libya, the allegations that her family foundation gave donors political access in exchange for their contributions, and the various accusations during her years as first lady, gave him lots of ammunition. Because Clinton could not match Trump's invective, innuendo, and slander, pundits advised her to simply denounce his barbs as untrue and focus on substantive issues.[124]

New York Times columnist David Brooks argued similarly that many Americans were wary of Clinton because she typically responded to attacks with secretiveness, thereby projecting coldness, weakness, and indignation. He encouraged her to "answer the 'Lock Her Up' enmity" by candidly describing what it feels like to be embroiled in political combat, encased in a "global celebrity role." If Clinton engaged in sincere self-appraisal and even displayed some remorse for her failures, the world would root for her instead of against her.[125]

Clinton's claim that FBI Director James Comey had confirmed the truthfulness of her answers regarding her private email account only increased doubts about her honesty, which Trump fueled. The *Washington Post*'s Fact Checker blog, operated by Glenn Kessler, rated Clinton's response as "Four Pinocchios," a label used to characterize "whoppers." Kessler accused Clinton of "cherry-picking" statements Comey made to avoid "the more disturbing findings of the FBI investigation."[126] "The *Washington Post* calls out #CrookedHillary for what she REALLY is," Trump tweeted. "A PATHOLOGICAL LIAR! Watch that nose grow!"[127] Fournier faulted Clinton for telling another unnecessary lie and giving undecided voters another reason to distrust her. Nevertheless,

Clinton's misdeed was "not as disturbing as Trump's mendacity, megalomania, intolerance, and intellectual slovenliness." Fournier urged Clinton's advisers, prominent Democrats, and liberal pundits to counsel her to stop lying. Disregarding this advice, she made no confessions and instead continued to argue that the "relentless" attacks on her since 1992 had been proven false.[128]

Clinton's financial practices also provoked controversy during the campaign and cost her votes. Detractors complained that the Clinton fortune (more than $50 million by 2016) clashed with the Methodist emphasis on helping others that she claimed guided her life. Clinton was especially criticized for raking in more than $21 million in speaking fees from various groups, including Wall Street firms, after resigning as secretary of state. Half of all prospective voters were bothered "a lot" by these honoraria. Trump argued that Clinton was "totally owned by Wall Street," while other Republicans contended that her cozy relationship with large firms would undermine her promise to regulate them.[129] Others protested that Hillary had not established appropriate boundaries between the State Department and the otherwise praiseworthy Clinton Foundation.[130]

Clinton, asserted Michael Tomasky of *The Daily Beast*, was not nearly as crooked as many Americans believed. Most of what had been written about her in the last twenty-five years was either grossly exaggerated or simply untrue. Upset that Clinton had defied so many social conventions, her conservative opponents were trying to persuade Americans that she was immoral, unfeminine, and a dangerous radical. Tomasky argued that two federal investigations had produced no proof that the first lady hid her billing records in the Whitewater case. Clinton had handled the White House travel office "scandal" ineptly, but it did not involve any ethical breaches. The claims that the Clintons had ordered the murder of Vince Foster and that he and Hillary had an affair were totally unsubstantiated. Three different bodies had investigated Filegate, and even Kenneth Starr had exonerated her on that issue. By 2016, forty-five books attacking Hillary had been published. Most of them ripped quotations out of context and used material from unconfirmed sources to depict her as "a scheming, lying, ambitious, unpatriotic harridan." Tomasky acknowledged that Clinton's use of a private e-mail server as secretary of state was indefensible, her acceptance of a huge speaking fee from Goldman Sachs was incomprehensible, and the Clintons' focus on wealth in the past few years was excessive. However, 80 percent of the criticisms of Hillary since 1992 were simply false. More than twenty official bodies employing very skilled investigators had painstakingly scrutinized her actions. If she had truly "done something unlawful or deeply unethical," Tomasky asked, would not one of these investigations have "found the goods?" More lies had been told about Clinton than any other figure in American history.[131]

An Illinois newspaper noted similarly that for a quarter century Clinton had endured "unabating, vicious political attacks," many caused by her own shortcomings, but most springing from a combination of conspiracy theories exaggeration, jealousy, and, sexism.[132] How many other people, a commentator asked, would be "so brave and open in our public personas after being subjected to 25 years of unrelenting and downright nasty criticism of what we say, what we do, and how we look?"[133]

Hillary and Hate Mongering: Clinton as the Devil

The 2016 presidential campaign was among the nastiest in American history. Clinton and Trump were not tarred and feathered, but their reputations were besmirched, and they were continually charged with grievous misdeeds. Although Trump was frequently compared with Adolf Hitler and accused of having a personality disorder, Clinton was castigated even more than her Republican rival. Trump repeatedly excoriated Clinton, as did twenty-five-year-old social media exploiter Emily Longworth, right-wing political commentator Dinesh D'Souza, and Texan radio host Alex Jones. Longworth's obscenity-laced tirades denouncing Clinton attracted hundreds of thousands of viewers on YouTube and Facebook. She was also the public face of an organization that sold T-shirts and merchandise emblazoned with "Hillary for Prison." Clinton, Longworth argued, "is a lying, manipulative, narcissistic woman who deserves" to be incarcerated for life. At Trump rallies, some of his zealous supporters shouted "Lock her up!," while others called Clinton "the servant of Satan" and used hashtags such as #Killary on social media.[134]

In his film *Hillary's America: The Secret History of the Democratic Party*, the top-grossing documentary of 2016, D'Souza accused Clinton of deceitful motives, dishonesty, and immoral actions. The review aggregation website Metacritic gave the film four Golden Raspberry Awards, including Worst Picture, the first one it ever awarded to a documentary, and the film received the second-lowest score in the site's history. A *Boston Herald* columnist decried *Hillary's America* as "an embarrassment to propaganda films," but a *National Review* article, while admitting that the documentary "is over the top in places and definitely selective," claimed that its "troubling facts are accurate." Jones, meanwhile, hosted a syndicated talk show broadcasted throughout the country and sponsored the InfoWars website, each of which had an audience of millions. Labeled "the most prolific conspiracy theorist in contemporary America," Jones censured Clinton as "a witch" who had embraced evil.[135]

The most damning (pun intended) and amazingly frequent accusation was that Clinton was the devil. The claim that women did the devil's work began in the Garden of Eden, and Clinton was not the first female presidential candidate to be linked with Satan. That "honor" belonged to Victoria Woodhull, who during her 1872 campaign for the nation's highest office was nicknamed "Mrs. Satan" because her views about "free love," marriage as a form of slavery, and easy divorce flouted conventional American norms.[136] Author Susan Faludi argued that the Hillary-as-devil motif began in 1992 when she "was anointed the feminine face of evil." Although she was not on the Democratic ticket in 1996, Hillary was cast as a demon helping subsidize the entire radical feminist agenda, held responsible for the murder of Vince Foster, and portrayed as a member of a satanic cult. Many men, Faludi maintained, blamed Clinton for their perceived decline in status and influence as society redefined power and success in terms of celebrity, downplayed the value of hard work, and challenged men's role as providers. Men protested that the first lady had used their tax dollars to fund women's rights around the world and pay for abortions and had called "the shots at the White House." Republican ideology combined with male insecurity, Faludi averred, led many to demonize Clinton. Right-wing politicians recognized that "the Hillary-with-horns specter" was a valuable fundraising tool, and she became a scapegoat for wounded male pride and anxiety about shifting values.[137]

At the July Republican National Convention, New Jersey Governor Chris Christie conducted a mock witch trial for Clinton. Former candidate Ben Carson compared Clinton with the devil because of her association with Saul Alinsky, the radical organizer who had admiringly referred to Satan on the dedication page of his 1971 book *Rules for Radicals*. Those who connected the dots, Carson argued, could easily see "the Alinsky-Lucifer-Clinton triangle." Americans, he contended, were being invited to elect a president "who has as their role model somebody who acknowledges Lucifer" and who rejected Christ's teachings by advocating killing babies, redefining marriage, and destroying the traditional family. If Americans continued to allow secular progressives "to take God out of our lives, God will remove himself from us," Carson warned.[138]

On August 1, Trump insisted that Clinton's leading Democratic challenger, Bernie Sanders, had "made a deal with the devil" by endorsing her. He had previously accused the Vermont senator of making this Faustian bargain, but this time Trump added, "She's the devil" (a claim he repeated during the October 9 presidential debate).[139] At the same time, a Public Policy Polling survey reported that 18 percent of likely voters believed that Clinton had a cordial relationship with Satan himself.[140] Dozens of websites claimed that "Hillary was actually a Satanist with demonic powers."[141] Henry Olsen, a senior fellow at the conservative Ethics and Public Policy Center, argued that in making this claim, Trump was "expressing what a lot of Republicans feel." No other mainstream American politician, Olsen added, would have dared to make such a declaration during the last one hundred years.[142] In late October, the Immaculate Conception Catholic Church in San Diego asserted in a leaflet and on its website that Satan was working through Clinton to promote abortion and declared voting for her a mortal sin. The devil had enticed many Christians to accept worldly values by using tactics outlined by Saul Alinsky to (in Clinton's own words) change "deep-seated cultural codes, religious beliefs and structural biases."[143]

Seeking to explain why so many Republicans accepted the premise that Clinton was, if not the devil incarnate, at least in league with him, a commentator contended in the *New Republic* that for more than two decades the political right had "caricatured Clinton as a power-hungry, corrupt she-devil." Republican leaders who had long depicted Clinton as a devious liar should not be surprised that many members of their base believed that she "really is the devil" and should be imprisoned. Ironically, after Trump secured their party's nomination, many prominent Republicans, who had at least tacitly accepted conspiracy theories about the Clintons and the Obamas, turned to "the 'corrupt,' 'crooked,' scandal—plagued, Benghazi-lying former secretary of state as their savior."[144] Mocking such claims, Alexandra Petri wrote in the *Washington Post* that before time began, "Hillary Clinton (Lucifer, Beelzebub, Lord of the Flies, Prince of Darkness, Satan) . . . [was] cast out of heaven for [her] overweening hubris." She was given two choices: reside in "eternal torment in a lake of fire surrounded by her fallen angels" or run for president as a female. After thousands of years of contemplation, she chose the second option.[145]

The *Access Hollywood* Tape and an "Excruciating" Choice

On October 7, a tape of *Access Hollywood*, a television program featuring events and celebrities in the entertainment industry, was released in which Trump made crude comments about groping women. The shocking revelation threatened to undercut religious conservatives' support of the Republican candidate. In his 1987 book, *The Art of the Deal*, Trump boasted about having sex with numerous married women, and in numerous interviews with Howard Stern in the 1990s and 2000s, he discussed his sexual exploits. But his vulgar remarks about grabbing women's genitals in this tape were especially offensive and came to public attention at a critical time in the campaign. Religious conservatives responded in a variety of ways.

Jerry Falwell Jr., James Dobson, Robert Jeffress, Tony Perkins, Ralph Reed, Franklin Graham, and Kenneth Copeland all continued to support Trump despite his lewd remarks. Either Democrats or establishment Republicans, they claimed, had released the video, which they had known about for weeks, strategically to inflict the maximum damage. Falwell called Trump's comments "reprehensible" and indefensible, but he emphasized that everyone sinned and that Trump was contrite and had apologized. Moreover, Falwell averred, the national debt was $20 trillion and the government needed to make major changes to prevent the nation from falling into the abyss. "I don't think the American people want this country to go down the toilet," Falwell declared, "because Donald Trump made some dumb comments on a videotape 11 years ago." If the Supreme Court became "stacked with liberals" who did not "honor the Constitution," Falwell added, no one would care about what Trump had said on a 2005 videotape. Instead, they would be wishing that "we had different Supreme Court justices."[146]

In December 2015, Dobson complained that Trump attacked people who disagreed with him, while also criticizing his operation of gambling enterprises. However, soon thereafter, Dobson declared his support for the entrepreneur, excusing his misbehavior and crude statements as resulting from him being a "baby Christian."[147] Dobson continued to endorse the Republican because he pledged to support "religious liberty and the dignity of the unborn," whereas Clinton "promises she will not."[148]

Jeffress insisted that Trump was "still the best candidate to reverse" the nation's "downward spiral." Although Trump's comments were "lewd, offensive, and indefensible," Hillary Clinton was not any more moral than him. Tony Perkins, the head of the Family Research Council, declared that he supported Trump not because of their shared values but because of their shared concerns about the Supreme Court, religious freedom, and national security.[149] During his second debate with Clinton two days after the tape was released, Trump argued that what Bill Clinton had done was "far worse." He had merely spoken, while Clinton had acted. No other politician, Trump claimed, had been "so abusive to women" as Bill Clinton.[150]

Ralph Reed, who headed Trump's religious advisory board, had argued in 1998 that the president's "character matters," but he downplayed Trump's

remarks about grabbing women's genitals.[151] Reed implored the religiously
devout to vote for the candidate who would "protect unborn life, defend religious freedom, grow the economy, appoint conservative judges and oppose the
Iran nuclear deal." A "10-year-old tape of a private conversation with a TV talk
show host," Reed claimed, was much less significant than Clinton's use of her
office to solicit funds from corporations and foreign governments to support
her family foundation, or her reckless and irresponsible use of a private email
server to handle classified material, thereby endangering national security.[152]

Trump's crude comments were indefensible, evangelist Franklin Graham
agreed, but so was "the godless progressive agenda of Barack Obama and
Hillary Clinton."[153] Graham advised Christians, "Hold your nose and go vote"
for the candidate "you would trust to appoint justices" who will "protect our
religious freedom as Christians."[154] Theologian Wayne Grunden renounced his
endorsement of Trump after the *Access Hollywood* tape was revealed, but he
reversed himself two weeks later and urged evangelicals to vote for Trump.
Committing adultery was immoral, he argued, but in a sinful world, voting
for morally flawed individuals was unavoidable. Christians should vote for
candidates who would best promote the United States' interests.[155]

Prosperity gospel proponent Kenneth Copeland warned Christians that
God would hold them morally accountable if they did not vote for Trump.
They would be complicit in the murder of every baby who was aborted after
the 2016 election. God would judge those who abandoned Trump as "guilty of
an abomination" because doing so might lead to "eight years of Hillary Clinton
and the worst mess anybody could make out of a nation." "This is God's nation,"
Copeland declared, "and nobody is going to take it away from him."[156]

Several prominent evangelical women, including Bible teacher Beth Moore,
singer Sara Groves, mental-health advocate Kay Warren (wife of Saddleback
Church's Rick Warren), popular authors Jen Hatmaker and Rachel Held Evans,
and Julie Roys, a host on the Moody Radio network, excoriated Trump's sexism
and misogyny and argued that his election would harm both women and the
Christian community. Warren tweeted, "As a victim of sexual assault, I tell you
firsthand of devastation wreaked on women & girls by predatory men & boys
who think women 'like it.'" On Instagram, Hatmaker called Trump's comments
a "travesty" and a "national disgrace," and insisted that Christians had several other options on election day.[157] Trump, she protested, had "consistently
normalized violence, sexual deviance, bigotry and hate speech. I wouldn't
accept this from my seventh-grade son, much less from a potential leader of
the free world."[158] Roys could not decide which made her sicker: "Listening to

Trump brag about groping women or listening to my fellow evangelicals defend him."[159] Evans exhorted evangelicals to castigate Trump for "calling women 'bitches' and 'pieces of ass.'"[160] More than twenty thousand women and men signed a petition on Change.org initiated by evangelicals, denouncing Trump's statements about women, Mexicans, immigrants, Muslims, and refugees.[161]

Some leading male evangelicals also denounced Trump's lewd comments, including megachurch pastor James MacDonald, a member of Trump's faith council. MacDonald labeled Trump's statement "misogynistic trash" that revealed him "to be lecherous and worthless" and declared he would not support the Republican nominee unless he demonstrated a "change of heart and direction."[162] Russell Moore and Albert Mohler continued to criticize Trump. Moore exhorted evangelicals to repudiate both the proabortion ethic of Margaret Sanger (represented by Clinton) and the lewd language of Howard Stern (exemplified by Trump).[163] Mohler argued that Trump's *Access Hollywood* video had "created an excruciating moment for evangelicals," a "crisis of conscience." How could they vote for Clinton, who threatened the values and causes they viewed "as vital to human flourishing"? Electing Clinton posed "a grave danger to unborn life and to values" that evangelicals considered "essential to America's cultural health and influence in the world." "Clinton's public positions and personal character," Mohler argued, disqualified her from serving as president. Her election would radically advance "liberal causes that will have lasting, perhaps irreversible consequences." On the other hand, Trump personified what evangelicals had long "preached (and voted) against": serial marriage, sexual immorality, and a fortune produced by promoting hedonism. Under normal circumstances, Trump would be viewed as embodying evangelicals' nightmares rather than carrying their hopes. Evangelical support for Trump, Mohler insisted, was "a horrifying embarrassment—a price for possible political gain that is simply unthinkable and too high to pay."[164] Was it morally defensible, Calvin University philosophy professor James K. A. Smith asked, to seek to preserve religious freedom by supporting a candidate who mocked Christian belief and practice?[165]

In mid-October, two leading evangelical magazines—*World* and *Christianity Today*—criticized both candidates. "Trump is generally reckless and Clinton generally ruthless," *World* editor Marvin Olasky declared. "Trump is a proud adulterer. Clinton is a proud pro-abortionist. Since character counts, both will almost certainly be presidential failures." He noted that many theologically and socially conservative Christians considered Clinton's platform and likelihood to appoint judges that would "turn federal courts much more aggressively to the left"—a sufficient reason to support Trump. However, judging Trump's character to be abysmal, Olasky implored him "to step aside and make room for another candidate."[166]

Christianity Today editor Andy Crouch agreed that the 2016 presidential contest presented Christians with a very difficult choice—between a woman who had "pursued unaccountable power through secrecy" and an unrepentant idolater who displayed no dependence "on God his Maker and Judge." Crouch noted that evangelicals correctly censured Clinton for not revering "the lives of the most vulnerable" and lambasted the Democratic Party for being "demonstrably hostile to expressions of traditional Christian faith." However, he complained, they did not subject Trump to the same critical analysis. Evangelicals largely, if reluctantly, overlooked his vulgarity, "vile and crude boasting about sexual conquest," and arrogance because he promised to appoint social conservatives to the Supreme Court to adjudicate such weighty issues as "the right of Christians and adherents of other religions to uphold their vision of sexual integrity and marriage even if they are in the cultural minority." Many evangelicals, he protested, were apparently so committed to protecting their self-interest that they were willing to ally themselves with a candidate who violated all that is sacred to them.[167]

As election day approached, Protestant pastors appeared more conflicted about whom to vote for than their parishioners were. A Lifeway Research poll in early October found that 40 percent of Protestant ministers were still undecided, a higher percentage than either the 32 percent supporting Trump or the 19 percent backing Clinton. This thirteen-point margin was much lower than in 2008 and 2012, when Protestant clergy favored Republican candidates by 35 to 40 percentage points. A *Washington Post*–ABC News poll reported that evangelical ministers favored Trump 39–9 over Clinton, but 45 percent were undecided. Mainline pastors preferred Clinton over Trump 43–15, with 35 percent still undecided. This poll also indicated that evangelicals of any race favored Trump by 52 to 40 percent, while nonevangelical Christians preferred Clinton by 56 to 36 percent.[168]

Courting the Catholic Vote

During the final month of the campaign, both Clinton and Trump saw opportunities to win the votes of Catholics, the country's second-largest religious bloc after evangelical Protestants. This diverse group included cultural conservatives, pro-life proponents, young political liberals, and Democratic-leaning

Hispanics. Earlier in the campaign, Trump had clashed with Pope Francis when the pope decried as un-Christian his plans to force Mexico to pay for a wall along its border with the United States and to deport many Latinos. Trump responded by calling Francis's comment "disgraceful." Some pundits argued that Trump's attack on the pontiff would help energize conservatives who wanted to halt illegal immigration, while others questioned the wisdom of criticizing the leader of 1.2 billion Catholics around the globe.[169] Some Catholics accused the pontiff of meddling in American politics, but Francis's emphasis on helping the poor and the appointment of more left-leaning cardinals and bishops in the United States had reduced Catholic support for the conservative Republican agenda.[170] Meanwhile, the Trump campaign tried to make political capital from hacked e-mails within the Clinton camp in October that disparaged Catholic conservatives.[171]

John McCarthy, Clinton's faith outreach director, reported that numerous Catholic lay leaders were uncomfortable with Trump and that his "divisive rhetoric" was repulsive to many Catholics. Several influential Catholic legislators campaigned on Clinton's behalf. For example, Sen. Richard Durbin (D-IL) hosted a roundtable discussion with nuns in Dubuque, Iowa. The Clinton campaign also created programs to appeal to voters with immigrant backgrounds, such as Italians and Irish, who are predominately Catholic.[172]

In March, Joseph Cella, a founder of Fidelis, a Catholic advocacy group, signed an open letter calling Trump "unfit to be president" because his "appeals to racial and ethnic fears and prejudice are offensive to any genuinely Catholic sensibility." He subsequently changed his mind, however, and agreed to serve as the Trump campaign's liaison to a committee of Catholic advisers. In mid-October, Cella exhorted Catholics to pray the rosary daily until election day and to ask God for "unity, peace and a Trump victory." In an open letter to the Annual Catholic Leadership Conference that month, Trump promised, "I am, and will remain, pro-life. I will defend your religious liberties and the right to fully and freely practice your religion, as individuals, business owners and academic institutions." Many Catholics who found Trump's language and some of his ideas repugnant still planned to vote for him because of his pro-life stance and promise to appoint socially conservative Supreme Court justices. Clinton was pleased that few bishops had endorsed Trump and hoped that their revulsion toward him would lead them to overlook her staff's negative e-mails and her position on abortion and same-sex marriage.[173]

Clinton's effort to win the vote of Catholics was made more difficult by the Democratic Party's platform pledge to overturn the Hyde Amendment, which prohibited using federal funds to pay for abortions, except to save the life of a pregnant woman or if the pregnancy resulted from rape or incest. This platform plank infuriated pro-life Democrats (the advocacy group Democrats for Life claimed that one of every three Democrats was pro-life) and irritated other Democrats who supported policies to reduce abortion. Many of these irate Democrats were Catholics whose votes Clinton needed to win the election. Sen. Joe Manchin of West Virginia denounced the plank as "crazy," while Pennsylvania senator Bob Casey implored the platform committee to change its position.[174]

Clinton and Mormons

Clinton also appealed to Mormons. Sensing an opportunity to win Utah, Clinton contributed an op-ed to the *Deseret News*, a Mormon-owned newspaper, in August. The Democrat accentuated the importance of religious freedom and compared Trump's proposal to ban Muslims from foreign nations from entering the United States with the persecution of Mormons during the nineteenth century. She also stressed that several prominent Mormons, including Mitt Romney, had criticized Trump. In a March 2016 speech, Romney, the 2012 Republican presidential candidate, had warned Utah residents that voting for Trump would greatly decrease "the prospects for a safe and prosperous future."[175]

After Trump's lewd comments on the *Access Hollywood* tape were reported, several leading Utah Republicans, including Gov. Gary Herbert and Rep. Jason Chaffetz, stated they could not support him. Lt. Gov. Spencer Cox had been a major voice in the Never Trump movement, and Sen. Mike Lee, a long-standing Trump critic, beseeched the Republican nominee to leave the ticket. A few days later, Clinton's campaign released a web ad titled "We are Mormons for Hillary," appealing directly to Church of Jesus Christ of Latter-Day Saints voters in Utah, Arizona, and Nevada. Mormons are required to serve for two years as missionaries (often overseas), and many of them were repelled by Trump's immigration policy and disagreed with his characterization of immigrants as job stealers and potential criminals.[176]

Tomicah Tillemann, a devout Mormon who served as a speechwriter for and adviser to Clinton during her tenure as secretary of state, warned that "Trump's election would be a catastrophe for the country and the principle of religious freedom." Those unsure about how she would handle *policy* issues should "remember that Hillary Clinton is, at her core, a Midwestern

Methodist." As secretary of state, Clinton repeatedly stated that she sought to help all children "realize their God-given potential." In addition, Clinton had championed religious freedom. Under her leadership, the State Department had created a groundbreaking task force on religion in foreign policy and had established a new office devoted to this issue. Clinton had frequently denounced the persecution of religious minorities and assembled faith leaders around the world to protect people's right to worship as they pleased. Tillemann also admired Clinton's knowledge of the Mormon Church and her compassion. She had praised the Mormon welfare system, visited some of the communion's leading historical sites, and credited the church with inspiring her family's practice of spending an evening together at home every week. Clinton often brought soup to the sick or visited people in the hospital. The caricature of her as cold and uncaring, Tillemann insisted, was blatantly false.[177]

Dissatisfied with the choice between Clinton and Trump, some Christians urged people of faith to choose a Mormon alternative. J. M. N. Reynolds, a professor at The King's College in New York City, argued that religiously devout Americans did not need to vote based on their fears or cast a ballot for the lesser of two evils. Reynolds argued that independent candidate Evan McMullin, a Mormon, Republican CIA agent, investment banker, and political adviser with exemplary character, presented a viable option for voters repulsed by Clinton's abortion rights advocacy and financial improprieties and by Trump's racism, misogynism, conspiracy theories, and lack of character.[178]

Sarah Pulliam Bailey, the *Washington Post's* chief writer on religion, observed in late October that the 2016 election was agonizing for many Mormons who believed that neither Clinton nor Trump met their moral standards. Consequently, many members of the church, headquartered in Salt Lake City, were leaning toward McMullin, their coreligionist. Several leading Utah Republicans endorsed McMullin, and the *Deseret News* urged Trump to drop out of the race because he did not espouse "the ideals and values of this community."[179]

The Case for Clinton

A wide assortment of pundits and politicians supported Clinton in 2016, stressing her Methodist faith, commitment to social justice, personal traits, experience, and vast superiority to Trump. Jon Favreau, Barack Obama's speechwriter during the 2008 campaign, admitted that he had penned many uncomplimentary things about Clinton. He argued in February 2016, however, that "she was by far the most prepared, impressive person at every [Obama] Cabinet meeting" and that many who worked for her praised her uncommon warmth and thoughtfulness. New Yorkers, Republican senators, Obama's White House staff, and heads of state throughout the world who had initially distrusted Clinton from a distance had found her to be genuine and likable up close. Clinton's claim that she wanted her administration to inspire people to act kindly toward friends, neighbors, colleagues, and students, and to do more to help one another, Favreau argued, was not a "cynical ploy" but "a theme that she's repeated throughout her life" and one rooted in her Methodist faith. He pointed out that as first lady Clinton had emphasized the need for "a new ethos of individual responsibility" and "actually living by the Golden Rule," while as secretary of state she had discussed people's need to develop a deeply ingrained sense of purpose.[180]

Speaking for many Republicans who saw Trump as an unsavory, inexperienced swindler who was a danger to the nation, neoconservative James Kirchcick argued that "Clinton is the one person standing between America and the abyss." Trump was "a brashly authoritarian populist" and a "charlatan, a gruesome amalgamation of the Monopoly Man and Elmer Gantry," who venerated Vladimir Putin, encouraged his supporters to engage in violent acts, called for the proliferation of nuclear weapons, and believed that NATO was obsolete. Despite her manifold faults, Clinton was the "real conservative" in the race and "the obvious choice for those who don't want to see our country degenerate into a banana republic."[181]

A Religion News Service columnist asserted that Christians could confidently vote for Clinton because her policies were much more "consistent with the message of Jesus Christ" than Trump's. Her life demonstrated her commitment to Christian faith and values. She had long promoted the rights of women and children. The central issue in the campaign, he claimed, "is how our country should treat immigrants and refugees." The Old Testament contained ninety-two verses highlighting God's command to welcome strangers, and Jesus instructed his followers to take care of the least of these. During the last decade, many congregations and religious organizations had championed overhauling immigration laws, which Clinton had strongly supported. In addition, Clinton expressed much greater concern than Trump about protecting God's creation. She had devised a plan to provide greater renewable energy and stop climate change. The only social issue religious conservatives seemed to care about was abortion, but they failed to note that abortions had reached a record low during Obama's tenure or that Clinton's perspective on abortion mirrored the position of the United Methodist Church. Christians, this columnist concluded, were choosing between "a lifelong, active Church member whose public service is imperfect but laudable and a narcissistic demagogue who has never helped anyone but himself."[182] A former US ambassador to Trinidad agreed that Clinton's life choices demonstrated that she "is, a caring, compassionate person who tries to live" by the Methodist "do all the good you can" dictum.[183]

Peter Cooke, a retired major general and the Democratic Party's candidate for governor of Utah in 2012, insisted that Clinton had many attributes people respected in a leader. She had been active in the Methodist church from her youth onward, maintained a close relationship with her youth pastor for many years, often carried a Bible with her, participated in a prayer group as first lady, and had long expressed her commitment to Christ through public service.[184]

Almost every major American newspaper endorsed Clinton. For only the third time since its inception in 1857, *The Atlantic* endorsed a presidential candidate. Clinton, its editors wrote, "has flaws (some legitimately troubling, some exaggerated by her opponents), but she is among the most prepared candidates ever to seek the presidency" and had "demonstrated an aptitude for analysis and hard work." Trump, on the other hand, had "no record of public service and no qualifications for public office." The "infomercial huckster" trafficked in "conspiracy theories and racist invective"; he was "appallingly sexist," "erratic, secretive and xenophobic," and displayed authoritarian tendencies.[185] Many urged Americans to vote for Clinton rather than enable Trump to win by supporting third-party candidates or not voting.[186]

A Concluding Assessment

On the eve of the election, Dallas megachurch pastor Robert Jeffress, a Fox News contributor, whose program "Pathway to Victory" aired on thousands of radio and television stations, summarized why Christians should vote for Trump. The Republican had "pledged to nominate Supreme Court justices who will either overturn *Roe v. Wade* or at least curtail late-time abortions including the horrific practice of partial-birth abortion." By contrast, Clinton, who refused to restrict abortion in any way, would nominate justices who would uphold *Roe v. Wade*. The Supreme Court justices and dozens of federal judges Clinton would be likely to nominate espoused "an expansionist view of the Constitution" and would "force the secular progressive agenda down the throats of Americans." Moreover, she would escalate the war the Obama administration had waged against religious liberty by suing the Little Sisters of the Poor Catholic charity for not providing their employees with abortion coverage, compelling Christian schools to allow boys to use girls' locker rooms, and prosecuting Christians who refused to provide services to same-sex couples. The sanctity of life and the preservation of religious freedom, Jeffress argued, were not "among the top ten concerns of most voters," but these issues should be the major concern of Christians.[187]

In October 2016, writing in *Christianity Today*, evangelicals' flagship magazine, Ed Stetzer, the executive director of the Billy Graham Center at Wheaton College, offered six reasons for evangelicals' antipathy toward Clinton: a clash over core values, her personification of progressivism, her alleged rejection of religious liberty, their angst over social trends, the perception that Clinton was a dishonest hypocrite, and their visceral hostility toward her. The principal issue over which evangelicals and Clinton clashed, Stetzer asserted, was abortion. The Democratic Party's platform stated, "We believe unequivocally, like the majority of Americans, that every woman should have access to quality reproductive health care services, including safe and legal abortion." The omission of the word "rare" from the usual triad of "safe, legal, and rare," Stetzer argued, signified the party's "much more aggressive approach" toward abortion. Furthermore, Planned Parenthood, an organization that had never previously endorsed a candidate during the primaries and was "plutonium" to religious conservatives, had strongly supported Clinton from the beginning of her campaign.[188]

According to Stetzer, many evangelicals saw Clinton as personifying secular, progressive values, which overshadowed in their minds her statements about her religious beliefs and practices. Clinton declared at an Al Smith charity dinner in October that Methodists, like Catholics, believed that to "achieve salvation we need both faith and good works." Although this statement was congruent with Catholicism since the Counter-Reformation, Stetzer labeled it as consistent with Pelagianism, a fifth-century heresy that viewed both grace and works as necessary to obtain salvation. Stetzer contended that her strenuous efforts to improve the lives of others fit well with John Wesley's emphasis on social holiness, but that she ignored the Methodist founder's stress on salvation by grace. Stetzer, however, misrepresented both Pelagianism and Clinton's theological position. Pelagius (354–420), a British monk, denied the doctrine of original sin, affirmed humanity's essential goodness, and taught that people could perfectly fulfill God's commands and achieve salvation without divine grace. Clinton's statement, by contrast, suggests that salvation results from a combination of grace and works, as Stetzer himself noted. However, as I will further document in the final chapter, Clinton affirmed numerous times that salvation is a gift of God based on people's faith, not works.[189]

Stetzer argued that Clinton's views of religious liberty clashed with those of evangelicals, but he focused on how little her campaign had done, despite being "awash in donations," to appeal to evangelicals or people of faith in general. Stetzer also insisted that numerous aspects of Clinton's campaign caused angst for evangelicals. Some of them opposed women playing leadership roles in politics. More importantly, Stetzer alleged, Clinton had said little during the campaign about religious matters or substantive issues that mattered to religious conservatives. Stetzer claimed that unlike Obama, who had based his support of same-sex marriage on Scripture and clearly described his conversion experience, Clinton had not spoken overtly about her faith in a significant way since 1993. Actually, as described in detail in this book, Clinton did discuss her faith numerous times between 1993 and 2016. Moreover, she could not point to a specific conversion experience because, as with many people raised in Christian settings, her faith had developed gradually through her family and church. She certainly could have done more to explain her positions on issues about which religious conservatives cared, but her differences with them on policy matters made it very challenging to do so.[190]

Stetzer noted correctly that Clinton was widely viewed as an untrustworthy hypocrite by many Americans, not just evangelicals. He argued that she faced a dilemma: if she did not speak about matters of faith, evangelicals would "continue to feel under-represented and under-valued"; if she did discuss how her policies reflected "core Christian values," many would see it "as a political tactic." Stetzer insisted that most religious Americans were repelled by Clinton because they perceived her positions and personality as "the perfect storm": her values and policies clashed with theirs and she could not be trusted.[191]

Although Clinton enjoyed cordial relationships with some prominent evangelicals, her campaign did not solicit their votes as enthusiastically or effectively as Obama's team did in 2008 or 2012. Clinton failed to exploit the opening to win religious voters offered by Trump's lewd, profane character nearly as fully as she could have. Michael Wear explained that Democrats focused on turning out the party's base to vote instead of trying to appeal to religious conservatives, in large part because those conservatives' antipathy toward Clinton was so great. It was "complicated psychologically" for religious conservatives who had strongly opposed Clinton for twenty years to support her in 2016.[192]

Numerous commentators pointed out the irony, if not the hypocrisy, of evangelicals' decision to back Trump while either ignoring or denigrating Clinton's faith. Evangelicals had long argued that politicians' faith helped determine their policies and had insisted that they cared deeply about candidates' character. Conservative Republican presidential nominees from Gerald Ford to Mitt Romney had long-standing connections with religious communities, robust professions of personal faith (except for John McCain), and generally upright characters. Trump, by contrast, had only recently adopted conservative stances on some issues, displayed little Christian piety or understanding of the Bible, and exhibited abysmal character. Clinton's faith and involvement with the Methodist church had been detailed in numerous biographies, articles, and interviews. Despite this extensive record of spiritual activity, Clinton's policy positions doomed her to the same fate suffered by Jimmy Carter, the devout Georgian Baptist Sunday school teacher whose actions as president provoked his opponents to create the powerful political movement known as the Christian Right.[193]

7

"God Grant That I May Never Live to Be Useless!"

In one of the major upsets in American political history, Donald Trump defeated Hillary Rodham Clinton in November 2016, astounding most pundits and pollsters. *New York Times* columnist David Brooks argued in July 2016 that if Clinton failed to defeat Trump, she would be viewed as "America's most hapless political loser and be vilified forever for enabling an era of American Putinism."[1] Brooks's assessment may be overly harsh, but Clinton was deeply wounded by her defeat and feared that Trump's presidency would severely harm the nation. Although she conceded defeat graciously, Clinton was devastated by her shocking loss, which seemingly ended her longstanding dream of becoming the nation's first female president and greatly expanding the good she could do by occupying its highest office. Losing to a man who had viciously attacked her, for whom she had little respect personally or politically, and whose political agenda and vision for America were radically at odds with hers was a crushing blow. Clinton won almost three million more votes than Trump, but she lost the electoral vote by 306 to 232, as Trump captured Michigan, Florida, Wisconsin, and Pennsylvania by razor-thin margins.

Although many people question God's goodness, love, or providence when they suffer significant setbacks and some even abandon their faith, Clinton, like countless others, relied on her strong faith to cope with her deeply disappointing defeat and to continue to undergird her efforts to improve the lives of women and children. Clinton ruminated extensively on her loss and offered explanations for it in her 2017 book *What Happened*. She also resumed her work with the Bill, Hillary and Chelsea Clinton Foundation and talked about her faith in several interviews. She coauthored books with her daughter and a best-selling mystery with novelist Louise Penny. In addition, Clinton criticized many of Trump's policies and hosted a podcast to discuss current events and philosophical issues.

What Happened?

During the campaign, scores of Republican leaders criticized Trump publicly and many others refused to support him. Only two of the nation's hundred largest newspapers endorsed Trump, while fifty-seven of them endorsed Clinton.[2] Almost all prognosticators predicted Clinton would win. What explains her shocking defeat? In *Shattered: Inside Hillary Clinton's Doomed Campaign* (2017), journalists Jonathan Allen and Amie Parnes attribute her loss to her inability to articulate a vision that inspired Americans and to capture the populist anger that was evident in her primary battle against Bernie Sanders. Bill Clinton biographer David Maraniss offered several reasons why Clinton lost: she had more baggage than any other candidate in modern times, she suffered both in comparison with and because of her husband, and she was hurt by her "tendency toward secrecy and lack of transparency" and many Americans' desire to end the Clinton political dynasty.[3]

Journalist Lawrence Tabak had attended a rodeo in Kansas City in 1994, where a clown introduced a talented donkey named Hillary, evoking hearty laughter. Clinton was not electable, Tabak concluded, because millions of Americans still viewed her as "a figure of ridicule." Electing her president was as absurd as electing a rodeo clown. Many voters despised Clinton but had difficulty explaining why. "Was it because she was smart, educated, powerful, or all of the above and a woman?" Most of them would have simply responded, "I don't know. . . . [I] just can't stand her."[4]

Sexism clearly played a major role in the 2016 campaign, as it had eight years earlier when Clinton lost the Democratic presidential nomination to Barack Obama. In 2016, the slurs by her openly misogynist opponent and her undeniable qualifications, Anne Helen Petersen asserted, "prompted both journalists and voters to question the standards by which politicians are judged—standards that are unquestionably masculine."[5] The criteria many Americans used to evaluate candidates were detrimental to Clinton. For a February 2016 *Esquire* article, Tom Junod surveyed dozens of men of various ages and occupations about Clinton, and most of them displayed sexual prejudice in their responses. Expressing a common perspective, a sixty-three-year-old teacher from Stillwater, Oklahoma, bluntly stated, "I do not trust that she, a woman, would be able to do what a man could with the same capabilities." Other men described Clinton as "cold and stiff" and "a little abrasive and a little arrogant."[6] Many men complained that Clinton was overly ambitious. The same traits that helped male politicians gain supporters—intellect, experience, and self-confidence—turned many voters off in Clinton's case. The major issue, Petersen argued, was "the real, if unconscious, fear" among many men "that women will take the reins of power, the keys to the system, the position of the presidency."[7]

Trump fueled such concerns. Although he repeatedly asserted that "no one respects women more than I do," Trump frequently insulted Clinton and women in general.[8] He insisted that Clinton would not be able to "satisfy" Americans because she had failed to satisfy her husband and accused her of playing "the woman card" to win the election. If Clinton "were a man," he opined, "I don't think she'd get 5 percent of the vote."[9] Trump called Clinton "a nasty woman" and tweeted that she did not "look presidential," implying that a woman could not serve effectively as president.[10] Meanwhile, Trump rallies featured T-shirts proclaiming "Trump That Bitch" and "Hillary Sucks But Not Like Monica."[11]

Throughout her campaign, Clinton emphasized feminist ideology and interests and appealed to female voters. Her campaign slogan was "I'm With Her," and the Democrat promised to improve political and economic opportunities for women. Pantsuits Nation was created in 2016 to support Clinton. While campaigning for her, its nearly three million female members promoted immigration reform, racial justice, religious freedom, and women's reproductive rights.[12]

Widespread beliefs that women were not as competent, strong, tough, and forceful as men handicapped Clinton despite her extensive experience as secretary of state, especially among voters concerned about national security issues and terrorist threats.[13] Although women are viewed as better able to promote "compassion issues" such as poverty, education, health care, and childcare, many prospective voters see them as less effective in dealing with "masculine" issues such as crime, the military, and the economy.[14] Some investigators concluded that sexism, as reflected in voters' attitudes and media coverage, played a decisive role in preventing the most qualified candidate from winning the 2016 election. An exit poll of 1,300 voters and a national survey of more than 10,000 white and Black Americans found that those who believed that men are better suited emotionally to govern were much more likely to cast ballots for Trump. Respondents who espoused sexism were significantly more likely to view Trump favorably than those who did not.[15] Some scholars contend that sexism reduced support for Clinton, increased support for Trump, and encouraged those Americans who were most hostile toward feminists and women to vote in greater numbers. They insist that sexism powerfully predicted voters' choices "even after controlling for authoritarianism, partisanship, and other predispositions."[16] Trump's misogynism and sexist affronts appear to have helped him gain the votes of sexists more than Clinton's gender appears to have lost those votes, despite the frequent condemnation of Trump's treatment of women by Democrats and women's groups.[17]

In the months following her defeat, Clinton was viewed more negatively than other candidates who had lost close elections for the presidency—Henry Clay, Thomas Dewey, Hubert Humphrey, Gerald Ford, and Al Gore. Many Americans treated Clinton as a pariah; pundits disparaged her, some on the left wing of the Democratic party blamed her for Trump's victory, and numerous Republicans and independents despised her. Although several factors played a role in this historically unprecedented vitriol, gender was significant. She was the first woman who ran as a major party nominee, a burden none of the other near-miss candidates bore. Since becoming first lady, Clinton had "served as a prism through which America has refracted its social anxieties." Detractors castigated her as "a radical feminist and left-wing agitator" when she lived in the White House, "a cutthroat opportunist when she ran for the Senate," and a millionaire defender of Wall Street when she campaigned in 2016.[18]

Commentators on the far right and far left agreed that Clinton lost the election in large part because she disrespected white working-class male voters in key midwestern states. During the Democratic primaries, Bernie Sanders insisted that Clinton did not support the interests of their party's working-class base and would sell them out to Wall Street.[19] Moreover, many white working-class men espoused a narrative of victimization, complaining that they were being displaced by women, people of color, and immigrants. They feared that the country they valued was slipping away, as evidenced by the legalization of same-sex marriage, the provision of gay and transgender rights, and the rising power of religious and racial minorities. Trump accentuated these complaints and fears during the general campaign. Nationwide, working-class white men supported Trump over Clinton by 71 to 23 percent. Clinton won only two of the 660 counties in the United States that in 2016 were at least 85 percent white and had per-capita incomes below the national median, whereas her husband had won almost half of these counties in 1996. Trump won a significantly higher percentage of the votes of whites without college degrees than McCain and Romney. Clinton received more support from women than Trump (54 to 39 percent), but white women without college degrees favored Trump by 64 to 28 percent, apparently sharing the same perspective and concerns as working-class white men.[20] Scholars and journalists offered many explanations for this outcome, including working-class Americans' economic displacement, reduced status compared with earlier generations, concern that Christian values were under attack, racial prejudice, grievances about the advancement of minorities, and preference for an entrepreneurial outsider over an entrenched political insider. A major reason for this outcome, however, was the same factor that led many evangelicals to cast ballots for Trump—their aversion to Clinton rather than their positive view of Trump. And for many in this category, their sexist attitudes contributed significantly to their antipathy toward Clinton.[21]

Clinton's inability to explain cogently and concisely why she wanted to be president also hurt her. Trump distilled his basic message into four often-repeated words: "Make America Great Again." Even in the more than five hundred pages of *What Happened*, Clinton did not clearly articulate why she ran.[22] She felt compelled to run because she thought she would "be good at the job" and "had the most relevant experience, meaningful accomplishments, and ambitious but achievable proposals, as well as the temperament to get things done in Washington."[23] Clinton claimed she wanted to strengthen the American economy and that Obama and some political gurus had encouraged her to seek the presidency. The job, she insisted, was "too important to pass up," and she wanted to improve the nation. Not surprisingly, Clinton also cited her Methodist faith as a key motivation. "We Methodists," she wrote, "are taught to 'do all the good you can.' I knew that if I ran and won, I could do a world of good and help an awful lot of people." She added, "In just one day at the White House, you can get more done for more people than in months anywhere else."[24]

Trump won in large part because he expressed the outrage many authoritarian-leaning white Americans, especially those without a college education, felt toward a political system they believed was failing them, undermining their economic and social stability, and diminishing their influence. Trump fanned their fears about economic stagnation, national security, and immigration.[25] He enabled them to direct their anger upward toward social elites and downward toward minorities. Clinton, meanwhile, focused too much on portraying "Trump as a dangerous aberration, an outsider unfit for office" instead of discussing how to improve the lives of average Americans. Her response to Trump's promise to "Make America Great Again" seemed to be "America Is Already Great," which did not resonate with the majority of voters.[26] In his speeches, on social media, and in their debates, Trump exploited America's "lingering sexism and the popular perception" of Clinton as part of "an arrogant and corrupt elite that believes it is above the law."[27]

Elections are sometimes significantly affected by candidates' statements that their opponents effectively employ against them. Such statements include James G. Blaine's claim in 1884 that the Democrats were the party of "rum, Romanism, and rebellion" and George H. W. Bush's subsequently abandoned pledge in 1988 to propose "no new taxes." Hillary Clinton made several statements that negatively impacted her 2016 candidacy. Soon after launching her campaign, she declared at a global women's conference that "deep-seated cultural codes, religious beliefs and structural biases" had to be changed in countries where women struggled to receive education and reproductive rights. A Fox News headline proclaimed in response, "Hillary: 'Religious Beliefs' Must Change for Sake of Abortion.'" Many Republican politicians and Christian media outlets also censured her remark.[28] So did Kirsten Powers, a Catholic Democratic political activist and commentator, who protested that Clinton appeared to view religious doctrines that opposed her political agenda as "biases" to be "dismantled by those who know better."[29]

A comment Clinton made at a fund-raising rally on September 9 also cost her votes. "To just be grossly generalistic," she declared, "you can put half of Trump supporters into what I call the basket of deplorables. Right? Racist, sexist, homophobic, xenophobic, Islamophobic, you name it." Republicans quickly pounced on her remark. Pundits compared it with Barack Obama's comments about clinging to "guns and religion" at a 2008 campaign fundraiser and Mitt Romney's remark in 2012 that "47 percent" of the people would vote for Obama "no matter what" because they were "dependent upon government," believed that "they are victims," thought "the government has a responsibility to care for them," and paid no income tax. Clinton quickly apologized for overgeneralizing, but many Americans were insulted by her comment.[30]

Yet another factor contributing to Clinton's defeat was the lack of or lukewarm support she received from many secular and religious progressives. Prominent voices, including Union Seminary professor Gary Dorrien and public-policy analyst Jeffrey Sachs, as well as many other Democrats who had supported Bernie Sanders in the 2016 primaries, accused Clinton of rejecting many of the fundamental tenets of progressivism. They complained, she argued, that Sanders's ambitious proposals "just won't work" and "the numbers don't add up." Progressives maintained that after the health care reform debacle in 1993, Clinton had moved from political liberalism toward the political center. Her husband's administration, with her enthusiastic support, had totally repudiated the Franklin Roosevelt–Lyndon Johnson legacy.[31] Moreover, progressives accused Clinton of being the candidate of both corporate greed and the military-industrial complex. Equally damning, Sachs argued, Clinton was "a staunch neocon" whose promotion of "American war adventures explains much of our current security danger." Her record as secretary of state is one of "the most militaristic, and disastrous, of modern US history."[32] While many older Democrats viewed her as a left-of-center politician who had skillfully navigated the political realities of Washington, numerous younger Democrats lambasted her for embodying "everything that's wrong with the current political system." To win in November, some pundits asserted, Clinton would have needed to convince Sanders's supporters that her disagreements with him were principally about tactics and the scope of his proposals and that "she isn't a neoconservative or a tool of Wall Street."[33] Clinton's failure to do this, coupled with the campaigning of some religious progressives such as Cornel West for Green Party nominee Jill Stein, cost Clinton much-needed votes.[34]

Clinton blamed her loss on several factors: the media, FBI director James Comey's investigation, several rash remarks she made, and her difficulty expressing her feelings. Clinton complained that the media had not focused on substantive political issues. According to Harvard's Shorenstein Center, she noted, "discussion of public policy accounted for just 10 percent of all campaign news coverage in the general election." Many journalists, she griped, hated her "attempt to talk unguardedly about what I thought was wrong in the country."[35] In a 2017 interview, Clinton attributed her loss to Comey's announcement in late October that the agency was again reviewing her e-mails as secretary of state, which intensified concerns about her integrity and judgment.[36]

Fox News commentators argued that Clinton blamed racism, sexism, Comey, and Russia rather than herself for her defeat. Her explanations, one of them contended, would be like Matt Ryan, the Atlanta Falcons' quarterback, blaming his uniform, the ball, the turf, the crowd, the referees, the defense, and his coach for his team's embarrassing loss to the New England Patriots in the 2017 Super Bowl after the Falcons led by 28–3 at halftime. They also ridiculed Clinton for complaining that Russia spent $100,000 on Facebook ads criticizing her, a paltry sum compared with the $141 million her campaign spent on promotional ads.[37]

In *What Happened*, Clinton did, however, accept blame for her defeat. "At every step, I felt that I had let everyone down," she wrote. "Because I had." She regretted several comments she made during the campaign, especially the one that half of Trump's supporters could be put in a "basket of deplorables."[38] In a 2020 Hulu documentary, Clinton discussed her difficulty in connecting with voters and seeming authentic. She argued that her emotional equanimity, which had served her well as she confronted unbridled sexism at Yale Law School and throughout her political career, was "a liability on the campaign trail." Clinton's thick skin helped her deal with America's "entrenched power structures" and the constant attacks on her character and actions, but it hindered her from discussing and displaying her inward self and feelings while campaigning. Both her gender and age contributed to this approach. Baby boomers were "taught to keep a stiff upper lip," whereas younger cohorts placed more value on vulnerability.[39] Had Clinton discussed more frequently and candidly how her religious beliefs inspired her political activism, it might have helped many voters to view her more positively.

Some pundits argued that Clinton lost because she had been expected to win so easily that her supporters did not work vigorously enough. Others, including Allen and Parnes, contended that the Clinton campaign was dysfunctional, plagued by "infighting and an out-of-touch candidate."[40]

Religious factors were also important in Trump's triumph, as the votes of religiously devout Americans propelled him to victory. The percentage of religiously committed citizens who voted for Democratic presidential candidates declined from 2008 to 2016. In 2008, 26 percent of evangelicals, 45 percent of all Protestants, and 54 percent of Catholics cast ballots for Obama. Four years later, he received the votes of 20 percent of evangelicals, 42 percent of all Protestants, and 50 percent of Catholics. Clinton performed even worse: only 16 percent of evangelicals, 39 percent of all Protestants, and 46 percent of Catholics supported her.[41] Trump bested Clinton by 60 to 37 percent among white Catholics, giving him a 52–45 percent overall lead among Catholics, even though Hispanic Catholics supported Clinton by 67 to 26 percent. Voters who attended church weekly backed Trump over Clinton by 56 to 40 percent; those who attended a few times a month to a few times a year were evenly divided between the two candidates. On the other hand, 71 percent of Jews, 70 percent of "nones," and 62 percent of voters who identified with religions other than Christianity or Judaism voted for Clinton, and those who never attended religious services supported Clinton by 62 to 31 percent.[42]

Evangelicals played a major role in Trump's victory. They favored Trump by 81 to 16 percent, representing the highest percentage of evangelical support a Republican presidential candidate had received since George W. Bush's 78 percent in 2004. Pundits have extensively debated why so many evangelicals voted, many reluctantly but others enthusiastically, for a candidate whose personal lifestyle, demeanor, and belittling of his opponent, women, immigrants, and people with disabilities clashed with their own values and perspectives. Why did four-fifths of evangelicals vote for the candidate who displayed ignorance about the Bible and Christian theology, rarely attended church, had been married three times, and engaged in sexual practices that deviated from scriptural norms instead of his rival, who had long expressed a strong commitment to Christ, regularly worshipped and prayed, taught Sunday school, knew the Bible well, frequently read Christian literature, stayed with her unfaithful husband, and professed to be guided in her policies by her understanding of Holy Writ? Numerous explanations have been offered, most importantly evangelicals' antipathy toward Clinton and Trump's support for conservative social values, including his opposition to abortion, defense of religious liberty, and promise to appoint conservative judges to the Supreme Court and other federal benches. Influenced by conservative talk radio shows and publications, many evangelicals associated Clinton's name with "fear, anxiety, corruption, sliminess, conniving, [and] big government," Alan Noble, a professor at Oklahoma Baptist University and editor of *Christ and Pop Culture*, explained.[43] Religious scholar Andrew Chesnut argued that Trump's "charismatic, almost messianic, personality and public speaking style" and his promise to "make America great again" echoed the "impassioned preaching heard at many evangelical churches, especially in the South." To many religious conservatives, Trump's signature slogan called for a return to an earlier era when they had more influence, American values were more biblically based, life was simpler, and the nation was more homogeneous. Moreover, Trump's flaunted affluence fit well with the gospel of prosperity, popular among some religious conservatives, in which wealth provided evidence for divine approval.[44] Evangelical radio host Erick Erickson contended that religious conservatives were more willing to believe that Trump was a Christian, even though he had not professed that Jesus was his savior and Lord, than they were to believe Clinton's frequent affirmations of basic Christian doctrines. "It was just baffling to me," declared Joshua

DuBois, who directed faith outreach for the 2008 Obama campaign, "that so many other Americans . . . didn't accept that she was Christian."[45]

For millions of evangelicals, Trump's pledges to defend their religious liberty and nominate socially conservative Supreme Court justices and federal judges were more important than his character flaws and moral transgressions. These so-called values voters overlooked claims that Trump lied repeatedly, sexually harassed women, refused to pay taxes, or stiffed contractors.[46] No other candidate in history, the president of Ohio Right to Life asserted, had pledged to nominate only "pro-life justices" to the Supreme Court. That prompted evangelicals on the fence about Trump to overlook "his bombastic and offensive comments." These voters believed that he would deliver what was most important to them—"a conservative court for a generation to come."[47]

Many evangelical leaders, Ed Stetzer claimed, "probably voted for Trump begrudgingly, because they felt they had no other choice." Clinton's stance on abortion, he avowed, prevented many evangelicals from casting ballots for her. Clinton's position pleased her core constituents but turned off many moderates and conservatives who wanted to vote for her because of their intense dislike of Trump. On the other hand, Franklin Graham, president of both the Billy Graham Evangelistic Association and Samaritan's Purse, probably spoke for many evangelicals when he attributed Trump's triumph to God's providence. God's answer to Christians' prayers, Graham asserted, brought about "the biggest political upset of our lifetime."[48]

Clinton made numerous mistakes during her 2016 campaign. Given how close the race was, her loss can be attributed to any of them. One that especially stands out, however, is her failure to appeal to religious constituencies, especially evangelicals. More targeted campaigning to religious groups could have enabled Clinton to win. Michael Wear, who directed Obama's efforts in this area in 2008 and 2012, contended that Obama had utilized the three principal elements "of successful faith outreach: direct engagement, policy commitments, and rhetoric." Obama appealed to people of faith in both campaigns through his staff, his website, and the media. Obama had discussed the importance of faith in his own life and the positive role the religiously devout could play if he were elected. Obama strove to explain how his policies were consistent with the values and priorities of people of faith and promised to limit "how far his policies would go on social issues where he generally disagreed with religious conservatives." Unfortunately, Wear argued, Clinton ignored almost all these strategies. Her campaign did little to appeal to religious constituencies (especially white evangelicals and Catholics), did not ask people of faith to vote for her, and took policy positions that enabled "Trump to prey on their sense" of being under attack. Trump understood that evangelicals felt embattled and isolated, Wear added, "and appealed to them on completely Machiavellian terms."[49] Unlike Clinton, Wear argued, future Democratic candidates must appeal to people of faith on such issues as poverty reduction, profamily work and tax policies, adoption, criminal-justice reform, immigration, environmental stewardship, and efforts to end human trafficking. Democrats must promise to preserve churches' tax-exempt status and to permit religious institutions to operate without government interference. Not doing this in 2016 had permitted fear-mongering to flourish. Moreover, Clinton's neglect of evangelicals and conservative Catholics led them to believe they would have no voice in her administration.[50]

Doug Pagitt, executive director of Vote Common Good, an organization that sought to mobilize liberal evangelicals and other Christian voters for Clinton, argued that her "faith mattered a lot to her," but her "campaign did nothing to share that story line, to encourage people to understand that or to even take religious voters seriously."[51] Many evangelicals resonated with the Democratic Party's planks on environmental issues and racial justice, but Clinton did little to link these positions to Scripture or to use her stances on these issues to appeal to religious conservatives.[52] When asked if Clinton lost in part because she did not speak enough about her faith, her Methodist adviser Bill Shillady responded that she had discussed her faith frequently at town halls and political rallies and with individuals she met, but that these statements were rarely reported in the media.[53]

Clinton's campaign unwisely ignored numerous interview requests from *Christianity Today*, *World* magazine, and other religious publications. Obama, by contrast, spoke with *Christianity Today* in 2008 about his conversion experience, church involvement, and belief in "the redemptive death and resurrection of Jesus Christ." He stressed the moral aspects of abortion and called for reducing the number of abortions by helping to prevent unwanted pregnancies and promoting adoption.[54] The Clinton campaign did not hire anyone to focus specifically on outreach to evangelicals or accept Tony Campolo's offer to create an Evangelicals for Hillary organization. She gave no major speeches to evangelical groups and did not meet publicly with evangelical leaders. Clinton also did little to explain her views on either abortion or religious freedom to evangelicals. "Obama asked for the votes of white evangelicals" whereas "Clinton did not," Wear lamented.[55] In 2008 Obama met with theologian Ronald Sider, founder of Evangelicals for Social Action, and other Christian leaders to discuss various issues including the right of faith-based organizations to consider individuals' religious commitments in their hiring decisions. Sider called the failure of the Clinton campaign to reach out to white evangelicals' "dumbfounding and incredibly stupid." He added, "Apparently they thought they could win without us."[56] Clinton also turned down an offer to speak at a prestigious St. Patrick's Day event at the University of Notre Dame, an invitation Obama and his running mate, Joe Biden, had previously accepted. Her campaign concluded incorrectly that other groups were more worthy of their attention than white Catholics.[57] Biden also appealed more effectively to religious constituencies in 2020 than Clinton did in 2016. He hired evangelical Joshua Dickson as his national faith engagement director and spoke frequently and explicitly about his faith. His campaign produced a digital ad promoting his Catholic faith, and his friends and numerous political supporters argued that his faith shaped his values and that his values directed his politics. Ronald Sider and Richard Mouw created "Pro-Life Evangelicals for Biden." Its adherents disagreed with Biden's position on abortion, but they argued that his "policies are more consistent with the biblically shaped ethic of life than those of Donald Trump."[58]

Historian Kristin Du Mez agreed that Clinton should have appealed more to religious voters, especially evangelicals. Clinton, she argued, could have provided a biblical justification for why abortion was a right worth protecting and supplied "a more nuanced vision of religious pluralism" that balanced religious freedom and civil rights to help refute Republican claims that, if elected, she would prevent conservative Christians from practicing their faith as they desired. On the other hand, Du Mez averred, the Democratic National Convention could have been mistaken for a religious revival, and Clinton's progressive, social-justice-oriented faith did resonate with many African Americans and mainline Protestants. Nevertheless, although Trump did not speak articulately about matters of faith and blatantly defied biblical values in his behavior and rhetoric, most religious conservatives ignored, rejected, or even ridiculed Clinton's faith.[59] Clinton, Du Mez asserted, had "long sought to reconcile the values of the left and the right, to call for a more compassionate politics" based on her faith. However, Americans' many political and social divisions and heated disagreements, coupled with the negative perception many citizens had of Clinton, denied her the political capital and moral authority she needed to bridge these gaps, heal a fractured nation, and provide a vision to enable Americans to find greater meaning and deal with their political, social, and spiritual crises.[60] Du Mez further argued that Americans have become so politically divided and their understanding of Scripture, theological perspectives, and religious values have become so strongly connected with their political commitments that politicians can no longer "speak a language of faith that transcends politics" or communicate religious truths across the nation's political factions. This polarization of Christianity inadvertently hastens the secularization of public life.[61]

Clinton's campaign staff may have seen the attempt to win evangelical votes as hopeless. After all, evangelicals had voted in large numbers for Republicans since the 1970s. Moreover, Clinton faced a large obstacle in trying to appeal to religious voters. Democrats espoused clashing religious perspectives. In 2016, only 47 percent of white, college-graduate registered Democrats identified as Christians, whereas 81 percent of African-American Democrats and 76 percent of Latino Democrats did. Moreover, 35 percent of millennials indicated that they had no religious affiliation, whereas only 17 percent of Baby Boomers and fewer than 11 percent of Americans born before 1945 reported being religiously unaffiliated. The party, therefore, contained many younger, well-educated, secular whites and numerous Hispanics, African Americans, and older whites whose faith mattered to them. In earlier elections, Eugene McCarthy and Robert Kennedy (both practicing Catholics), Methodist George McGovern, Southern Baptists Jimmy Carter and Bill Clinton, and United Church of Christ member Barack Obama had all spoken from their faith traditions in ways that resonated with many Democrats.[62] Ironically, Hillary Clinton, who arguably was more personally devout than any of these other candidates except Carter, was deeply influenced by Methodist social-justice stances, and had discussed religious topics more often in nonpolitical venues than any of them except McGovern and Carter, rarely explicitly connected her political positions to biblical precepts.

Various factors indicate that the outcome of the 2016 election might have been different if the Clinton campaign had reached out more effectively to religiously devout voters. As a twice-divorced casino magnate who had rarely attended church or knew little about the Bible and had bragged about behaviors that clashed with biblical morality, Trump was potentially repulsive to most evangelicals.[63] As discussed in chapter 6, numerous prominent evangelicals excoriated him in interviews, op-eds, and tweets. After Trump locked up the nomination in May, half of the one hundred leading evangelicals surveyed by *World* magazine declared that they could not vote for him. As noted, Clinton spoke at numerous Black churches and expounded on her faith in some interviews and campaign speeches. Clearly, however, she did not do enough to publicize her Christian commitment because, despite her twenty-five years in the limelight, 43 percent of Americans believed in 2016 that she was not a religious person.[64] Had Clinton met with evangelical leaders and groups, talked about issues that mattered to evangelicals, assured them that she would protect their religious freedom, listened to their concerns, and promised to give them a voice in her administration, she "might have peeled away" enough religiously committed Americans seeking a reason not to vote for Trump to win the election.[65] Had Clinton assured evangelicals more fervently that she would protect religious liberty and proposed a specific plan to decrease abortions, she might have captured more of their votes.[66] Three states Clinton lost by small margins—Pennsylvania, Wisconsin, and Michigan—had many mainline Protestant and Catholic voters. Many of these voters either did not recognize the depth or importance of Clinton's faith or thought that her faith was not genuine because of Republican misrepresentations. Had Clinton been more outspoken about her Christian convictions and focused more on faith outreach to these groups, she might have won these closely contested states.[67] Moreover, as noted, she received only 16 percent of the evangelical vote, 4 percent less than Obama garnered in 2012. Because white evangelicals accounted for about a fifth of the electorate in these three states, this difference could have enabled Clinton to win them.[68]

Dealing with Defeat

Clinton's concession speech the day after her heartbreaking loss was gracious and upbeat. Displaying "spiritual stamina," she stressed that her campaign had sought to build a "hopeful, inclusive and big-hearted" nation. Clinton insisted that Americans owed Trump "an open mind and the chance to lead." In sharp contrast to Trump's response to the 2020 election results, she emphasized that "our constitutional democracy enshrines the peaceful transfer of power and we don't just respect that, we cherish it." Clinton acknowledged that "this loss hurts," but she urged her supporters to "please never stop believing that fighting for what's right is worth it." After once again quoting Galatians 6:9, Clinton concluded, "Let us have faith in each other, let us not grow weary, let us not lose heart, for there are more seasons to come. And there is more work to do."[69]

Bill Shillady compared Clinton's shocking and shattering loss to Good Friday and her potential return to politics to Jesus's resurrection. In an e-mail the day after the election, Shillady told Clinton that for Christ's followers,

Good Friday was "the day that everything fell apart. All was lost." They denied him, "mourned, fled and hid."[70] "Their leader, master and Savior was dead and gone and they didn't know what to do."[71] Today, Shillady asserted, "you are experiencing a Friday. . . . But Sunday is coming!" He promised her that hope would be restored after enduring "the darkness and seeming hopelessness of Friday."[72] Clinton, Shillady argued, "was heartbroken, but her faith helped her move through that darkness." Because she knew the Bible "remarkably well," she understood which passages to read to gain inspiration and comfort.[73]

A week after the election, Clinton exhorted the audience at a Children's Defense Fund event in Washington to continue fighting for American children, but she also confessed that several times during the past week she wanted to "curl up with a good book or our dogs, and never leave the house again."[74] Clinton strove to accept defeat graciously, but she was fuming inside and fearful for the nation, and her natural inclination was to fight back. To cope with losing this "weird and wild election," Clinton went on long walks in the woods, practiced yoga, and drank her "fair share of chardonnay."[75] Clinton testified numerous times that her faith enabled her to withstand her electoral failure. She prayed passionately and reread the books by Dutch cleric Henri Nouwen that had helped her during the crisis caused by Bill's dalliance with Monica Lewinsky.[76] After the election, the Clintons continued attending the Mount Kisco Methodist Church near Chappaqua, New York, where they had worshipped since 2006. Their pastor described them as friendly, engaging, and low-key.[77]

"I prayed a lot," Clinton explained, "as fervently as I can remember ever doing . . . for help to put the sadness and disappointment of my defeat behind me; to stay hopeful and openhearted rather than becoming cynical and bitter . . . to find a new purpose and start a new chapter," and for wisdom. In addition, "I prayed that my worst fears about Donald Trump wouldn't be realized, and that people's lives and America's future would be made better, not worse, during his presidency."[78] Reflecting again on Nouwen's *The Return of the Prodigal Son*, she concluded that "my task was to be grateful for the humbling experience of losing the presidential election. Humility can be such a painful virtue. . . . Because of our limitations and imperfections . . . we must reach out beyond ourselves, to God and one another."[79] She added, "I was lifted up and blessed by a lot of people" who sent prayers and spiritual readings. "Through it all," she declared, "my faith was really holding me together in a very central way. It gave me a lot of courage to get up and keep going."[80] Both David Gergen, a former advisor to Bill Clinton, and biographer Carl Bernstein stated that Clinton's faith helped her cope with her devastating defeat.[81]

After her loss, Clinton seemed more willing to publicly discuss her faith. Since the election, Shillady declared, "I think her faith is stronger." In an *Atlantic* article, Emma Green contended that Clinton appeared to be "finally becoming a more straightforward version of herself: a woman whose fondest ambition is teaching scripture in church." Clinton had chosen to "celebrate a part of herself that she cherishes, just as millions of other Americans cherish their faith."[82] Clinton told Shillady that she wanted to preach, and he thought she would enjoy sharing the gospel in contexts that were not "politically charged."[83] Shillady predicted that Clinton might become a lay Methodist preacher, and articles in several major publications discussed this possibility. She would be a powerful pulpiteer, he argued, because of her ability to exposit the Bible, knowledge of Methodist history, passion for the disenfranchised and poor, and life experiences.[84]

Despite praying, reading many enjoyable books, exercising, and drinking Chardonnay, in late April 2017 Clinton was still reeling from her profoundly disappointing loss to Trump and was feeling bitter and angry about the attacks she had endured during the campaign. At that point, she listened to a TED Talk by Pope Francis on the importance of love, gentleness, and hope. While walking in the woods near her home in Chappaqua, Clinton decided to follow the pope's admonition to open her heart to everyone, even those who had mistreated her. As she explained in *What Happened*, Clinton was especially moved by the pontiff's call for "a 'revolution of tenderness.' What a phrase! He said, 'We all need each other, none of us is an island, an autonomous and independent 'I,' separated from the other, and we can only build the future by standing together." Francis implored people, Clinton quoted, "to use our eyes to see the other, our ears to hear the other, to listen to the children, the poor, [and] those who are afraid of the future." The pope also warned that the rancor people harbored in their hearts toward others and the offenses they did not forgive were open wounds that must be healed before they could experience peace. Pondering the pope's words, Clinton concluded, "I can carry around my bitterness forever, or I can open my heart once more to love and kindness. That's the path I choose."[85]

Out of the Woods

The day before Trump's inauguration, Eleanor Clift predicted in *The Daily Beast* that Clinton would rise to the occasion as she always did—whether it had been gracefully enduring her husband's infidelity, testifying to Congress about Benghazi for eleven hours, or volleying Trump's insults during the presidential debates. That she had not lost to Mitt Romney, John Kasich, or Marco Rubio but to Donald Trump, who for much of 2016 had been considered a joke and a sideshow by most politicians and pundits, made Clinton's defeat much more painful. She could blame her loss on being a woman or on the media lambasting her use of a private email server while largely ignoring "Trump's numerous and far more serious and consequential conflicts," Clift contended, and she could take solace in her very narrow margin of defeat. If she had won 78,000 more votes in Pennsylvania, Michigan, and Wisconsin combined, she would have been president. What must especially "hurt Clinton as a devout Methodist," Clift argued, was her belief she had failed to fulfill her moral duty to defeat a man who had violated "all the norms that govern political behavior in a democracy." However, her long-standing resilience would save her. Clinton would continue to promote the causes she had cared about since her days at the Children's Defense Fund in the mid-1970s. Clinton recognized that she had more work to do and would strive to complete her calling.[86] Many people have asked, another columnist noted, what caused Clinton "to continue to fight for the values we all hold so near and dear" despite all the difficulties she has gone through. The answer may be "in her quiet and steely Methodist upbringing where she was taught to 'do all the good you can.'"[87]

After her loss, Clinton continued her diligent efforts to improve the lives of children. At a Children's Defense Fund event in Washington in mid-November 2016, she reiterated her often-repeated argument: "Every child deserves to have the opportunity to live up to his or her God-given potential, and I believe the measure of any society is how we treat our children." Despite the progress the United States had made under President Obama, Clinton lamented, more than thirty-one million children still lived in or near poverty. She exhorted businesses, foundations, philanthropists, and religious congregations to help children. She asserted that the Bible tells us "Love never fails," and "I believe that."[88]

In May 2017, Clinton founded Onward Together, a political advocacy organization designed to encourage grassroots engagement to advance progressive causes. Its website highlighted the slogan Clinton called her new motto: "Resist, insist, persist and enlist."[89] Onward Together sought to "recruit and train future leaders" and to promote "real and lasting change."[90] It supported leaders, particularly young ones, who initiated projects and founded new organizations to fight for progressive values.[91]

Bill Shillady edited a book titled *Strong for a Moment Like This: The Daily Devotions of Hillary Rodham Clinton*, containing the devotionals he and others, primarily younger female Methodist pastors, had written for the Democrat during her campaign. The book included a foreword by Clinton and some e-mails she wrote to Shillady describing the inspiration she derived from the devotionals. Clinton's speechwriters had incorporated some ideas from them into her addresses.[92] However, Abingdon Press stopped the book's publication in August 2017, when it was discovered that Shillady had plagiarized some of its key devotionals.[93] The next year, many women who had contributed to this edited volume published *We Pray with Her: Encouragement for All Women Who Lead*.

Clinton's account of the 2016 election, titled *What Happened* and published in September 2017, sold 300,000 copies in its first week, the highest debut of a nonfiction book since 2012. Its sales revealed the great desire of Americans "to learn about and experience, from Hillary Clinton's singular perspective, the historic events of the 2016 election," declared Simon and Schuster's CEO.[94] By December, sales reached 450,000. During the last four months of 2017, Clinton spoke at more than thirty venues in the United States and Canada on a book tour. She also traveled to the United Kingdom, Australia, and New Zealand to promote *What Happened*. Writing in the *Chicago Tribune*, Heidi Stevens argued, "Tens of millions of people feel invested in Clinton's narrative." They "see themselves reflected in her story, and they see her story reflected in their country."[95] Clinton added a new epilogue to the 2018 paperback edition of *What Happened*, detailing how Trump's presidency was fulfilling her worst fears, although she was delighted by the swell of civic activism, women seeking public office, and young Americans protesting social injustices.

In 2019, Hillary and Chelsea coauthored *The Book of Gutsy Women: Favorite Stories of Courage and Resilience*. In it, they recounted the stories of abolitionist Harriet Tubman, environmentalist Rachel Carson, LGBTQ activist Edie Windsor, swimmer Diana Nyad, historian Mary Beard, civil rights activist Dorothy Height, author Chimamanda Ngozi, Pakistani female education advocate Malala Yousafzai, and other women whose bold actions had improved the world.

Speaking at the funeral of longtime congressman Elijah Cummings (D-MD) in 2019, Clinton declared that it was "the homegoing celebration of a great man, a moral leader and a friend." It was appropriate that Cummings shared the name of an Old Testament prophet, because the politician had "used the power and the wisdom that God gave him, to uphold the moral law" to which all people are responsible. Like the prophet, Clinton declared, Cummings called "down fire from heaven," "prayed and worked for healing," opposed corrupt leaders, and endured storms and earthquakes without losing his faith.[96]

In March 2020, Hulu released a four-part documentary on Clinton's life titled *Hillary*. Originally intended to celebrate the election of the nation's first female president, it instead told the history of modern feminism through the prism of Clinton's life by portraying a country "still grappling with a daunting degree of gender bias." In the documentary, Clinton again accepted some of the blame for her electoral loss.[97]

In September 2020, Clinton launched a podcast on iHeartRadio to discuss faith, resilience, grief, current political issues, and other topics with athletes, Broadway stars, advice givers, and political leaders. In one episode, Clinton chatted with Sybrina Fulton, the mother of Trayvon Martin, who was fatally shot in 2012 in Sanford, Florida, by George Zimmerman. They talked about finding "moments of joy in the midst of grief" and "reasons to get out of bed." Fulton's faith, Clinton reported, "was instrumental to her" as she coped with the loss of her son.[98] After the United States pulled its remaining troops from Afghanistan in August 2021, Clinton worked with the US government, foreign governments, and aid organizations to remove about one thousand at-risk women from the country.[99]

Although Clinton generally maintained a low public profile following her loss to Trump, she occasionally addressed issues troubling the nation and censured the president's actions. In her 2017 commencement address at Wellesley, Clinton deplored the "full-fledged assault on truth and reason" in the United States. Many denied science; concocted "elaborate, hurtful conspiracy theories"; fueled rampant fears about Muslims, minorities, undocumented immigrants, and the poor; and sowed "division at a time when we desperately need unity." She denounced the proposed federal budget as "an attack of unimaginable cruelty on the most vulnerable among us, the youngest, the oldest, the poorest and hard-working people" trying to rise into the middle class. The budget proposal grossly underfunded public education and efforts to combat the opioid crisis and jeopardized the world's future by "reversing our commitment to fight climate change." By lying about the problems confronting the nation, she argued, many American leaders were undermining confidence in government, which bred more cynicism and anger. They were also undercutting the belief that people "possess the capacity for reason and critical thinking, and that free and open debate is the lifeblood of a democracy." Clinton had derived great hope and joy after the 2016 election from meeting thousands of young people who told her that her "defeat had not defeated them." She urged graduates to dream bigger, set their sights higher, "stand up for truth and reason," and invest "love and time into your relationships."[100]

A year later, in her Class Day address at Yale, Clinton claimed that "fundamental rights, civic virtue, freedom of the press—even facts and reason"—were being assaulted more vigorously than at any other time in American history. On the other hand, she rejoiced that moral conviction, civic engagement, and devotion to democracy and the nation were increasing. Clinton argued that the nation's wounds could be healed only if people practiced "radical empathy" in their personal lives, families, communities, and public life. She urged Americans "to reach across divides of race, class and politics," to restore rational debate, to "disagree without being disagreeable," and "to recapture a sense of community and common humanity." Clinton contended that those who waged war on the rule of law, delegitimized elections, perpetrated "shameless corruption," and rejected the idea that political leaders "should be public servants" undermined national unity. She implored her audience to have faith that Americans could forge "honorable, practical compromise in the pursuit of ends that will lift us all up and move us forward."[101]

Criticizing Trump's immigration policies, Clinton tweeted in June 2018, "The test of any nation is how we treat the most vulnerable among us." She added, "Those who selectively use the Bible to justify this cruelty [of separating immigrant children from their parents] are ignoring a central tenet of Christianity. Jesus said 'Suffer the little children unto me.' He did not say 'let the children suffer.'"[102] Clinton also denounced the Trump administration's plan to end Deferred Action for Childhood Arrivals (DACA) as inconsistent with Christian values.[103] At an event organized by the Jewish Labor Committee in December 2019, she slammed the president for waging war against democracy and expressing "contempt for the values that we pledge allegiance to" and are "embodied in our constitution." She urged her listeners to be guided by the Jewish concept of *tikkun olam*, which taught that everyone had a responsibility to help repair the world, "or as I learned growing up in the Methodist church, 'Do all the good you can, for all the people you can, in all the ways you can, as long as ever you can.'"[104]

Clinton argued in a *Washington Post* op-ed that Trump should be impeached for his role in inciting the January 6, 2021, attack on the Capitol. Trump had given white supremacists, leaders of the far right, and conspiracy theorists a powerful platform by exalting whiteness over everything else. He had "whipped a dangerous element of our country into a frenzy" to try to "stop the steal." In addition to removing Trump from office, Clinton contended, elected leaders should demand the resignation of members of Congress who had helped him subvert democracy, expel people who conspired to overthrow the government, and pass laws to hold white supremacists accountable for their reprehensible acts. Clinton noted that conspiracy theorists had continued to portray her as "evil incarnate." She had been "burned in effigy for fighting for health-care reform," was accused of operating a pedophilia ring out of a pizza parlor, and received a mail bomb from a fanatical Trump supporter.[105]

In a November 2021 interview with Rachel Maddow on her show on MSNBC, Clinton urged Americans to "be much more sensitive to, [and] understanding and empathetic toward each other," especially to minority groups, "because we truly rise or fall together." Clinton explained that *State of Terror*, a 2021 novel she coauthored with Louise Penny, depicted a situation similar to the attack on the Capitol by Trump's followers; the book's protagonists sought to stage a coup because they felt threatened by civil rights advancement and cultural changes. Clinton also contended that Trump, like the autocratic leaders of Russia, Turkey, Hungary, and Brazil, was "driven by personal power and greed and corruption" and used people's fears about social change to cause them to feel insecure and hate one another, so that they could be easily manipulated by disinformation and demagogues.[106]

The Faith of Hillary Clinton: A Final Assessment

Clinton's understanding of the Bible, God, Jesus, prayer, human nature, the importance of good deeds, salvation, and morality have been quite consistent throughout her life. In explaining her faith, Clinton noted that the Methodist *Book of Discipline* taught that four streams shaped people's faith: Scripture, tradition, experience, and reason. Although a Christian's faith should be based on the Bible, she asserted, individuals should use reason to determine what their faith meant to them, deepen it, and decide how to follow it in their daily lives. To sustain their faith over time, she insisted, people needed to believe with both their heads and hearts. Clinton agreed with thirteenth-century Catholic theologian Thomas Aquinas that God's revelation is "eminently rational," which strengthened her faith.[107] In interviews, books, and speeches, Clinton stressed that she had a personal relationship with God, centered on reading the Bible and Christian literature and on praying.[108] Even though she had not talked much about her faith during some periods of her life, Clinton declared, it had always been foremost in her mind. Throughout her public career, she had tried to explain her faith, "sometimes more effectively than other times," but more importantly, she had "tried to be guided by it."[109] Figuring "out how best to translate your faith into your daily life," Clinton confessed, is challenging.[110]

The Bible, Clinton declared, is "the biggest influence on my thinking." She explained that "I was raised reading it, memorizing passages from it and being guided by it. I still find it a source of wisdom, comfort and encouragement."[111] When a South Carolina pastor told Clinton that he always learned something new whenever he studied the Bible, she responded, "Well, it's alive. It's the living Word."[112] The Bible, she insisted, provides "a glimpse of God and God's desire for a personal relationship" with individuals.[113] She argued further that scriptural passages are timeless as human experience had demonstrated.[114] In 1994, Clinton reported that she was "spending a lot of time thinking about the Sermon on the Mount, and particularly the Beatitudes." Christ's sermon, she admitted, was very challenging and hard "to fully understand." Clinton also greatly valued the book of James because as a Methodist, she was "big on deeds as well as words."[115] When asked in a 2007 interview what her favorite part of the Bible was, she replied, "It depends upon what's going on in my life" on "the challenges and questions that I'm coping with. Psalms is always a favorite. It's both comforting and challenging." She valued the Old Testament and found Isaiah "very intriguing and provocative," but spent most of her time reading the New Testament.[116]

Clinton affirms her belief in the Trinity: God the Father, Jesus the Son, and the Holy Spirit. She stresses God's unconditional love and forgiveness.[117] Clinton believes that Christ died on the cross to atone for human sin and reconcile the penitent with God the Father and in Jesus's bodily resurrection.[118] Jesus, she declared, "provided the ultimate vision of being the Way, the Truth and the Life."[119] Clinton avowed that she has often felt guided and empowered by the Holy Spirit.[120] Clinton professes to have a personal, intimate relationship with God. She noted that "for some people a personal relationship with God, a sense that you're saved, a real belief in your salvation is incredibly both moving and comforting."[121] Clinton, however, disagreed with the idea that a person's Christian faith was "sealed" the moment he or she accepted Christ as his or her savior. Being a Christian, she argued, was a "never-ending challenge." Every day she falls short of what she "should be achieving."[122]

As noted, prayer is extremely important to Clinton. She emphasizes that her parents taught her to pray as a child and that she prays every day.[123] She shares her father's "belief in the power and importance of prayer. I've often told audiences that if I hadn't believed in prayer before 1992, life in the White

House would have persuaded me." Prayer, she declared, is an "all-pervasive gift" that "lifts me up, that helps me let off steam, that guides me."[124] The prayers of her friends and "countless other people around the world . . . helped so much," Clinton asserted.[125] "I had friends who prayed for me, I prayed for myself, I prayed for other people, [and] I felt like I was sustained by prayer." After Bill decided to run for president, she reported, countless people promised that "they were praying for us," and after he was elected, there was a great "outpouring" of prayer for them.[126] She benefited from special prayers people sent her and carried many written prayers with her. Habitual prayer and contemplation, she averred, sustained, comforted, and empowered people.[127] At the 2007 Sojourners Presidential Forum, Clinton maintained that she prayed for discernment, wisdom, strength, and courage and joked that sometimes her plea was, "Oh, Lord, why can't you help me lose weight?"[128] She believes in the power of intercessory prayer. "I think there is increasing evidence" of the impact of such prayer, she explained, pointing to "an interesting hospital study in which patients of comparable medical condition" were treated exactly in the same way medically, but those who were prayed for recovered more quickly than those who were not.[129]

Although Clinton has certainly prayed, attended church, and read Christian literature extensively, her faith has revolved around practical action and good deeds. "I was raised to believe that actions spoke louder than words," she explained. An individual's faith, she insisted, "should be evident in how you treated other people and what kind of life you lived."[130] The biblical passages she cited most often exhorted Christians to do good works and to respond to other people's spiritual, material, physical, and social needs. "She didn't believe it was how high you jumped for joy in church," declared Ed Matthews, Clinton's pastor in Little Rock, Arkansas, "but what you did when you came down."[131]

Clinton praised Methodism for emphasizing both personal salvation and "active applied Christianity." Christians, she stressed, were obliged to help alleviate suffering.[132] Clinton asserted that "the Social Principles of the Methodist Church" and the denomination's history of promoting social justice undergirded many of her own positions and policies. She expressed pride that the Methodist Church had helped lead "the fight to improve the quality of education, promote parental responsibility, curb smoking among young people, expand comprehensive health care, strengthen marriages," and assist people of all ethnicities, races, and social classes.[133] Nevertheless, Clinton complained that her denomination had overemphasized the social gospel in the 1960s, 1970s, and 1980s "to the exclusion of personal faith and growth." She rejoiced that her communion began reemphasizing individual salvation in the 1990s.[134]

Clinton argued that human dignity and worth are based on our "being creatures of God" who have a spiritual nature.[135] However, because of our sinful nature, she insisted, "we do need boundaries. We need guardrails."[136] She praised America's founders for "their almost brutally realistic understanding of human nature" and their recognition that people needed to constrain their appetites. Her religious upbringing and faith, Clinton asserted, had given her "a rock-solid belief in individual responsibility and hard work," but she also believed that community was essential to human flourishing.[137]

Clinton has striven to live as a moral, responsible individual. She has tried to follow what she had been taught years earlier in Sunday school. The Golden Rule, she asserted, "is the best rule for life and for politics."[138] Clinton has looked to God for guidance and sought his wisdom. She has asked for forgiveness and has tried to start over again when she falls short.[139]

People's rights and responsibilities, Clinton contended, are connected. Unfortunately, the United States had often given people "rights without responsibilities," which had contributed to a massive decline in moral behavior. She agreed with New York senator Daniel Patrick Moynihan that American society was "defining deviancy down." Americans, she protested, had gradually accepted more deviant behavior as they embraced moral relativism. Clinton insisted that some behaviors were morally right and that others were morally wrong. She argued that people did and should "pass judgments all the time." She remembered a discussion about terrorists in a Yale Law School class in which many classmates "tried to explain away or rationalize their behavior." "There is another alternative," Clinton avowed—some people are evil. They may be able to devise "elaborate rationalizations" to explain their malevolent deeds and the circumstances of their lives may help account for their deplorable acts, "but their behavior is still evil."[140]

Because transcendent moral standards exist, Clinton contended, certain behaviors are indeed aberrant. This, journalist Michael Kelly asserted, was what social conservatives had argued for years. By contrast, social liberals, who dominated the national Democratic Party, averred that neither government nor society should put forth "a set of behavioral standards based on moral absolutes," because "individual freedom necessitates moral relativism." Clinton countered that many people still believed in and tried to live by absolute moral norms, and society rewarded them for doing so. The Ten Commandments, she claimed, provided the yardstick for human conduct. Almost every religion as well as secular humanism, she added, affirmed the Golden Rule in some form. The assumption underlying the Golden Rule and Christ's commandment to "Love thy neighbor as thyself," she maintained, is "that you will value yourself, that you will be a responsible being who will live by certain behaviors that enable you to have self-respect," which in turn would lead individuals "to respect and care for other people."[141]

Many people incorrectly believed, Clinton complained, that all Christians must affirm "one set of political beliefs" and that anyone who deviated from those particular convictions is "not really a Christian." Although she enjoyed meeting with Christians who espoused a variety of political perspectives in two Capitol Hill fellowship groups, in her speeches Clinton was often critical of Christians who did not share her political views. She wanted her faith to "be integrated and to inform my public life." Clinton insisted that the "great arc of justice" she strove to promote "keeps moving toward a better life, a better time, a better place, on this earth as well as after."[142]

As noted, Clinton is a progressive mainline Methodist. During the middle decades of the twentieth century, Christian progressives changed the focus of their foreign missionary enterprises from converting individuals to Christ to providing a wide array of social services. Progressive members of various Protestant denominations joined together to advance education and improve social conditions through numerous ventures, most notably the World Council of Churches, founded in 1948. They promoted individual freedom, democracy, religious and ideological pluralism, tolerance, reason, and scientific inquiry. In the 1960s, many mainline Protestant ministers made social reform their chief priority; they led rent strikes, organized picket lines, chaired community organizations, promoted low-cost urban housing projects, and urged the government to provide more welfare benefits. Progressive Christians also denounced racism, sexism, imperialism, and fervent nationalism. They were generally more concerned about people's interpersonal relationships and material conditions than the state of their souls. They typically focused more on mobilizing resources to reform society than on helping people develop a close relationship with God. Far more than evangelicals, progressive Christians affirmed the strict separation of church and state; supported abortion rights and the Equal Rights Amendment; and accepted premarital sex, cohabitation, and same-sex relationships.[143] Clinton shares most of the perspectives and priorities of progressive Christians, but she has been more interested in spirituality than many of them.

The Road Not Fully Taken

To analyze how Clinton's faith affected her political philosophy, policy pre-
scriptions, and two campaigns for the presidency, it is instructive to compare
her views and actions with those of another Democratic presidential candidate—George McGovern, a fellow Methodist (in fact, both attended Foundry
Methodist Church in Washington) who shared her commitment to the social
gospel. McGovern, who lost decisively to Richard Nixon in 1972, had some
significant advantages over Clinton in his efforts to apply biblical teaching to
public policy. He was the son of a minister, graduated from and later taught
for several years at Dakota Wesleyan University, attended Garrett Theological
Seminary, and served briefly as a pastor. McGovern is the only major-party
candidate in the twentieth century who worked as a minister. He is only the
second major-party nominee to hold a PhD (Woodrow Wilson was the first),
which he earned in history at Northwestern University, and he read social
gospel literature extensively, including the books of Walter Rauschenbusch.
McGovern participated in the World Council of Churches' meeting in Uppsala,
Sweden, in 1968 and chaired the WCC's Council on Racism in 1969.

In *My Brother's Keeper: George McGovern and Progressive Christianity* (2017),
Mark Lempke argued that the South Dakota senator presents an "example of
the possibilities for a prophetic and politically progressive form of Christianity." Rauschenbusch, Lempke contended, strongly influenced McGovern's
understanding of the role of government. McGovern called for basing politics
on compassion and using government funds to aid the most vulnerable, and he
demonstrated how Judeo-Christian and humanist ethics could reinforce each
other in the political arena. McGovern's worldview was shaped not only by his
education and life experiences but through his networking with prominent
mainline pastors throughout the 1960s. His close friend James Armstrong,
a Methodist bishop, helped him apply social gospel principles to his work.
However, like Clinton, McGovern was reluctant to discuss his personal faith.[144]

Religious groups created two organizations to campaign for the senator in
1972. Religious Leaders for McGovern, founded by Armstrong, another Methodist bishop, and a rabbi, "attracted support from the highest echelons of American
Protestantism." College professor and author Ronald Sider established Evangelicals for McGovern (EFM), which enlisted a cadre of socially activist theological
conservatives including Jim Wallis of *Sojourners*; Fuller Seminary professor Lewis
Smedes; John Alexander, editor of *The Other Side*; Calvin professors Richard
Mouw, Nicholas Wolterstorff, and Stephen Monsma; and historians Richard

Pierard and Robert Linder. Like McGovern, this small but influential group of evangelicals opposed the Vietnam War, and they were alarmed by the political conservatism of many of their compatriots. To help woo evangelicals, McGovern delivered a campaign speech at Wheaton College, a flagstaff evangelical institution near Chicago. EFM members did little grassroots work; they mainly tried to appeal to fellow believers through periodicals such as *Christianity Today*. Their arguments largely fell on deaf ears because most evangelicals saw McGovern as a liberal Protestant who was not open to their political or social perspectives and knew that Nixon enjoyed a close relationship with Billy Graham. Many of them were also repulsed by his commitment to the social gospel, which evangelicals faulted for exalting social transformation over personal conversion. EFM's efforts were ineffective as Nixon won 84 percent of the evangelical vote.[145]

Unlike McGovern, Clinton did not attend a Christian college or seminary or read social gospel literature widely. No specifically religious organizations were created to campaign for her in 2016. Moreover, she did not have relationships with as many ministers as McGovern did, nor did she have a spiritual confidant as Bishop Armstrong was for McGovern. However, Clinton knew at least four men who could have helped her better understand how her faith and biblical teaching could shape public policy: Jim Wallis, Wesley Pippert, Philip Wogaman, and Tony Campolo. During the first two decades of the twenty-first century, Wallis advised numerous Democratic candidates, including Barack Obama, on how to appeal to religious voters, and penned several books on Christianity and politics, including *Great Awakening: Seven Ways to Change the World* (2009) and *Living God's Politics: A Guide to Putting Your Faith into Action* (2009).[146] Pippert, a journalist who attended Foundry Methodist Church with Clinton, wrote *Memo for 1976: Some Political Options* (1974) and *The Hand of the Mighty: Right and Wrong Uses of Our Power* (1991). Wogaman, Foundry's senior pastor, published *Christian Perspectives on Politics* (2000). Campolo, a Baptist professor and pastor who counseled Bill Clinton after his affair with Monica Lewinsky, authored *Is Jesus a Republican or Democrat?* (1995) and *Red Letter Christians: A Citizen's Guide to Faith and Politics* (2013). Had Clinton discussed with these men how scriptural principles could direct her political philosophy and policy formation, her faith might have more deeply influenced her political career. Many of her political views were shaped during a period when she was not actively religious, and as a result her integration of faith and politics has been shallow. She frequently cited Galatians 6:9 on not growing weary in doing good and James's epistle on faith and works, but she did not develop a Christian philosophy of politics like these four men expressed.

Religion and Politics

This religious biography of Hillary Clinton sheds light on the significant role that religion plays in American politics, the importance of religion in America, the challenges the Democratic Party faces in appealing to religious voters, and the varied ways in which faith can direct or affect the work of Christian politicians.

Although the percentage of Americans attending church regularly has declined and the percentage of Americans professing to have no faith ("nones") has increased substantially during the past decade, religion remains important to many Americans and affects their understanding of and participation in politics, much more so than among citizens of other highly developed nations. A recent survey reported that 65 percent of Americans stated that religion is important in their daily lives, compared to only 24 percent of Japanese, 19 percent of Danes, and 17 percent of Swedes.[147] Another survey found that 53 percent of Americans reported that religion was "very important" in their lives, far more than the 14 percent of French, 11 percent of Japanese, and 3 percent of Chinese.[148] According to a third survey, 55 percent of Americans pray daily compared with only 25 percent of Canadians, 22 percent of Europeans, 18 percent of Australians, and a mere 6 percent of British.[149] Moreover, almost half of Americans believe the Bible should have at least "some" influence on the nation's laws, and 23 percent maintain that Scripture should have a "great deal" of influence. More than two-thirds of Christians and almost 90 percent of white evangelicals insist that biblical teaching should help shape US laws. Twice as many Republicans as Democrats want the Bible to influence the nation's laws.[150]

Various exit polls confirm that faith influences how many Americans vote and prompts them to campaign and donate money to candidates, run for office, or lobby to pass or defeat legislative proposals at the federal, state, and local levels. As a result, most American politicians pay at least lip service to religion in their rhetoric, policy proposals, and campaigning. Discussing religious issues and especially their personal faith, however, makes many politicians uncomfortable. Nevertheless, because of public expectations and in some cases their own convictions, officeholders, especially presidents, continually ask God to bless America, ask for prayers for victims of disasters, meet with religious leaders, speak at religious gatherings, create religious advisory groups, hire religious outreach directors for their campaigns, and extol religious values. Little of this occurs in Western Europe.[151]

As discussed, Clinton has a robust, deep faith that has helped to shape her life and her approach to politics. Nevertheless, she has struggled to discuss her personal faith, connect with religious voters (especially theologically conservative ones), and develop a consistently Christian approach to politics. Her personality, life experiences, negative perceptions of her, the recent history of the Democratic Party, and the complexity of religion in America have all made her quest more difficult. A 2019 Pew Research Center survey reported that 54 percent of adults viewed the Republican Party as "friendly" toward religion, whereas only 19 percent of respondents said the same about the Democratic Party.[152]

Nevertheless, the policies Clinton and other mainline Protestant politicians promote may become increasingly acceptable as the nation becomes less religious and many younger evangelical Protestants, especially Black and Latino ones, do not share older evangelicals' opposition to abortion, same-sex marriage, or gay and transgender rights, and endorse other progressive causes such as public investment in childcare and health care for all.[153]

Americans are divided over whether religious groups should focus on shaping the consciences of lawmakers and voters and on participating directly in the political process. Numerous Christians argue that legislative decisions and policies inevitably reflect particular values. Americans debate whether a democratic government should base its policies solely on the will of the people or consider an external reference point in decision-making. Many Americans insist that the nation's policies should be based on transcendent values so as to best preserve human dignity and protect people from the vagaries of public opinion and the challenges of non-Christian philosophies.[154] In a recent Pew Research Poll, 28 percent of American adults said that biblical principles "should take precedence over the will of the people" in formulating governmental policies. More than two-thirds of white evangelical Protestants (68 percent) and half of Black Protestants insisted that "the Bible should override the will of the people when the two conflict."[155]

Some of Clinton's actions clashed with her Christian faith. She engaged in questionable financial practices, appears to have knowingly made false statements at times, and sometimes promoted her own political interests instead of the common good. Moreover, like most other Christian politicians, she did not carefully study how biblical teaching could best direct her work and help determine her political positions and decisions. As noted previously, she could have taken much greater advantage of Christian friends, advisers, books, and articles to help her reflect more deeply about scriptural principles that are relevant to statecraft and to design policies that more fully resonated with biblical tenets. But politics is a messy, complicated, convoluted enterprise that involves making many compromises. That fact, coupled with dealing with colleagues who espouse different worldviews, provides immense challenges for Christian politicians.

Moreover, although hundreds of books have been written about a biblical view of government, Christians' responsibility to participate in politics, and the best ways to do so,[156] few books or articles instruct Christian politicians on how to perform their duties. There are no manuals or training courses for Christian politicians. Christians since Augustine have suggested characteristics and practices that Christian rulers should exude and implement. In The City of God, Augustine maintained that a Christian emperor should promote God's majesty, provide people with opportunities to worship God, be "slow to punish and ready to pardon," seek heavenly rewards rather than earthly glory, and offer God "sacrifices of humility, contrition, and prayer for their sins."[157] Following Augustine's lead, Martin Luther and John Calvin insisted that faithful Christian princes would act very differently from non-Christian ones.

The best resources for contemporary Christian politicians are arguably the autobiographies of fellow believers who strove to be guided by their faith in their work. The most notable recent US example is probably Mark Hatfield, who served as governor and US senator from Oregon. Widely known as both a Republican maverick and a man of strong Christian commitment, Hatfield authored Conflict and Conscience (1971), Between a Rock and a Hard Place (1976), and Against the Grain: Reflections of a Rebel Republican (2000) to describe the challenges he faced in trying to faithfully follow his Christian convictions in the political arena. Hatfield denounced the military-industrial complex, opposed the Vietnam War, drafted a nuclear freeze resolution that Congress passed in 1983, and decried both abortion and the death penalty. He worked to improve health care, education, housing, and employment opportunities, and strove to reduce poverty and racial discrimination. Hatfield argued that a desire to promote the kingdom of God should direct Christian political engagement. While participating actively in politics, he stated, Christians should not force others to accept their views. He urged believers to neither withdraw from the world nor uncritically accept the world's standards. Christians' "fundamental allegiance and loyalty," he argued, is to God's kingdom, the aims and values of which often clash with those of American society.[158]

Political activist Jim Wallis challenges Christians in *God's Politics* (2005) to evaluate politicians by whether they enhance human life, dignity, and rights; "whether they strengthen family life and protect children; whether they promote racial reconciliation and support gender equality"; whether they advance social justice and peace; and whether they further the common good. He exhorts Americans to elevate the public good over their own ethnic, religious, gender, economic, and cultural self-interest and give preference to the poor, marginalized, and vulnerable. Rejecting the belief that God is on our side, which always leads to self-righteousness and triumphalism and often to pursuing dangerous foreign policies, citizens should instead ask "if we are on God's side," which typically leads to repentance, humility, and accountability.[159] He urges citizens to practice civility and compassion and assume that their political opponents "are operating out of good will" instead of seeing them as not simply incorrect but as immoral.[160]

Jack Kemp, whose wife Joanne participated in a prayer group with Clinton while she was first lady, called for a more limited government and celebrated the accomplishments of free enterprise more than Hatfield and Wallis, but he shared many of their commitments. Directed by his faith, the eight-term US congressman, Secretary of Housing and Urban Development, and 1996 Republican vice-presidential candidate strongly promoted civil rights, supported unions, championed affordable housing, combatted poverty, and opposed abortion.[161]

The Principles of Christian Political Engagement adopted by the National Association of Evangelicals in 2003 also provide a solid biblical foundation for Christian politicians. The document's tenets include "Protecting Religious Freedom and Liberty of Conscience," "Safeguarding the Nature and Sanctity of Human Life," "Strengthening Marriages, Families and Children," "Seeking Justice and Compassion for the Poor and Vulnerable," "Preserving Human Rights," "Pursuing Racial Justice and Reconciliation," "Promoting Just Peace and Restraining Violence," and "Caring for God's Creation."[162] Judged by the similar standards put forth by evangelicals from the left to the right (and others including sociologist James Davison Hunter, former George W. Bush speechwriter Michael Gerson, Christians for Social Action founder Ronald Sider, and devotees of Abraham Kuyper such as Richard Mouw), Clinton, with the major exception of her position on abortion, receives high marks.[163] And while strongly advocating the prochoice position, she strove to reduce the number of abortions by working to change the life circumstances and social structures that led women to abort their fetuses.

Given the lack of civility, even bellicosity, that characterizes contemporary American politics, and the deep divisions, not simply between Republicans and Democrats, but within both parties, it is good to remember that many Christians across the political spectrum (including sizable numbers of evangelicals) and numerous proponents of other ideologies share similar attitudes and principles and agree on some basic objectives for what government should do. This can help us cope with the natural human tendency James Madison warned about in "Federalist No. 10" to divide into factions that are so driven by "mutual animosity" that people are "much more disposed to oppress each other than to cooperate for the common good."[164]

Clinton's ability to work with people across the political spectrum at various points in her career illustrates that Americans still share a substantial core of values. The problem, however, is that she could not make common cause with everyone at the same time. When she pleased the right (on issues such as sexual abstinence and welfare reform), the left was unhappy. More often, her policies pleased the left, making the right unhappy. Arguably, her experience confirms the depth of American political polarization in that her attempt to work with both sides proved untenable, contributing to her playing much more to the left than the right on religious issues in 2016.

Throughout her long and impressive career, Clinton's faith has been consistent, deep, and very important to her life and work. As Clinton has frequently testified herself, and many others have affirmed, her Methodist convictions and spirituality have guided and inspired her from her youth to the present. Her faith has helped shape her personality and worldview, determine her goals, drive her to work arduously, stimulate her to care about the downtrodden and destitute, and strive to improve the lives of women and children. It has helped direct and empower her work as a lawyer, first lady of Arkansas and the United States, US senator, secretary of state, and presidential candidate.

Nevertheless, critics complain that Clinton's faith has contributed to her strong sense of moral superiority and stubbornness that damaged her greatly at times, including "crippling her efforts to produce universal health care and rendering her [2016] presidential campaign a joyless death march."[165] Religious conservatives protest that Clinton's theological progressivism has led her to adopt policies on abortion, same-sex marriage, and religious liberty that clash with biblical teaching. Despite ample evidence that her faith is authentic and life-directing, her detractors have often bashed her faith as politically motivated, and the negative appraisals of Clinton described in this book have led many Americans to believe that her faith is either inconsequential or disingenuous. However, by inspiring her to engage in public service and enabling her to cope with substantial adversity and massive criticism, Clinton's faith has played a very positive role in her life.

Throughout her life, Hillary Rodham Clinton has worked tirelessly and passionately to use her various public positions to do all the good she could for all the people she could, in all the ways she could. Although her efforts have been made more difficult by her personality flaws and the ridicule and resistance of her political opponents, her years of public service, especially her herculean efforts to aid women and children, should be commended and celebrated.

Notes

Preface

1. Paul Kengor, *God and Hillary Clinton: A Spiritual Life* (New York: HarperCollins, 2006), xii; Bernstein is quoted in Julie Mazziotta, "How Hillary Clinton's Faith Will Help Her Cope with Shocking Presidential Defeat," *People*, November 9, 2016, https://people.com/politics/clinton-faith-after-presidential-loss/; Huckabee is cited in Michael Luo, "Faith Intertwines with Political Life for Clinton," *New York Times*, July 7, 2007, https://www.nytimes.com/2007/07/07/us/politics/07clinton.html; Jones is quoted in Meredith Oakley, *On the Make: The Rise of Bill Clinton* (Washington, DC: Regnery, 1994), 97; Strider is cited in Dan Merica, "From Park Ridge to Washington: The Youth Minister Who Mentored Hillary Clinton," CNN, April 25, 2014, https://www.cnn.com/2014/04/25/politics/clinton-methodist-minister/.

Introduction

1. Michael O' Loughlin, "The (Mostly) Secret Faith Life of Hillary Clinton," *America*, August 15, 2016, https://www.americamagazine.org/politics-society/2016/08/15/mostly-secret-faith-life-hillary-clinton.

2. Kristin Du Mez, "Can Hillary Clinton's Faith Help Her Lead a Fractured Nation?" Religion and Politics, July 25, 2016, https://religionandpolitics.org/2016/07/25/can-clintons-faith-help-her-lead-a-fractured-nation/.

3. Jon Meacham, "Letting Hillary Be Hillary," *Newsweek*, January 21, 2008, https://www.newsweek.com/letting-hillary-be-hillary-86471.

4. Jack Hitt, "Harpy, Hero, Heretic: Hillary," *Mother Jones*, January–February 2007, https://www.motherjones.com/politics/2007/01/harpy-hero-heretic-hillary/.

5. Christopher Andersen, *American Evita: Hillary Clinton's Path to Power* (New York: HarperCollins, 2004), ix.

6. Joe Conason and Gene Lyons, *The Hunting of the President: The Ten-Year Campaign to Destroy Bill and Hillary Clinton* (New York: St. Martin's, 2000), xiii.

7. Anderson, *American Evita*, 268–69, 271.

8. Katha Pollitt, "Rotten Hillary," in *Thirty Ways of Looking at Hillary: Reflections by Women Writers*, ed. Susan Morrison (New York: HarperCollins, 2008), 16–17, 22.

9. Jason Ripley, "Judging Hillary," *Christian Century* 124 (October 30, 2007), 32–34.

10. Maureen Dowd, "Liberties; Icon and I Will Survive," *New York Times*, December 9, 1998, A29.

11. Susanna Moore, "Cold Snap: The Sorceress Problem," in *Thirty Ways of Looking at Hillary*, 217.

12. Sady Doyle, *Trainwreck: The Women We Love to Hate, Mock, and Fear . . . and Why* (Brooklyn: Melville House, 2016), xviii.

13. "Hating Hillary," *Christianity Today*, March 3, 2008, https://www.christianitytoday.com/ct/2008/march/14.26.html.

14. Both Bordo and Atwood are quoted in Hillary Rodham Clinton, *What Happened* (New York: Simon and Schuster, 2017), 126.

15. Judy Fahys, "Carl Bernstein Paints Full-Spectrum Portrait of Hillary Rodham Clinton," *The Salt Lake Tribune*, October 19, 2007 (first quotation); Carl Bernstein, *A Woman in Charge: The Life of Hillary Rodham Clinton* (New York: Knopf, 2007), 40 (second quotation).

16. Kenneth Woodward, "Soulful Matters," *Newsweek*, October 30, 1994, https://www.newsweek.com/soulful-matters-189302.

17. "Transcript of Interview with Senator Clinton," *New York Times*, July 6, 2007, https://www.nytimes.com/2007/07/06/us/politics/07clinton-text.html.

18. Bernstein interview with an unnamed aide, *Woman in Charge*, 36.

19. William Chafe, *Bill and Hillary: The Politics of the Personal* (New York: Farrar, Straus and Giroux, 2012), 40.

20. See, for example, Hillary Rodham Clinton, *Living History* (New York: Simon and Schuster, 2003), 22.

21. Quoted in "Obama, Clinton Found Faith in Land of Lincoln," NPR, February 3, 2008, https://www.npr.org/templates/story/story.php?storyId=18619707.

22. Wade Clark Roof and William McKinney, *American Mainline Religion: Its Changing Shape and Future* (New Brunswick, NJ: Rutgers University Press, 1987), 73 (quotation); Randall Balmer, *Grant Us Courage: Travels along the Mainline of American Protestantism* (New York: Oxford University Press, 1996), 148.

23. Mark Lempke, *My Brother's Keeper: George McGovern and Progressive Christianity* (Amherst: University of Massachusetts Press, 2017), 8 (quotation), 56, 89.

24. Matthew Hedstrom, "The Rise of Spiritual Cosmopolitanism: Liberal Protestants and Cultural Politics," in *Faithful Republic: Religion and Politics in Modern America*, ed. Andrew Preston, Bruce Schulman, and Julian Zelizer (Philadelphia: University of Pennsylvania Press, 2015), 73. See also N. Jay Demerath III, "Cultural Victory and Organizational Defeat in the Paradoxical Decline of Religious Liberalism," *Journal for the Scientific Study of Religion* 34 (July 1995), 458–69; William Hutchison,

The Modernist Impulse in American Protestantism (New York: Oxford University Press, 1976).

25. See Steven M. Tipton, *Public Pulpits: Methodists and Mainline Churches in the Moral Argument of Public Life* (Chicago: University of Chicago Press, 2008); Jason Lantzer, *Mainline Christianity: The Past and Future of America's Majority Faith* (New York: New York University Press, 2012); James Hudnut-Beumler and Mark Silk, *The Future of Mainline Protestantism in America* (New York: Columbia University Press, 2018); Robert Wuthnow, *The Quiet Hand of God: Faith-Based Activism and the Public Role of Mainline Protestantism* (Berkeley: University of California Press, 2002); Glenn Utter, *Mainline Christians and U.S. Public Policy: A Reference Handbook* (Santa Barbara, CA: ABC-CLIO, 2007); Elesha Coffman, *The Christian Century and the Rise of the Protestant Mainline* (New York: Oxford University Press, 2013); Margaret Bendroth, *The Last Puritans: Mainline Protestants and the Power of the Past* (Chapel Hill: University of North Carolina Press, 2016); Corwin Smidt et al., "The Political Attitudes and Activities of Mainline Protestant Clergy in the Election of 2000: A Study of Six Denominations," *Journal for the Scientific Study of Religion* 42 (December 2003), 515–32; Mark Chaves, Helen Giesel, and William Tsitsos, "Religious Variations in Public Presence: Evidence from the National Congregations Study," in *The Quiet Hand of God: Faith-Based Activism and the Public Role of Mainline Protestantism*, ed. Robert Wuthnow and John Evans (Berkeley: University of California Press, 2002), 108–28.

26. Scholars have defined the social gospel in a variety of ways; the movement consisted of numerous groups and its proponents engaged in a wide variety of activities. Christopher Evans argued that the social gospel "integrated evangelical and liberal theological strands" to advocate for "systemic, structural changes" in American political, social, and economic life (*The Social Gospel in American Religion: A History* [New York: New York University Press, 2017], 2). Susan Hill Lindley defined the social gospel as a movement whose proponents believed that the kingdom of God was "at least partly realizable in this world," recognized the corporate and structural nature of sin, and worked to redeem social institutions ("Deciding Who Counts: Toward a Revised Definition of the Social Gospel," in *The Social Gospel Today*, ed. Christopher Evans [Louisville, KY: Westminster John Knox Press, 2001], 24). See also Gary Scott Smith, *The Search for Social Salvation* (Lanham, MD: Lexington Books, 2000), 3, 6–9, 24, 37, 400–401, 409, 416. Although the social gospel is most connected with the 1880–1920 period, as Evans documents, it helped spark the civil rights movement in the 1960s and 1970s and has continued to have many advocates, especially among mainline and Black Protestants. On this point, see the chapters in part 2 of *The Social Gospel Today*, 101–69. Methodists have long played a major role in propagating the social gospel. See Smith, *Social Salvation*, 8, 11, 31–32, 371–72, 446–49; Robert Moats Miller, "Methodism and Society, 1900–1939," in *The History of American Methodism*, ed. Emory Bucke (New York: Abingdon, 1964), vol. 3, 328–406; Donald Gorrell, "The Methodist Federation for Social Service and the Social Creed," *Methodist History* 13 (January 1975), 3–32; Donald Gorrell, "The Social Creed of Methodists through Eighty Years," *Methodist History* 26 (July 1988), 213–28; Kenneth Collins and Ryan

Danker, eds., *The Next Methodism: Theological, Social, and Missional Foundations for Global Methodism* (Franklin, TN: Seedbed, 2022).

27. Frederick Norwood, *The Story of American Methodists* (Nashville: Abingdon Press, 1974); Russell Richey, Kenneth Rowe, and Jean Miller Schmidt, *American Methodism: A Compact History* (Nashville: Abingdon Press, 2012); Russell Richey, Kenneth Rowe, and Jean Miller Schmidt, *Perspectives on American Methodism: Interpretive Essays* (Nashville: Kingswood Books, 1993); William Abraham and James Kirby, *The Oxford Handbook of Methodist Studies* (Oxford: Oxford University Press, 2011); Jason Vickers, ed., *The Cambridge Companion to American Methodism* (Cambridge: Cambridge University Press, 2013).

28. Mark Tooley, "Hillary Clinton, Methodism and Progressivism," August 11, 2017, https://juicyecumenism.com/2017/08/11/hillary-clinton-methodism -progressivism/. See also James Heidinger, *The Rise of Theological Liberalism and the Decline of American Methodism* (Franklin, TN: Seedbed, 2017); Margaret Bendroth, *Growing Up Protestant: Parents, Children and Mainline Churches* (New Brunswick, NJ: Rutgers University Press, 2002).

29. Tooley, "Hillary Clinton, Methodism and Progressivism."

30. See Lempke, *My Brother's Keeper.*

31. Woodward, "Soulful Matters."

32. See Ashley Boggan Dreff, *Entangled: A History of American Methodism, Politics, and Sexuality* (Nashville: New Room Books, 2018).

33. John Brummett, "Hillary Clinton Strikes a Conciliatory Tone on Abortion." *Las Vegas Review-Journal*, February 13, 2005, 4J.

34. Barbara Amiel, "Holy Crusader," *Wall Street Journal,* October 22, 1996, A20.

35. Chafe, *Bill and Hillary*, 185.

36. Sarah Pulliam Bailey, "The Deep Disgust for Hillary Clinton that Drives So Many Evangelicals to Support Trump," *Washington Post*, October 9, 2016, https:// www.washingtonpost.com/news/acts-of-faith/wp/2016/10/09/the-deep-disgust -for-hillary-clinton-that-drives-so-many-evangelicals-to-support-trump.

37. Woodward, "Soulful Matters." Woodward mentions only the first two criticisms.

38. Daniel Silliman, "Hillary Clinton Showed Up for Church Today. Will Faith Help or Hurt Her on the Campaign?" *Washington Post*, September 13, 2015, https://www.washington post.com/news/acts-of-faith/wp/2015/09/13/hillary-clinton-showed-up-for-church -today-will-faith-help-or-hurt-her-on-the-campaign/; Bailey, "Deep Disgust."

39. Jack Jenkins, "Hillary Clinton Is Now the Most Religious Candidate Running for President," ThinkProgress, May 6, 2016, https://archive.thinkprogress.org/ hillary-clinton-is-now-the-most-religious-candidate-running-for-president-heres -why-that-matters-7cd6819374e5/.

40. Ruth Graham, "Why Hillary Clinton Bombed with White Evangelical Voters," *Slate*, December 15, 2016, https://slate.com/news-and-politics/2016/12/why-hillary -clinton-bombed-with-white-evangelical-voters.html.

41. Graham, "Why Hillary Clinton Bombed."

42. Madhuri Sathish, "Hillary Clinton Is Interested in Becoming A Preacher— REPORT," Bustle, August 11, 2017, https://www.bustle.com/p/hillary-clinton-is -considering-preaching-her-methodist-faith-report-76003.

Chapter 1. "I Felt My Heart Strangely Warmed"

1. Clinton's paternal grandparents claimed they became Methodists because their great-grandparents were converted in the small coal-mining villages in northern England and South Wales by John Wesley. See Hillary Rodham Clinton, *Living History* (New York: Simon and Schuster, 2003), 21.

2. Clinton, *Living History*, 2–3.

3. On Dorothy's early life, see Kathleen Gronnerud, *Hillary Clinton: A Life in American History* (Santa Barbara, CA: ABC-CLIO, 2021), 4–5.

4. Bob Secter and Dawn Turner Trice, "Clinton: Most Famous. Least Known?" *Chicago Tribune*, November 27, 2007, https://www.chicagotribune.com/lifestyles/chi-1127hillaryclintonnov27-story.html.

5. Dan Zak, "Always Running, Always Prepared: Hillary Clinton as a High School Politician," *Washington Post*, October 17, 2016, https://www.washingtonpost.com/lifestyle/style/hillary-clinton-high-school-years-always-running-always-prepared/2016/10/17/35dd9e4a-8c08–11e6-bf8a-3d26847eeed4_story.html.

6. William Chafe, *Bill and Hillary: The Politics of the Personal* (New York: Farrar, Straus and Giroux, 2012), 34.

7. Carl Bernstein, *A Woman in Charge: The Life of Hillary Clinton* (New York: Knopf, 2007), 12.

8. Amy Chozick, "Hillary Clinton Draws Scrappy Determination from a Tough, Combative Father," *New York Times*, July 19, 2015, https://www.nytimes.com/2015/07/20/us/politics/hillary-clinton-draws-scrappy-determination-from-a-tough-combative-father.html.

9. Secter and Trice, "Most Famous. Least Known?"

10. Roger Morris, *Partners in Power: The Clintons and Their America* (Washington, DC: Regnery, 1996), 115.

11. Paul Kengor, *God and Hillary Clinton: A Spiritual Life* (New York: HarperCollins, 2007), 4.

12. Clinton, *Living History*, 11.

13. Hillary Clinton, *It Takes a Village: And Other Lessons Children Teach Us* (New York: Simon and Schuster, 1996), 25, 24; quotations in that order.

14. Clinton, *It Takes a Village*, 24.

15. Chafe, *Bill and Hillary*, 36–37.

16. Chozick, "Hillary Clinton."

17. Kengor, *God and Hillary Clinton*, 7.

18. Clinton, *Living History*, 12.

19. Bernstein, *Woman in Charge*, 13.

20. "Wake Up the World! Transcript of Hillary Rodham Clinton's Address to Assembly 2014," United Women in Faith, April 26, 2014, https://www.unitedmethodistwomen.org/news/wake-up-the-world!.

21. Quoted in Daniel Burke, "The Public and Private Faith of Hillary Clinton," CNN, October 30, 2016, https://www.cnn.com/2016/10/30/politics/clinton-faith-private/index.html.

22. Clinton, *Living History*, 22. Leon Osgood, one of Hillary's Sunday school teachers and a lifelong member of First Methodist, reported that "Hugh was not active at

all" at Park Ridge perhaps because "he traveled a lot on business" (quoted in Peter and Timothy Flaherty, *The First Lady* [Lafayette, LA: Vital Issues Press, 1995], 21). Others agree that Hugh was "seldom seen" at church (Kenneth Woodward, "Soulful Matters," *Newsweek*, October 30, 1994, https://www.newsweek.com/soulful-matters-189302).

23. Hillary Rodham Clinton, "Address to the General Conference," April 24, 1996, http://catalog.gcah.org/DigitalArchives/conference/GC96/hilltext.html.

24. Martha Sherrill, "In 1993 We Interviewed Hillary Clinton about Religion," *Washington Post*, October 17, 2016, https://www.washingtonpost.com/news/post -politics/wp/2016/10/17/in-1993-we-interviewed-hillary-clinton-about-religion-and -politics-heres-what-she-said/.

25. Hillary Clinton, *Hard Choices* (New York: Simon and Schuster, 2014), 587.

26. Clinton, *It Takes a Village*, 171.

27. Quoted in Norman King, *Hillary: Her True Story* (New York: Birch Lane Press, 1993), 8.

28. Chafe, *Bill and Hillary*, 37.

29. Martha Sherrill, "The Education of Hillary Clinton," *Washington Post*, January 11, 1993, https://www.washingtonpost.com/archive/lifestyle/1993/01/11/the-education -of-hillary-clinton/371300bc-40ef-408b-8f52-b9d7d55adc97/.

30. Morris, *Partners in Power*, 123.

31. Bernstein, *Woman in Charge*, 30.

32. Zak, "Always Running."

33. Zak, "Always Running."

34. Martha Sherrill, "Hillary Clinton's Inner Politics," *Washington Post*, May 6, 1993, https://www.washingtonpost.com/archive/lifestyle/1993/05/06/hillary-clintons -inner-politics/799e9d5d-0dff-4017-be98-00253b76e974/.

35. Clinton, *Living History*, 21.

36. Charles Kenney, "Hillary: The Wellesley Years," *Boston Globe*, January 12, 1993, https://www.bostonglobe.com/news/politics/1993/01/12/hillary-the-wellesley -years/OEapzWGuzSNAFiIHL2zm9K/story.html.

37. Clinton, *It Takes a Village*, 26, 173, 182–83. In 1994, Clinton shared that she had recently reread this essay that in many ways "was very simple," but it also contained much that was "as profound as any theology" she had read ("The First Lady's Remarks to the National Prayer Luncheon," February 2, 1994, https://clintonwhitehouse4 .archives.gov/media/text/1994–02–02-first-lady-remarks-to-the-national-prayer -luncheon.text).

38. Clinton, *Living History*, 21.

39. Clinton, *It Takes a Village*, 27.

40. Clinton, "Address to the General Conference."

41. Neo-Orthodoxy is a Protestant theological movement that strongly impacted European and American academic theology from the 1930s until the late 1960s. Rejecting the exuberant optimism of liberal theology and the belief in biblical in-fallibility of theological conservatism, its proponents emphasized major themes of Reformation theology, especially the transcendence of God, the radical sinfulness of humanity, Jesus Christ as savior and lord, and the kingdom of God. Its principal proponents included Swiss theologians Karl Barth and Emil Brunner, German pastor

Dietrich Bonhoeffer, and American theologians Reinhold Niebuhr and Paul Tillich. Most Neo-Orthodox Christians were deeply concerned about ethical issues, including war and peace and racial discrimination. See Heather Warren, *Theologians of a New World Order* (New York: Oxford University Press, 1997), and John Wilson, *Introducing Modern Theology: Trajectories in the German Tradition* (Louisville: Westminster John Knox Press, 2007).

42. Zak, "Always Running."

43. Marcella Bombardieri, "From Conservative Roots Sprang a Call for Change," *Boston Globe,* October 21, 2007, A1.

44. Zak, "Always Running."

45. Kengor, *God and Hillary Clinton*, 14.

46. Morris, *Partners in Power*, 121.

47. Clinton, *Living History*, 22.

48. See Gail Sheehy, *Hillary's Choice* (New York: Random House, 1999), 33–37; David Maraniss, *First in His Class* (New York: Simon and Schuster, 1995), 250–54; Chafe, *Bill and Hillary*, 38.

49. Clinton, *Living History*, 23.

50. Burke, "The Public and Private Faith."

51. Flaherty and Flaherty, *The First Lady*, 21.

52. Sherrill, "We Interviewed Hillary Clinton."

53. Jones and Bentzinger, as cited in Zak, "Always Running."

54. Martin Kasindorf, "Meet Hillary Clinton. She's Raised Hackles and Hopes, But One Thing's Certain: She'll Redefine Role of First Lady," *Newsday*, January 10, 1993, 7.

55. Clinton, *It Takes a Village*, 27.

56. Kasindorf, "Meet Hillary Clinton."

57. Bernstein, *Woman in Charge*, 34 (first two phrases); Chafe, *Bill and Hillary*, 38 (third phrase).

58. Morris, *Partners in Power*, 120.

59. Sherrill, "We Interviewed Hillary Clinton."

60. "Wake Up the World!"

61. Quoted in Sherrill, "Inner Politics."

62. Morris, *Partners in Power*, 121.

63. Bombardieri, "From Conservative Roots."

64. Clinton, *Living History*, 23.

65. Clinton, *Living History*, 23.

66. Bombardieri, "From Conservative Roots."

67. Clinton, *Living History*, 23.

68. Morris, *Partners in Power*, 121.

69. David Brock, *The Seduction of Hillary Clinton* (New York: Free Press, 1996), 6 (first two quotations), 7 (third quotation).

70. Michael Kelly, "Saint Hillary," *New York Times*, May 23, 1993, https://www.nytimes.com/1993/05/23/magazine/saint-hillary.html.

71. Dan Merica, "From Park Ridge to Washington: The Youth Minister Who Mentored Hillary Clinton," CNN, April 25, 2014, https://www.cnn.com/2014/04/25/politics/clinton-methodist-minister/.

72. Joyce Milton, *The First Partner* (New York: William Morrow, 1999), 22.

73. King, *Hillary*, 9.

74. Bombardieri, "From Conservative Roots."

75. Clinton, *Living History*, 23.

76. Sheehy, *Hillary's Choice*, 34.

77. Bernstein, *Woman in Charge*, 35–36.

78. Bombardieri, "From Conservative Roots."

79. Bernstein, *Woman in Charge*, 37.

80. David Hollinger, *After Cloven Tongues of Fire: Protestant Liberalism in Modern American History* (Princeton, NJ: University Press, 2013), 22–23.

Chapter 2. "Let Your Light Shine to All"

1. Charles Kenney, "Hillary: The Wellesley Years," *Boston Globe*, January 12, 1993, https://www.bostonglobe.com/news/politics/1993/01/12/hillary-the-wellesley-years/OEapzWGuzSNAFiIHL2zm9K/story.html.

2. "How to Steal $500 Million," Frontline, November 8, 1994, http://www.shoppbs.pbs.org/wgbh/pages/frontline/programs/transcripts/1304.html.

3. Why Clinton attended church infrequently during these years is unclear. Being preoccupied with her studies at Yale and then with adjusting to new jobs, marriage, and her role as Arkansas's first lady perhaps was a factor. Arguably, during these years, her faith was not as important to her as earlier and later in her life.

4. Roger Morris, *Partners in Power: The Clintons and Their America* (New York: Henry Holt, 1996), 124.

5. This is a description of the *Time* article by the *Wellesley News*. See Kenney, "Hillary: The Wellesley Years."

6. Michael Kelly, "Saint Hillary," *New York Times Magazine*, May 23, 1993, https://www.nytimes.com/1993/05/23/magazine/saint-hillary.html.

7. "The Inheritor," *Time*, January 6, 1967, 18–23.

8. "Notes of Mr. Durant's Sermon on 'The Spirit of the College,'" in *Sermons Preached by Henry Fowle Durant on September 23, 1877* (Boston: Frank Wood, 1890).

9. H. F. Durant, "A Few Thoughts on the Study of the Bible" (undated sermon on Psalms 139:7–12 [1877?]), 2, Wellesley College Archives, as cited by A. Donald MacLeod, "Hillary Clinton and the Evangelical Feminism of the Start-up of Wellesley College," October 2016, http://adonaldmacleod.com/2016/10/hillary-clinton-and-the-evangelical-feminism-of-the-start-up-of-wellesley-college/.

10. File in the Wellesley College Archives titled "Mr. Durant's Last Words," with the notation "Copied by me [Marion Payson Guild] from Mrs. Durant's own mss record lent me by Fanny Massil in summer of 1915," as cited by MacLeod, "Hillary Clinton." See also Florence Morse Kingsley, *The Life of Henry Fowle Durant: Founder of Wellesley College* (New York: Century, 1924).

11. On Wellesley's history, see Arlene Cohen, *Wellesley College* (Charleston, SC: Arcadia Publishing, 2006). In 1965, Article I of Wellesley's By-Laws still stated, "The College was founded for the glory of God and the service of the Lord Jesus Christ by the education and culture of women. To realize this design it is required that the

Trustees shall be in manifest sympathy with the traditional religious purpose of the College, that members of the faculty shall be selected with a view to maintaining the Christian purpose of the College; and that every undergraduate shall study the Sacred Scriptures." Quoted in Manning Pattillo and Donald Mackenzie, *Church-Sponsored Higher Education in the United States* (Washington, DC: American Council on Education, 1966), 20.

12. Michael Kruse, "The First Time Hillary Clinton Was President," *Politico* magazine, August 26, 2016, https://www.politico.com/magazine/story/2016/08/hillary-clinton-2016-wellesley-president-214188/.

13. Martha Sherrill, "The Rising Lawyer's Detour to Arkansas; At Wellesley, She Found Her Calling. At Yale, She Met Her Future," *Washington Post*, January 12, 1993, B1.

14. Kristin Du Mez, "Can Hillary Clinton's Faith Help Her Lead a Fractured Nation?" Religion and Politics, July 25, 2016, https://religionandpolitics.org/2016/07/25/can-clintons-faith-help-her-lead-a-fractured-nation/.

15. Kenney, "Hillary: The Wellesley Years."

16. Kruse, "First Time Hillary Was President."

17. Kenney, "Hillary: The Wellesley Years."

18. Gail Sheehy, *Hillary's Choice* (New York: Random House, 1999), 124.

19. Carl Bernstein, *A Woman in Charge: The Life of Hillary Clinton* (New York: Knopf, 2007), 49.

20. Kenneth Woodward, "Soulful Matters," *Newsweek*, October 30, 1994, https://www.newsweek.com/soulful-matters-189302.

21. Barbara Olson, *Hell to Pay* (Washington, DC: Regnery Publishing, 1999), 35.

22. Bernstein, *Woman in Charge*, 50.

23. Michael Luo, "Faith Intertwines with Political Life for Clinton," *New York Times*, July 7, 2007, https://www.nytimes.com/2007/07/07/us/politics/07clinton.html.

24. Hillary Rodham Clinton, *Living History* (New York: Simon and Schuster, 2003), 28.

25. Hillary Rodham Clinton, *What Happened* (New York: Simon and Schuster, 2017), 197.

26. Bernstein, *Woman in Charge*, 40 (first quotation), 50 (second and third quotations).

27. Kenney, "Hillary: The Wellesley Years."

28. Quoted in Donnie Radcliffe, *Hillary Rodham Clinton: A First Lady for Our Time* (New York: Warner, 1993), 69.

29. Douglas Sloan, *Faith and Knowledge: Mainline Protestantism and American Higher Education* (Lexington: University of Kentucky Press, 1994), 83.

30. "Methodists: A Jester for Wesleyans," *Time*, October 21, 1966, 69.

31. "Dr. Harold Ehrensperger Dies; Active in Theater and Religion," *New York Times*, November 10, 1973, 34.

32. July 7, 1969, letter to subscribers, *motive*, May 1969, 1. The May 1969 issue consists only of this letter.

33. Stephen Weissman and Doug Tuthill, "Freedom and the University," *motive*, October 1965, 4–13.

34. Jack Newfield, "Revolt without Dogma," *motive*, October 1965, 20–22; Keith Bridston, "The Student Generation and the Ecumenical Movement," *motive*, October 1965, 25–28; Elmra Kendricks, "Vietnam: Our Common Task," *motive*, October 1965, 36.

35. Julian Bond, "Impetus and Impact: Students and the Civil Rights Movement," *motive*, October 1965, 41–44.

36. George McLain, "Education for a Reconstructed America," *motive*, October 1965, 45–46.

37. Roger Shinn, "Living in a World That Won't Stand Still," *motive*, October 1965, 50–52.

38. "A Student Manifesto: A Model for Revolutionary Mission," *motive*, October 1965, 30–32.

39. Woodward, "Soulful Matters." In her interview with Woodward, Clinton referred to Oglesby's article as "Change or Containment," and numerous biographers and journalists have cited this title. The actual title of the essay is "World Revolution and American Containment."

40. Margalit Fox, "Carl Oglesby, Antiwar Leader in 1960s, Dies at 76," *New York Times*, September 14, 2011, https://www.nytimes.com/2011/09/14/us/carl-oglesby -antiwar-leader-in-1960s-dies-at-76.html.

41. Carl Oglesby, "Let Us Shape the Future," https://www.sds-1960s.org/sds_wuo/ sds_documents/oglesby_future.html.

42. Carl Oglesby, "World Revolution and American Containment," *motive*, October 1966, 21.

43. Oglesby, "World Revolution and American Containment," 24. Oglesby elaborated on these arguments in his "Vietnam Crucible: An Essay in the Meanings of the Cold War," 3–176, in Oglesby and Richard Shaull, *Containment and Change: Two Dissenting Views of American Foreign Policy* (New York: Macmillan, 1967).

44. Oglesby, "World Revolution and American Containment," 23.

45. Bernstein, *Woman in Charge*, 45–46.

46. MacLeod, "Hillary Clinton."

47. Jennifer Siegel, "Clinton's Thesis on Leftist Icon Reveals Roots," *Forward,* December 7, 2007, A1, A7.

48. Wayne A. R. Leys, "Machiavelli in Modern Dress," *Christian Century* 76 (November 11, 1959), 1308; Saul Alinsky, *Reveille for Radicals* (Chicago: University of Chicago Press, 1946), 112.

49. "Justice and Beyond Justice," *Christian Century* 82 (February 24, 1965), 228.

50. "The Professional Radical: A Conversation with Saul Alinsky," introduced by Marion Sanders, *Harper's*, June 1965, 37–46.

51. "The Greatest Good of All," *Christian Century* 82 (July 30, 1965), 827.

52. Kruse, "First Time Hillary Clinton Was President."

53. Hillary Rodham, "'There is Only the Fight' . . . An Analysis of the Alinsky Model," senior thesis, Wellesley College, 1969, chapter 1, p. 11, http://www.hillaryclinton quarterly.com/documents/HillaryClintonThesis.pdf.

54. Siegel, "Clinton's Thesis on Leftist Icon." On Alinsky, see P. David Finks, *The Radical Vision of Saul Alinsky* (New York: Paulist Press, 1984); Nicholas von Hoffman, *Radical: A Portrait of Saul Alinsky* (New York: Nation Books, 2010).

55. Clinton, *Living History*, 38.

56. Kenney, "Hillary: The Wellesley Years."

57. David Brock, *The Seduction of Hillary Rodham* (New York: Free Press, 1996), 11.

58. Gist, Adams, and Shield are quoted in Kenney, "Hillary: The Wellesley Years."

59. Kenney, "Hillary: The Wellesley Years."

60. Will Herberg, *Judaism and Modern Man: An Interpretation of Jewish Religion* (New York: Farrar, Straus and Young, 1951).

61. Bob Secter and Dawn Turner Trice, "Clinton: Most Famous. Least Known?" *Chicago Tribune*, November 27, 2007, https://www.chicagotribune.com/lifestyles/chi-1127hillaryclintonnov27-story.html.

62. George Cornell, AP, "New First Lady Practices What She Preaches; Hillary Clinton Reads Scriptures, Acts in Methodist Tradition," *Salt Lake Tribune,* December 5, 1992, C1.

63. "The Choice," 2016 documentary, PBS, https://www.pbs.org/wgbh/frontline/film/the-choice-2016/transcript/.

64. Quoted in Tamara Keith, "Taking on a US Senator as a Student Propelled Clinton into the Spotlight," UPR Presents, July 28, 2016, https://www.upr.org/post/taking-us-senator-student-propelled-clinton-spotlight#stream/0.

65. Quoted in Mark Jacob, "When the Chicago Tribune Scolded a 'Girl' Named Hillary Rodham," *Chicago Tribune*, September 30, 2016, https://www.chicagotribune.com/news/ct-clinton-trump-tribune-archives-met-20160930-story.html.

66. Edward Brooke, "Progress in the Uptight Society: Real Problems and Wrong Procedures," Wellesley College, May 31, 1969, https://www.wellesley.edu/events/commencement/archives/1969commencement/commencementaddress.

67. Clinton, *Living History*, 40.

68. Nancy Wanderer, as quoted in the "The Choice."

69. Brock, *Seduction*, 22.

70. "Hillary D. Rodham's 1969 Student Commencement Speech," https://www.wellesley.edu/events/commencement/archives/1969commencement/studentspeech.

71. Kenney, "Hillary: The Wellesley Years."

72. "Miss Rodham's Discourtesy to Sen. Brooke Was Unjustified," *Chicago Tribune*, June 3, 1969. See also "Park Ridge Girl Raps Brooke," *Chicago Tribune*, June 2, 1969.

73. Amy Chozick, "5 Things You Might Not Know about Hillary Clinton," *New York Times*, May 19, 2015, https://www.nytimes.com/2015/05/20/us/politics/5-things-you-might-not-know-about-hillary-clinton.html; Michelle Theriault Boots and Erica Martinson, "The Untold Story of Hillary Clinton's 1969 Summer in Alaska," *Anchorage Daily News*, October 5, 2016, https://www.adn.com/politics/2016/10/05/the-untold-story-of-hillary-clintons-1969-summer-in-alaska/. Boots and Martinson argue that some of Clinton's accounts on the campaign trail of her work in the cannery are suspect. Clinton has not offered any other explanations for why she spent the summer in Alaska. In his speech introducing Hillary in July 2016, Bill called her decision to go to Alaska "a total lark."

74. Bernstein, *Woman in Charge*, 63.

75. Clinton, *Living History*, 38.

76. Valerie Hudson and Patricia Leidl, *The Hillary Doctrine: Sex and American Foreign Policy* (New York: Columbia University Press, 2015), 11.

77. Bernstein, *Woman in Charge*, 73–74.

78. Paul Kengor, *God and Hillary Clinton: A Spiritual Life* (New York: HarperCollins, 2006), 47.

79. William Chafe, *Bill and Hillary: The Politics of the Personal* (New York: Farrar Strauss and Giroux, 2012), 77 (first quotation), Bernstein, *Woman in Charge*, 86–87 (all the Ehrman material); David Maraniss, *First in His Class* (New York: Simon and Schuster, 1995), 265–67; Bill Clinton, *My Life* (New York: Random House, 2004), 190–200; Sheehy, *Hillary's Choice*, 84. On Ehrman, see Amy Chozick, "Sara Ehrman, Outspoken Feminist with Deep Ties to Clintons, Dies at 98," *New York Times*, June 3, 2017, https://www.nytimes.com/2017/06/03/us/sara-ehrman-dead-adviser-to-clintons.html.

80. Martha Sherrill, "Hillary Clinton's Inner Politics," *Washington Post*, May 6, 1993, https://www.washingtonpost.com/archive/lifestyle/1993/05/06/hillary-clintons-inner-politics/799e9d5d-0dff-4017-be98-00253b76e974/. See Marian Wright Edelman, *Guide My Feet: Prayers and Meditations for Our Children* (New York: HarperCollins, 1995).

81. Martin Kasindorf, "Meet Hillary Clinton. She's Raised Hackles and Hopes, But One Thing's Certain: She'll Redefine Role of First Lady," *Newsday*, January 10, 1993, 7. The *Wall Street Journal* noted that Edelman had been hailed as "an American Mother Teresa" whose numerous accolades included one hundred honorary degrees (Dana Milbank, "Children's Defense Fund and Its Lauded Leader Lose Clout as Social Policy Shifts to the States," *Wall Street Journal*, May 28, 1996, A28).

82. Bernstein, *Woman in Charge*, 92.

83. Clinton, *Living History*, 66.

84. Bernstein, *Woman in Charge*, 92.

85. Clinton, *Living History*, 64.

86. Rebecca Savransky, "Trump Mocks Clinton for Failing DC Bar Exam," The Hill, August 29, 2016, https://thehill.com/blogs/ballot-box/presidential-races/293643-trump-mocks-clinton-for-failing-dc-bar-exam.

87. Mark Miller, "Saint or Sinner?" *Newsweek*, April 10, 1994, https://www.newsweek.com/saint-or-sinner-187072 (first quotation); Amy Chozick, "The Road Trip That Changed Hillary Clinton's Life," *New York Times*, October 28, 2016, https://www.nytimes.com/2016/10/29/us/politics/hillary-clinton-road-trip.html (second and third quotations).

88. Deborah Sale, interview with Bernstein, *Woman in Charge*, 62.

89. Connie Bruck, "Hillary the Pol," *New Yorker*, May 30, 1993, https://www.newyorker.com/magazine/1994/05/30/hillary-the-pol.

90. Bernstein, *Woman in Charge*, 62 (first and third quotations), 63 (second quotation).

91. Amy Chozick, "Family Disputes and a Nasty Can of Beans: Hillary Clinton as Litigator," *New York Times*, November 3, 2016, https://www.nytimes.com/2016/11/04/us/politics/hillary-clinton-lawyer.html.

92. Margaret Carlson, "A Different Kind of First Lady," *Time*, November 16, 1992, 40–41.

93. Bernstein, *Woman in Charge*, 162.

94. Amy Chozick, "Stress Over Family Finances Propelled Hillary Clinton into Corporate World," *New York Times*, August 10, 2016, https://www.nytimes.com/2016/08/11/us/politics/hillary-clinton-money.html.

95. Tom Dillard, "Frank Durward White (1933–2003)," *Encyclopedia of Arkansas*, https://encyclopediaofarkansas.net/entries/frank-durward-white-125/ (quotation); David Maraniss, "Lessons of Humbling Loss Guide Clinton's Journey," *Washington Post*, June 14, 1992, https://www.washingtonpost.com/archive/politics/1992/07/14/lessons-of-humbling-loss-guide-clintons-journey/be11571f-088f-4df8-b11c-d1d276954a52/.

96. Joyce Milton, *The First Partner* (New York: William Morrow, 1999), 139–40.

97. Brock, *Seduction*, 148.

98. Maraniss, *First in His Class*, 432–33.

99. Richard Wilke, introducing Clinton, in Hillary Rodham Clinton, "Address to General Conference," April 24, 1996, http://catalog.gcah.org/DigitalArchives/conference/GC96/hilltext.html.

100. Janet Cawley, "Leading Lady: The First Lady Takes Her Place on the National Stage," *Chicago Tribune*, May 9, 1993, 10.

101. Daniel Burke, "The Public and Private Faith of Hillary Clinton," CNN, October 30, 2016, https://www.cnn.com/2016/10/30/politics/clinton-faith-private/index.html.

102. "Our History," First United Methodist Church—Little Rock, https://fumclr.org/about/our-history/.

103. Kengor, *God and Hillary Clinton*, 72.

104. Bernstein, *Woman in Charge*, 162.

105. Sheehy, *Hillary's Choice*, 173.

106. Clinton, *It Takes a Village*, 9.

107. Claire Osborne, ed., *The Unique Voice of Hillary Rodham Clinton: A Portrait in Her Own Words* (New York: Avon Books, 1997), 18.

108. David Maraniss, "Roots of Clinton's Faith Deep, Varied," *Washington Post*, June 29, 1992, https://www.washingtonpost.com/archive/politics/1992/06/29/roots-of-clintons-faith-deep-varied/081f58ca-5974-4329-a675-0936011e96ac/.

109. Cornell, "New First Lady Practices What She Preaches," C1.

110. Clinton, *It Takes a Village*, 171–72, 177; quotation from 172.

111. Norman King, *Hillary: Her True Story* (New York: Birch Lane Press, 1993), 120. Matthews told Paul Kengor that he did not counsel the Clintons (*God and Hillary Clinton*, 84).

112. Brock, *Seduction*, 147–48; quotations 148.

113. Quoted in Woodward, "Soulful Matters."

114. Kasindorf, "Meet Hillary Clinton."

115. Brock, *Seduction*, 161.

116. Chafe, *Bill and Hillary*, 118.

117. Brock, *Seduction*, 162.

118. "Hillary Clinton: Activist and Scholar," *Telegram and Gazette* (Worcester, MA), April 21, 1992, D1.

119. Chafe, *Bill and Hillary*, 119.

120. Both Starr and Blair are quoted in Ruth Marcus, "Now, a Different Kind of First Lady," *Washington Post*, January 20, 1993, F20.

121. "Hillary Clinton: Activist and Scholar," D1.

122. Chafe, *Bill and Hillary*, 119.

123. Chafe, *Bill and Hillary*, 83 (first quotation), 136 (second quotation).

124. Marcus, "Different Kind of First Lady."

125. Martha Sherrill, "The Education of Hillary Clinton," *Washington Post*, January 11, 1993, https://www.washingtonpost.com/archive/lifestyle/1993/01/11/the-education-of-hillary-clinton/371300bc-40ef-408b-8f52-b9d7d55adc97/.

126. Marcus, "Different Kind of First Lady."

127. Morris, *Partners in Power*, 142.

128. Hillary Clinton, *What Happened* (New York: Simon and Schuster, 2017), 433.

129. Chafe, *Bill and Hillary*, 153.

130. Maureen Dowd, "The 1992 Campaign: Candidate's Wife; Hillary Clinton as Aspiring First Lady: Role Model, or a 'Hall Monitor' Type?" *New York Times*, May 18, 1992, A15.

131. Michael Kruse, "The TV Interview That Haunts Hillary Clinton," *Politico*, September 23, 2016, https://www.politico.com/magazine/story/2016/09/hillary-clinton-2016-60-minutes-1992-214275/.

132. William Safire, "The Hillary Problem," *New York Times*, March 26, 1992, A23.

133. Kruse, "The TV Interview."

134. Dowd, "The 1992 Campaign," A15.

135. Karen Ball, "Move Over Status Quo—Name of Her Game Is Change," *Salt Lake Tribune,* July 12, 1992, A21.

136. "Wife, Mother, Lawyer, Scholar; Hillary Clinton's Juggling Act," *Telegram and Gazette* (Worcester, MA), November 5, 1992, A4.

137. Ball, "Move Over Status Quo," A21.

138. Ball, "Move Over Status Quo," A21.

139. Christopher Lasch, "Hillary Clinton, Child Savior," *Harper's*, October 1992, 74–83.

140. Cal Thomas, "Hillary Clinton Plans to Redesign Family," *St. Louis Dispatch*, October 27, 1992, B3.

141. Clinton had argued in 1973 that "the basic rationale for depriving people of rights in a dependency relationship is that certain individuals are incapable or undeserving of the right to take care of themselves and consequently need social institutions specifically designed to safeguard their position." She added, "Along with the family, past and present examples of such arrangements include marriage, slavery and the Indian reservation system." See Hillary Rodham, "Children Under the Law," *Harvard Educational Review* 43, no. 4 (1973): 493.

142. Felicity Barringer, "The 1992 Campaign: Hillary Clinton; From Lawyer to Mother; Now, Both of the Above," *New York Times*, October 30, 1992, A18.

143. Chafe, *Bill and Hillary*, 139.

144. Donald Baer, Matthew Cooper, and David Gergen, "Bill Clinton's Hidden Life," *US News and World Report*, July 20, 1992, 30.

145. "Clinton Calls Attack Offensive," *St. Louis Post-Dispatch,* August 24, 1992, A1.

146. See Meredith Oakley, *On the Make: The Rise of Bill Clinton* (Washington, DC: Regnery, 1994), 97. Oakley cites an interview with Jones in "The Real Woman, Hillary Clinton," *People*, January 25, 1993.

147. Patt Morrison, "Time for a Feminist as First Lady?" *Los Angeles Times*, July 14, 1992, 1.

148. "Clinton Calls Attack Offensive," 1A.

149. Morrison, "Time for a Feminist," 1.

150. Morrison, "Time for a Feminist," 1.

151. Kelly, "Saint Hillary."

152. Clinton, *Living History*, 117.

Chapter 3. "Light Yourself on Fire with Passion"

1. James Stewart, *Blood Sport: The President and His Adversaries* (New York: Simon and Schuster, 1996), 368.

2. Bob Secter and Dawn Turner Trice, "Clinton: Most Famous. Least Known?" *Chicago Tribune*, November 27, 2007, https://www.chicagotribune.com/lifestyles/ chi-1127hillaryclintonnov27-story.html.

3. Angie Cannon, "Trail-Blazing First Lady Inspires Admiration, Antipathy," *Salt Lake Tribune,* September 24, 1996, A4.

4. Patt Morrison, "With Hillary Clinton, East Meets West in White House Power," *Los Angeles Times*, January 17, 1993, 1.

5. Carl Bernstein, *A Woman in Charge: The Life of Hillary Clinton* (New York: Knopf, 2007), 9–10; quotation from 9.

6. Kenneth Woodward, "Soulful Matters," *Newsweek*, October 30, 1994, https:// www.newsweek.com/soulful-matters-189302.

7. Kenneth Woodward, "The Democrats' Methodist Moment," *Wall Street Journal*, September 22, 2016, https://www.wsj.com/articles/the-democrats-methodist -moment-1474586097.

8. "Statement to the Methodist News Service in 1992," as cited in George Cornell, "Hillary Brings Theology to the White House," *Washington Post*, December 5, 1992, https://www.washingtonpost.com/archive/local/1992/12/05/hillary-clinton-brings -theology-to-white-house/64647e92–9d8a-476b-bb35–69fc5e7e8e10/.

9. Woodward, "Soulful Matters."

10. Hillary Rodham Clinton, *It Takes a Village* (New York: Simon & Schuster, 1996), 173, 178; quotations in that order.

11. Hillary Rodham Clinton, *Living History* (New York: Simon & Schuster, 2003), 428.

12. Woodward, "Democrats' Methodist Moment."

13. See Gary Scott Smith, *Faith and the Presidency: From George Washington to George W. Bush* (New York: Oxford University Press, 2006); and Smith, *Religion in the Oval*

Office: The Religious Lives of American Presidents (New York: Oxford University Press, 2015).

14. *Live with Regis and Kathie Lee*, June 10, 1996, in Claire Osborne, ed., *The Unique Voice of Hillary Rodham Clinton: A Portrait in Her Own Words* (New York: Avon Books, 1997), 89.

15. Bernstein, *Woman in Charge*, 296.

16. Felicity Barringer, "The President-Elect's Wife: Hillary Clinton's New Role: The Job Description Is Open," *New York Times*, November 16, 1992, https://www.nytimes.com/1992/11/16/us/transition-president-elect-s-wife-hillary-clinton-s-new-role-job-description.html.

17. Richard Berke, "The Other Clinton Helps Shape the Administration," *New York Times*, December 14, 1992, https://www.nytimes.com/1992/12/14/us/the-transition-the-other-clinton-helps-shape-the-administration.html.

18. David Lauter, "Mrs. Wonk Goes to Washington: If Hillary Clinton Succeeds, She Could Revolutionize the Role of First Lady. If She Fails, She Could Take the Whole Administration Down with Her," *Los Angeles Times*, May 23, 1993, 12.

19. Mary Leonard, "So Far, Hillary Clinton Is Suffering in Silence," *Boston Globe*, September 14, 1998, A3.

20. Clinton, *Living History*, 110.

21. Margaret Carlson, "A Different Kind of First Lady," *Time*, November 16, 1992, 40–41.

22. Berke, "The Other Clinton."

23. Carlson, "Different Kind of First Lady."

24. Martin Kasindorf, "Meet Hillary Clinton. She's Raised Hackles and Hopes, But One Thing's Certain: She'll Redefine Role of First Lady," *Newsday*, January 10, 1993, 7.

25. Myriam Marquez, "Media Can't Seem to Explain Hillary Clinton without Resorting to Caricature," *Sun Sentinel* (Fort Lauderdale, FL), May 1, 1993, 18A.

26. Cornell, "Hillary Brings Theology."

27. Mimi Hall, "The Unseen Side of Hillary Clinton," *USA Today*, November 27, 1992, 4A. See also "Hillary Clinton Schooled in Doctrine of Methodism Theology," *Los Angeles Times*, December 5, 1992, 4.

28. As quoted in Janet Cawley, "Leading Lady: The First Lady Takes Her Place on the National Stage," *Chicago Tribune*, May 9, 1993, 10.

29. Carol Jouzaitis, "First Lady Is Gaining New Respect," *Chicago Tribune*, May 23, 1993, C6.

30. As quoted in Cawley, "Leading Lady," 10.

31. Lauter, "Mrs. Wonk Goes to Washington," 12.

32. Cawley, "Leading Lady," 10.

33. Jouzaitis, "First Lady."

34. Lauter, "Mrs. Wonk Goes to Washington."

35. Martha Sherrill, "Hillary Clinton's Inner Politics," *Washington Post*, May 6, 1993, https://www.washingtonpost.com/archive/lifestyle/1993/05/06/hillary-clintons-inner-politics/799e9d5d-0dff-4017-be98-00253b76e974/.

36. Lauter, "Mrs. Wonk Goes to Washington."

37. Sherrill, "Inner Politics."

38. Lauter, "Mrs. Wonk Goes to Washington."

39. Bernstein, *Woman in Charge*, 297, 298; quotations in that order.

40. "Remarks by First Lady Hillary Rodham Clinton," April 7, 1993, https://clinton whitehouse3.archives.gov/WH/EOP/First_Lady/html/generalspeeches/1993/19930407 .html.

41. Sherrill, "Inner Politics."

42. All quotations in this paragraph from "Remarks by First Lady Hillary Rodham Clinton."

43. Woodward, "Soulful Matters."

44. "Remarks by First Lady."

45. "Remarks by First Lady." Clinton also argued that when dealing with the crucial issues of "When does life start" and "When does life end?," people must decide if what "we believe is morally and ethically and spiritually correct and do the best we can with God's guidance."

46. Michael Kelly, "Saint Hillary," *New York Times Magazine*, May 23, 1993, https:// www.nytimes.com/1993/05/23/magazine/saint-hillary.html.

47. Michael Luo, "Faith Intertwines with Political Life for Clinton," https://www .nytimes.com/2007/07/07/us/politics/07clinton.html.

48. "Remarks by First Lady."

49. Bernstein, *Woman in Charge*, 301.

50. Kelly, "Saint Hillary."

51. Bernstein, *Woman in Charge*, 299.

52. Quoted in Kelly, "Saint Hillary."

53. Hillary Clinton, "The First Lady's Remarks to the National Prayer Luncheon," February 2, 1994, https://clintonwhitehouse4.archives.gov/media/text/1994 -02-02-first-lady-remarks-to-the-national-prayer-luncheon.text.

54. Kelly, "Saint Hillary"; Daniel Burke, "The Public and Private Faith of Hillary Clinton," CNN, October 30, 2016, https://www.cnn.com/2016/10/30/politics/clinton -faith-private/index.html.

55. Luo, "Faith Intertwines." Critics pointed to her use of such terms as growth and wellness. See John Leo, "Hillary Clinton Wins Points with 'Politics of Meaning,'" *Tampa Bay Times*, May 31, 1993, https://www.tampabay.com/archive/1993/05/31/ hillary-clinton-wins-points-with-politics-of-meaning/.

56. Kelly, "Saint Hillary." Neither Stowe nor Day are part of the social gospel tradition.

57. Burke, "The Public and Private Faith."

58. Bernstein, *Woman in Charge*, 301.

59. Kelley, "Saint Hillary."

60. Quoted in Sherrill, "Inner Politics."

61. Paul Kengor, *God and Hillary Clinton: A Spiritual Life* (New York: HarperCollins, 2007), 119. Clinton was also influenced by the publications and speeches of Czech president Vaclav Havel and communitarian William Galson, the deputy assistant to the president for domestic policy.

62. Quoted in Sherrill, "Inner Politics."

63. Sherrill, "Inner Politics." Lerner is quoted in ibid.

64. Michael Lerner, "Hillary's Politics, My Meaning," *Washington Post*, June 13, 1993, https://www.washingtonpost.com/archive/opinions/1993/06/13/hillarys-politics -my-meaning/9d9136fb-9c84–40e7-a1e5-ca0ff2581116/.

65. Kelly, "Saint Hillary."

66. Kelly, "Saint Hillary."

67. David Brock, *The Seduction of Hillary Clinton* (New York: Free Press, 1996), 385.

68. Sherrill, "Inner Politics."

69. William Chafe, *Bill and Hillary: The Politics of the Personal* (New York: Farrar Strauss and Giroux, 2012), 185.

70. "First Lady's Remarks."

71. Clinton, *It Takes a Village*, 148.

72. Bernstein, interview with Wright, *Woman in Charge*, 310–11.

73. Chafe, *Bill and Hillary*, 228.

74. Kengor, *God and Hillary Clinton*, 140.

75. Kenneth Walsh, "Being There for Bill," *US News and World Report* 118 (February 27, 1995), 36.

76. Hillary Rodham Clinton, *Living Faith* (New York: Simon & Schuster, 2003), 267.

77. Woodward, "Soulful Matters." Clinton did not explain why she read *Christianity Today*; it may have been to keep abreast of the thinking of evangelicals, a major American religious community.

78. Clinton, *Living Faith*, 267.

79. Mark Miller, "Saint or Sinner?" *Newsweek*, April 10, 1994, https://www.newsweek .com/saint-or-sinner-187072. See also "Hillary in the Pits," *Wall Street Journal*, March 30, 1994, A16.

80. Brock, *Seduction*, v-vi.

81. Brock, *Seduction*, v-vi.

82. Kenneth Walsh and Bruce Auster, "Her Time of Travail," *US News and World Report* 120 (February 5, 1996), 26.

83. Brock, *Seduction*, vi; these quotations are all Brock's words except for Quinn's.

84. William Safire, "Blizzard of Lies," *New York Times*, January 8, 1996, 1:27; Anne Helen Petersen, *Too Fat, Too Slutty, Too Loud: The Rise and Reign of the Unruly Woman* (New York: Plume, 2017), 143 (survey results).

85. Safire, "Blizzard of Lies."

86. Ronald Brownstein, "Two Books about Hillary Rodham Clinton," Chron, June 10, 2007, https://www.chron.com/life/books/article/Two-books-about-Hillary-Rodham -Clinton-1808569.php.

87. Michael Ruane, "Historic D.C. Church Lands on Most-Endangered List," *Washington Post*, May 19, 2010, https://www.washingtonpost.com/wp-dyn/content/story/2010/ 05/18/ST2010051806169.html?sid=ST2010051806169. See also Jacqueline Trescott, "Clinton's Big Day to Start at Black Church," *Washington Post*, December 5, 1992, C1.

88. Lynne Marek, "Behind the Scenes, First Lady Plays Role," *Chicago Tribune*, January 21, 1993, A15. See also DeNeen Brown and Patricia Davis, "'Our President . . . Our

Neighbor'; Historic Black Church Near White House Plays Host to First Worshipper," *Washington Post*, January 21, 1993, B6. See also Clinton, *Living History*, 123.

89. Stephanie Griffith, "Churches Praying for a President in Their Pews," *Washington Post*, January 2, 1993, B1.

90. Lynne Marek, "Church and State," *Chicago Tribune*, June 5, 1994, https://www.chicagotribune.com/news/ct-xpm-1994–06–05–9406050104-story.html.

91. Burke, "Public and Private Faith."

92. Melissa Lauber, "Former First Family Visits, Speaks, at Foundry UMC's 200th Anniversary Celebration," Baltimore-Washington Conference Archives, September 14, 2015, https://www.bwcumc.org/archives/former-first-family-visits-speaks-at-foundry-umcs-200th-anniversary-celebration/.

93. "Doles Drop Church They Shared with Clintons," *St. Louis-Dispatch*, May 21, 1995, G74.

94. Laurie Goodstein, "Pastor to President Says Morality Includes Courage, Caring and Proportion," *New York Times*, March 1, 1998, https://www.nytimes.com/1998/03/01/us/pastor-to-president-says-morality-includes-courage-caring-and-proportion.html.

95. Bill Broadway, "Methodist Minister and Ethicist Sees God's Will in the Exceptions," *Washington Post*, June 22, 2002, B9.

96. John Harris, "Clinton 'Always Believed' He Would Get 2nd Term," *Washington Post,* January 20, 1997, A13.

97. Cal Thomas, "The Moral Nurture of the Clintons," *Baltimore Sun*, https://www.baltimoresun.com/news/bs-xpm-1995–04–28–1995118129-story.html.

98. Goodstein, "Pastor to President Says."

99. Woodward, "Soulful Matters."

100. "First Lady's Remarks."

101. Goodstein, "Pastor to President Says"; Thomas, "Moral Nurture of the Clintons."

102. Marek, "Church and State."

103. Amy Goldstein, "Part of, But Apart From, It All; Clintons Have Complex Relationship with City," *Washington Post*, January 20, 1997, E17.

104. "Troubles Follow Clinton to Church," *Baltimore Sun,* April 25, 1994, 8A.

105. Harris, "Clinton 'Always Believed.'"

106. Paul Duggan, "For Clinton and Nation, the Big Day," *Washington Post*, January 20, 1997, A1.

107. Hamil Harris, "Clintons Appear to Find Solace and Support at Church Service," *Washington Post*, January 26, 1998, A9. For other examples, see Kenneth Bazinet, "Bill, Hil Hear about True Love," *New York Daily News,* March 15, 1999, 8; "It's Church, Shakespeare for First Family," *Milwaukee Journal Sentinel,* December 28, 1998, 3; "The Old and the New Mark Holiday," *Chicago Tribune*, December 25, 2000, 22.

108. Luo, "Faith Intertwines."

109. Clinton, *Living History*, 168.

110. "First Lady's Remarks."

111. "First Lady's Remarks" (first seven quotations); Linda Feldman, "Candidate Clinton Goes Public with Her Private Faith," *The Christian Science Monitor,* December 20, 2007, 1 (eighth quotation).

112. Bernstein, *Woman in Charge*, 314.

113. The Foundation Fellowship, https://thefellowshipfoundation.org/history/.

114. "The 25 Most Influential Evangelicals in America," *Time*, February 7, 2005, http://content.time.com/time/specials/packages/article/0,28804,1993235 _1993243_1993261,00.html. On Coe and the Fellowship, also see Zach Montague, "Doug Coe, Influential Evangelical Leader, Dies at 88," *New York Times*, February 22, 2017, https://www.nytimes.com/2017/02/22/us/obituary-doug-coe-fellowship -foundation.html; Emily Belz and Edward Lee Pitts, "All in the Family," *World Magazine*, August 14, 2009, https://wng.org/articles/all-in-the-family-1620658185; Jeff Sharlet, *The Family: The Secret Fundamentalism at the Heart of American Power* (New York: HarperCollins, 2008).

115. Clinton, *Living History*, 168.

116. Jeff Sharlet and Kathryn Joyce, "Hillary's Prayer: Hillary Clinton's Religion and Politics," *Mother Jones*, September 1, 2007, https://www.motherjones.com/politics/ 2007/09/hillarys-prayer-hillary-clintons-religion-and-politics/.

117. Bernstein, *Woman in Charge*, 296–97; quotation from 297.

118. Bernstein, *Woman in Charge*, 413.

119. Bernstein, *Woman in Charge*, 414.

120. Bernstein, *Woman in Charge*, 415 (quotations), 414.

121. Francis Clines, "White House Plays Down a New Age Visitor," *New York Times*, June 24, 1996, https://www.nytimes.com/1996/06/24/us/white-house-plays-down -a-new-age-visitor.html.

122. Osborne, ed., *Unique Voice of Hillary Rodham Clinton*, 121.

123. Joseph Berger, "Performing Seances? No, Just 'Pushing the Membrane of the Possible,'" *New York Times*, June 25, 1996, https://www.nytimes.com/1996/06/25/ us/performing-seances-no-just-pushing-the-membrane-of-the-possible.html. See also Paula Span, "Spirits Lifted, Not Summoned," *Washington Post*, June 24, 1996, https://www.washingtonpost.com/archive/lifestyle/1996/06/25/spirits-lifted-not -summoned/407d20de-0db7-4873-9cea-c77c7a55285c/.

124. Burke, "Public and Private Faith."

125. Maureen Dowd, "Liberties: The Inner Life of Cheese," *New York Times*, June 27, 1996, A23.

126. "Hillary Clinton Denies Book's Claim; Seeks to Blunt Report She Has 'Spiritual' Guru," *The Record* (Bergen County, NJ), June 25, 1996, A15 (quotation); James Pinkerton, "Pause before Tossing Stones at First Lady," *Newsday* (Long Island, NY), June 27, 1996, A47.

127. "Clinton Denies Book's Claim," A15.

128. Dowd, "Liberties," A23.

129. Brigid Schulte, "'Spiritual Event' Is Denied: Hillary Clinton Says She Was Brainstorming for a Book," *Philadelphia Inquirer*, June 25, 1996, A3 (Greeley quotations); Clines, "White House Plays Down" (Bateson quotation).

130. "Clinton Denies Book's Claim."

131. David Gibson, "A Spiritual Adviser in N.J. Minister Has Guided the First Lady," *The Record* (Bergen County, NJ), July 15, 1996, A3.

132. Schulte, "'Spiritual Event.'"

133. Clines, "White House Plays Down."

134. David Maraniss and Susan Schmidt, "Hillary Clinton and the Whitewater Controversy: A Close-Up; Her Public Record Suggests Conflicts with Self-Portrait of Naivete," *Washington Post*, June 2, 1996, A1.

135. Clinton, *Living Faith*, 334 (first and second quotation), 335 (third and fourth quotation).

136. Clinton, *It Takes a Village*, 179.

137. Richard Bernstein, "A Few Hints on Nurture from the First Lady," *New York Times*, February 5, 1996, https://www.nytimes.com/1996/02/05/books/books-of-the-times-a-few-hints-on-nurture-from-the-first-lady.html.

138. Bernstein, *Woman in Charge*, 448 (quotation), 449.

139. "Hillary's Right: It Takes a Village to Raise a Child," *Palm Beach Post* (West Palm Beach, FL), January 20, 1996, D1.

140. Phyllis Burke, "Primary Education; *It Takes a Village: And Other Lessons Children Teach Us*, by Hillary Rodham Clinton," *Los Angeles Times*, January 28, 1996, 1.

141. Hillary Rodham Clinton, "Address to General Conference," April 24, 1996, http://catalog.gcah.org/DigitalArchives/conference/GC96/hilltext.html.

142. Clinton, "Address to General Conference."

143. Clinton, "Address to General Conference."

144. Kengor, *God and Hillary Clinton*, 159, 158; quotations in that order. On Clinton's speech, see also Linda Bloom, "Hillary Speaks to United Methodists," April 24, 1996, https://www.umnews.org/en/news/hillary-speaks-to-united-methodists; Steve Rabey, "Hillary Clinton Urges Methodists to Take Their Faith into the World," https://religionnews.com/1996/04/25/news-story-hillary-clinton-urges-methodists-to-take-their-faith-into-the-wo/.

145. Allida Black, *The First Ladies of the United States of America* (Washington, DC: White House Historical Association, 2013).

146. Woodward, "Soulful Matters."

147. Hillary Clinton, "What Plan Will Do for You," *USA Today*, September 21, 1993, 13A.

148. David Anderson, "Hillary Clinton, Catholic Leaders Discuss Health Care," *St. Petersburg Times*, May 8, 1993, 4E.

149. Christopher Andersen, *American Evita: Hillary Clinton's Path to Power* (New York: William Morris, 2004), 140.

150. Brownstein, "Two Books."

151. Brock, *Seduction*, 67.

152. John Farrell, "Hillary Clinton Stands Her Ground," *Boston Globe*, December 1, 1994, A1.

153. Hamil Harris and Vanessa Williams, "Churches Rally, Offering Plan to Revive D.C.; First Lady, Others Pledge Aid to WIN," *Washington Post*, May 29, 1996, B3; David Vise, "A Rising New Force in D.C. Wins First Lady's Attention," *Washington Post*, December 22, 1996, B1.

154. Hillary Rodham Clinton, "Talking It Over," April 8, 1998, https://clintonwhitehouse3.archives.gov/WH/EOP/First_Lady/html/columns/HRC0408.html.

155. Clinton on *Larry King Live*, May 5, 1994, in Osborne, *Unique Voice*, 181.

156. "Clinton: Focus on Best Candidate, Not Race, Gender," NPR, January 25, 2008, https://www.npr.org/templates/story/story.php?storyId=18418848.

157. See Andrew Ujifusa, "Reviewing Hillary Clinton's Role in the Creation of Early Head Start," EdWeek, August 17, 2016, https://www.edweek.org/policy-politics/reviewing-hillary-clintons-role-in-the-creation-of-early-head-start/2016/08?print=1.

158. Hillary Clinton, "The Fight Over Orphanages," *Newsweek*, January 16, 1995, 22.

159. Clinton, "Fight Over Orphanages," 22.

160. Clinton, "Fight Over Orphanages," 23.

161. Hillary Clinton, "Spirit of Compassion for Children Attacked," *Arizona Republic*, March 16, 1995.

162. Elizabeth Mehren, "The First Lady's Family Values Parenting," *Los Angeles Times*, June 15, 1995, 1.

163. Brock, *Seduction*, 118

164. Clinton, *It Takes a Village*, 170 (first quotation), 171 (second, third and fourth quotations), 316 (fifth quotation).

165. Clinton, "Address to General Conference."

166. Hillary Clinton, "Our Chance for Healthier Children," *New York Times*, August 5, 1997, https://www.nytimes.com/1997/08/05/opinion/our-chance-for-healthier-children.html.

167. Harrison interview with Kengor, *God and Hillary Clinton*, 49–50.

168. Kengor, *God and Hillary Clinton*, 99.

169. George Weigel, *Witness to Hope: The Biography of Pope John Paul II* (New York: HarperCollins, 2001), 715.

170. Transcript of August 12, 1993, remarks by Pope John Paul II. Also see Weigel, *Witness to Hope*, 681.

171. Raymond Hernandez and Patrick Healy, "The Evolution of Hillary Clinton," *New York Times*, July 13, 2005, https://www.nytimes.com/2005/07/13/nyregion/the-evolution-of-hillary-clinton.html.

172. Quoted in Peggy Noonan, "Still, Small, Voice," *Crisis Magazine*, February 1, 1998, https://peggynoonan.com/71/.

173. Clinton, *Living History*, 417–18.

174. Hillary Clinton, "Secretary Clinton's Keynote at the National Prayer Breakfast," Real Clear Politics, February 4, 2010, https://www.realclearpolitics.com/articles/2010/02/04/hillary_clinton_keynote_transcript_the_national_prayer_breakfast_100176.html.

175. Kengor, *God and Hillary Clinton*, 130; Ines Murzaku, "Can Mother Teresa Help Clinton Embrace Adoption over Abortion?" *Crux*, August 19, 2016, https://cruxnow.com/commentary/2016/08/can-mother-teresa-help-clinton-embrace-adoption-abortion/.

176. Clinton, *Living History*, 417–18.

177. Brigid Schulte, "Controversies Have Not Broken Hillary Clinton the First Lady," *The Record* (Bergen County, NJ), January 24, 1998, A10.

178. Clinton, *Living History*, 466.

179. Luo, "Faith Intertwines."

180. Chafe, *Bill and Hillary*, 280.

181. "Monica Lewinsky Won't Testify Before Next Week," CNN, February 11, 1998, https://www.cnn.com/ALLPOLITICS/1998/02/11/lewinsky.scandal/.

182. Brigid Schulte, "Crisis Finds Hillary Clinton Stoic as Ever," *Philadelphia Inquirer*, January 25, 1998, A1.

183. Goodstein, "Pastor to President Says," 1:16.

184. Peter Baker and Dan Balz, "Clinton Prepares for Historic Test; Relationship with Lewinsky May Be Termed 'Inappropriate," *Washington Post*, August 17, 1998, A1.

185. Leonard, "Clinton Is Suffering," A3.

186. Quoted in Chafe, *Bill and Hillary*, 288.

187. Clinton, *Living History*, 468 (first quotation), 469 (second and third quotations).

188. Clinton, *Living History*, 488 (first and second quotations), 478 (third quotation).

189. Chafe, *Bill and Hillary*, 292; Elizabeth Dias, "Hillary Clinton: Anchored by Faith," *Time*, June 27, 2014, https://time.com/2927925/hillary-clintons-religion/.

190. Burke, "Public and Private Faith." See also Clinton, *Living History*, 470.

191. Gail Sheehy, *Hillary's Choice* (New York: Random House, 1999), 322–23.

192. Dias, "Hillary Clinton."

193. "Remarks of First Lady."

194. Burke, "Public and Private Faith."

195. Luo, "Faith Intertwines."

196. Brian Knowlton, "'I Sinned,' He Says in Apology that Includes Lewinsky," *New York Times*, September 12, 1998, https://www.nytimes.com/1998/09/12/news/i-sinned-he-says-in-apology-that-includes-lewinsky-clinton-vows-he-will.html. In his sermon on September 13 Wogaman praised the president for repenting of his sin rather than trying to excuse his behavior. The Clintons did not attend the service that Sunday, but Wogaman discussed his sermon on the phone with Bill. In his sermon the next week, Wogaman criticized politicians who sought "not just to defeat but to destroy their opponents." Wogaman argued that Clinton's impeachment and removal from office would be a victory for his long-standing political opponents and would undermine the presidency as an institution. See *From the Eye of the Storm: A Pastor to the President Speaks Out* (Louisville, KY: Westminster John Knox Press, 1998), 40, 47 (quotation), 132.

197. Zev Chafets, "When It Comes to Faith, This Senator's Full of It," *New York Daily News*, June 9, 2003, 4.

198. Leonard, "Hillary Clinton Is Suffering," A3.

199. Emma Green, "Hillary Wants to Preach," *The Atlantic*, August 6, 2017, https://www.theatlantic.com/politics/archive/2017/08/hillary-clinton-devotionals/535941/.

200. Jesse Jackson, "Keeping Faith in a Storm," *Newsweek*, August 31, 1998, 43.

201. Bob Woodward, *Shadow: Five Presidents and the Legacy of Watergate* (New York: Simon & Schuster, 1999), 451.

202. Hillary Rodham Clinton, *What Happened* (New York: Simon & Schuster, 2017), 161.

203. "Clinton Says Faith Got Her through Marital Woes," *NBC News*, June 5, 2007, https://www.nbcnews.com/id/wbna19039626.

204. Luo, "Faith Intertwines."

205. Chafe, *Bill and Hillary*, 332.

206. Clinton, *Living History*, 489.

207. Bernstein, *Woman in Charge*, 36.

208. Burke, "Public and Private Faith."

209. Gil Troy, "The Nine Lives of Hillary Clinton: From Goldwater Girl to Presidential Candidate, Hillary Clinton's Changing Incarnations Have Defined Her," *Daily Beast*, April 4, 2015, https://www.proquest.com/usnews/docview/1680253984/C9E6F137D0414719PQ/4?accountid=5657.

210. "First Lady Says Husband Faced 'Abuse' as Child," *Milwaukee Journal Sentinel*, August 2, 1999, 1. The interview is in *Talk* magazine.

211. Andersen, *American Evita*, 97–98, 141; Bernstein, *Woman in Charge*, 36 (quotation).

212. Pam Platt, "Dynamics of a Duo: Professor Dissects Power Couple Bill and Hillary Clinton, Together and Separately," *Courier-Journal* (Louisville, KY), November 4, 2012, https://www.proquest.com/usnews/docview/1125737381/CA82CA9C9D684E0EPQ/1?accountid=5657.

213. Joyce Milton, *The First Partner* (New York: William Morrow, 1999), 378.

214. Maureen Dowd, "Liberties: Dragon Lady Politics," *New York Times*, October 13, 1999, https://www.nytimes.com/1999/10/13/opinion/liberties-dragon-lady-politics.html.

215. Bernstein, *Woman in Charge*, 345 (first and second quotations), 199 (third and fourth quotations).

216. Carl Bernstein, "Portrait of the Candidate as a Young Climber," *Washington Post*, June 3, 2007, B3.

217. Quoted in John Farrell, "Hillary Clinton's Role Modeling: The First Lady's Toughest Challenge Has Been Defining Her Image, Influence," *Boston Globe*, February 4, 1996, 1.

218. Chafe, *Bill and Hillary*, 230.

219. Quoted in Farrell, "Clinton's Role Modeling."

Chapter 4. "Be Rigorous in Judging Ourselves and Gracious in Judging Others"

1. Fred Kaplan, "The Politics of Hillary Clinton," *Boston Globe*, March 2, 1999, A1.

2. Hillary Clinton, *Living History* (New York: Simon and Schuster, 2003), 140–41; quotations in that order.

3. Michael Powell, "Hillary Clinton, the New Ideal," *Washington Post*, March 25, 1999, C1.

4. John Zogby, as quoted in David Daley, "Election 2000: Hillary Clinton Leaves No Room for in Between; Some Love Her, Others Despise Her, but Almost No One Is Indifferent," *Milwaukee Journal Sentinel*, December 19, 1999, 8.

5. Jodi Enda, "A Hillary Clinton Run," *Philadelphia Inquirer*, June 2, 1999, A1.

6. Paul Kengor, *God and Hillary Clinton: A Spiritual Life* (New York: HarperCollins, 2007), 188–89.

7. Enda, "A Hillary Clinton Run," A1.

8. Michael Powers, "Just Listening: As Hillary Clinton Makes Her First New York Swing, She Asks More Than She Answers," *Washington Post*, July 10, 1999, C1.

9. Peggy Noonan, *The Case against Hillary Clinton* (New York: Regan Books, 2000), xviii.

10. Daley, "Election 2000," 8. Weyrich, Coulter, Corn, and Sheehy are all quoted in Daley.

11. "Forum: Ethics: Hillary Clinton Should Run," *The Atlanta Journal-Constitution*, July 17, 1999, C3.

12. Lynne Duke, "How Hillary Got Her Groove Back," *Washington Post*, November 13, 2000, C1.

13. Noonan, *Case against Hillary Clinton*, 8 (first quotation), 12 (second quotation), 11 (third quotation), 13.

14. Noonan, *Case against Hillary Clinton*, 103, 27 (first quotation), 177 (second and third quotations), 180 (fourth quotation).

15. Michael Powell, "Why Is This Candidate Smiling?," *Washington Post*, August 7, 2000, C1.

16. Beth Harpaz, "Hillary Clinton Steps Out as a New Yorker," *Los Angeles Times*, February 6, 2000, A1.

17. Duke, "How Hillary Got Her Groove Back," C1.

18. Harpaz, "Hillary Clinton Steps Out," A1.

19. "Mayor Unfairly Using Religion, First Lady Says," *New York Times*, February 10, 2000, A1; John Harris, "Giuliani Letter Has Clinton 'Outraged,'" *Washington Post*, February 10, 2000, A10. Both sources cite the first quotation; the *Times* article includes the second quotation, and the *Post* article includes the third quotation.

20. Rick Brand and Dan Janison, "CAMPAIGN 2000 / Religion Differences / Clinton, Giuliani Spar over Letter Hitting Her on Tradition," *Newsday* (Long Island, NY), February 10, 2000, A5.

21. "New Book Exposes Hillary Clinton's Attitudes toward Religious Traditionalists, Faith-Based Social Organizations," US Newswire, February 10, 2000, 1.

22. Jean Williams Booker, "AME Church Endorses Clinton and McCall," *New York Amsterdam News*, June 1, 2000, 4.

23. Elizabeth Moore and John Riley, "An Emotional Denial/ Clinton Slams Allegation of Anti-Semitic Remark," *Newsday*, July 17, 2000, A7.

24. Beth Harpaz, "Emotional Hillary Clinton Denies Anti-Semitic Slur Alleged in Book," *Charleston Gazette* (Charleston, WV), July 17, 2000, 2A.

25. Harpaz, "Clinton Denies Anti-Semitic Slur."

26. Beth Harpaz, *The Girls in the Van: A Reporter's Diary of the Campaign Trail* (New York: St. Martin's, 2001), 135.

27. William Godschlag and David Saltonstall, "Synagogue Offers Hil Relief," *New York Daily News*, July 23, 2000, 5.

28. "Campaign 2000: The New York Senate Debate," *New York Times*, October 9, B6.

29. Kengor, *God and Hillary Clinton*, 196.

30. Harpaz, *Girls in the Van*, 1.

31. Karen Carrillo, "Hillary Clinton Joins Churchgoers for Service at First Baptist Church of Crown Heights," *New York Amsterdam News*, September 12, 2000, 4.

32. Elizabeth Moore, "Harlem Sings Hillary's Praise," *Newsday*, October 2, 2000, A16.

33. Harpaz, *Girls in the Van*, 198–99.

34. Harpaz, *Girls in the Van*, 184.

35. Adam Nagourney, "Mrs. Clinton Preaches to the Party Faithful," *New York Times*, November 6, 2000, A1.

36. Maggie Habberman, "Mass Appeal as 'Sister' Hillary Tours Churches," *New York Post*, November 6, 2000, https://nypost.com/2000/11/06/mass-appeal-as-sister-hillary-tours-churches/.

37. Cheryl Lavin, "The Clinton Campaign Magazine Writer Tells How Hillary Became the Senator from New York," *Chicago Tribune*, February 28, 2001, E4.

38. Harpaz, *Girls in the Van*, 141.

39. Lynne Duke, "Hillary Clinton Accelerates into Her Own Orbit," *Washington Post*, November 8, 2000, https://www.washingtonpost.com/archive/lifestyle/2000/11/08/hillary-clinton-accelerates-into-her-own-orbit/0a7fa92f-2b1a-4bfa-9884-35e2531e00f1/.

40. John Harris, "Hillary's Big Adventure: A Supportive Spouse, Surprisingly Accepting Colleagues, and a Mandate to Legislate," *Washington Post*, January 27, 2002, https://www.washingtonpost.com/politics/hillarys-big-adventure-a-supportive-spouse-surprisingly-accepting-colleagues-and-a-mandate-to-legislate/2016/07/11/f041d082-4791-11e6-90a8-fb84201e0645_story.html.

41. Harris, "Hillary's Big Adventure."

42. Ronald Brownstein, "Two Books about Hillary Rodham Clinton," Chron, June 10, 2007, https://www.chron.com/life/books/article/two-books-about-hillary-rodham-clinton-1808569.php.

43. Michael Wear, "The Temptation of Hillary Clinton," *USA Today*, June 29, 2016, https://www.usatoday.com/story/opinion/2016/06/29/temptation-hillary-clinton-warren-evangelical-brownback-unifier-bible-study-senate-new-york-lgbt-olumn/86288776/.

44. Carl Bernstein, *A Woman in Charge: The Life of Hillary Clinton* (New York: Knopf, 2007), 548.

45. "Carl Bernstein on Hillary Clinton." *The Charlie Rose Show* transcripts, June 5, 2007.

46. Shawn Zeller, "As a Senator, Hillary Clinton Got Along with the GOP. Could She Do So as President?," Roll Call, September 26, 2016, https://www.rollcall.com/2016/09/26/as-a-senator-hillary-clinton-got-along-with-the-gop-could-she-do-so-as-president/.

47. Joshua Green, "Take Two," *The Atlantic*, November 1, 2006, 73 (first quotation), 74 (second and third quotations). Compare Brownstein, "Two Books."

48. Rebecca Traister, *Big Girls Don't Cry: The Election That Changed Everything for American Women* (New York: Simon and Schuster, 2011), 27.

49. Zeller, "Clinton Got Along with the GOP."

50. Alfred Lubrano, "Who Is Hillary Clinton?" *Philadelphia Inquirer*, July 24, 2016, K2.

51. Zeller, "Clinton Got Along with the GOP."

52. For example, Stephen Zunes, "Support for Iraq War Still Haunts Hillary Clinton's Candidacy," *National Catholic Register*, August 3, 2015, https://www.ncronline .org/blogs/ncr-today/support-iraq-war-still-haunts-hillary-clinton-s-candidacy.

53. Jeff Gerth and Don Van Natta Jr., *Her Way: The Hopes and Ambitions of Hillary Rodham Clinton* (New York: Little, Brown, 2008), 273–74. See also Michael Kranish, "Hillary Clinton Regrets Her Iraq Vote," *Washington Post*, September 15, 2016, https://www.washingtonpost.com/politics/hillary-clinton-regrets-her-iraq-vote -but-opting-for-intervention-was-a-pattern/2016/09/15/760c23d0–6645-11e6-96c0 -37533479f3f5_story.html.

54. Green, "Take Two."

55. Lubrano, "Who Is Hillary Clinton?"

56. D. Michael Lindsay, "Is the National Prayer Breakfast Surrounded by a 'Christian Mafia'? Religious Publicity and Secrecy within the Corridors of Power," *American Academy of Religion* 74 (June 2006), 391–92; Lisa Getter, "Showing Faith in Discretion," *Los Angeles Times*, September 27, 2002; Peter Boyer, "Frat House for Jesus," *New Yorker*, September 13, 2010, https://www.newyorker.com/magazine/2010/09/13/ frat-house-for-jesus.

57. "Clinton: Focus on Best Candidate, Not Race, Gender," NPR, January 25, 2008, https://www.npr.org/templates/story/story.php?storyId=18418848.

58. "Transcript: Chris Coons and James Lankford on 'Face the Nation,'" CBS News, December 29, 2019, https://www.cbsnews.com/news/transcript-chris-coons-and -james-lankford-on-face-the-nation/.

59. Green, "Take Two," 57.

60. Harris, "Hillary's Big Adventure."

61. Harris, "Hillary's Big Adventure."

62. "Hillary's '*Living History*' Is Making Sales History," *Baltimore Sun*, August 17, 2003, https://www.baltimoresun.com/news/bs-xpm-2003–08–17–0308160043-story.html.

63. Krista Larson, "2 Churches on Hillary Clinton's N.J. Swing," *The Record* (Bergen County, NJ), November 1, 2004, A14.

64. David Steinmetz, "Too Many Methodists? Presidential Politics and Mainline Religion," Knight Ridder Tribune News Service, August 6, 2004, 1, https://www .proquest.com/usnews/docview/457117327/B043AB7A73D24D92PQ/164?accountid =5657.

65. "The Truth about Hillary," Q&A with Kathryn Jean Lopez, *National Review Online*, June 20, 2005, https://www.nationalreview.com/2005/06/truth-about-hillary -interview/.

66. Christopher Flickinger, "Author Ed Klein Claims Clintons 'Sold Their Souls to the Devil in Order to Achieve Power,'" *Human Events Online*, July 8, 2005.

67. Al Mohler, "The Truth about the Truth about Hillary," https://albertmohler .com/2005/06/29/the-truth-about-the-truth-about-hillary.

68. Noonan and the *Economist* are quoted in Jeff Sharlet and Kathryn Joyce, "Hillary's Prayer: Hillary Clinton's Religion and Politics," *Mother Jones*, September 1, 2007, https://www.motherjones.com/politics/2007/09/hillarys-prayer-hillary-clintons -religion-and-politics/.

69. Michael Jonas, "Sen. Clinton Urges Use of Faith-Based Initiatives," *Boston Globe*, January 20, 2005, B1.

70. Quoted in John DiIulio, *Godly Republic: A Centrist Blueprint for America's Faith-Based Future* (Berkeley: University of California Press, 2007), 83.

71. See Marci Hamilton, *God vs. the Gavel: Religion and the Rule of Law* (Cambridge: Cambridge University Press, 2007).

72. Jonas, "Clinton Urges Use of Faith-Based Initiatives."

73. Suzanne Fields, "The Reinvention of Hillary Clinton," *Washington Times*, January 30, 2005, https://www.washingtontimes.com/news/2005/jan/30/20050130-094527-2313r/.

74. Kristen Lombardi, "God Is a Centrist Democrat," *Village Voice*, March 2, 2005, 30–31.

75. Quoted in "Hillary in the Middle on Values Issues," *Washington Times*, January 26, 2005, https://www.washingtontimes.com/news/2005/jan/26/20050126-121258-1641r/.

76. Peter Beinart, "No Shift to the Center; Stereotypes, Not Policy Changes, Drive Criticism of Hillary Clinton," *Washington Post*, May 9, 2005, A23.

77. Raymond Hernandez, "As Clinton Shifts Themes, Debate Arises on Her Motives," *New York Times*, February 1, 2005, https://www.nytimes.com/2005/02/01/politics/as-clinton-shifts-themes-debate-arises-on-her-motives.html.

78. Quoted in Ben Smith, "Hillary Enemies Find Her Cross Just Unbearable," *New York Daily News*, October 20, 2006, 25.

79. Sharlet and Joyce, "Hillary's Prayer." See also Jeff Sharlet, *The Family: Power, Politics and Fundamentalism's Shadow Elite* (Queensland: University of Queensland Press, 2008), 274ff.

80. Kengor, *God and Hillary Clinton*, 217. For a fuller account of the controversy Clinton's views on abortion provoked, see 239–43, 248–51.

81. "Mass Pro-Choice Rally Held in Washington," CBC News, April 25, 2004, https://www.cbc.ca/news/world/mass-pro-choice-rally-held-in-washington-1.470688.

82. "Sen. Hillary Clinton Floor Remarks on Samuel Alito Jr. SCOTUS nomination," C-SPAN, January 28, 2006, https://www.c-span.org/video/?c4580935/user-clip-hillary-clinton-floor-speech-alito.

83. Patrick Healy, "Clinton Seeking Shared Ground over Abortions," *New York Times*, January 25, 2005, https://www.nytimes.com/2005/01/25/nyregion/clinton-seeking-shared-ground-over-abortions.html.

84. Lombardi, "God Is a Centrist Democrat."

85. Marc Humbert, "Hillary Clinton Seems to Move toward Center," *The Record* (Bergen County, NJ), February 6, 2005, A4.

86. "Catholic Groups Boycott Hillary Speech," *Newsmax*, January 29, 2005.

87. "Senator Clinton Blasts Bush Administration over Abortion," *Catholic Exchange*, January 18, 2005.

88. "Catholic Group Opposes Honor for Senator Clinton," Catholic News Agency, April 21, 2005, https://www.catholicnewsagency.com/news/3710/catholic-group-opposes-honor-for-senator-clinton; Hillary Clinton, *It Takes a Village: And Other Lessons Children Teach Us* (New York: Simon and Schuster, 1996), 178.

89. Religious Coalition for Reproductive Choice, https://rcrc.org/.

90. "Democratic Candidates Compassion Forum at Messiah College," April 13, 2008, http://transcripts.cnn.com/transcripts/0804/13/se.01.html.

91. Kengor, *God and Hillary Clinton*, 270.

92. Michael McAuliff and Helen Kennedy, "Hil Has Holy Cow over Immigrant Bill," *New York Daily News*, March 23, 2006, 7.

93. Roger Mahony, "Called by God to Help," *New York Times*, March 22, 2005, https://www.nytimes.com/2006/03/22/opinion/called-by-god-to-help.html. For a refutation of Clinton's and Mahoney's position, see James Fitzpatrick, "Criminalizing the Good Samaritan," *Catholic Exchange*, April 17, 2006, https://catholicexchange.com/criminalizing-the-good-samaritan/.

94. Peter Wallsten and Nick Anderson, "The Nation; Democrats Map Out a Different Strategy," *Los Angeles Times*, November 6, 2004, A1.

95. David Paul Kuhn, "The Gospel According to Jim Wallis," *Washington Post*, November 26, 2006, https://www.washingtonpost.com/archive/lifestyle/magazine/2006/11/26/the-gospel-according-to-jim-wallis-span-classbankheadfor-democrats-to-win-back-the-white-house-they-may-well-have-to-rely-on-the-power-of-the-almighty-and-its-not-bill-clinton-span/096710d9–9741–4a80–8b8c-bdaf6ccbb8e7/.

96. Kuhn, "The Gospel According to Jim Wallis."

97. Lombardi, "God Is a Centrist Democrat."

98. Kuhn, "The Gospel According to Jim Wallis."

99. David Kirkpatrick, "Consultant Helps Democrats Embrace Faith, and Some in Party Are Not Pleased," *New York Times*, December 26, 2006, https://www.nytimes.com/2006/12/26/us/politics/26faith.html; Jason Byassee, "Democrats for Jesus," *Christian Century* 124 (October 30, 2007), 20–23.

100. Michael Gerson, "Can She Reach Religious Voters?" *Washington Post*, September 26, 2007, A19.

101. Paul Kengor, "Could Hillary Win the Religious Vote?" *USA Today*, November 5, 2007, A15.

102. "Hating Hillary," *Christianity Today*, March 3, 2008, https://www.christianitytoday.com/ct/2008/march/14.26.html.

103. Sara Pulliam, "Do Evangelicals Really Prefer Hillary to Obama?" *Christianity Today*, March 3, 2008, https://www.christianitytoday.com/ct/2008/marchweb-only/110-12.0.html.

104. David Guarino, "Hill at Tufts: Use the Bible to Guide Poverty Policy," *Boston Herald*, November 11, 2004, 23.

105. Lombardi, "God Is a Centrist Democrat."

106. "Sen. Hillary Clinton Delivers Remarks at a Selma Voting Rights March Commemoration," Political Transcript Wire (Lanham, MD), March 4, 2007, https://www.proquest.com/usnews/docview/467213137/C93C561C364C4147PQ/1?accountid=5657.

107. "Sen. Hillary Rodham Clinton Delivers Remarks at the National Hispanic Prayer Breakfast," Political Transcript Wire, Lanham, MD, June 15, 2007, https://www.proquest.com/usnews/docview/467227699/922C18B79DFD4AB0PQ/1?accountid=5657.

108. Special Edition: Sojourners Presidential Forum, June 4, 2007, http://transcripts.cnn.com/transcripts/0706/04/sitroom.03.html.

109. "Transcript of Interview with Senator Clinton," *New York Times*, July 6, 2007, https://www.nytimes.com/2007/07/06/us/politics/07clinton-text.html.

110. "Interview with Senator Clinton."

111. "Interview with Senator Clinton."

112. "Interview with Senator Clinton."

113. Cal Thomas, "Clinton Rewrites the Good Book," *Baltimore Sun*, July 11, 2007, https://www.baltimoresun.com/news/bs-xpm-2007–07–11–0707110063-story.html. See also James Armstrong, "Proud of Clinton's Faith; Ex-Bishop Defends 'Social Gospel,'" *Orlando Sentinel* (Orlando, FL), July 16, 2007, A17.

114. Hillary Clinton, "Remarks at the Global Summit on AIDS and the Church at Saddleback Church in Lake Forest, California," November 29, 2007, https://www.presidency.ucsb.edu/documents/remarks-the-global-summit-aids-and-the-church-saddleback-church-lake-forest-california.

115. Linda Feldman, "Candidate Clinton Goes Public with Her Private Faith," *Christian Science Monitor*, December 20, 2007, 1.

116. "Democratic Candidates Compassion Forum."

117. "Democratic Candidates Compassion Forum."

118. "Democratic Candidates Compassion Forum."

119. Laurie Goodstein and Neela Banerjee "Obama's Talk Fuels Easter Sermons," *New York Times*, March 23, 2008, https://www.nytimes.com/2008/03/23/us/politics/23churches.html.

120. Jeff Zeleny and Katharine Seelye "Obama Takes Heat for Remarks," *Monterey Herald*, April 13, 2008, https://www.montereyherald.com/2008/04/13/obama-takes-heat-for-remarks/.

121. George Curry, "Hillary Clinton Is 'Majoring in the Minor,'" *Afro-American Red Star* (Washington, DC), April 26, 2008, A7.

122. George Curry, "'Slick Hillary' Does Not Separate Church and State," *Afro-American Red Star*, April 19, 2008, A7. Snyder and Matthews are quoted in this article.

123. "Hillary Clinton Meets with Bay Area African-American Ministers and Community Leaders," Targeted News Service, Washington, DC, August 15, 2007, https://www.proquest.com/usnews/docview/468739476/B92E3DD1BECC4C65PQ/300?accountid=5657.

124. Martin Evans, "Hillary Clinton Finds Time for Her Base in Harlem," McClatchy-Tribune Business News, October 28, 2007, https://www.proquest.com/usnews/docview/458975597/77548EDD87E143BDPQ/165?accountid=5657.

125. Niele Anderson, "Hillary Clinton Converses with Faith Leaders," *Los Angeles Sentinel*, January 24, 2008, C5.

126. Kelly Punete, "Norwalk Church on Bill's Rounds," *Press-Telegram* (Long Beach, CA), February 3, 2008, https://www.proquest.com/usnews/docview/382071268/56D28A80222A4EF9PQ/749?accountid=5657.

127. "Bill Clinton Takes to the Churches," *New York Times*, February 10, 2008, https://www.proquest.com/usnews/docview/2222716184/4A3FCC7B20CF4A70PQ/1?accountid=5657.

128. Robin Toner, "Faith in Spotlight, Candidates Battle for Catholic Votes," *New York Times*, April 15, 2008, https://www.nytimes.com/2008/04/15/us/politics/15catholics.html.

129. "The Institute of Progressive Christianity Condemns the Recent Attack on the Christianity of Senator Hillary Rodham Clinton on MSNBC," PR Newswire, New York, June 28, 2007, https://www.proquest.com/usnews/docview/453392598/12156592B35C4565PQ/448?accountid=5657.

130. Renad Schafer Horton, "Hillary Clinton: Too Religious to Be President?" *Tucson Citizen*, February 8, 2008, B1.

131. Lilliam Mongeau, "Hillary Clinton Answers 10 Questions on Early Education," *Atlantic*, September 6, 2016, https://www.theatlantic.com/education/archive/2016/09/hillary-clinton-answers-10-questions-on-early-education/498659/.

132. Andrew Ujifusa, "Reviewing Hillary Clinton's Role in the Creation of Early Head Start," *Education Week*, August 17, 2016, https://www.edweek.org/policy-politics/reviewing-hillary-clintons-role-in-the-creation-of-early-head-start/2016/08.

133. Brent Bozell, with Tim Graham, *Whitewash: What the Media Won't Tell You about Hillary Clinton but Conservatives Will* (New York: Crown Forum, 2007), 10.

134. Dick Morris and Eileen McCann, *Condi vs. Hillary: The Next Great Presidential Race* (New York: HarperCollins, 2005), 1; Susan Estrich, *The Case for Hillary Clinton* (New York: HarperCollins, 2005), 4.

135. Robin Givhan, "Hillary Clinton's Tentative Dip into New Neckline Territory, *Washington Post*, July 20, 2007, http://www.washingtonpost.com/wp-dyn/content/article/2007/07/19/AR2007071902668.htm; Amanda Fortini, "The Feminist Reawakening: Hillary Clinton and the Fourth Wave," *New York Magazine*, April 13, 2008, http://nymag.com/news/features/46011/.

136. Diana Carlin and Kelly Winfrey, "Have You Come a Long Way, Baby? Hillary Clinton, Sarah Palin, and Sexism in 2008 Campaign Coverage," *Communication Studies* 60 (August 9, 2009), 327–31.

137. Ashleigh Crowther, "Sexist Language in Media Coverage of Hillary Clinton," *Media Crit*, December 12, 2007, http://mediacrit.wetpaint.com/page/Sexist+Language+in+Media+Coverage+of+Hillary+Clinton.

138. Megan Garber, "Play Misty for Me," *Columbia Journalism Review*, January 8, 2008, http://www.cjr.org/campaign_desk/play_misty_for_me_1.php?page=all&print=true.

139. Diane Blair, "Hillary Clinton's 18 Million Cracks: The Enduring Legacy of the Presidential Glass Ceiling," in ed. Michelle Lockhart and Kathleen Mollick, *Hillary Rodham Clinton and the 2016 Presidential Election: Her Political and Social Discourse* (Lanham, MD: Lexington Books, 2015), 6, 8 (quotation). See also Eleanor Clift and Tom Brazaitis, *Madam President: Women Blazing the Leadership Trail* (New York: Routledge, 2003).

140. Anne Helen Petersen, *Too Fat, Too Slutty, Too Loud: The Rise and Reign of the Unruly Woman* (New York: Plume, 2018), 146. See also Marie Cocco, "A Farewell to the 'Hillary Nutcracker' and Other Obscenities," Truthdig, May 13, 2008, https://www.truthdig.com/articles/a-farewell-to-the-hillary-nutcracker-and-other-obscenities.

141. Kathleen Seelye and Julie Bosman, "Media Charged with Sexism in Clinton Coverage," *New York Times*, June 13, 2008, https://www.nytimes.com/2008/06/13/us/politics/13women.html. See also Rebecca Traister, "Hey, Obama Boys; Back Off Already!" *Salon*, April 14, 2008, https://www.salon.com/2008/04/14/obama_supporters/; Fortini, "The Feminist Reawakening."

142. Quoted in Shawn Parry-Giles, *Hillary Clinton in the News: Gender and Authenticity in American Politics* (Urbana: University of Illinois Press, 2014), 136.

143. Carlin and Winfrey, "Have You Come a Long Way, Baby?" 339, 335 (quotation). See also Susan Carroll and Kelly Dittmar, "The 2008 Candidacies of Hillary Clinton and Sarah Palin: Cracking the 'Highest, Hardest Glass Ceiling,'" in ed. Susan Carroll and Richard Fox, *Gender and Elections: Shaping the Future of American Politics* (New York: Cambridge University Press, 2010), 44–77; Leonie Huddy and Tony Carey Jr., "Group Politics Redux: Race and Gender in the 2008 Democratic Presidential Primaries," *Politics and Gender* 5 (March 2009), 81–96; Regina Lawrence and Melody Rose, *Hillary Clinton's Race for the White House: Gender Politics and the Media on the Campaign Trail* (Boulder, CO: Lynne Rienner, 2010); David Paul and Jesse Smith, "Subtle Sexism? Examining Vote Preferences When Women Run against Men for the Presidency," *Journal of Women, Politics and Policy* 29, no. 4 (2008): 451–76.

144. Lori Cox Han, "Is the United States Really Ready for a Woman President?," in ed. Lori Cox Han and Caroline Heldman, *Rethinking Madam President: Are We Ready for a Woman in the White House?* (Boulder, CO: Lynne Rienner, 2007), 4–5. See also Dianne Bystrom et al., *Gender and Candidate Communication* (New York: Routledge, 2004), 21; Diane Heith, "The Lipstick Watch: Media Coverage, Gender and Presidential Campaigns," in *Anticipating Madam President: The First Female Presidency*, ed. Robert Watson and C. Ann Gordon (New York: Lynne Rienner, 2002), 124–26; and Caroline Heldman, Susan Carroll, and Stephanie Olson, "'She Brought Only a Skirt': Print Media Coverage of Elizabeth Dole's Bid for the Republican Presidential Nomination," *Political Communication* 22 (July 2005): 313–35; Diane Bystrom, "Advertising, Web Sites, and Media Coverage: Gender and Communication along the Campaign Trail," in *Gender and Elections: Shaping the Future of American* Politics, ed. Susan Carroll and Richard Fox (Cambridge: Cambridge University Press, 2005), 168–88; Barbara Burrell, "Likeable? Effective Commander in Chief? Polling on Candidate Traits in the 'Year of the Presidential Woman,'" *Political Science and Politics* 61 (2008): 747–52.

145. Kathleen Dolan, *Voting for Women: How the Public Evaluates Women Candidates* (Boulder, CO: Westview Press, 2004), 45. See also Ronnee Schreiber, *Righting Feminism: Conservative Women and American Politics* (New York: Oxford University Press, 2008).

146. R. Marie Griffith, *Mortal Combat: How Sex Divided American Christians and Fractured American Politics* (New York: Basic Books, 2017).

147. "Hillary Rodham Clinton Suspends Her Presidential Campaign," *Washington Post*, June 7, 2008, https://www.washingtonpost.com/wp-dyn/content/article/2008/06/07/AR2008060701029.html.

Chapter 5. "I Look upon All the World as My Parish"

1. Michael Hirsh, "How Hillary Found Her Groove with Obama," *Newsweek*, April 22, 2010, https://www.newsweek.com/how-hillary-found-her-groove-obama-70589.

2. Adam Beam, "For Hillary Clinton, Faith Means Caring for Others," *Sunday Gazette* (Charleston, WV), April 27, 2014, https://www.proquest.com/usnews/docview/1519310049/8739BFD6BDB340D4PQ/7?accountid=5657.

3. Walter Russell Mead, "Was Hillary Clinton a Good Secretary of State?" *Washington Post*, May 30, 2014, https://www.washingtonpost.com/opinions/was-hillary-clinton-a-good-secretary-of-state/2014/05/30/16daf9c0-e5d4-11e3-a86b-362fd5443d19_story.html.

4. "Hillary's Farewell Speech," *The Daily Beast*, February 1, 2013, https://www.thedailybeast.com/hillarys-farewell-speech-read-the-transcript.

5. Quoted in Gayle Tzemach Lemmon, "The Hillary Doctrine," *Newsweek*, March 6, 2011, https://www.newsweek.com/hillary-doctrine-66105.

6. Susan Glasser, "Head of State," *Foreign Policy*, June 18, 2012, https://foreignpolicy.com/2012/06/18/head-of-state/.

7. Tracy Wilkinson, "Clinton's Sullied Legacy; She Won Praise as Top Diplomat, but Global Crises Cast a Shadow," *Los Angeles Times*, August 22, 2016, A1.

8. "Remarks by First Lady Hillary Rodham Clinton at Celebration of International Women's Day, Copenhagen, Denmark," March 8, 1995, https://clintonwhitehouse4.archives.gov/WH/EOP/First_Lady/html/generalspeeches/1995/3-8-95.html.

9. Todd Purdum, "Hillary Clinton Discovers a New Role," *New York Times*, April 2, 1995, A7.

10. Hillary Rodham Clinton, *Living History* (New York: Simon and Schuster, 2003), 278.

11. Valerie Hudson and Patricia Leidl, *The Hillary Doctrine: Sex and American Foreign Policy* (New York: Columbia University Press, 2015), 18.

12. Hillary Rodham Clinton, "Remarks for the United Nations Fourth World Conference on Women," September 5, 1995, https://www.un.org/esa/gopher-data/conf/fwcw/conf/gov/950905175653.txt.

13. Clinton, "Remarks for the United Nations Fourth World Conference on Women."

14. Hudson and Leidl, *The Hillary Doctrine*, 7, 8; quotations in that order. On the speech's impact on America's approach to Afghanistan, see Karen Garner, *Gender and Foreign Policy in the Clinton Administration* (Boulder, CO: First Forum Press, 2013), 160.

15. Kate Grant, "20 Minutes That Changed the World: Hillary Clinton in Beijing," *Huffington Post*, February 4, 2013, https://www.huffpost.com/entry/hillary-clinton_b_2603159.

16. Alyse Nelson, as quoted in Lemmon, "The Hillary Doctrine."

17. Clinton, *Living History*, 306.

18. Beijing Declaration and Platform for Action, 1995, http://www.un.org/womenwatch/daw/beijing/platform/.

19. Sandra Sobieraj, "First Lady Decries Women's Repression; Hillary Clinton Says Brutality in Algeria, Afghanistan Perverts Spirit of Islam," *Austin American Statesman*, March 27, 1999, A8.

20. Hillary Clinton, "New Hope for Afghanistan," *Time*, November 24, 2001, http://content.time.com/time/nation/article/0,8599,185643,00.html.

21. Hudson and Leidl, *The Hillary Project*, 50.

22. Carl Bernstein, *A Woman in Charge: The Life of Hillary Clinton* (New York: Knopf, 2007), 553; Hudson and Leidl, *The Hillary Doctrine*, 51.

23. Hudson and Leidl, *The Hillary Doctrine*, 52.

24. "Senate Confirmation Hearing for Secretary of State Nominee Hillary Clinton," January 13, 2009, https://www.presidency.ucsb.edu/documents/senate-confirmation -hearing-for-secretary-state-nominee-hillary-clinton.

25. "Hillary Sees Subjugation of Women as Threat to Security," Dawn, March 14, 2010, https://www.dawn.com/news/857688/hillary-sees-subjugation-of-women-as -threat-to-security.

26. Hillary Clinton, "Remarks at the TEDWomen Conference," December 8, 2010, https://2009–2017.state.gov/secretary/20092013clinton/rm/2010/12/152670.htm.

27. Lemmon, "The Hillary Doctrine."

28. John Cassidy, "The Hillary Doctrine: 'Smart Power' or 'Back to the Crusades'?" *The New Yorker*, August 11, 2014, https://www.newyorker.com/news/john-cassidy/ hillary-doctrine-one.

29. Michael Jordan Smith, "Does Hillary Really Believe in the Hillary Doctrine?" *The New Republic*, June 23, 2015, https://newrepublic.com/article/122132/does-hillary -really-believe-hillary-doctrine.

30. Lemmon, "The Hillary Doctrine." A study that examined 156 countries from 1981 to 2005 furnished strong support for this aspect of the Hillary Doctrine. See Nilay Saiya, Tasneem Zaihra, and Joshua Fidler, "Testing the Hillary Doctrine: Women's Rights and Anti-American Terrorism," *Political Research Quarterly* 70 (March 2017), 421–32, https://journals.sagepub.com/doi/pdf/10.1177/1065912917698046. See also Valerie Hudson, Mary Caprioli, Bonnie Ballif-Spanvill, Rose McDermott, and Chad Emmett, "The Heart of the Matter: The Security of Women and the Security of States," *International Security* 33, no. 3 (2009): 7–45.

31. US Department of State and US Agency for International Development, *Leading through Civilian Power: The First Quadrennial Diplomacy and Development Review* (Washington, DC: US Department of State, 2010), x, https://2009–2017.state.gov/ documents/organization/153108.pdf.

32. *Leading through Civilian Power*, 23.

33. "A New Gender Agenda," interview by Mark Landler, *New York Times*, August 18, 2009, https://www.nytimes.com/2009/08/23/magazine/23clinton-t.html?page wanted=all.

34. Hillary Clinton, "Keynote Address at the 58th National Prayer Breakfast," February 4, 2010, https://2009–2017.state.gov/secretary/20092013clinton/rm/2010/ 02/136501.htm.

35. Lemmon, "The Hillary Doctrine,"

36. Lemmon, "The Hillary Doctrine."

37. Mary Jordan, "'Hillary Effect' Cited for Increase in Female Ambassadors to U.S.," *Washington Post*, January 11, 2010, https://www.washingtonpost.com/wp-dyn/content/article/2010/01/10/AR2010011002731.html?hpid=topnews.

38. Hillary Rodham Clinton, "Remarks at the Women in the World Summit," March 10, 2012, https://2009–2017.state.gov/secretary/20092013clinton/rm/2012/03/185604.htm.

39. Hudson and Leidl, *The Hillary Doctrine*, 62. Adopted by the United Nations in 1979 and endorsed by almost one hundred nations by 1989, the convention established "an international bill of rights for women" and "an agenda for action by countries to guarantee the enjoyment of those rights" ("Convention on the Elimination of All Forms of Discrimination against Women New York, 18 December 1979," https://www.ohchr.org/en/professionalinterest/pages/cedaw.aspx). The US senate repeatedly refused to ratify the treaty, influenced by the argument of conservative politicians and theologically conservative religious leaders that it is unnecessary because the United States already abides by its stipulations and would subject the nation "to the whims of an international agency" (Linda Lowen, "Why Won't the U.S. Ratify the CEDAW Human Rights Treaty?" ThoughtCo, January 3, 2020, https://www.thoughtco.com/why-wont-u-s-ratify-cedaw-3533824).

40. Hudson and Leidl, *The Hillary Doctrine*, 169–77; quotation from 172.

41. Clinton, "Keynote Address."

42. "Wake Up the World!" Transcript of Hillary Rodham Clinton's Address to Assembly 2014, https://www.unitedmethodistwomen.org/news/wake-up-the-world!

43. Lemmon, "The Hillary Doctrine."

44. "Secretary Clinton Announces Global Alliance for Clean Cookstoves," September 2, 2010, https://unfoundation.org/media/secretary-clinton-announces-global-alliance-for-clean-cookstoves/.

45. Quoted in Stephanie McCrummen, "The Secretary of 1,000 Things," *Washington Post*, November 27, 2012, A1.

46. Hillary Rodham Clinton, *Hard Choices: A Memoir* (New York: Simon and Schuster, 2014), 584–85; quotations in that order.

47. "No Ceilings," http://www.noceilings.org/.

48. "Wake Up the World!"

49. *Hard Choices*, 562.

50. John Campbell, "Gay Rights in Africa," Council on Foreign Relations, December 7, 2011, https://www.cfr.org/blog/gay-rights-africa.

51. Clinton, *Hard Choices*, 582 (all quotations), 583, 576.

52. See Alexis Okeowo, "Out in Africa: A Gay-Rights Struggle with Deadly Stakes," *New Yorker*, December 16, 2012, https://www.newyorker.com/magazine/2012/12/24/out-in-africa.

53. Hillary Rodham Clinton, "Secretary of State Remarks at Swearing-In Ceremony for Suzan Johnson Cook, Ambassador-at-Large for International Religious Freedom," June 2, 2011, https://2009–2017.state.gov/secretary/20092013clinton/rm/2011/06/164867.htm.

54. Clinton, *Hard Choices*, 574 (first two quotations), 575, 293 (third and fourth quotations). See also Nina Shea and Paul Marshall, "Hillary Clinton Chats up the Organization of Islamic Cooperation, Which Demands World-Wide Bans on Criticizing Islam," *Wall Street Journal*, December 5 2011, https://www.proquest.com/usnews/docview/907870900/77548EDD87E143BDPQ/168?accountid=5657); Charles Hoskinson, "Blaming the Video for Benghazi Highlights Hillary Clinton's Weak Defense of American Values," *Washington Examiner*, May 31, 2014, https://www.proquest.com/usnews/docview/1530739888/2E851755203D4334PQ/1?accountid=5657.

55. Hillary Clinton, "Remarks at Reception Marking Eid ul-Fitr," September 13, 2012, https://2009–2017.state.gov/secretary/20092013clinton/rm/2012/09/197735.htm.

56. Clinton, "2010 National Prayer Breakfast."

57. Clinton, "2010 National Prayer Breakfast."

58. Clinton, "2010 National Prayer Breakfast."

59. Clinton, "2010 National Prayer Breakfast" (first quotation); Kevin den Dulk, "What Do We Know about Hillary Clinton and Religious Freedom?" Religious Freedom Institute, October 20, 2016, https://www.religiousfreedominstitute.org/cornerstone/2016/10/20/what-do-we-know-about-hillary-clinton-and-religious-freedom (second quotation).

60. Clinton, "2010 National Prayer Breakfast."

61. Clinton, "2010 National Prayer Breakfast."

62. Quoted in McCrummen, "The Secretary of 1,000 Things," A1.

63. McCrummen, "The Secretary of 1,000 Things," including the Ebeling quotation.

64. Bill Keller, "Just the Ticket," *New York Times*, January 8, 2012, https://www.nytimes.com/2012/01/09/opinion/keller-just-the-ticket.html.

65. Steven Lee Myers, "Hillary Clinton's Last Tour as a Rock-Star Diplomat," *New York Times*, June 27, 2012, https://www.nytimes.com/2012/07/01/magazine/hillary-clintons-last-tour-as-a-rock-star-diplomat.html?pagewanted=all; Schmidt and Graham are quoted in Myers.

66. Hudson and Leidl, *The Hillary Doctrine*, xiii–xiv.

67. Myers, "Hillary Clinton's Last Tour."

68. Wilkinson, "Clinton's Sullied Legacy," A1.

69. For example, "The Case for Our Union: Hillary Clinton for President," *Daily Herald* (Arlington Heights, IL), October 23, 2016, 14; Peter Cooke, "Clinton Has the Attributes We Respect in a Leader," *Deseret News* (Salt Lake City), November 6, 2016, https://www.proquest.com/usnews/docview/1838211157/847AD226ED944614PQ/682?accountid=5657.

70. Quoted in Myers, "Hillary Clinton's Last Tour."

71. Swanee Hunt, "Marshall and Clinton: A Shared Legacy," *Huffington Post*, January 30, 2013, https://www.huffpost.com/entry/george-marshall-hillary-clinton_b_2585790.

72. Mead, "Was Hillary Clinton a Good Secretary of State?"

73. Mead, "Was Hillary Clinton a Good Secretary of State?"

74. Hudson and Leidl, *The Hillary Doctrine*, 333.

75. Michael Rubin, "Hillary Clinton's Legacy," *Commentary*, July 17, 2013, https://www.commentary.org/michael-rubin/hillary-clinton-legacy/.

76. Hudson and Leidl, *The Hillary Doctrine*, 60.

77. Stephen Walt, "Is Hillary Clinton a Great Secretary of State?" *Foreign Policy*, July 10, 2012, https://foreignpolicy.com/2012/07/10/is-hillary-clinton-a-great-secretary -of-state/.

78. Alfred Lubrano, "Who Is Hillary Clinton?" *Philadelphia Inquirer*, July 24, 2016, K2.

79. Sean Hannity, "Karl Rove on Hillary Clinton," CQ Roll Call, June 17, 2014, https://www.proquest.com/usnews/docview/1795788560/77548EDD87E143BDPQ/ 184?accountid=5657.

80. Bret Stephens, "The Hillary Myth: Can Anyone Name an Achievement to Justify the Adulation of Our Secretary of State?" *Wall Street Journal,* July 16, 2012, https://www.proquest.com/usnews/docview/1025746642/2A5E74E006A34E71PQ/ 3?accountid=5657.

81. Gil Troy, "The Nine Lives of Hillary Clinton: From Goldwater Girl to Presidential Candidate, Hillary Clinton's Changing Incarnations Have Defined Her," *The Daily Beast*, April 4, 2015, https://www.proquest.com/usnews/docview/1680253984/C9 E6F137D0414719PQ/4?accountid=5657. See also Walt, "Is Hillary Clinton a Great Secretary of State?"

82. Sally Quinn, "Hillary Clinton on Twitter: A Loss of Faith," *Washington Post*, June 13, 2013, https://www.washingtonpost.com/national/on-faith/hillary-clinton-on-twitter -a-loss-of-faith/2013/06/13/a77da32e-d446–11e2–8cbe-1bcbee06f8f8_story.html.

83. Quinn, "Hillary Clinton on Twitter."

84. Linda Bloom, "Clinton Salutes Mission Work of UM City Society," UMC, November 5, 2013, https://www.nyac.com/newsdetail/75897.

85. "Public Sees Religion's Influence Waning," https://www.pewforum.org/ 2014/09/22/public-sees-religions-influence-waning-2/.

86. Daniel Silliman, "Hillary Clinton Showed Up for Church Today. Will Faith Help or Hurt Her on the Campaign?" *Washington Post*, September 13, 2015, https://www .washingtonpost.com/news/acts-of-faith/wp/2015/09/13/hillary-clinton-showed -up-for-church-today-will-faith-help-or-hurt-her-on-the-campaign/.

87. Lloyd Green, "GOP's Biggest 2016 Problem: Clinton's Numbers among White Voters," *The Daily Beast*, June 9, 2014, https://www.thedailybeast.com/gops-biggest -2016-problem-clintons-numbers-among-white-voters.

88. Katie Zezima, "Web Site Launches to Woo Voters of Faith for Hillary Clinton," *Washington Post*, April 25, 2014, https://www.washingtonpost.com/news/post-politics/ wp/2014/04/25/web-site-launches-to-woo-voters-of-faith-for-hillary-clinton/; Dallas Kelsey, "Hillary Clinton Praises Bible, Own Methodist Upbringing," *Deseret News* (Salt Lake City), June 24, 2014, https://www.proquest.com/usnews/docview/15394 01581/77548EDD87E143BDPQ/160?accountid=5657.

89. Burns Strider, "'Grace Notes': The Quiet, Unshakable Faith of Hillary Clinton (COMMENTARY)," *Religion News*, April 4, 2015, https://religionnews.com/ 2015/04/08/grace-notes-quiet-unshakable-faith-hillary-clinton-commentary/. The quoted words are Clinton's.

90. "Wake Up the World!"

91. "Wake Up the World!"

92. Quoted in Katie Zezima, "Hillary Clinton: Speaking to Methodist Women Feels Like a 'Homecoming,'" *Washington Post*, April 26, 2014, https://www.washingtonpost .com/news/post-politics/wp/2014/04/26/hillary-clinton-speaking-to-methodist-women-feels-like-a-homecoming/. On this speech, see also Michael O'Loughlin, "The (Mostly) Secret Faith Life of Hillary Clinton," *America*, August 15, 2016, https://www .americamagazine.org/politics-society/2016/08/15/mostly-secret-faith-life-hillary -clinton; Adam Beam, "For Hillary Clinton, Faith Means Caring for Others," *Sunday Gazette* (Charleston, WV), April 27, 2014, https://www.proquest.com/usnews/doc view/1519310049/8739BFD6BDB340D4PQ/7?accountid=5657.

93. Cal Thomas, "Newfound Faith among Liberal Democrats Like Hillary Clinton Is Still Mostly for Show," *Washington Examiner*, April 30, 2014, https://www.proquest .com/usnews/docview/1520191235/8094B357385494FPQ/40?accountid=5657.

94. Sue Stolzmann Hoffmann, "Hillary Far from a 'Liberal Skeptic,'" *Sheboygan Press* (Sheboygan, WI), May 14, 2014, 4.

95. Silliman, "Clinton Showed Up."

96. Quoted in Perry Stein, "Clinton Helps Mark D.C. Church's Bicentennial," *Washington Post*, September 13, 2015, A4. Chelsea Clinton declared at this celebration, "I am so grateful that through the Youth Group, we not only went on Appalachian Service Project trips, but we did a lot of work right here in Washington, D.C. We could never escape how intimately connected our faith should be, and must be, connected to our works" (Melissa Lauber, "Former First Family Visits, Speaks, at Foundry UMC's 200th Anniversary Celebration," September 14, 2015, https://www.bwcumc.org/archives/former-first-family-visits-speaks-at-foundry -umcs-200th-anniversary-celebration/).

97. Dan Merica, "With Scripture, Hillary Clinton Wins Over a Voter," CNN, May 27, 2015, https://www.cnn.com/2015/05/27/politics/hillary-clinton-2016-election-faith/index .html. See also Czarina Og, "Hillary Clinton's Knowledge of Scripture Impresses South Carolina Pastor," *Christian Today*, June 3, 2015, https://www.christiantoday.com/article/ hillary.clintons.knowledge.of.scripture.impresses.south.carolina.pastor/55219.htm.

98. Chris Cillizza, "Hillary Clinton's 'Apology' Interview, Annotated: What She Said—and What She Meant," *Washington Post*, September 9, 2015, https://www .washingtonpost.com/news/the-fix/wp/2015/09/09/annotating-hillary-clintons -apology-interview-with-abc/.

99. Tony Campolo, "Why Christians Should Vote for Hillary," *Washington Post*, April 13, 2015, https://www.washingtonpost.com/national/religion/pointcounter-point-why-christians-should-_-or-shouldnt-_-vote-for-hillary/2015/04/13/e590e83e -e221-11e4-aeof-f8c46aa8c3a4_story.html; David French, "Why Christians Should Not Vote for Hillary," *Washington Post*, April 13, 2015.

100. Eleanor Clift, "Everyone Sees the Hillary They Want to See," *The Daily Beast*, June 17, 2014, https://www.thedailybeast.com/everyone-sees-the-hillary-they-want -to-see.

101. Maureen Dowd, "When Will Hillary Let It Go?" *New York Times*, June 15, 2014, https://www.nytimes.com/2014/06/15/opinion/sunday/maureen-dowd-when-will -hillary-let-it-go.html.

102. For example, Hannity, "Karl Rove on Hillary Clinton."

103. Gil Troy, "How to Handle Hillary Haters: Hillary Clinton Has to Make the Case That Her Presidency Will Accomplish Something, Despite the Hate That Goes Back to the 1980s," *The Daily Beast*, February 15, 2015, https://www.proquest.com/usnews/docview/1675909514/D7F00EB3891941E1PQ/101?accountid=5657.

104. Troy, "How to Handle Hillary Haters." See also Gil Troy, *Hillary Rodham Clinton: Polarizing First Lady* (Lawrence: University Press of Kansas, 2006).

105. Troy, "How to Handle Hillary Haters."

106. Troy, "How to Handle Hillary Haters."

107. Jeff Greenberg, "Why Hillary Clinton Should Go a-Knocking on Ralph Reed's Door," *The Daily Beast*, June 15, 2014, https://www.proquest.com/usnews/docview/1649002214/8094B357385494FPQ/43?accountid=5657.

Chapter 6. "Be Not Weary of Well Doing"

1. Ron Fournier, "Why Can't Hillary Clinton Stop Lying?" *The Atlantic*, August 1, 2016, https://www.theatlantic.com/politics/archive/2016/08/why-hillary-clinton-keeps-lying/493841/.

2. "Faith and the 2016 Campaign," Pew Forum, January 27, 2016, https://www.pewforum.org/2016/01/27/faith-and-the-2016-campaign/. An October poll revealed almost 80 percent of Black Protestants stated that Clinton's religious beliefs were stronger than Trump's; influenced by their animosity toward Clinton, only 28 percent of white evangelicals agreed. Robert Jones et al., "The Divide Over America's Future: 1950 or 2050? Findings from the 2016 American Values Survey," PRRI, October 25, 2016, https://www.prri.org/research/poll-1950s-2050-divided-nations-direction-post-election.

3. David Gibson, "Can Hillary Clinton Finally Close the 'God Gap'?" Religion News, July 24, 2016, https://religionnews.com/2016/07/24/can-hillary-clinton-finally-close-the-god-gap/.

4. Gibson, "Can Hillary Clinton Finally Close the 'God Gap'?"

5. Michael Wear, "The Temptation of Hillary Clinton," *USA Today*, June 29, 2016, https://www.usatoday.com/story/opinion/2016/06/29/temptation-hillary-clinton-warren-evangelical-brownback-unifier-bible-study-senate-new-york-lgbt-olumn/86288776/.

6. Jack Jenkins, "Hillary Clinton Is Now the Most Religious Candidate Running for President," ThinkProgress, May 6, 2016, https://archive.thinkprogress.org/hillary-clinton-is-now-the-most-religious-candidate-running-for-president-heres-why-that-matters-7cd6819374e5/.

7. Quoted in Sarah Pulliam Bailey, "The Deep Disgust for Hillary Clinton That Drives So Many Evangelicals to Support Trump," *Washington Post*, October 9, 2016, https://www.washingtonpost.com/news/acts-of-faith/wp/2016/10/09/the-deep-disgust-for-hillary-clinton-that-drives-so-many-evangelicals-to-support-trump/.

8. John Fea, "The No. 1 Reason Evangelicals Still Put Their Hopes in Trump," Religion News Service, August 9, 2016, http://religionnews.com/2016/08/09/the-no-1-reason-evangelicals-still-put-their-hopes-in-trump/.

9. Quoted in Farai Chideya, "Evangelicals, Once Skeptical of Trump, Have Rallied to His Side," FiveThirtyEight, September 27, 2016, https://fivethirtyeight.com/features/evangelicals-have-rallied-to-trumps-side/.

10. Bailey, "Disgust for Hillary Clinton."

11. Bailey, "Disgust for Hillary Clinton."

12. Laurie Goodstein, "Donald Trump Reveals Evangelical Rifts That Could Shape Politics for Years," *New York Times*, October 17, 2016, https://www.nytimes .com/2016/10/17/us/donald-trump-evangelicals-republican-vote.html.

13. Russell Moore, "Have Evangelicals Who Support Trump Lost Their Values?" *New York Times*, September 17, 2015, https://www.nytimes.com/2015/09/17/opinion/ have-evangelicals-who-support-trump-lost-their-values.html.

14. Russell Moore, "Why This Election Makes Me Hate the Word 'Evangelical,'" *Washington Post*, February 29, 2016, https://www.washingtonpost.com/news/acts-of -faith/wp/2016/02/29/russell-moore-why-this-election-makes-me-hate-the-word -evangelical/.

15. Sarah Eekhoff Zylstra, "Why Trump Tape Caused Only One Evangelical Leader to Abandon Him," *Christianity Today*, October 10, 2016, https://www.christianity today.com/news/2016/october/why-trump-tape-cause-evangelical-leader-switch -wayne-grudem.html.

16. David Gushee, "Christians Are 'Called to Resist' Trump," Religious New Service, May 1, 2016, https://religionnews.com/2016/05/01/christian-resistance-donald-trump/.

17. Bob Allen, "Mohler Says Likely Trump/Clinton Showdown a Dilemma for Christian Voters," *Baptist News*, March 2, 2016, https://baptistnews.com/article/ mohler-says-likely-trumpclinton-showdown-a-dilemma-for-christian-voters/.

18. Ruth Graham, "Can America's Largest Protestant Denomination Stop Trump?" *Slate*, April 28, 2016, https://slate.com/news-and-politics/2016/04/can-americas -largest-protestant-denomination-do-anything-to-stop-donald-trump.html.

19. "Why Max Lucado Broke His Political Silence for Trump," interview by Richard Clark, *Christianity Today*, February 26, 2016, https://www.christianitytoday.com/ct/ 2016/february-web-only/why-max-lucado-broke-his-political-silence-for-trump.html.

20. Emma Green, "Trump Is Surrounding Himself with Evangelical Pastors," *The Atlantic*, June 21, 2016, https://www.theatlantic.com/politics/archive/2016/06/tr026 ump -is-surrounding-himself-with-evangelical-pastors/488114/.

21. Kate Shellnutt and Sarah Eekhoff Zylstra, "Who's Who of Trump's 'Tremendous' Faith Advisers," *Christianity Today*, June 22, 2016, https://www.christianitytoday .com/ct/2016/june-web-only/whos-who-of-trumps-tremendous-faith-advisors.html.

22. Sarah McCammon, "Inside Trump's Closed-Door Meeting, Held to Reassure 'the Evangelicals,'" NPR, June 21, 2016, https://www.npr.org/2016/06/21/483018976/ inside-trumps-closed-door-meeting-held-to-reassures-the-evangelicals.

23. Beth Reinhard and Erica Orden, "Donald Trump Questions Hillary Clinton's Religious Faith," *Wall Street Journal*, June 21, 2016, https://www.proquest.com/ usnews/docview/1798440839/8094B357385494FPQ/25?accountid=5657.

24. John Corrales, "Donald Trump Asks for Evangelicals' Support and Questions Hillary Clinton's Faith," *New York Times*, June 21, 2016, https://www.nytimes .com/2016/06/22/us/politics/donald-trump-asks-for-evangelicals-support-and -questions-hillary-clintons-faith.html.

25. Kristin Du Mez, "Can Hillary Clinton's Faith Help Her Lead a Fractured Nation?" *Religion and Politics*, July 25, 2016, https://religionandpolitics.org/2016/07/25/can-clintons-faith-help-her-lead-a-fractured-nation/.

26. Andrew Kirell and Andrew Desiderio, "Donald Trump Goes Truther on Hillary Clinton's Religion," *The Daily Beast*, June 21, 2016, https://www.proquest.com/usnews/docview/1811377184/C9E6F137D0414719PQ/5?accountid=5657.

27. Reinhard and Orden, "Donald Trump Questions Hillary Clinton's Religious Faith." Fikes added that "Trump's proposals are not just un-Christian—they're un-American and at odds with the values our country holds dearest" (Corrales, "Trump Asks for Evangelicals' Support").

28. Maggie Haberman, "Donald Trump Returns Fire, Calling Hillary Clinton a 'World-Class Liar,'" *New York Times*, June 22, 2016, https://www.nytimes.com/2016/06/23/us/politics/trump-speech-clinton.html.

29. Neelesh Moorthy, "What Do We Know about Hillary Clinton's Religion? A Lot, Actually," June 24, 2016, https://www.politifact.com/factchecks/2016/jun/24/donald-trump/what-do-we-know-about-hillary-clintons-religion-lo/. See also Robert Farley, "We Know Plenty about Clinton's Religion," Factcheck Posts, June 22, 2016, https://www.factcheck.org/2016/06/we-know-plenty-about-clintons-religion/.

30. Lawrence O'Donnell, "The Last Word for June 21, 2016," MSNBC, https://www.msnbc.com/transcripts/the-last-word/2016-06-21-msna868516.

31. McCammon, "Inside Trump's Closed-Door Meeting."

32. Haberman, "Trump Returns Fire."

33. Bailey, "Disgust for Hillary Clinton."

34. Bailey, "Disgust for Hillary Clinton,"

35. Laurie Goodstein, "Nearly Four-Fifths of White Evangelicals Say They'll Vote for Donald Trump," *New York Times*, July 14, 2016, https://www.nytimes.com/2016/07/14/us/donald-trump-white-evangelical-voters-poll.html.

36. "In Their Own Words: Why Voters Support—and Have Concerns about—Clinton and Trump," Pew Research Center, September 21, 2016, https://www.pewresearch.org/politics/2016/09/21/in-their-own-words-why-voters-support-and-have-concerns-about-clinton-and-trump/. In a *Washington Post-ABC News* poll, 70 percent of white evangelicals said they had an unfavorable view of Clinton, primarily because they thought that she was not honest and trustworthy. See "Poll: Clinton, Trump in Virtual Dead Heat on Eve of First Debate," *Washington Post*, September 24, 2016, https://www.washingtonpost.com/politics/poll-clinton-trump-in-virtual-dead-heat-on-eve-of-first-debate/2016/09/24/b99c95de-81cb-11e6-8327-f141a7beb626_story.html.

37. Bailey, "Disgust for Hillary Clinton."

38. "Evangelicals Rally to Trump, Religious 'Nones' Back Clinton," Pew Research Center, July 13, 2016, https://www.pewforum.org/2016/07/13/evangelicals-rally-to-trump-religious-nones-back-clinton/.

39. Ralph Benko, "God Bless America: Donald Trump, Presbyterian, vs. Hillary Clinton, Methodist," *Forbes*, August 7, 2016, https://www.forbes.com/sites/ralph

benko/2016/08/07/god-bless-america-donald-trump-presbyterian-vs-hillary-clinton
-methodist/?sh=4161cfc16168.

40. Goodstein, "White Evangelicals Say They'll Vote for Donald Trump."

41. Katelyn Beaty, "'Jesus Feminists' See Hillary Clinton as a Role Model. They Just Won't Vote for Her," *Washington Post*, July 20, 2016, https://www.washingtonpost.com/news/acts-of-faith/wp/2016/07/20/why-some-young-evangelical-women-are-drawn-to-feminism-and-to-hillary-clinton/.

42. Eliza Collins, "Hillary Clinton: Planned Parenthood Videos 'Disturbing,'" *Politico*, July 29, 2015, https://www.politico.com/story/2015/07/hillary-clinton-questions-planned-parenthood-videos-disturbing-120768.

43. Paul Kengor, "Hillary Clinton's Church Problem," *Crisis Magazine*, June 1, 2016, https://www.crisismagazine.com/2016/hillary-clintons-church-problem. See also Ashley Boggan Dreff, *Entangled: A History of American Methodism, Politics, and Sexuality* (Nashville, TN: New Room Books, 2018). Dreff explains that since the early 1970s the commitment of Methodist evangelicals to a traditional understanding of biblical sexual morality has clashed with "the new morality" of theologically liberal Methodists, which endorsed sex education, abortion rights, and homosexuality, producing intense debates.

44. Paul Kengor, "The Changing Faith of Hillary Clinton," *The Daily News* (Lebanon, PA), August 17, 2016, https://www.proquest.com/usnews/docview/2306763876/8739BFD6BDB340D4PQ/12?accountid=5657. See also Paul Kengor, "Hillary Clinton's Evolution on Gay Marriage," *USA Today*, March 13, 2013, https://www.usatoday.com/story/opinion/2013/03/20/hillary-clinton-gay-marriage/2001229/.

45. Eliel Cruz, "Opinion: Clinton, Kaine Pro-LGBTQ Because of Faith, Not in Spite of It," NBC News, September 15, 2016, https://www.nbcnews.com/feature/nbc-out/opinion-clinton-kaine-pro-lgbtq-because-faith-not-spite-it-n648341. During the 2016 presidential campaign, the United Methodist Church appointed a commission to reassess its rules on the ordination and marriage of gays, lesbians, and transgender individuals. Based on its work, the *Book of Discipline*, the denomination's governing document, stated that the "practice of homosexuality" is "incompatible with Christian teaching." See Laurie Goodstein, "United Methodists to Revisit Rules on Gays and Marriage," *New York Times*, May 19, 2016, A18.

46. Hillary Rodham Clinton, *It Takes A Village: And Other Lessons Children Teach Us* (New York: Simon and Schuster, 1996).174–75; quotation from 174.

47. Kevin den Dulk, "What Do We Know about Hillary Clinton and Religious Freedom?" Religious Freedom Institute, October 20, 2016, https://www.religiousfreedominstitute.org/cornerstone/2016/10/20/what-do-we-know-about-hillary-clinton-and-religious-freedom.

48. Kengor, "Changing Faith of Hillary Clinton."

49. Marc Thiessen, "Hillary Clinton Is a Threat to Religious Liberty," *Washington Post*, October 13, 2016, https://www.washingtonpost.com/opinions/hillary-clinton-is-a-threat-to-religious-liberty/2016/10/13/878cdc36–9150–11e6-a6a3-d50061aa9fae_story.html.

50. Alexandra Desanctis, "Hillary Clinton Is No Champion of Religious Freedom," *National Review*, August 11, 2016, https://www.nationalreview.com/2016/08/hillary -clinton-opposes-religious-liberty/.

51. den Dulk, "Hillary Clinton and Religious Freedom."

52. Beaty, "Jesus Feminists."

53. Linda Bloom, "Viewing Clinton's Campaign through Faith, Gender," *United Methodist News*, February 6, 2016, https://www.umnews.org/en/news/viewing -clintons-campaign-through-faith-gender.

54. Daniel Burke, "The Public and Private Faith of Hillary Clinton," CNN, October 30, 2016, https://www.cnn.com/2016/10/30/politics/clinton-faith-private/index .html.

55. Burke, "Public and Private Faith."

56. Kristin Kobes Du Mez, "Hillary Clinton's History of Faith Is Long and Rich," *Washington Post*, July 26, 2016, https://www.washingtonpost.com/news/acts-of -faith/wp/2016/07/26/hillary-clintons-history-of-faith-is-long-and-rich-this-week -she-should-talk-about-it/.

57. Burke, "Public and Private Faith."

58. Kyrie O'Connor, "Trump and Clinton's Religious Backgrounds Aren't That Different," *Houston Chronicle*, July 1, 2016, https://www.houstonchronicle.com/lifestyle/houston -belief/article/Trump-and-Clinton-s-religious-backgrounds-aren-t-8337207.php.

59. Salena Zito, "Hillary Clinton Stresses Need for Civility, Unity," *TCA Regional News*, May 1, 2016, https://www.proquest.com/usnews/docview/1785592076/B043A B7A73D24D92PQ/175?accountid=5657; "Here's What Hillary Clinton Says Her 'Creed' Is," *Washington Post*, September 30, 2016, https://www.washingtonpost.com/video/ politics/heres-what-hillary-clinton-says-her-creed-is/2016/09/30/b9cd1e2c-872d -11e6-b57d-dd49277af02f_video.html.

60. Amy Chozick, "Hillary Clinton Gets Personal on Christ and Her Faith," *New York Times*, January 25, 2016, https://www.nytimes.com/politics/first-draft/2016/01/25/ hillary-clinton-gets-personal-on-christ-and-her-faith/.

61. David Gushee, "Hillary on Christian Faith: It's about Love and Service, Not Judgment," *Religious News*, January 26, 2016, https://religionnews.com/2016/01/26/ hillary-faith-iowa-love-christianity/.

62. Jonathan Capehart, "The Importance of What Hillary Clinton Did and Said in Philadelphia," *Washington Post*, January 29, 2016, https://www.washingtonpost .com/blogs/post-partisan/wp/2016/01/29/the-importance-of-what-hillary-clinton -did-and-said-in-philadelphia/.

63. Wilford Shamlin III, "Hillary Clinton visits Mother Bethel AME," *Philadelphia Tribune,* January 29, 2016, 1A, 4A.

64. Heather Clark, "'Pastors' Lay Hands on 'President-to-Be Clinton' to 'Decree and Declare Favor of the Lord,'" *Christian News*, February 2, 2016, https://christian news.net/2016/02/04/pastors-lay-hands-on-president-to-be-clinton-to-decree-and -declare-favor-of-the-lord/.

65. Clark, "Pastors' Lay Hands."

66. Eugene Scott, "Candidates Discuss the Importance of Their Faith," CNN, February 4, 2016, https://www.cnn.com/2016/02/04/politics/bernie-sanders-hillary-clinton-faith/index.html. See also Abby Phillip, "Hillary Clinton Opens Up about Running for President," *Washington Post*, February 4, 2016, https://www.washingtonpost.com/news/post-politics/wp/2016/02/04/hillary-clinton-opens-up-about-running-for-president-this-is-hard-for-me/.

67. Jeff Stein, "Hillary Clinton's New Hampshire Concession Speech," Vox, February 9, 2016, http://www.vox.eom/2016/2/9/.

68. Chris Dixon, "Hillary Clinton Makes Appeals to Black Voters in South Carolina," *New York Times*, February 25, 2016, https://www.nytimes.com/politics/first-draft/2016/02/25/hillary-clinton-makes-appeals-to-black-voters-in-south-carolina/; David Catanese, "Hillary Clinton's South Carolina Salvation," *US News and World Report*, February 26, 2016, https://www.usnews.com/news/blogs/run-2016/2016/02/26/hillary-clintons-south-carolina-salvation?context=amp.

69. Heather Clark, "Hillary Clinton Says She Is 'Person of Faith,'" *Christian News*, February 24, 2016, https://christiannews.net/2016/02/24/hillary-clinton-says-she-is-person-of-faith-cheered-at-gospel-musics-stellar-awards/.

70. Cathaleen Chen, "How Hillary Clinton Finally Addressed Bill's Infidelity," *Christian Science Monitor*, March 7, 2016, https://www.csmonitor.com/USA/2016/0307/how-hillary-clinton-finally-addressed-bill-s-infidelity.

71. Samuel Freedman, "For Hillary Clinton and Democrats, a Public Shift toward 'God-Talk,'" *New York Times*, August 27, 2016, https://www.nytimes.com/2016/08/28/us/for-hillary-clinton-and-democrats-a-public-shift-toward-god-talk.html.

72. Zito, "Clinton Stresses Need for Civility, Unity."

73. Amy Chozick, "Hillary Clinton Says Confederate Flag 'Shouldn't Fly Anywhere,'" *New York Times*, June 23, 2015, https://www.nytimes.com/2015/06/24/us/politics/hillary-clinton-says-confederate-flag-shouldnt-fly-anywhere.html.

74. Du Mez, "Can Hillary Clinton's Faith Help Her Lead."

75. Hillary Rodham Clinton, "African Methodist Episcopal Church National Convention," July 8, 2016, https://awpc.cattcenter.iastate.edu/2017/03/21/remarks-at-the-african-methodist-episcopal-church-national-convention-jul-8–2016/.

76. Kenneth Miller, "Hillary Clinton Makes Surprises," *Call and Post* (Cleveland), August 3, 2016, 1A.

77. Jennifer Rubin, "What Hillary Clinton Should Say to the Baptists," *Washington Post*, September 8, 2016, https://www.washingtonpost.com/blogs/right-turn/wp/2016/09/08/what-hillary-clinton-should-say-to-the-baptists/.

78. Amy Chozick, "Hillary Clinton Returns to the Campaign Trail, Vowing New Approach," *New York Times*, September 15, 2016, https://www.nytimes.com/2016/09/16/us/politics/hillary-clinton-campaign.html.

79. Emily McFarlan Miller, "Clinton Describes Her 'Activist, Social Justice Faith' to Baptists," *Religion News*, September 8, 2016, https://religionnews.com/2016/09/08/clinton-describes-activist-social-justice-faith-to-baptists/ (first, third, fourth, fifth, sixth, and eighth quotations); Amy Chozick, "Hillary Clinton Emphasizes Impor-

tance of Faith to Black Audience," *New York Times*, September 8, 2016, https://www
.nytimes.com/2016/09/09/us/politics/hillary-clinton-emphasizes-importance-of
-faith-to-black-audience.html (second and seventh quotations).

80. Hillary Rodham Clinton, "Remarks at the National Baptist Convention—Sep.
8, 2016," Iowa State University, https://awpc.cattcenter.iastate.edu/2017/03/21/
remarks-at-the-national-baptist-convention-in-kansas-city-mo-sep-8-2016/.

81. Clinton, "Remarks at the National Baptist Convention."

82. Clinton, "Remarks at the National Baptist Convention."

83. Miller, "Clinton Describes Her 'Activist, Social Justice Faith.'"

84. Laura Meckler and Colleen McCain Nelson, "Hillary Clinton's Team Aims for a
More Positive Message," *Wall Street Journal*, September 8, 2016, https://www.proquest
.com/usnews/docview/1817582035/8823E05329EE4A1DPQ/353?accountid=5657.

85. Matt Flegenheimer and Amy Chozick, "Hillary Clinton's Positive Message?"
New York Times, October 1, 2016, https://www.nytimes.com/2016/10/02/us/politics/
hillary-clinton-campaign.html.

86. Philip Rucker, "For Clinton, Attacking Trump May Not Be Enough," *Washington
Post*, September 21, 2016, https://www.washingtonpost.com/politics/for-clinton
-attacking-trump-may-not-be-enough/2016/09/21/c90c8018-7f75-11e6-8d0c-fb6c
00c90481_story.html.

87. Flegenheimer and Chozick, "Clinton's Positive Message?"

88. Burke, "Public and Private Faith."

89. Hemant Mehtais, "Hillary Clinton Needs to Reach Out to Nonreligious Americans," The District Chronicles, Howard University, Washington DC, July 21, 2016,
https://www.proquest.com/usnews/docview/1805823178/77548EDD87E143BDPQ/
278?accountid=5657.

90. Michael Gerson, "Republicans Have Ceded the Ground on Faith," *Washington Post*,
July 26, 2016, https://www.washingtonpost.com/opinions/republicans-have-ceded
-the-ground-on-faith/2016/07/25/b551da8e-528c-11e6-88eb-7dda4e2f2aec_story.html.

91. Du Mez, "Hillary Clinton's History of Faith Is Long and Rich."

92. Amy Sullivan, "'Do All the Good': The Methodist Saying that Became a Clinton Campaign Slogan," Yahoo, July 29, 2016, https://www.yahoo.com/news/hillary
-good-000000095.html.

93. David Gibson, "The Divided Soul of the Democratic Party," *Religion News*, July
28, 2016, https://religionnews.com/2016/07/28/the-divided-soul-of-the-democratic
-party/.

94. Emily VanDerWerff, "The Democratic Convention's Most Surprising Argument:
Christianity Is a Liberal Religion," Vox, July 29, 2016, https://www.vox.com/2016/
7/29/12320252/democrats-christian-religion-dnc-convention.

95. Freedman, "A Public Shift Toward 'God-Talk.'"

96. Michael Gerson, "Clinton vs. Trump: A Choice between the Uninspiring and
the Unfit," *Washington Post*, July 29, 2016, https://www.washingtonpost.com/
opinions/a-choice-between-the-uninspiring-and-the-unfit/2016/07/29/9fab8178
-55aa-11e6-b7de-dfe509430c39_story.html.

97. Karen Tumulty and Dan Balz, "How Hillary Clinton Proposed to Tim Kaine," *Washington Post*, July 23, 2016, https://www.washingtonpost.com/politics/how-clinton-proposed-to-tim-kaine/2016/07/23/c9bb4572–50d0–11e6-a7d8–13d06b37f256_story.html.

98. Tom Gjelten, "Clinton, Kaine Driven by Their Faith in the 'Social Gospel,'" NPR, August 3, 2016, https://www.npr.org/2016/08/03/488544556/clinton-kaine-driven-by-their-faith-in-the-social-gospel.

99. Kimberly Winston, "5 Faith Facts about Tim Kaine: 'I Do What I Do for Spiritual Reasons,'" *Religion News*, July 22, 2016, https://religionnews.com/2016/07/22/5-faith-facts-about-tim-kaine-i-do-what-i-do-for-spiritual-reasons/.

100. Travis Fain, "Catholic Virtue: Kaine Connects in Rust Belt Over Religion," *Daily Press,* July 30, 2016, https://www.dailypress.com/government/dp-nws-kaine-pennsylvania-20160730-story.html.

101. Gibson, "Divided Soul of the Democratic Party."

102. Winston, "5 Faith Facts about Tim Kaine."

103. "Kaine: Campaigns Face New Firestorms," CQ Roll Call, October 16, 2016, https://www.proquest.com/usnews/docview/1829839070/A320B2CE9B034B35PQ/479?accountid=5657.

104. Jay Michaelson, "How Tim Kaine, Hillary Clinton's VP, Defies the Religious Stereotype," *The Daily Beast*, July 22, 2016, https://www.thedailybeast.com/how-tim-kaine-hillary-clintons-vp-defies-the-religious-stereotype.

105. Elaine Quijano, "Senator Tim Kaine and Governor Mike Pence Participate in Vice Presidential Debate," CQ Roll Call, October 4, 2016, https://www.proquest.com/usnews/docview/1940504947/389A4585504641CFPQ/1?accountid=5657.

106. Cal Thomas, "Faith and the VP Debate," October 4, 2016, *Commercial Appeal*, https://www.commercialappeal.com/story/opinion/columnists/2016/10/04/cal-thomas-faith-and-vp-debate/91516712/.

107. Dan Merica, "Bill Clinton: To Understand Hillary, Look to Her Faith," *CNN Wire Service,* January 28, 2016, https://www.proquest.com/usnews/docview/1760778661/A320B2CE9B034B35PQ/489?accountid=5657.

108. "Trump $40 Million behind Clinton on Fundraising," CQ Roll Call, June 21, 2016, https://www.proquest.com/usnews/docview/1800015434/A320B2CE9B034B35PQ/490?accountid=5657.

109. "Tim Kaine and Hillary Clinton Delivered the Following Remarks at a Rally in Youngstown, Ohio," *Targeted News Service* (Washington, DC), August 1, 2016, https://www.proquest.com/usnews/docview/1808026033/EFA2B527B3EB4EA9PQ/331?accountid=5657.

110. "President Obama Stumps for Hillary Clinton in North Carolina," *Atlanta* CQ Roll Call, November 2, 2016, https://www.proquest.com/usnews/docview/1835861556/9F34551F0DC34951PQ/1?accountid=5657.

111. E. J. Dionne, "This Election's Faith-Based Candidate," *Washington Post*, September 11, 2016, https://www.washingtonpost.com/opinions/this-elections-faith-based-candidate/2016/09/11/4c9893c2–76c5–11e6–8149-b8d05321db62_story.html.

112. William Chafe, "If She Wins the White House, Which Hillary Clinton Governs," *East Bay Times* (Walnut Creek, CA), October 16, 2016, A18.

113. Chris Cormier Maggiano, "Public Servant in Chief," *Huffington Post*, November 4, 2016, https://www.huffpost.com/entry/public-servant-in-chief_b_581c873ae4b0334571e09a0d.

114. Otis Moss Jr., "Why I Support Secretary Hillary Rodham Clinton," *Call and Post* (Cleveland), February 10, 2016, 4A.

115. E. J. Dionne, "The Five Days in 2008 that Propelled Clinton Today: Her Grueling 2008 Campaign and Methodist Upbringing Made Her a Formidable Fighter," *Washington Post*, June 8, 2016, https://www.washingtonpost.com/opinions/the-five-days-in-2008-that-propelled-clinton-to-today/2016/06/08/9c6755fa-2db4-11e6-9b37-42985f6a265c_story.html.

116. Garrison Keillor, "Hillary Clinton's Concrete Shoes," *Washington Post*, September 14, 2016, https://www.washingtonpost.com/opinions/hillary-clintons-concrete-shoes/2016/09/14/eb033ef8-7a90-11e6-ac8e-cf8e0dd91dc7_story.html.

117. Bill Moyers and Michael Winship, "Hillary Clinton's Wall Street Address," *Huffington Post*, June 19, 2015, https://www.huffpost.com/entry/hillary-clintons-wall-str_1_b_7622148.

118. Goldie Taylor, "Hillary and 'The Discipline of Gratitude,'" *The Daily Beast*, February 7, 2016, https://www.thedailybeast.com/goldie-taylorhillary-and-the-discipline-of-gratitude.

119. Marc Fisher, "Allies Try to Coax Out the Clinton They Know," *Washington Post*, September 25, 2016, A1.

120. William Chafe, "Time for Real Hillary to Step Forward," *Oakland Tribune, East Bay Times edition,* May 14, 2016, https://www.proquest.com/usnews/docview/1789105434/AB91027C3B342DCPQ/1?accountid=5657.

121. Cathleen Decker, "Election 2016; Democratic National Convention," *Los Angeles Times,* July 29, 2016, B1.

122. Ron Fournier, "Hillary's Challenge with Trust," *The Atlantic*, February 22, 2016, https://www.theatlantic.com/politics/archive/2016/02/hillarys-challenge-with-trust/470289/. See also Vann Newkirk II, "On Hillary Clinton's Pandering," *The Atlantic*, April 2016, https://www.theatlantic.com/politics/archive/2016/04/hillary-clinton-pandering-radio/479004/.

123. Jeremy Silk Smith, "Clinton's Trustworthiness Remains a Drag on Her Candidacy," Roll Call, August 11, 2016, https://www.rollcall.com/2016/08/11/clintons-trustworthiness-remains-a-drag-on-her-candidacy/.

124. Linda Feldmann, "How Hillary Clinton Learned to Become a Street Fighter," *Christian Science Monitor*, June 4, 2016, https://www.proquest.com/usnews/docview/1793756554/CCD3EB7A031744C2PQ/1?accountid=5657.

125. David Brooks, "Hillary, This Is Why Democrats Are Still Struggling," *New York Times*, July 26, 2016, https://www.nytimes.com/2016/07/26/opinion/hillary-this-is-why-democrats-are-still-struggling.html.

126. Glenn Kessler, "Clinton's Claim that the FBI Director Said Her Email Answers Were 'Truthful,'" *Washington Post*, July 31, 2016, https://www.washingtonpost.com/

news/fact-checker/wp/2016/07/31/clintons-claim-that-the-fbi-director-said-her-email-answers-were-truthful/.

127. Donald J. Trump (@realDonaldTrump), http://pic.twitter.com/FsrUGByuuD, August 2, 2016.

128. Smith, "Clinton's Trustworthiness."

129. Amy Chozick, "Stress over Family Finances Propelled Hillary Clinton into Corporate World," *New York Times*, August 10, 2016, https://www.nytimes.com/2016/08/11/us/politics/hillary-clinton-money.html.

130. For example, see "The Case for Our Union: Hillary Clinton for President," *Daily Herald* (Arlington Heights, IL), October 23, 2016, 14; Guthrie Graves-Fitzsimmons, "Christians Can Stand Confidently Voting for Clinton," *Courier-Journal* (Louisville, KY), October 30, 2016, H2.

131. Michael Tomasky, "Straight Talk about 'Crooked Hillary' Clinton," *The Daily Beast*, October 4, 2016, https://www.proquest.com/usnews/docview/1831317844/8094B357385494FPQ/66?accountid=5657.

132. "The Case for Our Union," 14.

133. Jon Favreau, "Why Electing Hillary in '16 Is More Important Than Electing Obama in '08," *The Daily Beast*, February 26, 2016, https://www.thedailybeast.com/why-electing-hillary-in-16-is-more-important-than-electing-obama-in-08.

134. Jasmine Taylor-Coleman, "The Dark Depths of Hatred for Hillary Clinton," BBC, October 12, 2016, https://www.bbc.com/news/magazine-36992955.

135. Taylor-Coleman, "Dark Depths of Hatred."

136. Rick Sampson, "First Woman to Run for President—'Mrs. Satan'—Was No Hillary Clinton," October 18, 2016, https://www.usatoday.com/story/news/politics/elections/2016/10/18/victoria-woodhull-hillary-clinton-first-woman/92051476/.

137. Susan Faludi, "How Hillary Clinton Met Satan," *New York Times*, October 29, 2016, https://www.nytimes.com/2016/10/30/opinion/sunday/how-hillary-clinton-met-satan.html.

138. Jessie Hellman, "Carson Defends 'Lucifer' Comment: Clinton and Alinsky 'on a First-name Basis,'" *The Hill*, July 20, 2016, https://thehill.com/blogs/ballot-box/presidential-races/288457-carson-explains-lucifer-comment-clinton-and-alinksy-on-a?rl=1 (first quotation); Gideon Resnick, "Ben Carson Ties Hillary Clinton to Lucifer as GOP Swaps Campaign for Witch Trial," *The Daily Beast*, July 20, 2016, https://www.thedailybeast.com/ben-carson-ties-hillary-clinton-to-lucifer-as-gop-swaps-campaign-for-witch-trial (second quotation); Aaron Blake and Francis Stead Sellers, "Hillary Clinton, Saul Alinsky and Lucifer, Explained: Sympathy for the Devil?" *Washington Post*, July 20, 2016, https://www.washingtonpost.com/news/the-fix/wp/2016/07/20/hillary-clinton-saul-alinsky-and-lucifer-explained/.

139. Jeremy Diamond, "Donald Trump Calls Hillary Clinton 'the Devil,'" CNN, August 1, 2016, https://www.cnn.com/2016/08/01/politics/donald-trump-hillary-clinton-devil-election-2016/index.html; David Jackson, "Donald Trump Just Called Hillary Clinton 'the Devil,'" *USA Today*, https://www.usatoday.com/story/news/politics/onpolitics/2016/08/01/donald-trump-just-called-hillary-clinton-devil/87938974/.

140. Katie Dowd, "Poll Finds 18 Percent of Voters Believe Hillary Clinton Has 'Ties to Lucifer,'" August 1, 2016, https://www.sfgate.com/politics/article/poll-hillary

-clinton-hangs-with-satan-8993306.php; Public Policy Polling, July 30, 2016, https://www.publicpolicypolling.com/wp-content/uploads/2017/09/PPP_Release_National_7302016.pdf. See also Ian Philbrick, "That Poll Asking Voters If Hillary Is the Devil Was Doing Trump's Dirty Work for Him," *Slate*, August 11, 2016, https://slate.com/human-interest/2016/08/poll-asking-voters-if-hillary-clinton-is-the-devil-only-helps-trump.html.

141. Hillary Rodham Clinton, *What Happened* (New York: Simon and Schuster, 2017), 126.

142. Quoted in Lucy Schouten, "Why Donald Trump Calls Hillary Clinton 'the Devil,'" *Christian Science Monitor*, August 6, 2016, https://www.proquest.com/usnews/docview/1809162106/77548EDD87E143BDPQ/169?accountid=5657.

143. "San Diego Catholic Church Says Devil Works through Hillary Clinton," Reuters, November 5, 2016, https://www.deccanchronicle.com/world/america/051116/san-diego-catholic-church-says-devil-works-through-hillary-clinton.html.

144. Eric Sasson, "Republicans Can't Decide If Hillary Is a She-Devil or Not," *New Republic*, August 12, 2016, https://newrepublic.com/article/136016/republicans-cant-decide-hillary-she-devil-not.

145. Alexandra Petri, "The Hideous, Diabolical Truth about Hillary Clinton," *Washington Post*, October 14, 2016, https://www.washingtonpost.com/blogs/compost/wp/2016/10/14/the-hideous-diabolical-truth-about-hillary-clinton/.

146. Sarah Pulliam Bailey, "Standing by Donald Trump, Pat Robertson Calls Lewd Video 'Macho Talk,'" *Washington Post*, October 10, 2016, https://www.proquest.com/usnews/docview/1827571543/F9D507405B7B4C2DPQ/1?accountid=5657; Sarah Pulliam Bailey "'We're All Sinners': Jerry Falwell Jr Defends Donald Trump after Video of Lewd Remarks," *Washington Post*, October 10, 2016, https://www.washingtonpost.com/news/acts-of-faith/wp/2016/10/10/jerry-falwell-jr-the-gop-establishment-could-be-behind-donald-trump-video-leak/.

147. Sarah Pulliam Bailey, "'Still the Best Candidate': Some Evangelicals Still Back Trump Despite Lewd Video," *Washington Post*, October 8, 2016, https://www.washingtonpost.com/news/acts-of-faith/wp/2016/10/08/still-the-best-candidate-some-evangelicals-still-back-trump-despite-lewd-video/.

148. Zylstra, "Trump Tape."

149. Bailey, "Still the Best Candidate."

150. Bailey, "We're All Sinners."

151. Lauren Goodstein, "The Testing of a President," *New York Times*, September 20, 1998, 1:34; Bailey, "Still the Best Candidate."

152. Bailey, "Still the Best Candidate."

153. Tim Funk, "Franklin Graham: Trump Comments 'Cannot Be Defended,' but Supreme Court Is Top Issue," *Charlotte Observer*, October 8, 2016, https://www.charlotteobserver.com/living/religion/article106936232.html.

154. Joel Burgess and Mark Barrett, "'Hold Your Nose and Vote,' Graham Tells Christians," *Asheville Citizen-Times* (Asheville, NC), October 16, 2016, A6.

155. Sarah Pulliam Bailey, "The Trump Effect? A Stunning Number of Evangelicals Will Now Accept Politicians' 'Immoral' Acts," *Washington Post*, October 19, 2016, https://www.washingtonpost.com/news/acts-of-faith/wp/2016/10/19/the-trump

-effect-evangelicals-have-become-much-more-accepting-of-politicians-immoral
-acts/.

156. Sarah Pulliam Bailey, "Televangelist: Christians Who Don't Vote Are Going to Be Guilty of Murder,'" *Washington Post*, October 11, 2016, https://www.washington post.com/news/acts-of-faith/wp/2016/10/11/televangelist-christians-who-dont-vote -are-going-to-be-guilty-of-murder/.

157. Katelyn Beaty, "'No More': Evangelical Women Are Done with Donald Trump and His Misogyny," *Washington Post*, October 13, 2016, https://www.washington post.com/news/acts-of-faith/wp/2016/10/13/no-more-evangelical-women-are-done -with-donald-trump-and-his-misogyny/.

158. Laurie Goodstein, "Donald Trump Reveals Evangelical Rifts That Could Shape Politics for Years," *New York Times*, October 17, 2016, https://www.nytimes.com/ 2016/10/17/us/donald-trump-evangelicals-republican-vote.html.

159. Beaty, "No More." See also Ruth Graham, "These Evangelical Women Speaking Out against Trump Have More Influence Than You Think," *Slate*, October 12, 2016, https:// slate.com/human-interest/2016/10/the-evangelical-women-speaking-out-against -trump-have-more-influence-than-you-think.html.

160. Bailey, "Still the Best Candidate."

161. Emily Miller, "Will Evangelical Women Turn the Tide against Trump?" Religion News Service, October 17, 2016, https://religionnews.com/2016/10/17/will-evangelical women-turn-the-tide-against-trump/.

162. Sarah Pulliam Bailey, "'Lecherous and Worthless': Megachurch Pastor from Trump's Own Evangelical Council Denounces Him," *Washington Post*, October 10, 2016, https://www.washingtonpost.com/news/acts-of-faith/wp/2016/10/10/misogynistic -trash-megachurch-pastor-from-trumps-own-evangelical-council-denounces-him/.

163. Pulliam, "Still the Best Candidate."

164. Al Mohler Jr., "Opinion: Donald Trump Has Created an Excruciating Moment for Evangelicals," *Washington Post*, October 9, 2016, https://www.washingtonpost.com/news/ acts-of-faith/wp/2016/10/09/donald-trump-has-created-an-excruciating-moment -for-evangelicals/.

165. Bailey, "Still the Best Candidate."

166. Marvin Olasky, "Unfit for Power," *World Magazine*, October 11, 2016, https:// wng.org/articles/unfit-for-power-a1617305343.

167. Andy Crouch, "Speak Truth to Trump," October 10, 2016, https://www.christianity today.com/ct/2016/october-web-only/speak-truth-to-trump.html.

168. Sarah Pulliam Bailey, "Donald Trump's Pastor Problem: 40 Percent of Protes- tant Ministers Are Still Undecided," *Washington Post*, October 7, 2016, https://www .washingtonpost.com/news/acts-of-faith/wp/2016/10/07/donald-trumps-pastor -problem-40-percent-of-protestant-pastors-are-still-undecided/.

169. Patrick Healy, "Donald Trump Fires Back at Sharp Rebuke by Pope Francis," *New York Times*, February 18, 2016, https://www.nytimes.com/2016/02/19/us/politics/ donald-trump-fires-back-at-sharp-rebuke-by-pope-francis.html; Jim Yardley, "Pope Francis Suggests Donald Trump Is 'Not Christian,'" *New York Times*, February 18, 2016, https://www.nytimes.com/2016/02/19/world/americas/pope-francis-donald -trump-christian.html.

170. Jason Horowitz, "Clinton Challenges Trump for a Traditional Republican Bloc, White Catholics," *New York Times*, October 18, 2016, https://www.nytimes.com/2016/10/19/us/politics/catholic-voters-clinton-trump.html.

171. In a 2012 e-mail, Voices for Progress president Sandy Newman told John Podesta, who served as the chair of the 2016 Clinton campaign, that Catholics needed to call for gender equality in their church. Newman exhorted the Clinton team to "plant the seeds of the revolution" to change Catholic teaching. Podesta replied that Catholics in Alliance for the Common Good and Catholics United had been created to accomplish this goal. John Halpin, a senior fellow at the Center for American Progress, complained in a 2011 email to Jennifer Palmieri, the White House director of communications from 2013 to 2015, that many powerful conservative leaders were Catholics who were attracted to the faith's "systematic thought and severely backwards gender relations" (Marc Thiessen, "Hillary Clinton Is a Threat to Religious Liberty," *Washington Post*, October 13, 2016). See also Sarah Pulliam Bailey, "WikiLeaks Emails Appear to Show Clinton Spokeswoman Joking about Catholics and Evangelicals," *Washington Post*, October 12, 2016, https://www.washingtonpost.com/news/acts-of-faith/wp/2016/10/12/wikileaks-emails-show-clinton-spokeswoman-joking-about-catholics-and-evangelicals/.

172. Horowitz, "Clinton Challenges Trump."

173. Horowitz, "Clinton Challenges Trump."

174. Gibson, "God Gap."

175. Gretel Kauffmann, "Hillary Clinton Writes Op-ed to Win Over Mormons in Utah: Will It Work?" *Christian Science Monitor*, August 11, 2016, https://www.proquest.com/usnews/docview/1810672278/77548EDD87E143BDPQ/198?accountid=5657.

176. Chris Cillizza, "Why Hillary Clinton Is Making a New Mormon Pitch," *Washington Post*, October 11, 2016, https://www.washingtonpost.com/news/the-fix/wp/2016/08/16/why-donald-trump-is-like-radioactive-waste-in-utah/.

177. Tomicah Tillemann, "What Mormons Should Know about Hillary," *Deseret News* (Salt Lake City), October 16, 2016, https://www.proquest.com/usnews/docview/1830406167/56D28A80222A4EF9PQ/710?accountid=5657.

178. J. M. N. Reynolds, "Why People of Faith Don't Have to Vote between the Lesser of Two Evils," *Washington Post*, October 17, 2016, https://www.washingtonpost.com/news/acts-of-faith/wp/2016/10/17/why-people-of-faith-dont-have-to-vote-between-the-lesser-of-two-evils/.

179. Sarah Pulliam Bailey, "Why Donald Trump Could Lose Red Utah: Mormon America Has Found Another Candidate," *Washington Post*, October 26, 2016, https://www.washingtonpost.com/news/acts-of-faith/wp/2016/10/26/why-donald-trump-could-lose-red-utah-mormon-america-has-found-another-candidate/.

180. Favreau, "Why Electing Hillary in '16 Is More Important."

181. James Kirchick, "Hillary Clinton Is 2016's Real Conservative—Not Donald Trump," *The Daily Beast*, June 9, 2016, https://www.thedailybeast.com/hillary-clinton-is-2016s-real-conservativenot-donald-trump.

182. Graves-Fitzsimmons, "Christians Can Stand Confidently," H2.

183. Terry Shumaker, "Another View: Hillary Clinton Can Bring Us Back Together," *The Union Leader* (Manchester, NH), October 26, 2016, A1.

184. Peter Cooke, "Clinton Has the Attributes We Respect in a Leader," *Deseret News*, November 6, 2016, https://www.proquest.com/usnews/docview/1838211157/847AD226ED944614PQ/682?accountid=5657.

185. "Against Donald Trump," *The Atlantic*, November 2016, https://www.the atlantic.com/magazine/archive/2016/11/the-case-for-hillary-clinton-and-against -donald-trump/501161/. *The Atlantic* had previously endorsed Abraham Lincoln and Lyndon Johnson.

186. For example, see Ilya Somin, "Why Hillary Clinton Is a Lesser Evil than Donald Trump," *Washington Post*, May 5, 2016, https://www.washingtonpost.com/news/volokh-conspiracy/wp/2016/11/03/hillary-clinton-is-still-the-lesser-evil/.

187. Robert Jeffress, "Why Christians Must Vote in This Election (Staying Home Is Not an Option)," Fox News, November 1, 2016, https://www.foxnews.com/opinion/why-christians-must-vote-in-this-election-staying-home-is-not-an-option.

188. Ed Stetzer, "Why Evangelicals Dislike and Distrust Hillary Clinton So Much," *Christianity Today*, October 2016, https://www.christianitytoday.com/edstetzer/2016/october/why-evangelicals-dislike-and-distrust-hillary-clinton-so-mu.html.

189. Stetzer, "Why Evangelicals Dislike and Distrust Hillary Clinton."

190. Stetzer, "Why Evangelicals Dislike and Distrust Hillary Clinton."

191. Stetzer, "Why Evangelicals Dislike and Distrust Hillary Clinton."

192. Bailey, "The Deep Disgust for Hillary Clinton."

193. See Kurt Eichenwald, "Donald Trump's God Problem," *Newsweek*, August 22, 2016, https://www.newsweek.com/2016/09/02/donald-trump-god-christianity -evangelicals-492385.html, and Gary Scott Smith, "Why the Devil Are Evangelicals Supporting Trump?" *Newsweek*, January 13, 2016, https://www.newsweek.com/why-devil-are-evangelicals-backing-trump-415379. Evangelicals could have supported other candidates for the 2016 Republican nomination whose faith commitments were similar to theirs and had been very involved in the church: Mike Huckabee, Ben Carson, Ted Cruz, Jeb Bush, Carly Fiorina, Marco Rubio, and Rick Santorum.

Chapter 7. "God Grant That I May Never Live to Be Useless!"

1. David Brooks, "Hillary, This Is Why Democrats Are Still Struggling," *New York Times*, July 26, 2016, https://www.nytimes.com/2016/07/26/opinion/hillary-this-is -why-democrats-are-still-struggling.html.

2. Reid Wilson, "Final Newspaper Endorsement Count: Clinton 57, Trump 2," The Hill, November 6, 2016, http://thehill.com/blogs/ballot-box/presidential-races/304606-finalnewspaper-endorsement-count-clinton-57-trump-2.

3. Jonathan Allen and Amie Parnes, *Shattered: Inside Hillary Clinton's Doomed Campaign* (New York: Crown, 2017). See also George Packer, "Hillary Clinton and the Populist Revolt," *New Yorker*, October 31, 2016, https://www.newyorker.com/magazine/2016/10/31/hillary-clinton-and-the-populist-revolt; David Maraniss, "A Dynasty Undone by Its Building Blocks," *Washington Post*, November 10, 2016, A1.

4. Lawrence Tabak, "Why Hillary Lost—Bring in the Clowns," *Madison Capital Times*, November 16, 2016, 42. See also Megan Carpentier, "Why Do People Dislike Hillary Clinton? The Story Goes Far Back," *The Guardian*, https://www.theguardian

.com/us-news/2016/oct/18/hillary-clinton-why-hate-unlikeable-us-election. Reagan biographer Craig Shirley argued, "There's something about her manner, persona, voice, smirk that just grates on a lot of people," while pundit Elaine Kamarck declared, Clinton "reminds people of their mothers, or the schoolteacher they didn't like."

5. Anne Helen Petersen, *Too Fat, Too Slutty, Too Loud: The Rise and Reign of the Unruly Woman* (New York: Plume, 2017), 136.

6. Tom Junod, "The Last Optimist at the Apocalypse," *Esquire*, February 2016, http://classic.esquire.com/article/2016/2/1/the-last-optimist-at-the-apocalypse.

7. Petersen, *Too Fat, Too Slutty, Too Loud*, 159. See also Amy Chozick, "Hillary Clinton Raises Her Voice, and a Debate over Speech and Sexism Rages," *New York Times*, February 4, 2016, https://www.nytimes.com/2016/02/05/us/politics/hillary-clinton-speeches-sexism.html; Caroline Heldman, Meredith Conroy, and Alissa Ackerman, *Sex and Gender in the 2016 Presidential Election* (Santa Barbara, CA: ABC-CLIO, 2018); Dustin Harp, *Gender in the 2016 US Presidential Election* (New York: Routledge, 2019). For a dissenting view that women candidates usually do not suffer a penalty from voters, see Deborah Jordan Brooks, *He Runs, She Runs: Why Gender Stereotypes Do Not Harm Women Candidates* (Princeton, NJ: Princeton University Press, 2013); Kathleen Dolan, "Gender Stereotypes, Candidate Evaluations, and Voting for Women Candidates: What Really Matters?" *Political Research Quarterly* 67 (March 2014), 96–107; Kathleen Dolan *When Does Gender Matter? Women Candidates and Gender Stereotypes in American Elections* (New York: Oxford University Press, 2014); and Ryan Claassen and John Barry Ryan, "Social Desirability, Hidden Biases, and Support for Hillary Clinton," *PS: Political Science and Politics* 49 (October 2016): 730–35.

8. Aaron Blake, "21 Times Donald Trump Has Assured Us He Respects Women," *Washington Post*, March 8, 2017, https://www.washingtonpost.com/news/the-fix/wp/2017/03/08/21-times-donald-trump-has-assured-us-he-respects-women/; Nina Bahadur, "18 Real Things Donald Trump Has Actually Said about Women," *Huffington Post*, October 10, 2016, https://www.huffpost.com/entry/18-real-things-donald-trump-has-said-about-women_n_55d356a8e4b07addcb442023.

9. Libby Nelson, "Donald Trump Says Women Don't Like Hillary Clinton. They Dislike Him Even More," Vox, April 26, 2016, http;//www.vox.com/2016/4/26/11514948/trump-clinton-women; Tamara Keith, "Sexism Is Out in the Open in the 2016 Campaign. That May Have Been Inevitable," National Public Radio, October 23, 2016, https://tinyurl.com/yyrej36j.

10. Daniella Diaz, "Trump Calls Clinton 'a Nasty Woman,'" CNN, October 19, 2016, https://www.cnn.com/2016/10/19/politics/donald-trump-hillary-clinton-nasty-woman/index.html; Ashley Parker, "Donald Trump Says Hillary Clinton Doesn't Have 'a Presidential Look,'" *New York Times*, September 6, 2016, https://www.nytimes.com/2016/09/07/us/politics/donald-trump-says-hillary-clinton-doesnt-have-a-presidential-look.html.

11. Chris D'Angelo, "Trump Supporters Are Peddling Disgustingly Sexist Anti-Hillary Clinton Swag," *Huffington Post*, May 3, 2016, https://www.huffpost.com/entry/deplorable-anti-clinton-merch-at-trump-rallies_n_572836e1e4b016f378936c22; Kris-

tin Bellstrom, "Trump Supporters Are Selling 'Trump That Bitch' T-Shirts Featuring Hillary Clinton," *Forbes*, April 24, 2016, https://fortune.com/2016/04/25/trump -clinton-misogynistic-merch/.

12. Emanuella Grinberg, "Hillary Clinton's 'Pantsuit Nation' Suits Up for Election Day," CNN, November 6, 2016, https://www.cnn.com/2016/11/06/politics/pantsuit -nation-trnd/index.html; Libby Chamberlain, *Pantsuit Nation* (New York: Flatiron Books, 2017).

13. See Kathleen Dolan, "The Impact of Gender Stereotyped Evaluations on Support for Women Candidates," *Political Behavior* 32 (March 2010), 69–88; Nichole Bauer, "Emotional, Sensitive, and Unfit for Office? Gender Stereotype Activation and Support for Female Candidates," *Political Psychology* 36:6 (2015), 691–708; Mirya Holman, Jennifer Merolla, and Elizabeth Zechmeister, "Terrorist Threat, Male Stereotypes, and Candidate Evaluations," *Political Research Quarterly* 69 (March 2016), 134–47.

14. Tessa Ditonto, "A High Bar or a Double Standard? Gender, Competence, and Information in Political Campaigns," *Political Behavior* 39 (June 2017), 304; Michelle Swers, *Women in the Club: Gender and Policy Making in the Senate* (Chicago: University of Chicago Press, 2013); Debra Dobson, *The Impact of Women in Congress* (New York: Oxford University Press, 2006). See also Barry Burden, Yoshikuni Ono, and Masahiro Yamada, "Reassessing Public Support for a Female President," *Journal of Politics* 79 (May 2017), 1073–78.

15. For example, see Ana Bracic, Mackenzie Israel-Trummel, and Allyson Shortle, "Is Sexism for White People? Gender Stereotypes, Race, and the 2016 Presidential Election," *Political Behavior* 41 (July 2019), 281–82, 291, 299–300.

16. Carly Wayne, Marzia Oceno, and Nicholas Valentino, "How Sexism Drives Support for Donald Trump," *Washington Post*, October 23, 2016, https://www.washington post.com/news/monkey-cage/wp/2016/10/23/how-sexism-drives-support-for -donald-trump/; Nicholas Valentino, Carly Wayne, and Marzia Oceno, "Mobilizing Sexism: The Interaction of Emotion and Gender Attitudes in the 2016 US Presidential Election," *Public Opinion Quarterly* 82 (2018; supplement), 220. Compare Lori Cox Han, *In It to Win: Electing Madam President* (New York: Bloomsbury Academic, 2015); Meredith Conroy, *Masculinity, Media, and the American Presidency* (New York: Palgrave Macmillan, 2015); Jackson Katz, *Man Enough? Donald Trump, Hillary Clinton, and the Politics of Presidential Masculinity* (Northampton, MA: Interlink Books, 2016); Brian Schaffner, Matthew MacWilliams, and Tatishe Nteta, "Understanding White Polarization in the 2016 Vote for President: The Sobering Role of Racism and Sexism," *Political Science Quarterly* 33 (Spring 2018), 9–34; Jane Junn, "The Trump Majority: White Womanhood and the Making of Female Voters in the U.S.," *Politics, Groups, and Identities*, 5, no. 2 (2017), 343–52; Erin Cassese and Tiffany Barnes, "Reconciling Sexism and Women's Support for Republican Candidates: A Look at Gender, Class, and Whiteness in the 2012 and 2016 Presidential Races," *Political Behavior* 41, no. 3 (2019): 677–700. Cassese and Barnes define hostile sexism as "antipathy toward women who are viewed as usurping men's power or making illegitimate claims on government to advance their own status" (685).

17. Bracic, Israel-Trummel, and Shortle, "Is Sexism for White People?" 299–300.

18. Joshua Zeitz, "Why Do They Hate Her?" *Politico Magazine*, June 3, 2017, https://www.politico.com/magazine/story/2017/06/03/why-do-they-hate-her-215220/.

19. Valentino, Wayne, and Oceno, "Mobilizing Sexism," 214.

20. "An Examination of the 2016 Electorate, Based on Validated Voters," August 9, 2018, https://www.pewresearch.org/politics/2018/08/09/an-examination-of-the-2016-electorate-based-on-validated-voters/.

21. John Sides and Henry Farrell, eds., *The Science of Trump: Explaining the Rise of an Unlikely Candidate* (Washington, DC: Monkey Cage, 2016); Jim Tankersly, "How Trump Won: The Revenge of Working-Class Whites," *Washington Post*, November 9, 2016; Zeitz, "Why Do They Hate Her?"; Robert Francis, "Him, Not Her: Why Working-class White Men Reluctant about Trump Still Made Him President of the United States," *Sociological Research for a Dynamic World 4* (January 2018), 1–11; Junn, "The Trump Majority," 343–52; Clyde Haberman, "Religion and Right-Wing Politics: How Evangelicals Reshaped Elections," *New York Times*, October 28, 2018, https://www.nytimes.com/2018/10/28/us/religion-politics-evangelicals.html; Erin Cassese, "Straying from the Flock? A Look at How Americans' Gender and Religious Identities Cross-Pressure Partisanship," *Political Science Quarterly* 73, no. 1 (2019): 169–83; Erin Cassese and Mirya Holman, "Playing the Woman Card: Ambivalent Sexism in the 2016 US Presidential Race." *Political Psychology* 40, no. 1 (2019): 55–74.

22. Becket Adams, "Hillary Clinton Still Can't Say Why She Wanted to Be President," *Washington Examiner*, September 13, 2017. Amy Chozick reports in *Chasing Hillary: Ten Years, Two Presidential Campaigns and One Intact Glass Ceiling* (New York: Harper, 2018) that the Clinton camp considered eighty-four potential campaign slogans.

23. Hillary Rodham Clinton, *What Happened* (New York: Simon and Schuster, 2017), 39.

24. Clinton, *What Happened*, 51, 54, 52.

25. Matthew MacWilliams, "The One Weird Trait That Predicts Whether You're a Trump Supporter," *Politico Magazine*, January 17, 2016, https://www.politico.com/magazine/story/2016/01/donald-trump-2016-authoritarian-213533; Matthew Mac-Williams, "Who Decides When the Party Doesn't? Authoritarian Voters and the Rise of Donald Trump," *PS: Political Science and Politics* 49: 716–21.

26. Sarah Jaffe, "The Democrats' Deadly Error," *New York Times*, November 9, 2016, https://www.nytimes.com/interactive/projects/cp/opinion/election-night-2016/it-is-possible-for-trump-to-bea-good-president.

27. Will Wilkinson, "The Majesty of Trump," *New York Times*, November 9, 2016, https://www.nytimes.com/interactive/projects/cp/opinion/election-night-2016/it-is-possible-for-trump-to-bea-good-president.

28. "5 Faith Facts about Hillary Clinton: Social Gospel Methodist to the Core," January 29, 2016, https://religionnews.com/2016/01/29/hillary-clinton-religion-methodist/.

29. Kirsten Powers, "Hillary Clinton's Message: Religious People Are Fools," *Daily Record* (Morristown, NJ), May 3, 2015, 5.

30. Dan Merica and Sophie Tatum, "Clinton Expresses Regret for Saying 'Half' of Trump Supporters Are 'Deplorables,'" CNN, September 9, 2016, https://www.cnn.com/2016/09/09/politics/hillary-clinton-donald-trump-basket-of-deplorables/index.html; Mark Memmott, "Romney's Wrong and Right about the '47 Percent,'" National Public Radio, September 18, 2012, https://www.npr.org/sections/thetwo-way/2012/09/18/161333783/romneys-wrong-and-right-about-the-47-percent.

31. Benjamin Studebaker, "Why Bernie vs Hillary Matters More than People Think," February 5, 2016, https://benjaminstudebaker.com/2016/02/05/why-bernie-vs-hillary-matters-more-than-people-think/.

32. Jeffrey Sachs, "Hillary Is the Candidate of the War Machine," *Huffington Post*, February 5, 2016, https://www.huffpost.com/entry/hillary-is-the-candidate_b_9168938.

33. Bill Scher, "Why Does the Left Hate Hillary?" *Politico Magazine*, May 31, 2016, https://www.politico.com/magazine/story/2016/05/hillary-clinton-2016-progressives-213916/. See also Gary Dorrien, "We Do Not Need Another Clinton Administration. If Only Sanders Would Say It," *Salon*, January 30, 2016, https://www.salon.com/2016/01/30/we_do_not_need_another_clinton_administration_if_only_sanders_would_say_it/.

34. "Cornel West: Why I Endorse Green Party's Jill Stein Over 'Neoliberal Disaster' Hillary Clinton," *Democracy Now*, July 18, 2016, https://www.democracynow.org/2016/7/18/why_a_member_of_the_democratic.

35. Clinton, *What Happened*, 222, 437; quotations in that order.

36. "Hillary Clinton's Full Conversation with Christiane Amanpour," *NBC News*, May 2, 2017, https://www.nbcnews.com/video/hillary-clinton-s-full-conversation-with-christiane-amanpour-934945859735.

37. Kimberly Guilfoyle, Jesse Watters, Greg Gutfeld, Dana Perino, and Juan Williams, "Hillary Clinton Cites Racism, Sexism, Comey, Russia, Bernie Sanders and More For Her Loss," CQ Roll Call, September 11, 2017, https://www.proquest.com/usnews/docview/1940475611/77548EDD87E143BDPQ/128?accountid=5657. Timothy Lee argued similarly that Clinton blamed "Russia, fake news, the sad state of the Democratic Party, sexism, and the media that covered the email scandal 'like Pearl Harbor.'" Compare Chris Cillizza, "In Election Blame Game, It's Time for Hillary Clinton to Take Her Share," CNN, June 1, 2017, https://www.cnn.com/2017/06/01/politics/hillary-clinton-2016/.

38. Clinton, *What Happened*, 18, 437; quotations in that order.

39. Kristin Du Mez, "Why Can't We Have Nice Feminists," Patheos, March 13, 2020, https://www.patheos.com/blogs/anxiousbench/2020/03/why-we-cant-have-nice-feminists/.

40. Jocelyn Noveck, "As Clinton Emerges from the Woods, What Will Her Role Be?" *Salt Lake Tribune*, May 26, 2017, https://www.proquest.com/usnews/docview/2066650557/56D28A80222A4EF9PQ/751?accountid=5657.

41. Jeffrey Cimmino, "Liberal Pastors Optimistic Democrats Can Rebound with Faith Voters After Lackluster Display in 2016," *Washington Examiner*, September 8, 2019, https://www.proquest.com/usnews/docview/2286791817/5827E93FC0FC4EF6PQ/788?accountid=5657.

42. Jessica Martinez and Gregory Smith, "How the Faithful Voted: A Preliminary 2016 Analysis," Pew Research Center, November 9, 2016, https://www.pewresearch .org/fact-tank/2016/11/09/how-the-faithful-voted-a-preliminary-2016-analysis/. Clinton won about the same percentage of Latinos that Obama won in 2008, but it was 6 percent less than he took in 2012. See Robert Suro, "Here's What Happened with the Latino Vote," *New York Times*, November 9, 2016, https://www.nytimes.com/ interactive/projects/cp/opinion/election-night-2016/heres-what-happened-with -the-latino-vote.

43. "The Deep Roots of Our Hillary Hostility," *Christianity Today*, July 27, 2016, https://www.christianitytoday.com/ct/podcasts/quick-to-listen/deep-roots-of-our -hillary-hostility-.html.

44. Lucy Schouten, "Why Donald Trump Calls Hillary Clinton 'the Devil,'" *Christian Science Monitor*, August 6, 2016, https://www.proquest.com/usnews/docview/1809 162106/77548EDD87E143BDPQ/169?accountid=5657.

45. Emma Green, "Hillary Wants to Preach," *The Atlantic*, August 6, 2017, https:// www.theatlantic.com/politics/archive/2017/08/hillary-clinton-devotionals/535941/.

46. Laurie Goodstein, "Religious Right Believes Donald Trump Will Deliver on His Promises," *New York Times*, November 11, 2016, https://www.nytimes.com/2016/11/12/ us/donald-trump-evangelical-christians-religious-conservatives.html.

47. Laura Bischoff, "Abortion Issue Key to Trump Support: Evangelicals Looked at Policy over Personality When They Voted," *Dayton Daily News*, December 25, 2016, A1. Exit polls in Ohio found that 78 percent of evangelicals and 54 percent of main-line Christians voted for Trump and that 69 percent of evangelicals viewed Clinton unfavorably.

48. "Franklin Graham: The Media Didn't Understand the 'God-factor' in Trump's Win," *Washington Post*, November 10, 2016. On evangelical support for Trump, see also Ryan Claassen, "Understanding the Political Motivations of Evangelical Vot-ers." In *The Evangelical Crackup? The Future of the Evangelical-Republican Coalition*, ed. Paul Djupe and Ryan Claassen (Philadelphia: Temple University Press, 2018), 49–62; Michele Margolis, "Who Wants to Make America Great Again? Understand-ing Evangelical Support for Trump," *Politics and Religion* 13, no. 1 (2019): 1–30.

49. Goodstein, "Religious Right Believes Donald Trump Will Deliver on His Promises."

50. Michael Wear, "Why Democrats Must Regain the Trust of Religious Voters," *The Atlantic*, November 21, 2017, https://www.theatlantic.com/politics/archive/2017/11/ why-democrats-must-regain-faith-among-religious-voters/546434/. Wear estimated the white evangelical vote to be more than 25 percent of the electorate, which is higher than the estimate of most pollsters. See also Michel Wear, *Reclaiming Hope* (Nashville: Thomas Nelson, 2017), 23–56, 159–76.

51. Cimmino, "Liberal Pastors Optimistic Democrats Can Rebound."

52. Ruth Graham, "Why Hillary Clinton Bombed with White Evangelical Voters," *Slate*, December 15, 2016, https://slate.com/news-and-politics/2016/12/why-hillary -clinton-bombed-with-white-evangelical-voters.html.

53. Daniel Burke, "How Faith Led Hillary Clinton 'Out of the Woods,'" CNN, August 10, 2017, https://www.cnn.com/2017/08/10/politics/clinton-daily-devotional/index.html.

54. "Q&A: Barack Obama," *Christianity Today*, January 23, 2008, https://www.christianitytoday.com/ct/2008/januaryweb-only/104–32.0.html.

55. Michael Wear, "Why Did Obama Win More White Evangelical Votes than Clinton? He Asked for Them," *Washington Post*, November 22, 2016, https://www.washingtonpost.com/posteverything/wp/2016/11/22/why-did-obama-win-more-white-evangelical-votes-than-clinton-he-asked-for-them/.

56. Graham, "Why Hillary Clinton Bombed."

57. Amy Chozick, "Hillary Clinton's Expectations, and Her Ultimate Campaign Missteps," *New York Times*, November 9, 2016, https://www.nytimes.com/2016/11/10/us/politics/hillary-clinton-campaign.html?mcubz=2.

58. Asma Khalid, "How Joe Biden's Faith Shapes His Politics," National Public Radio, September 20, 2020, https://www.npr.org/2020/09/20/913667325/how-joe-bidens-faith-shapes-his-politics; Daniel Silliman, "Joe Biden Campaigns on Faith," *Christianity Today*, August 17, 2020, https://www.christianitytoday.com/news/2020/august/joe-biden-catholic-evangelical-faith-vote-2020-convention.html; Ron Sider and Richard Mouw, "We Are Pro-Life Evangelicals for Biden," *Christian Post*, October 2, 2020, https://www.christianpost.com/voices/fri-2nd-embargo-for-noon-we-are-pro-life-evangelicals-for-biden.html.

59. Kristin Du Mez, "The Democrats Have a Religion Problem, but They Are Not the Only Ones," June 29, 2017, https://kristindumez.com/resources/the-democrats-have-a-religion-problem-but-theyre-not-the-only-ones/.

60. Kristin Du Mez, "Can Hillary Clinton's Faith Help Her Lead a Fractured Nation?" *Religion and Politics*, July 25, 2016, https://religionandpolitics.org/2016/07/25/can-clintons-faith-help-her-lead-a-fractured-nation/.

61. Du Mez, "The Democrats Have a Religion Problem."

62. Daniel Williams, "The Democrats' Religion Problem," *New York Times*, June 23, 2017, https://www.nytimes.com/2017/06/23/opinion/democrats-religion-jon-ossoff.html?mcubz=2&_r=0.

63. Graham, "Why Hillary Clinton Bombed."

64. "Faith and the 2016 Campaign," Pew Research Center, January 27, 2016, https://www.pewforum.org/2016/01/27/faith-and-the-2016-campaign/.

65. Graham, "Why Hillary Clinton Bombed."

66. John Fea, "Here's What Hillary Clinton Has to Do to Win Over Evangelicals," Penn Live, November 6, 2016, https://www.pennlive.com/opinion/2016/11/heres_what_hillary_clinton_has.html.

67. Madhuri Sathish, "Hillary Clinton Is Interested in Becoming a Preacher—REPORT," Bustle, August 11, 2017, https://www.bustle.com/p/hillary-clinton-is-considering-preaching-her-methodist-faith-report-76003.

68. In 2014, evangelicals were 25 percent of Michigan's population, 22 percent of Wisconsin's population, and 19 percent of Pennsylvania's population. "Evangelical Protestants," Pew Research Center, https://www.pewresearch.org/religion/religious-landscape-study/religious-tradition/evangelical-protestant/.

69. "Hillary Clinton's Concession Speech (Full Text)," CNN, November 9, 2016, https://www.cnn.com/2016/11/09/politics/hillary-clinton-concession-speech (all quotations except spiritual stamina); Kristin Kobes Du Mez, "Hillary Clinton's Spiritual Stamina," Patheos, November 17, 2016, https://www.patheos.com/blogs/anxiousbench/2016/11/hillary-clintons-spiritual-stamina/.

70. Daniel Burke, "First on CNN: The Email Hillary Clinton's Pastor Sent Her the Day after the Election," CNN, August 10, 2017, https://www.cnn.com/2017/08/10/politics/clinton-pastor-email/index.html.

71. Burke, "How Faith Led Hillary Clinton."

72. Burke, "First on CNN."

73. Burke, "How Faith Led Hillary Clinton." Bill Shillady reported that when he ate dinner with the Clintons on Christmas Eve in a restaurant, other diners gave her a standing ovation and many greeted her tearfully. People seemed to be "feeling like they personally had let her down" (Noveck, "As Clinton Emerges").

74. Hillary Rodham Clinton, "2016 Children's Defense Fund Gala Speech—November 16, 2016," Iowa State University, March 21, 2017, https://awpc.cattcenter.iastate.edu/2017/03/21/2016-childrens-defense-fund-gala-speech-nov-16-2016/.

75. Hillary Rodham Clinton, "Class Day Address at Yale University—May 20, 2018," Iowa State University, July 6, 2018, https://awpc.cattcenter.iastate.edu/2018/07/06/class-day-address-at-yale-university-may-20–2018/.

76. Michael Luo, "The Private Faith of Hillary Clinton," *New Yorker*, September 8, 2017, https://www.newyorker.com/news/news-desk/the-private-faith-of-hillary-clinton.

77. Steve Lieberman, "Clintons Attend Christmas Eve Service at Mount Kisco Methodist Church," Iohud, December 24, 2016, https://www.lohud.com/story/news/local/2016/12/24/clintons-christmas-mass-mount-kisco/95836442/.

78. Clinton, *What Happened*, 23, 30, 31 (first quotation), 32 (remaining quotations).

79. Clinton, *What Happened*, 34.

80. "Clinton: I Relied on Prayer, Yoga and 'My Fair Share of Chardonnay' after 'Devastating' 2016 Loss," GantNews, September 7, 2017, https://gantnews.com/2017/09/07/clinton-i-relied-on-prayer-yoga-and-my-fair-share-of-chardonnay-after-devastating-2016-loss/.

81. Julie Mazziotta, "How Hillary Clinton's Faith Will Help Her Cope with Shocking Presidential Defeat," *People*, November 9, 2016, https://people.com/politics/clinton-faith-after-presidential-loss/.

82. Green, "Hillary Wants to Preach."

83. Burke, "How Faith Led Hillary Clinton."

84. Martha Quillin, "Hillary Clinton Wants to Be a Lay Preacher. Here's What Her Spiritual Adviser Says," *News and Observer* (Raleigh, NC), August 9, 2017, https://www.newsobserver.com/news/politics-government/article166235497.html.

85. Clinton, *What Happened*, 443 (first and second quotations), 445 (third quotation). See Pope Francis, "Why the Only Future Worth Building Includes Everyone," TED.com, April 25, 2017, https://www.ted.com/talks/pope_francis_why_the_only_future_worth_building_includes_everyone/transcript?language=en; Colby Itkowitz, "Hillary Clinton Turned to a Surprising Source for Healing after Her Devastating

Loss: Pope Francis's TED Talk," *Washington Post*, September 15, 2017, https://www
.washingtonpost.com/news/acts-of-faith/wp/2017/09/15/hillary-clinton-turned-to
-a-surprising-source-for-healing-after-her-devastating-loss-pope-franciss-ted-talk/.

86. Eleanor Clift, "Hard-Luck Hillary Clinton's Second Case of the Inaugural
Blues: Unlike in 2009, There Is No Consolation Prize This Time for a Campaign that
Fell Short," *The Daily Beast*, January 19, 2017, https://www.proquest.com/usnews/
docview/1868376200/D15E4DF670994C74PQ/73?accountid=5657.

87. Minyon Moore, "Hillary Clinton Is Not Done Making History Yet," *The Daily
Beast*, January 2, 2017, https://www.proquest.com/usnews/docview/1856684796/
D15E4DF670994C74PQ/86?accountid=5657.

88. Clinton, "2016 Children's Defense Fund Gala Speech."

89. Noveck, "As Clinton Emerges."

90. "Hillary Clinton's Commencement Speech at Wellesley College: A Call to 'Defend
Truth,' and Jabs at Her Political Rival," CNBC, May 28, 2017, https://www.cnbc.com/
2017/05/28/hillary-clintons-2017-commencement-speech-at-wellesley.html.

91. "Our Program," https://www.onwardtogether.org/program/.

92. Green, "Hillary Wants to Preach."

93. Rachel Zoll, "Hillary Clinton's Pastor Plagiarized Prayer at Heart of Book," *The
Press Democrat* (Santa Rosa, CA), August 15, 2017; Daniel Burke, "Publisher Pulls Book
by Hillary Clinton's Pastor, Citing Plagiarism," CNN, September 5, 2017, https://www
.cnn.com/2017/09/05/politics/clinton-pastor-book-pulled-plagiarism/index.html.

94. Constance Grady, "Hillary Clinton's New Book Debuted to Higher Sales than
Any Nonfiction Hardcover Since 2012," Vox, September 20, 2017, https://www.vox
.com/culture/2017/9/20/16339516/hillary-clinton-what-happened-best-hardcover
-nonfiction-since-2012.

95. Heidi Stevens, "Hillary Clinton in New Book 'What Happened' Shoulders
Blame, Takes Aim," *Chicago Tribune*, September 12, 2017, https://www.proquest.com/
usnews/docview/1938143091/B92E3DD1BECC4C65PQ/27?accountid=5657.

96. "Live Coverage as Hillary Clinton Speaks at Elijah Cummings' Funeral," CQ
Roll Call, October 25, 2019, https://www.proquest.com/usnews/docview/23088893
30/77548EDD87E143BDPQ/254?accountid=5657.

97. Hank Stuever, "Hulu's 'Hillary' Turns a Tale of Defeat into a Personal History of
Modern Feminism," *Washington Post*, March 5, 2020, https://www.washingtonpost.com/
entertainment/tv/hulus-hillary-turns-a-tale-of-defeat-into-a-personal-history-of
-modern-feminism/2020/03/04/4fcfb65c-5d9d-11ea-b014-4fafa866bb81_story.html.

98. Rasha Ali, "Hillary Clinton Is Launching a Podcast Tackling Topics Like Faith, Resilience and Grief," *USA Today*, September 22, 2020, https://www.usatoday.com/story/
entertainment/celebrities/2020/09/22/hillary-clinton-launching-podcast-faith
-resilience-and-grief/5863622002/.

99. "Transcript: The Rachel Maddox Show, 11/23/21," MSNBC, November 23, 2021,
https://www.msnbc.com/transcripts/transcript-rachel-maddow-show-11-23-21
-n1284525.

100. "Hillary Clinton's Commencement Speech at Wellesley College."

101. Hillary Rodham Clinton, "Class Day Address at Yale University—May 20, 2018," Iowa State University, May 20, 2018, https://awpc.cattcenter.iastate.edu/2018/07/06/class-day-address-at-yale-university-may-20-2018/.

102. Hillary Clinton (@HillaryClinton), June 18, 2018, https://twitter.com/hillaryclinton/status/1008807317280870403.

103. Morgan Nelson, "Hillary Clinton: 'My Faith Was Really Holding Me Together' after 2016 Loss," *Juicy Ecumenism*, September 25, 2017, https://juicyecumenism.com/2017/09/25/hillary-clinton-faith-election-2016-loss/.

104. Josefin Dolsten, "Hillary Clinton Urges Jewish Labor Activists Not to 'Walk Away,'" *Jewish Journal* (Deerfield Beach, FL), December 18, 2019, A7.

105. Hillary Clinton, "Trump Should Be Impeached. But That Alone Won't Remove White Supremacy from America," *Washington Post*, January 11, 2021, https://www.washingtonpost.com/opinions/2021/01/11/hillary-clinton-impeach-trump-capitol-white-supremacy/. See also Amanda Robb, "Anatomy of a Fake News Scandal," *Rolling Stone*, November 16, 2017, https://www.rollingstone.com/feature/anatomy-of-a-fake-news-scandal-125877/.

106. "Transcript: The Rachel Maddow Show."

107. "Transcript of Interview with Senator Clinton," *New York Times*, July 6, 2007, https://www.nytimes.com/2007/07/06/us/politics/07clinton-text.html?pagewanted=2&sq=I%20Still%20Haven&st=cse%27t%20Found%20What%20I&scp=8%27m%20Looking%20For%20(Instrumental).

108. For example, see "Transcript of Interview with Senator Clinton."

109. Luo, "Private Faith of Hillary Clinton."

110. Nelson, "Hillary Clinton: 'My Faith Was Really Holding Me Together.'"

111. "Hillary Rodham Clinton: By the Book," *New York Times*, June 15, 2014, https://www.nytimes.com/2014/06/15/books/review/hillary-rodham-clinton-by-the-book.html?ref=review&_r=1.

112. Czarina Og, "Hillary Clinton's Knowledge of Scripture Impresses South Carolina Pastor," *Christian Today*, June 3, 2015, https://www.christiantoday.com/article/hillary.clintons.knowledge.of.scripture.impresses.south.carolina.pastor/55219.htm.

113. Luo, "Private Faith of Hillary Clinton."

114. Michael Kelly, "Saint Hillary," *New York Times Magazine*, May 23, 1993, https://www.nytimes.com/1993/05/23/magazine/saint-hillary.html.

115. Kenneth Woodward, "Soulful Matters," *Newsweek*, October 30, 1994, https://www.newsweek.com/soulful-matters-189302.

116. "Transcript of Interview with Senator Clinton,"

117. For example, see "Democratic Candidates Compassion Forum at Messiah College," April 13, 2008, http://transcripts.cnn.com/transcripts/0804/13/se.01.html.

118. Woodward, "Soulful Matters."

119. "First Lady's Remarks."

120. Luo, "Faith Intertwines."

121. "Transcript of Interview with Senator Clinton."

122. Woodward, "Soulful Matters."

123. "Transcript of Interview with Senator Clinton."

124. Hillary Rodham Clinton, "The First Lady's Remarks to the National Prayer Luncheon," February 2, 1994, https://clintonwhitehouse4.archives.gov/media/text/1994–02–02-first-lady-remarks-to-the-national-prayer-luncheon.text.

125. Clinton, *Living History*, 267 (first quotation), 167 (third quotation); Clinton, "First Lady's Remarks" (second quotation).

126. "Transcript of Interview with Senator Clinton,"

127. Claire Osborne, ed., *The Unique Voice of Hillary Rodham Clinton: A Portrait in Her Own Words* (New York: Avon Books, 1997), 88.

128. "Special Edition: Sojourners Presidential Forum," CNN, June 4, 2007, http://transcripts.cnn.com/TRANSCRIPTS/0706/04/sitroom.03.html.

129. Woodward, "Soulful Matters."

130. Luo, "Private Faith of Hillary Clinton."

131. Daniel Burke, "The Public and Private Faith of Hillary Clinton," CNN, October 30, 2016, https://www.cnn.com/2016/10/30/politics/clinton-faith-private/index.html.

132. Carl Bernstein, *A Woman in Charge: The Life of Hillary Clinton* (New York: Knopf, 2007), 297.

133. Hillary Rodham Clinton, "Address to General Conference," April 24, 1996, http://catalog.gcah.org/DigitalArchives/conference/GC96/hilltext.html.

134. Interview with United Methodist News Service, September 16, 1992, as quoted in Jeff Sharlet and Kathryn Joyce, "Hillary's Prayer: Hillary Clinton's Religion and Politics," *Mother Jones*, September 1, 2007, https://www.motherjones.com/politics/2007/09/hillarys-prayer-hillary-clintons-religion-and-politics/.

135. Kelly, "Saint Hillary."

136. "Transcript: The Rachel Maddox Show."

137. John Harris, "Hillary's Big Adventure; A Supportive Spouse, Surprisingly Accepting Colleagues, and a Mandate to Legislate," *Washington Post*, January 7, 2002, https://www.washingtonpost.com/politics/hillarys-big-adventure-a-supportive-spouse-surprisingly-accepting-colleagues-and-a-mandate-to-legislate/2016/07/11/f041d082-4791-11e6-90a8-fb84201e0645_story.html.

138. "Sen. Hillary Rodham Clinton Delivers Remarks at the National Hispanic Prayer Breakfast," *Political Transcript Wire* (Lanham, MD), June 15, 2007, https://www.proquest.com/usnews/docview/467227699/922C18B79DFD4AB0PQ/1?accountid=5657.

139. "Transcript of Interview with Senator Clinton."

140. Kelly, "Saint Hillary."

141. Kelly, "Saint Hillary."

142. "Clinton: I Relied on Prayer, Yoga and 'My Fair Share of Chardonnay' after 'Devastating' 2016 Loss."

143. David Hollinger, *After Cloven Tongues of Fire: Protestant Liberalism in Modern American History* (Princeton, NJ: Princeton University Press, 2013), 22, 39; Ward Clark Roof and William McKinney, *American Mainline Religion: Its Changing Shaping and Future* (New Brunswick, NJ: Rutgers University Press), 186–228; Dean Hoge, Benton Johnson, and Donald Luidens, *Vanishing Boundaries: The Religion of the Mainline*

Protestant Baby Boomers (Louisville, KY: Westminster John Knox Press, 1994); Christopher Evans, *Liberalism without Illusions: Renewing an American Christian Tradition* (Waco, TX: Baylor University Press, 2010); Gary Dorrien, *The Making of American Liberal Theology: Crisis, Irony, and Postmodernity, 1950–2005* (Louisville, KY: Westminster John Knox Press, 2006); Jill Gill, *Embattled Ecumenism: The National Council of Churches, the Vietnam War, and the Trials of the Protestant Left* (Ithaca, NY: Cornell University Press, 2011).

144. Mark Lempke, *My Brother's Keeper: George McGovern and Progressive Christianity* (Amherst: University of Massachusetts Press, 2017), 5 (quotation), 29, 63, 88–89.

145. Lempke, *My Brother's Keeper*, 129, 146–48, 159, 162

146. On Wallis's relationship with Obama, see Laurie Goodstein, "Without a Pastor of His Own, Obama Turns to Five," *New York Times*, March 15, 2009, https://www.nytimes.com/2009/03/15/us/politics/15pastor.html.

147. "Religiosity Highest in World's Poorest Nations," Gallup, August 31, 2010, https://news.gallup.com/poll/142727/religiosity-highest-world-poorest-nations.aspx. Compare David O'Reilly, "When You Say You Believe in God, What Do You Mean?" *Pew Trust Magazine*, Fall 2018, https://www.pewtrusts.org/en/trust/archive/fall-2018/when-you-say-you-believe-in-god-what-do-you-mean.

148. "Generally, Poorer Nations Tend to Be Religious; Wealthy Less So, Except for U.S.," Pew Research Center, December 21, 2015, https://www.pewresearch.org/fact-tank/2015/12/23/americans-are-in-the-middle-of-the-pack-globally-when-it-comes-to-importance-of-religion/ft_15-12-17_religioussaliencescatter/.

149. Dalia Fahmy, "Americans Are Far More Religious than Adults in Other Wealthy Nations," Pew Research Center, July 31, 2018, https://www.pewresearch.org/fact-tank/2018/07/31/americans-are-far-more-religious-than-adults-in-other-wealthy-nations/.

150. "White Evangelicals See Trump as Fighting for Their Beliefs, though Many Have Mixed Feelings about His Personal Conduct," Pew Research Center, March 12, 2020, https://www.pewresearch.org/religion/2020/03/12/white-evangelicals-see-trump-as-fighting-for-their-beliefs-though-many-have-mixed-feelings-about-his-personal-conduct/#half-of-americans-say-the-bible-should-influence-u-s-laws.

151. One exception is former German chancellor Angela Merkel, whom some argue has a thoughtfully articulated Christian political vision. See, for example, Nick Spencer, "Merkel's Strong, Unshowy Faith," *Church Times*, February 26, 2016, https://www.churchtimes.co.uk/articles/2016/26-february/comment/columnists/merkel-s-strong-unshowy-faith; Delphine Nerbollier, "Angela Merkel's Chancellorship and the Influence of Religion," *LaCroix International*, September 17, 2021, https://international.la-croix.com/news/politics/angela-merkels-chancellorship-and-the-influence-of-religion/14899.

152. "Americans Have Positive Views about Religion's Role in Society, but Want It Out of Politics," Pew Research Center, November 15, 2019, https://www.pewresearch.org/religion/2019/11/15/americans-have-positive-views-about-religions-role-in-society-but-want-it-out-of-politics/.

153. Haberman, "Religion and Right-Wing Politics."

154. Kenneth Wald and Allison Calhoun-Brown, *Religion and Politics in the United States* (Lanham, MD: Rowman and Littlefield, 2007), 363.

155. "White Evangelicals See Trump as Fighting for Their Beliefs."

156. See, for example, Paul Marshall, *Thine Is the Kingdom: A Biblical Perspective on the Nature of Government and Politics Today* (Grand Rapids: Eerdmans, 1986); Doug Bandow, *Beyond Good Intentions: A Biblical View of Politics* (Wheaton, IL: Crossway, 1988); David Gushee, ed., *Christians and Politics beyond the Culture Wars: An Agenda for Engagement* (Grand Rapids: Baker, 2000); Amy Black, *Honoring God in Red or Blue: Approaching Politics with Humility, Grace, and Reason* (Chicago: Moody, 2012).

157. Augustine, *City of God*, book V, chapter 24.

158. Stanley Carson-Thies, "Uncommon Contributor to the Common Good: The Legacy of Mark Hatfield, 1922–2011," November 4, 2011, Center for Public Justice, https://www.cpjustice.org/public/capital_commentary/article/669. See also Roy Herron, *How Can a Christian Be in Politics?: A Guide Toward Faithful Politics* (Wheaton, IL: Tyndale House Publishers, 2005). The Tennessee state senator's work was motivated by the Old Testament concept of shalom, Jeremiah's commandment to Jewish exiled to seek the welfare of Babylon, Micah's admonition to "do justice, and love kindness, and to walk humbly with God," and Jesus's Sermon on the Mount and his injunction to take care of the least of these.

159. Jim Wallis, *God's Politics: Why the Right Gets It Wrong and the Left Doesn't Get It* (San Francisco: HarperSan Francisco, 2005), xxiii (first quotation), xv, xiv (second quotation).

160. Ray Suarez, *The Holy Vote: The Politics of Faith in America* (New York: Rayo, 2006), 7.

161. Morton Kondracke and Fred Barnes, *Jack Kemp: The Bleeding-Heart Conservative Who Changed America* (New York: Sentinel, 2015); https://www.jackkempfoundation.org/; David Frum, "Why Jack Kemp's Legacy Is More Relevant than Ever," *The Atlantic*, October 12, 2015, https://www.theatlantic.com/politics/archive/2015/10/jack-kemp-legacy/410152/; David Rosenbaum, "A Passion for Ideas: Jack French Kemp," *New York Times*, August 11, 1996, https://www.nytimes.com/1996/08/11/us/a-passion-for-ideas-jack-french-kemp.html?sec=&spon=&pagewanted=print; Peggy Noonan, "He Had the Power of the Happy Man: Jack Kemp, Champion of Economic Freedom and the Little Guy," *Wall Street Journal*, May 8, 2009, https://www.wsj.com/articles/SB124173306994398011#mod=djemEditorialPage.

162. https://www.forthehealth.net/religious-freedom.

163. See James Davison Hunter, *To Change the World: The Irony, Tragedy, and Possibility of Christianity in the Late Modern World* (New York: Oxford University Press, 2010); Michael Gerson and Peter Wehner, *City of Man: Religion and Politics in a New Era* (Chicago: Moody, 2010); Ronald Sider, *Just Politics: A Guide for Christian Engagement* (Grand Rapids: Brazos, 2012). Many mainline Protestants and Catholics espoused similar views.

164. James Madison, Federalist Papers No. 10 (1787), https://billofrightsinstitute.org/primary-sources/federalist-no-10. For an analysis of why Americans are so

politically divided and suggestions about how to overcome this, see Jonathan Haidt, *The Righteous Mind: Why Americans Are Divided by Politics and Religion* (New York: Vintage Books, 2012), and Haidt, *Life after Babel: Adapting to a World We Can No Longer Share* (New York: Penguin, 2023).

165. Klein, "Why Have So Many Tried to Take Down Hillary?"

Index

comment, 200, 202; board memberships of, 41; call of for Trump's impeachment, 214; campaign of to reform Arkansas's public schools, 44–45; and channeling of Eleanor Roosevelt, 71–72, 73–74; on combatting AIDS, 115, 116, 149; comparison of with Joan of Arc, 3, 53, 89; comparison of with Lady Macbeth, 3, 48, 63, 89; criticism of Donald Trump by, 169, 170, 197, 212, 213, 214; and controversy over a Brooklyn Museum exhibit, 95; and criminalizing the Good Samaritan, 108–9; defense of the rule of law and peaceful transition of power, 208, 214; denunciation of racism by, 96, 167, 169; as the devil, viii, 3, 4, 121, 152, 181–82; distrust of, 104, 143, 158, 169, 171, 177–78, 193, 269n36; efforts of to end human trafficking, 100, 111, 132, 144, 205; efforts of to help Blacks, 164 (*see also* Clinton, Hillary, denunciation of racism by); efforts of to protect religious minorities, 137, 139, 189; efforts of to reconcile head and heart, 20, 28, 58, 166, 215; efforts of to woo religious voters, 10, 105, 112–13, 119, 167; emphasis of on doing good, 5, 52, 60, 75–76, 102, 119, 132, 144, 168 (*see also* Clinton, Hillary, "do all the good you can"; on faith and works; focus of on social justice; as a social activist); emphasis of on spiritual renewal, 54, 61; and environmental protection, 80, 140, 176, 190; exhorting of Democrats to discuss religion, 58, 112; exhorting of religious people to participate in politics, 116; and Feed the Future initiative, 175; as a feminist, 5, 45, 48, 49, 91, 146, 181, 197, 198; and Filegate, 2, 92, 93, 177, 179; focus of on social justice, 14, 20, 43, 96, 103, 112, 144, 168, 206; on forgiveness, 86, 115, 166, 168–69, 216, 218; and founding of Onward Together, 211; and gay marriage, 88, 92, 118, 160, 226; on global warming, 114, 115, 190; as a Goldwater girl, 15; hatred of, 4, 147–48, 158; helping of to end fighting between Israel and Hamas, 139; and the Hillary Doctrine, 124, 125–26, 129, 140; and Hobby Lobby, 161; image problem of, 121, 176–77; and immigration, 118, 162,

175, 190, 214; importance of, vii, 1–2; on the importance of fatherhood, 81; importance of studying the religious views of, ix, 222; on individual responsibility, 55–56, 78, 102, 204, 218; and the Iraq war, 101, 105; and Jews, 96–97, 98; as a lawyer, 2, 40–41; leadership of a health care initiative, 51, 55, 56, 71, 77–78, 91; and "Love and Kindness" campaign video, 166; and Martin Luther King Jr., 18, 33; and moral principles, 26–27, 49, 61, 218–19; and Mormons, 188–89; and the New Age controversy, 70–74, 76; and Pantsuits Nation, 197; and Pentecostals, 152, 165; personal morality of, 5, 9, 27, 156, 163; personal traits of, 21, 26, 27, 33, 38, 39, 46, 49, 64, 73, 100, 138, 176–77, 189, 197; perspective of US foreign policy of, 123, 124; philosophy of government of, 58, 59, 80, 89, 93, 100, 102, 104; and Planned Parenthood, 159, 192; policy similarities of with Obama, 147; political perspective of, 20, 22–23, 26, 55–56; political support for, 53, 96, 99, 112, 118, 143, 150, 163–64, 186, 189–91, 197, 198–99, 200–201, 202–3; as poorly understood, 1, 152; polls about the religious beliefs of, 111, 267n2, 269n36; and polls of religious voters, 112, 143, 151, 158, 186; and the practice of "the discipline of gratitude," 63, 86, 165, 166; praise of, 46, 55, 59, 63, 73, 75, 94, 106, 118, 138, 140, 175, 190; as a professor at University of Arkansas School of Law, 40; as a progressive, vii, 5, 8, 26, 27, 38, 49, 58, 92, 105, 160, 206, 211, 219; promotion of affordable housing by, 78, 118; promotion of cookstoves by, 132–33; promotion of gay rights by, 134, 136, 156, 158, 175; promotion of human rights by, 94, 125–29, 134, 136–37, 175; promotion of universal health care by, 76, 77, 92, 118, 119, 226; questioning of religious views by, 25–26; on "radical empathy," 213; and religious liberty, 100, 111, 134–37, 146, 152, 160–62, 183, 188, 189, 191–92, 193, 226; reluctance of to discuss personal life and feelings, 54, 177, 201, 202; as a Rockefeller Republican, 31, 34; role-playing of Barry Goldwater by, 15;

GARY SCOTT SMITH is a professor of history emeritus at Grove City College. His many books include *Mark Twain: Prophet, Preacher, and Social Philosopher*.

The University of Illinois Press
is a founding member of the
Association of University Presses.

———————————————

Composed in 10.25/14 Chaparral Pro
with Avenir LT Std display
by Lisa Connery
at the University of Illinois Press
Manufactured by Sheridan Books, Inc.

University of Illinois Press
1325 South Oak Street
Champaign, IL 61820–6903
www.press.uillinois.edu